So Hilarious You'll Bust a Gut! ISOBEYAN

You'll be the class star if you buy a graphic novel and T-shirt combo pack!

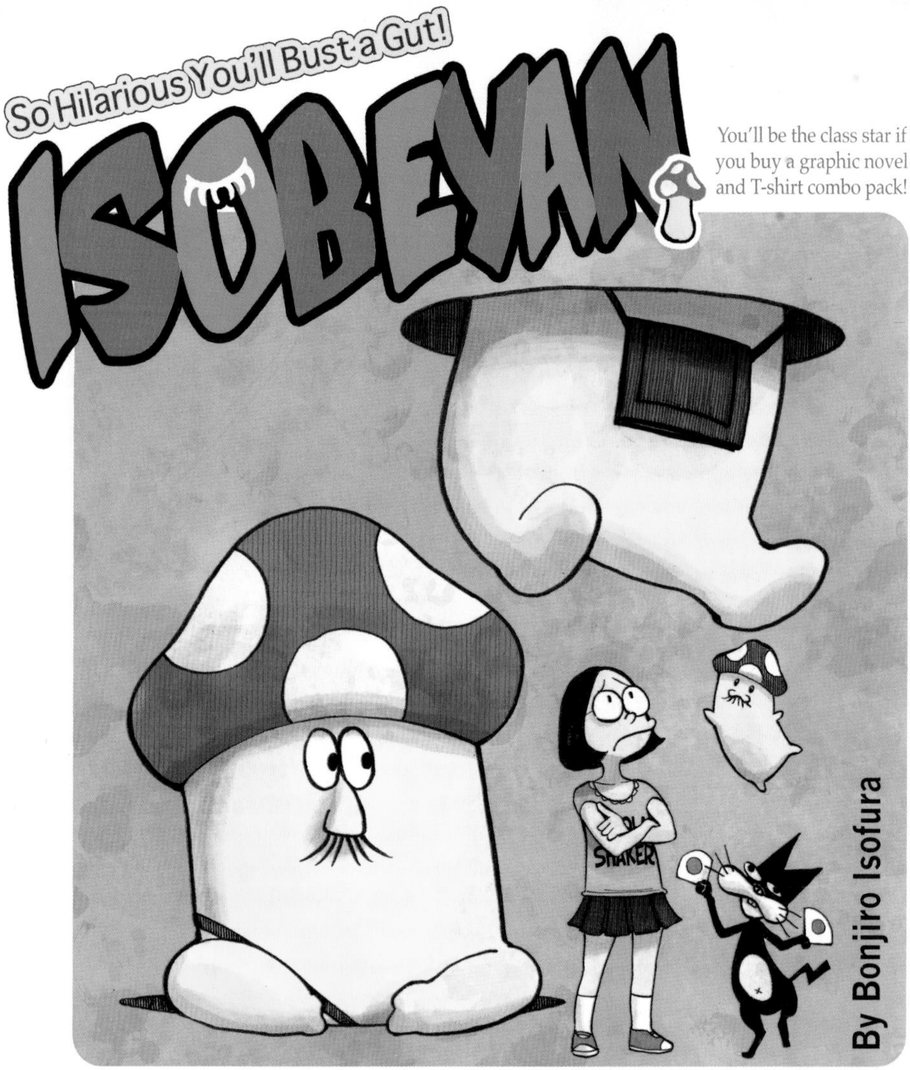
SHAKER
By Bonjiro Isofura

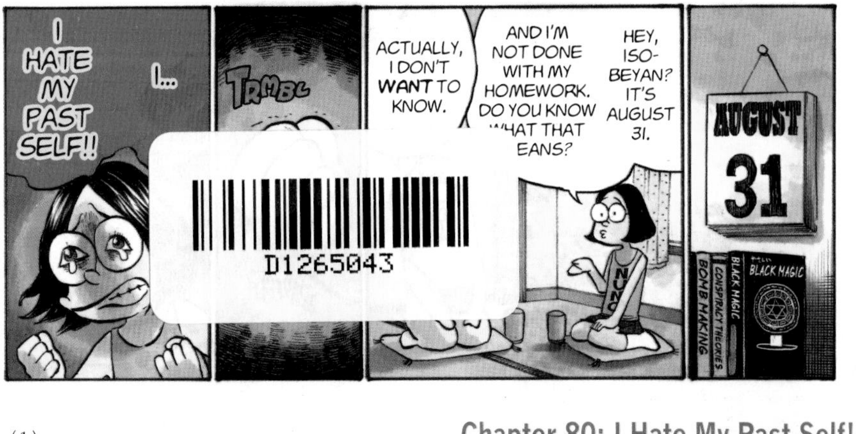
AUGUST
31
BLACK MAGIC
BLACK MAGIC
CONSPIRACY THEORIES
BOMB MAKING
HEY, ISO-BEYAN? IT'S AUGUST 31.
AND I'M NOT DONE WITH MY HOMEWORK. DO YOU KNOW
HAT THAT
EANS?
ACTUALLY, I DON'T WANT TO KNOW.
TRMBL
I...
I HATE MY PAST SELF!!

Chapter 80: I Hate My Past Self!

☆The past doesn't matter! Live in the moment! *Isobeyan* is for everyone!

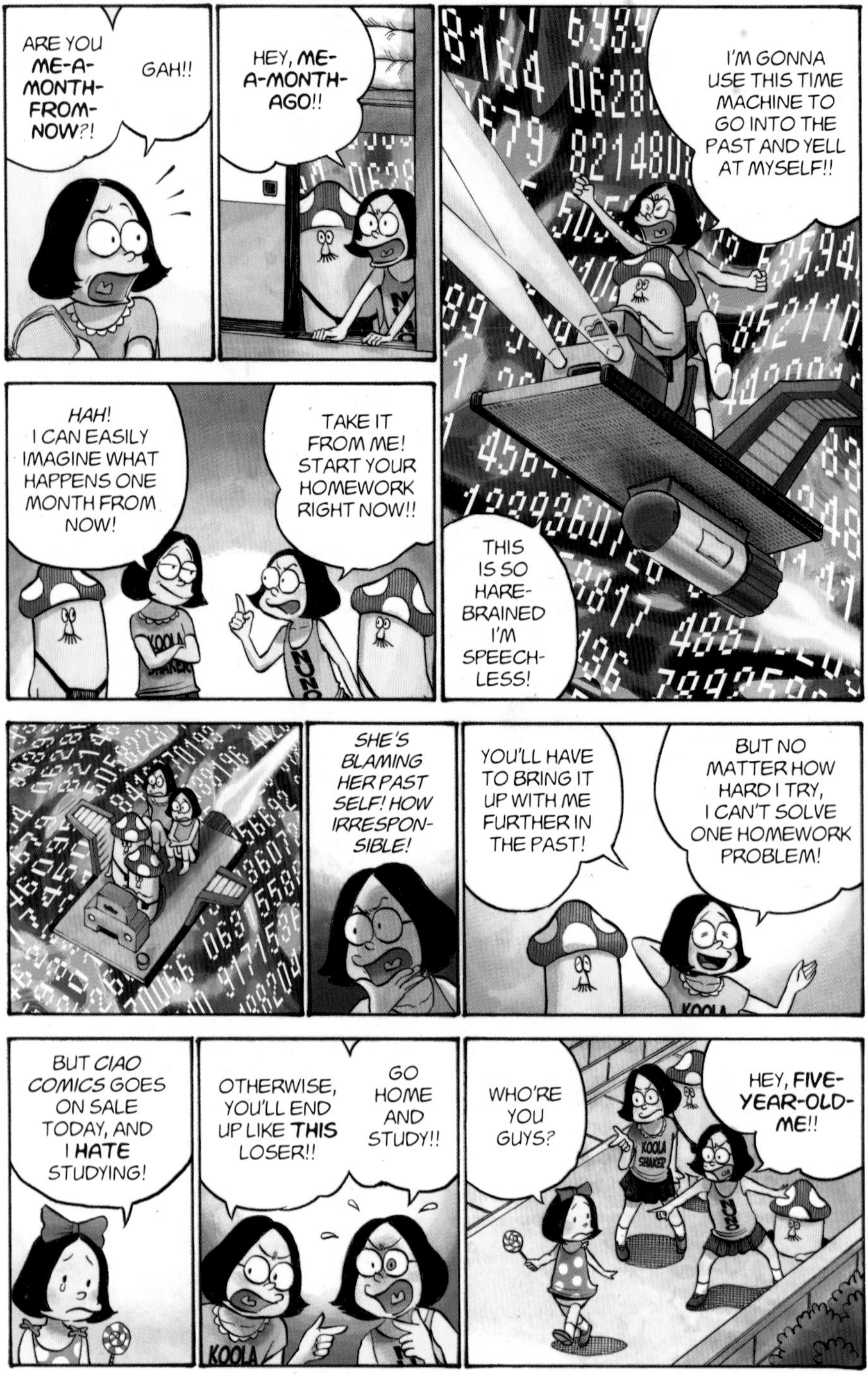
I'M GONNA USE THIS TIME MACHINE TO GO INTO THE PAST AND YELL AT MYSELF!!
THIS IS SO HARE-BRAINED I'M SPEECH-LESS!
HEY, ME-A-MONTH-AGO!!
GAH!!
ARE YOU ME-A-MONTH-FROM-NOW?!
TAKE IT FROM ME! START YOUR HOMEWORK RIGHT NOW!!
HAH! I CAN EASILY IMAGINE WHAT HAPPENS ONE MONTH FROM NOW!
BUT NO MATTER HOW HARD I TRY, I CAN'T SOLVE ONE HOMEWORK PROBLEM!
YOU'LL HAVE TO BRING IT UP WITH ME FURTHER IN THE PAST!
SHE'S BLAMING HER PAST SELF! HOW IRRESPON-SIBLE!
HEY, FIVE-YEAR-OLD-ME!!
WHO'RE YOU GUYS?
GO HOME AND STUDY!!
OTHERWISE, YOU'LL END UP LIKE THIS LOSER!!
BUT CIAO COMICS GOES ON SALE TODAY, AND I HATE STUDYING!

SUPER-POPULAR MASTERPIECE COMEDY **ISOBEYAN**

☆Tell Bonjiro Isofura about your ideas for Mysterious Items! He's waiting for your letters!

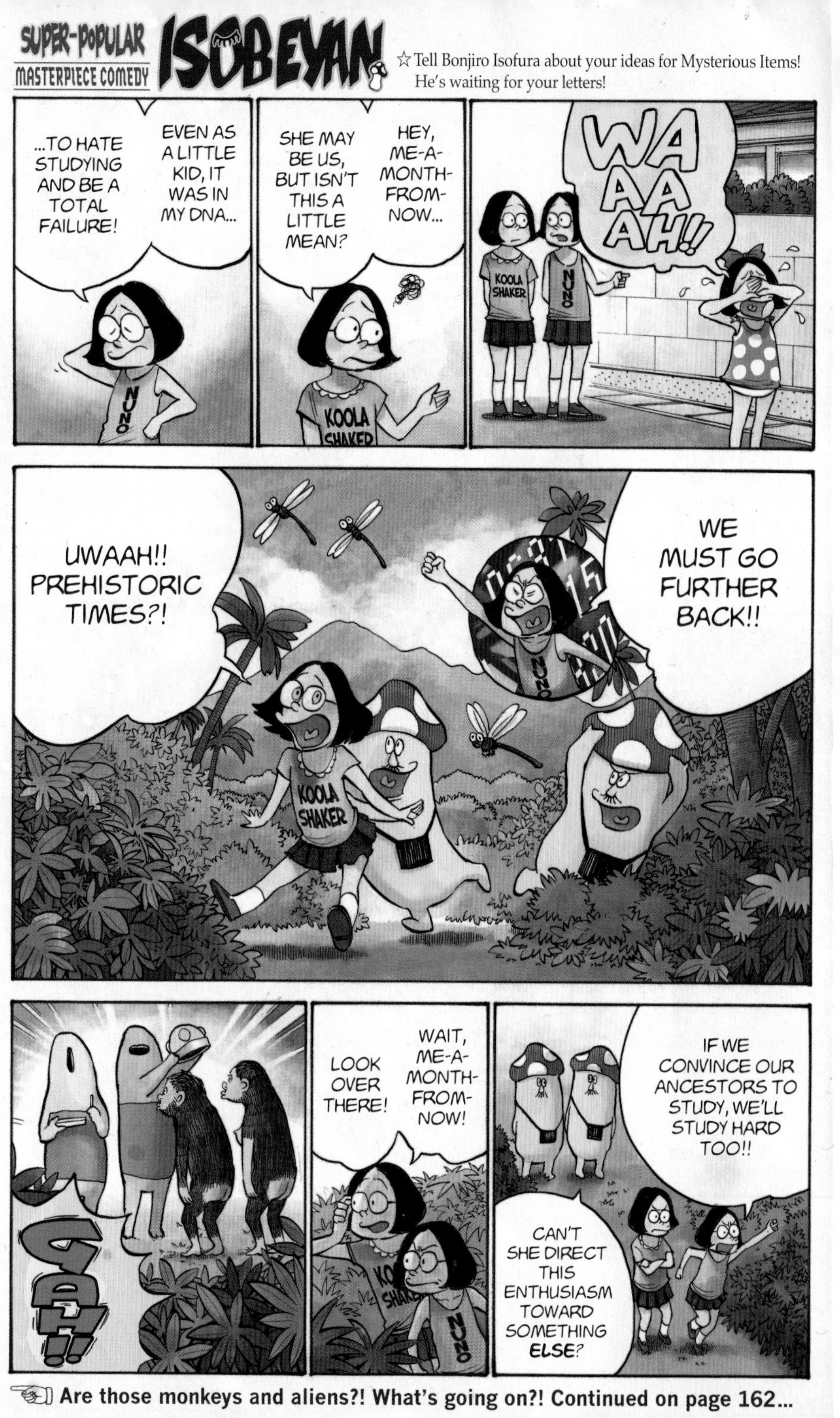
WAAAAAH!!
KOOLA SHAKER
NUNO
HEY, ME-A-MONTH-FROM-NOW...
SHE MAY BE US, BUT ISN'T THIS A LITTLE MEAN?
EVEN AS A LITTLE KID, IT WAS IN MY DNA...
...TO HATE STUDYING AND BE A TOTAL FAILURE!
WE MUST GO FURTHER BACK!!
UWAAH!! PREHISTORIC TIMES?!
IF WE CONVINCE OUR ANCESTORS TO STUDY, WE'LL STUDY HARD TOO!!
CAN'T SHE DIRECT THIS ENTHUSIASM TOWARD SOMETHING **ELSE**?
WAIT, ME-A-MONTH-FROM-NOW!
LOOK OVER THERE!
GAAH!!

☞ **Are those monkeys and aliens?! What's going on?! Continued on page 162...**

DEAD DEAD DEMON'S DEDE DEDE DESTRUCTION

4

Chapter 25   005

Chapter 26   023

Chapter 27   043

Chapter 28   063

Chapter 29   081

Chapter 30   103

Chapter 31   122

Chapter 32   143

CHAPTER 25

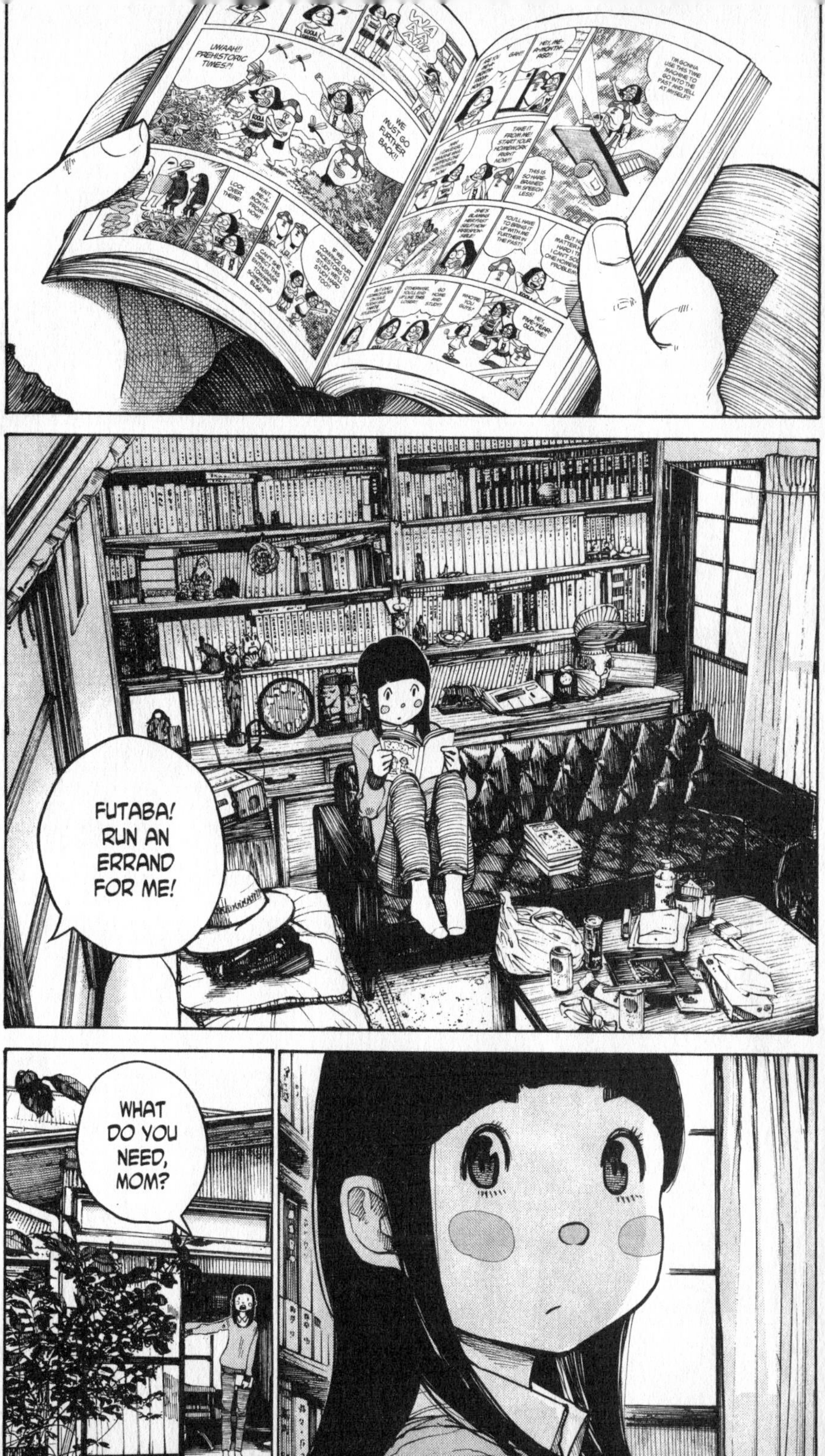
FUTABA! RUN AN ERRAND FOR ME!
WHAT DO YOU NEED, MOM?

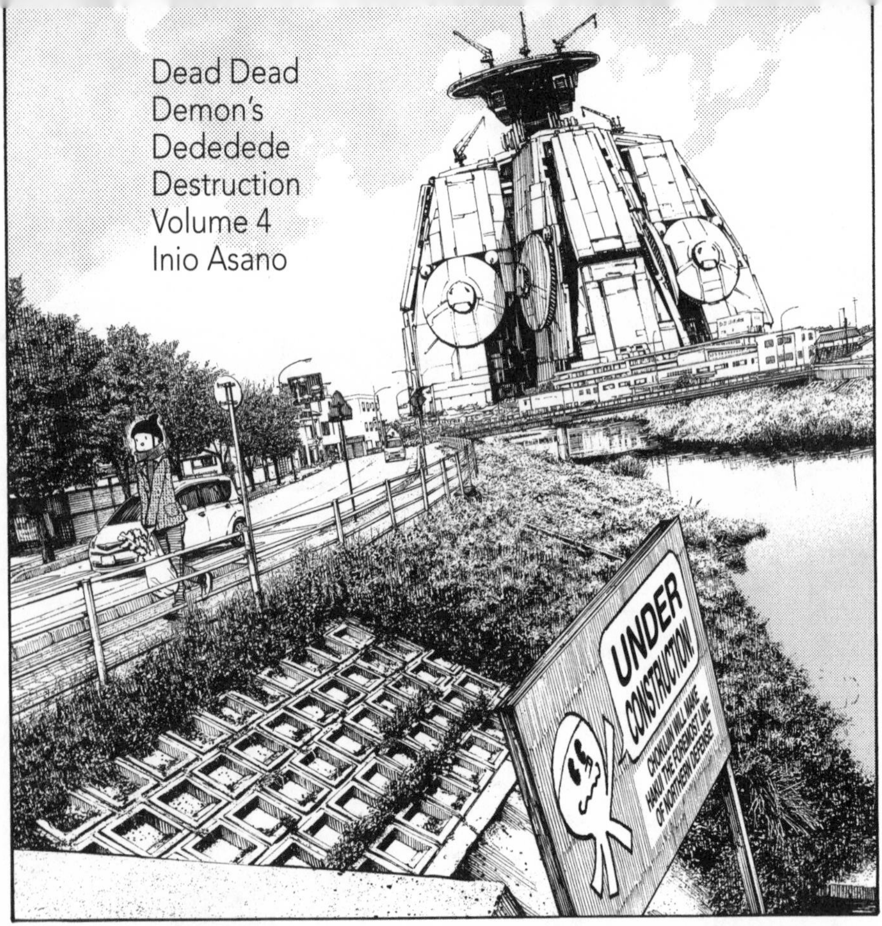
Dead Dead Demon's Dededede Destruction
Volume 4
Inio Asano
UNDER CONSTRUCTION!
CHOKUJIN WILL MAKE HAKUI THE FOREMOST LINE OF NORTHERN DEFENSE!

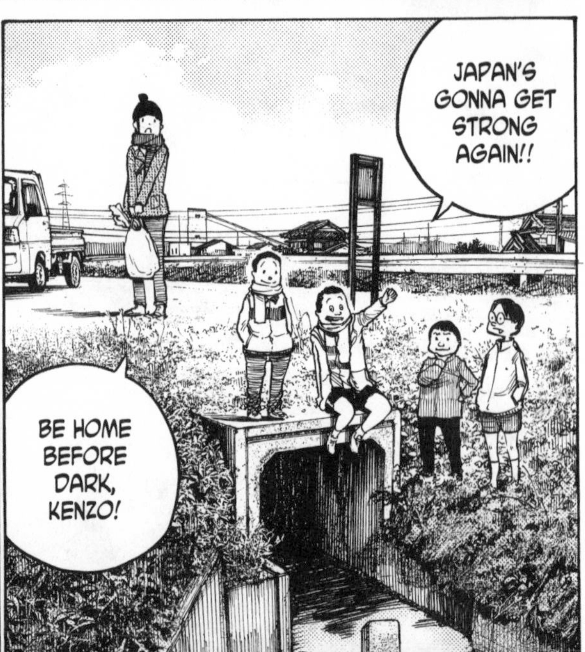
JAPAN'S GONNA GET STRONG AGAIN!!
BE HOME BEFORE DARK, KENZO!

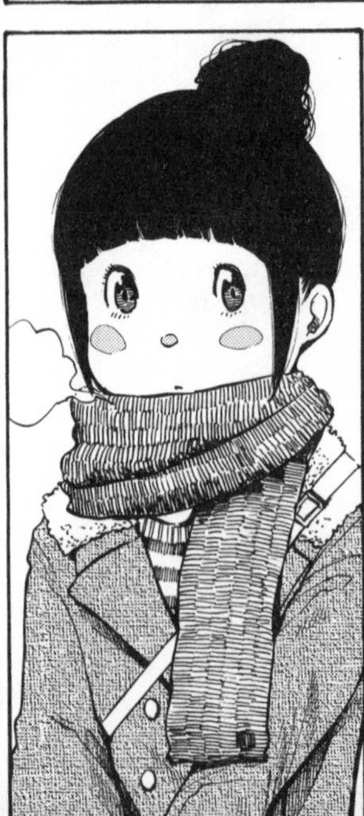

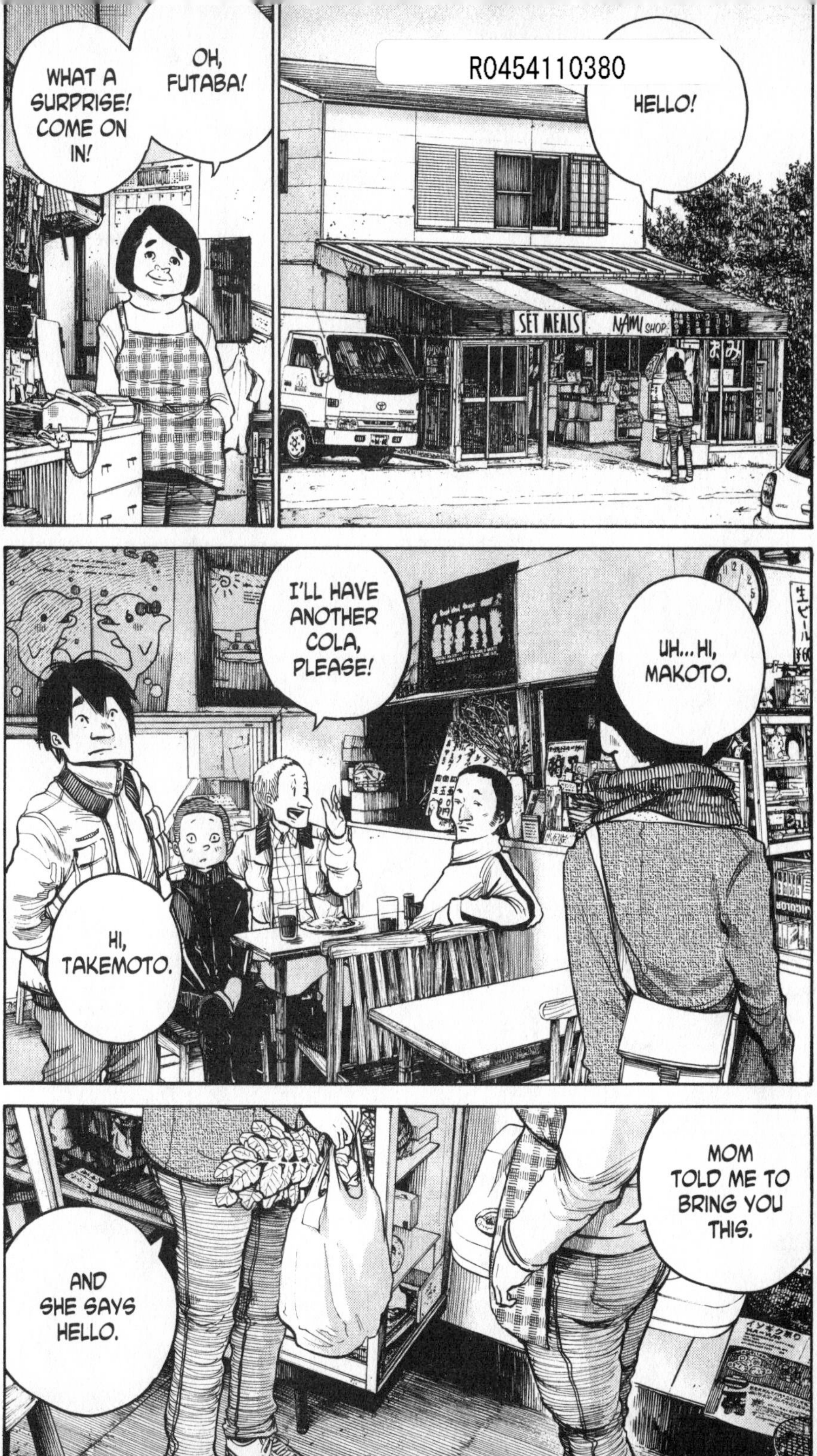
HELLO!
SET MEALS
NAMI SHOP
OH, FUTABA!
WHAT A SURPRISE! COME ON IN!
UH... HI, MAKOTO.
I'LL HAVE ANOTHER COLA, PLEASE!
HI, TAKEMOTO.
MOM TOLD ME TO BRING YOU THIS.
AND SHE SAYS HELLO.

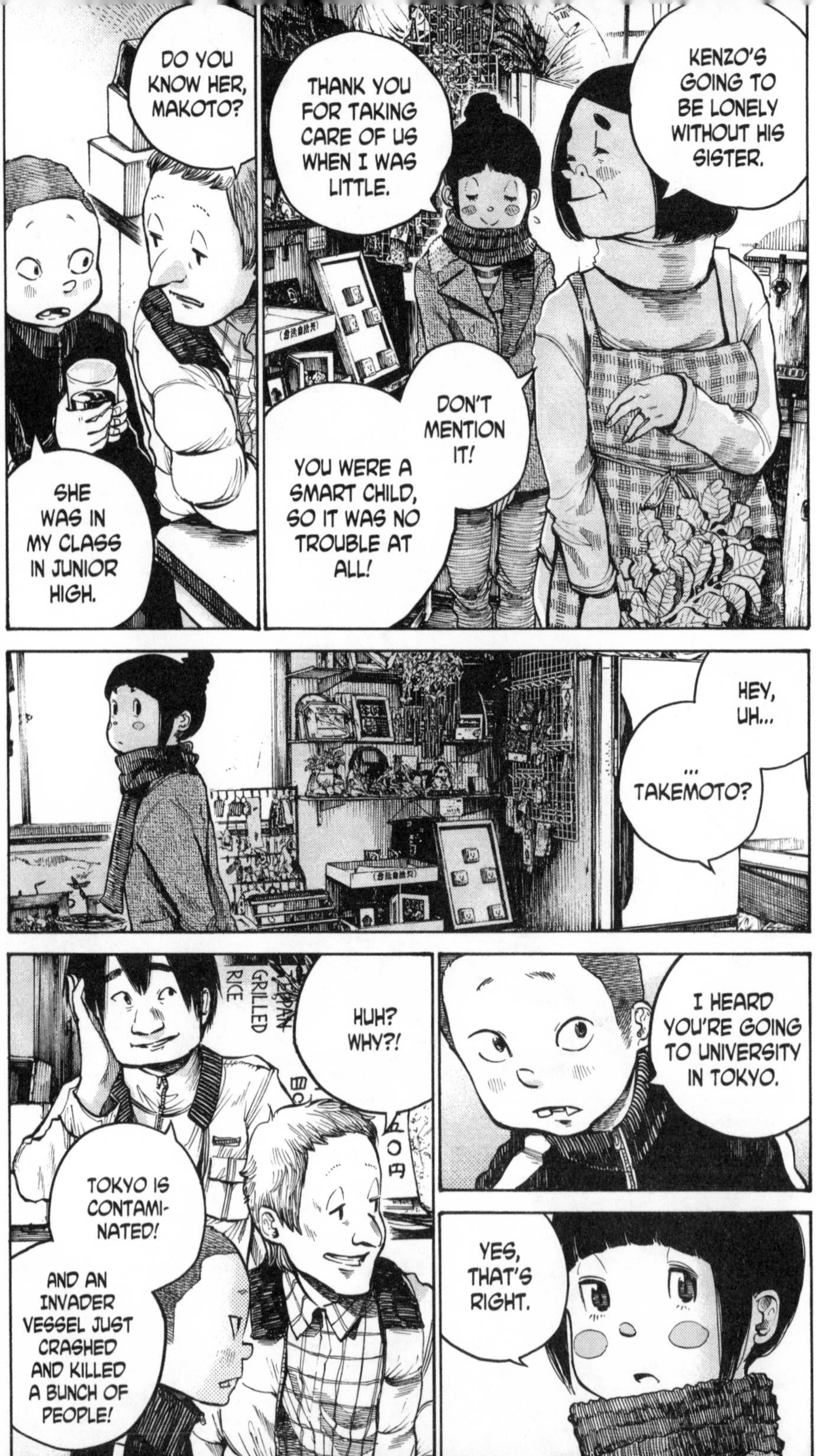
KENZO'S GOING TO BE LONELY WITHOUT HIS SISTER.
THANK YOU FOR TAKING CARE OF US WHEN I WAS LITTLE.
DON'T MENTION IT!
YOU WERE A SMART CHILD, SO IT WAS NO TROUBLE AT ALL!
DO YOU KNOW HER, MAKOTO?
SHE WAS IN MY CLASS IN JUNIOR HIGH.
HEY, UH...
... TAKEMOTO?
I HEARD YOU'RE GOING TO UNIVERSITY IN TOKYO.
YES, THAT'S RIGHT.
HUH? WHY?!
GRILLED RICE
TOKYO IS CONTAMINATED!
AND AN INVADER VESSEL JUST CRASHED AND KILLED A BUNCH OF PEOPLE!

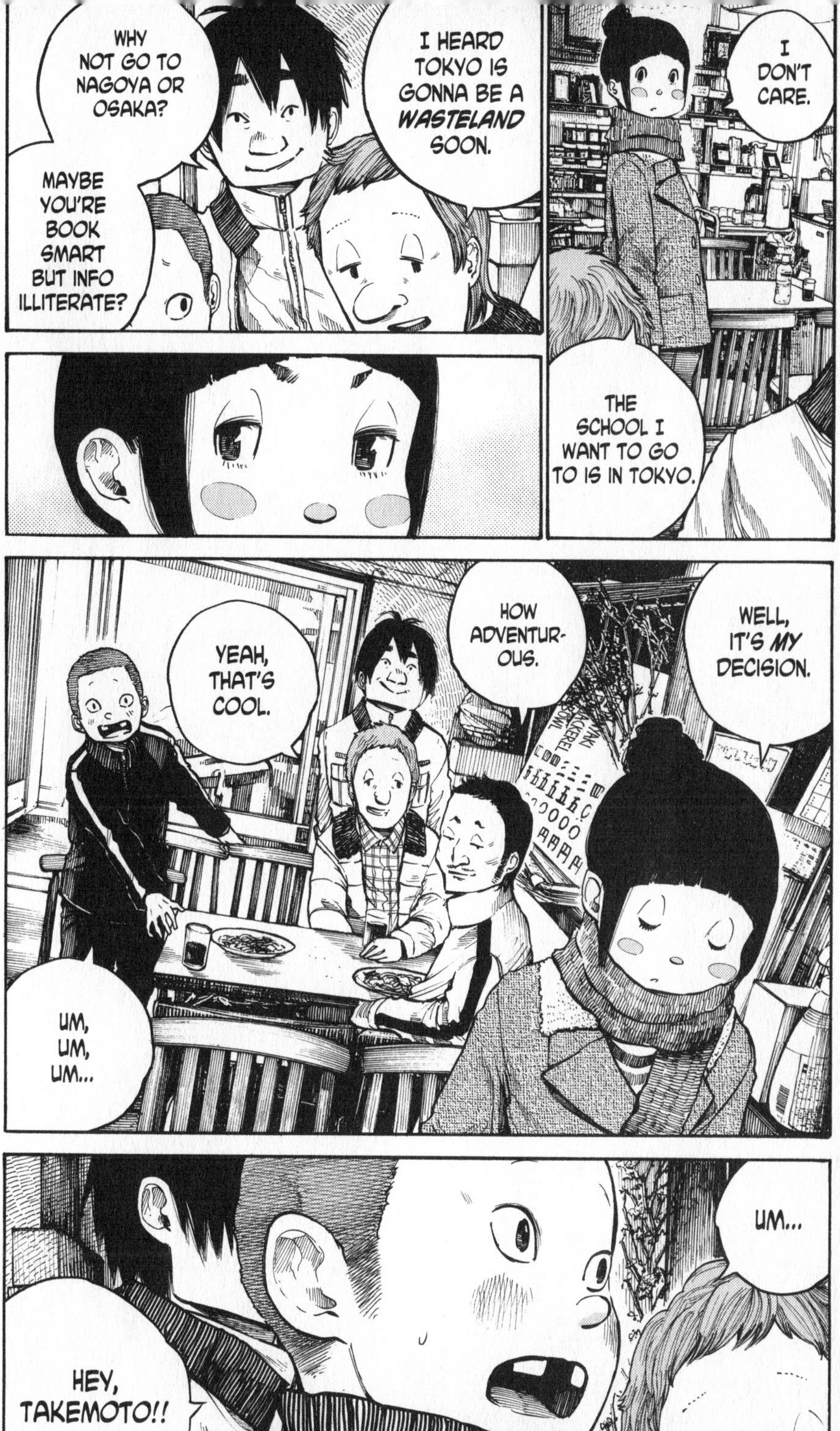
I DON'T CARE.
THE SCHOOL I WANT TO GO TO IS IN TOKYO.
I HEARD TOKYO IS GONNA BE A *WASTELAND* SOON.
WHY NOT GO TO NAGOYA OR OSAKA?
MAYBE YOU'RE BOOK SMART BUT INFO ILLITERATE?
WELL, IT'S *MY* DECISION.
HOW ADVENTUR-OUS.
YEAH, THAT'S COOL.
UM, UM, UM...
UM...
HEY, TAKEMOTO!!

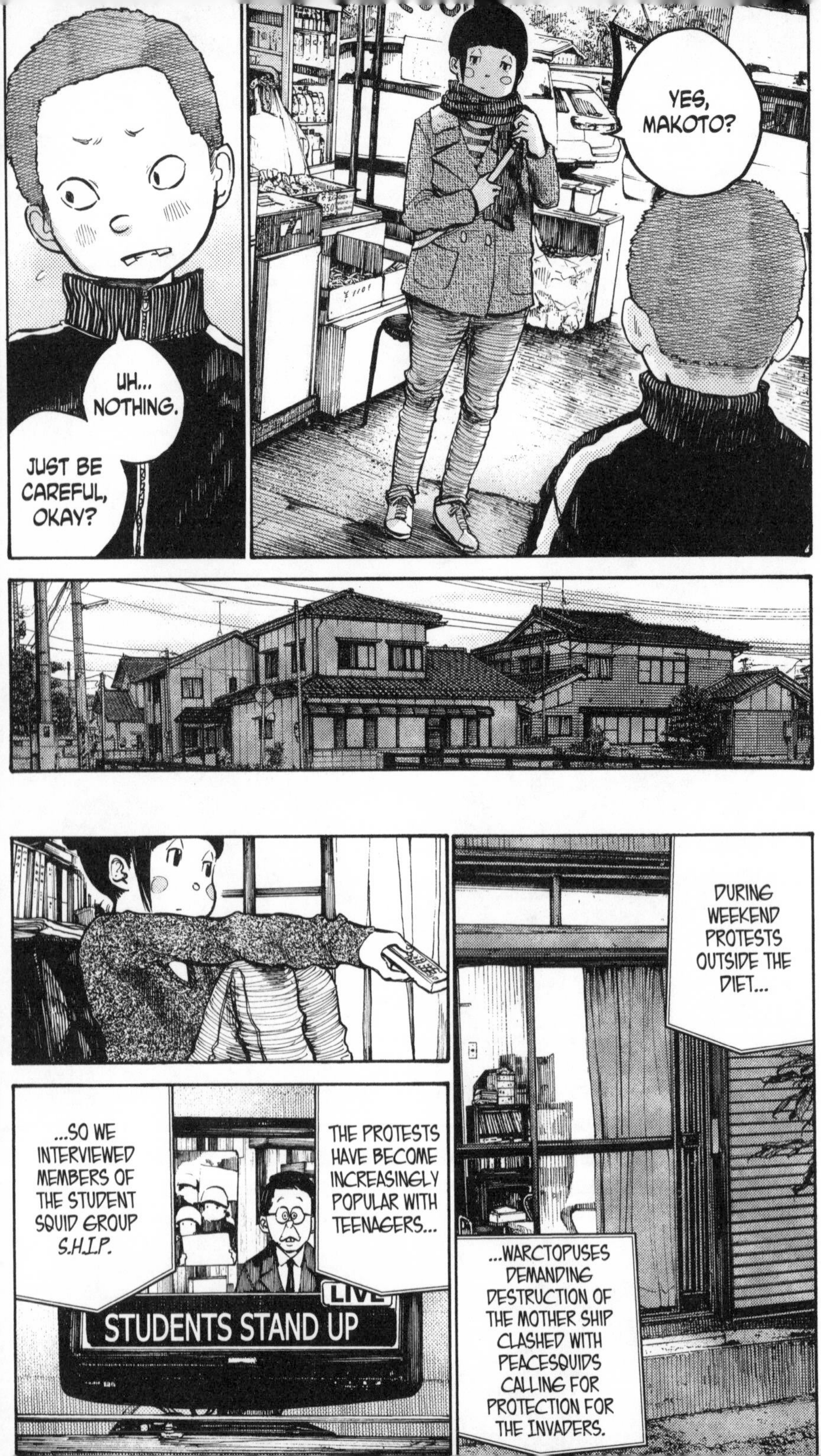
YES, MAKOTO?
UH... NOTHING.
JUST BE CAREFUL, OKAY?
DURING WEEKEND PROTESTS OUTSIDE THE DIET...
...WARCTOPUSES DEMANDING DESTRUCTION OF THE MOTHER SHIP CLASHED WITH PEACESQUIDS CALLING FOR PROTECTION FOR THE INVADERS.
THE PROTESTS HAVE BECOME INCREASINGLY POPULAR WITH TEENAGERS...
...SO WE INTERVIEWED MEMBERS OF THE STUDENT SQUID GROUP S.H.I.P.
LIVE
STUDENTS STAND UP

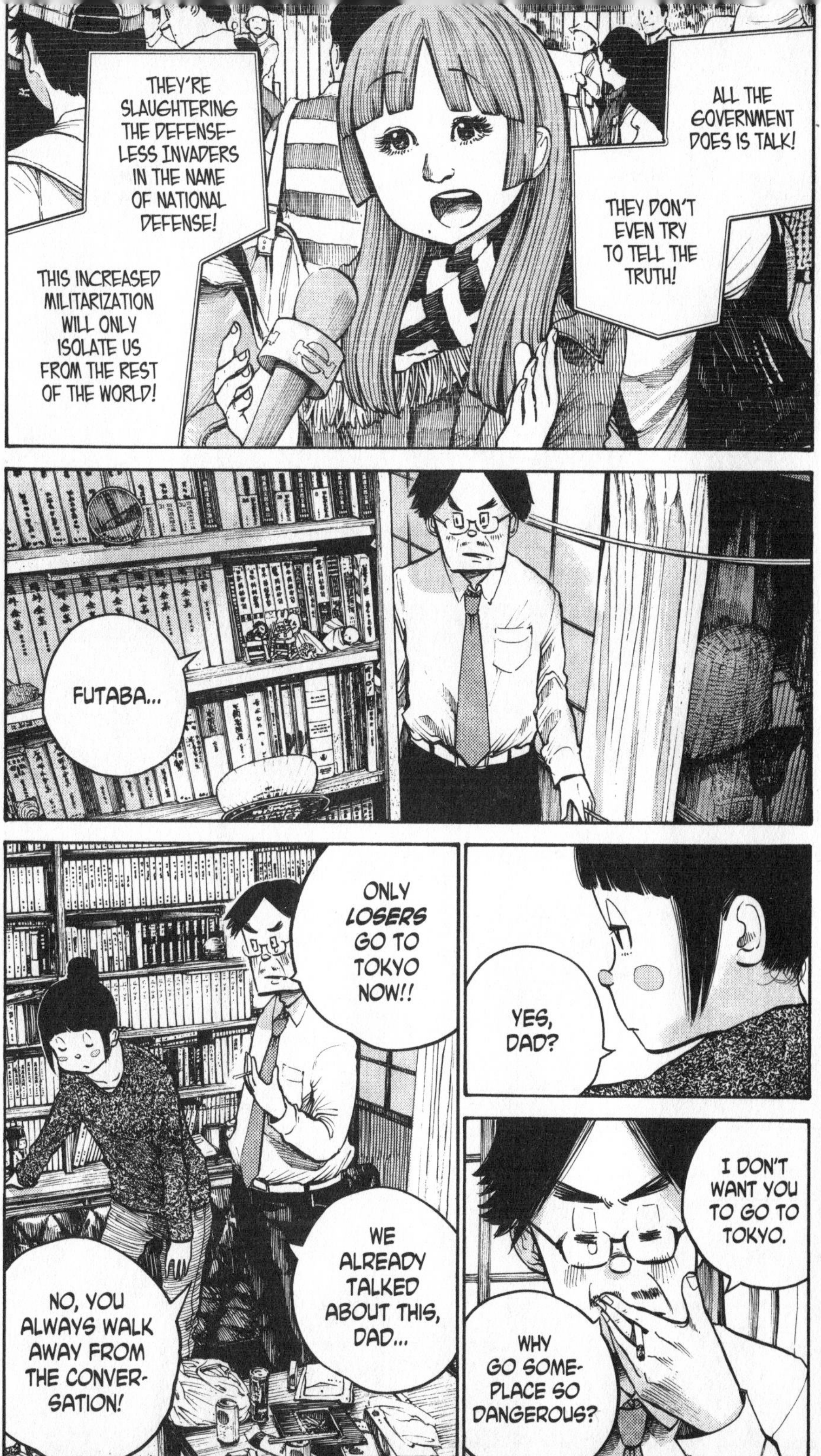
ALL THE GOVERNMENT DOES IS TALK!
THEY DON'T EVEN TRY TO TELL THE TRUTH!
THEY'RE SLAUGHTERING THE DEFENSE-LESS INVADERS IN THE NAME OF NATIONAL DEFENSE!
THIS INCREASED MILITARIZATION WILL ONLY ISOLATE US FROM THE REST OF THE WORLD!
FUTABA...
YES, DAD?
I DON'T WANT YOU TO GO TO TOKYO.
WHY GO SOME-PLACE SO DANGEROUS?
ONLY *LOSERS* GO TO TOKYO NOW!!
WE ALREADY TALKED ABOUT THIS, DAD...
NO, YOU ALWAYS WALK AWAY FROM THE CONVER-SATION!

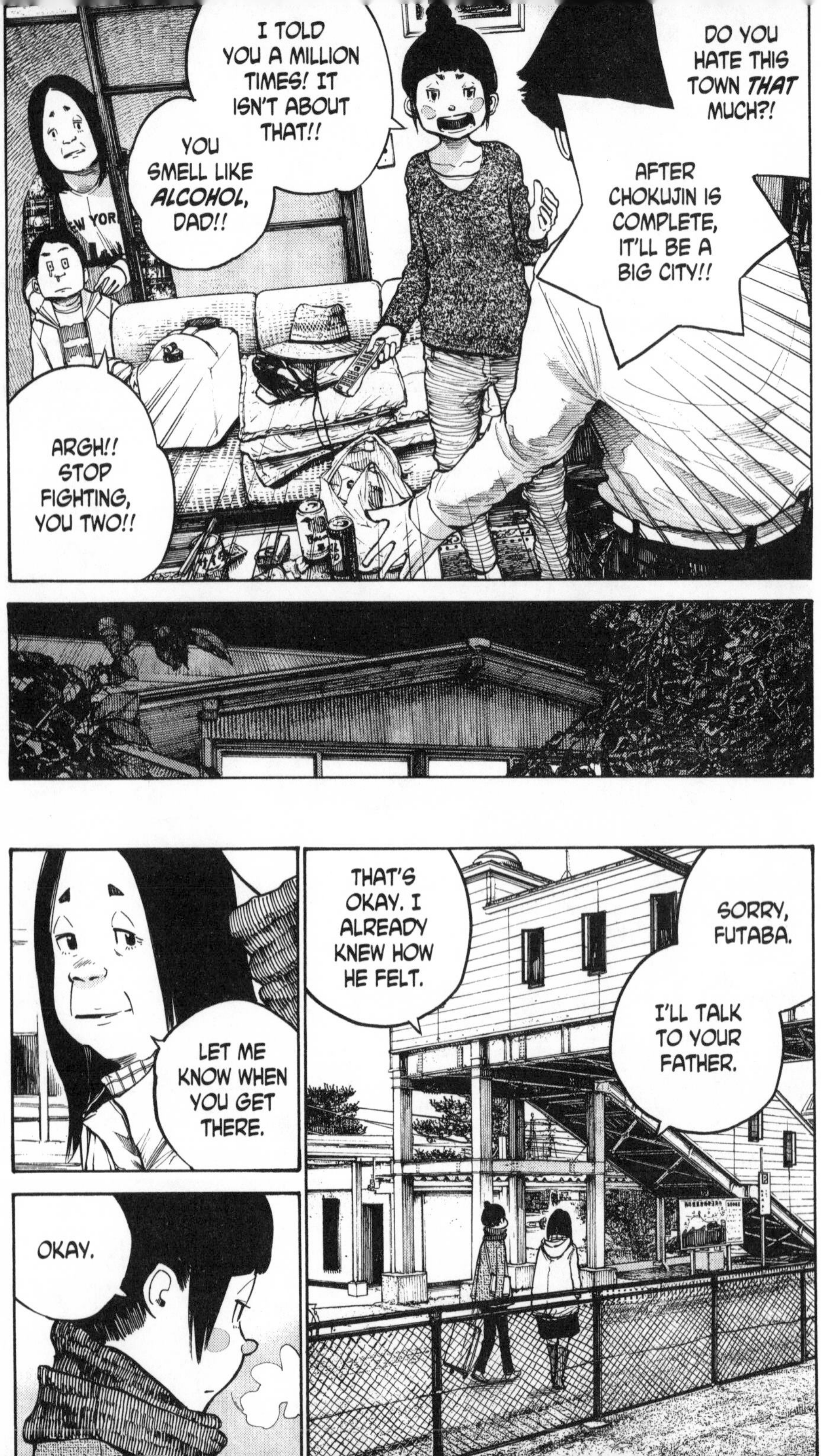
DO YOU HATE THIS TOWN *THAT* MUCH?!
AFTER CHOKUJIN IS COMPLETE, IT'LL BE A BIG CITY!!
I TOLD YOU A MILLION TIMES! IT ISN'T ABOUT THAT!!
YOU SMELL LIKE *ALCOHOL*, DAD!!
ARGH!! STOP FIGHTING, YOU TWO!!
SORRY, FUTABA.
I'LL TALK TO YOUR FATHER.
THAT'S OKAY. I ALREADY KNEW HOW HE FELT.
LET ME KNOW WHEN YOU GET THERE.
OKAY.

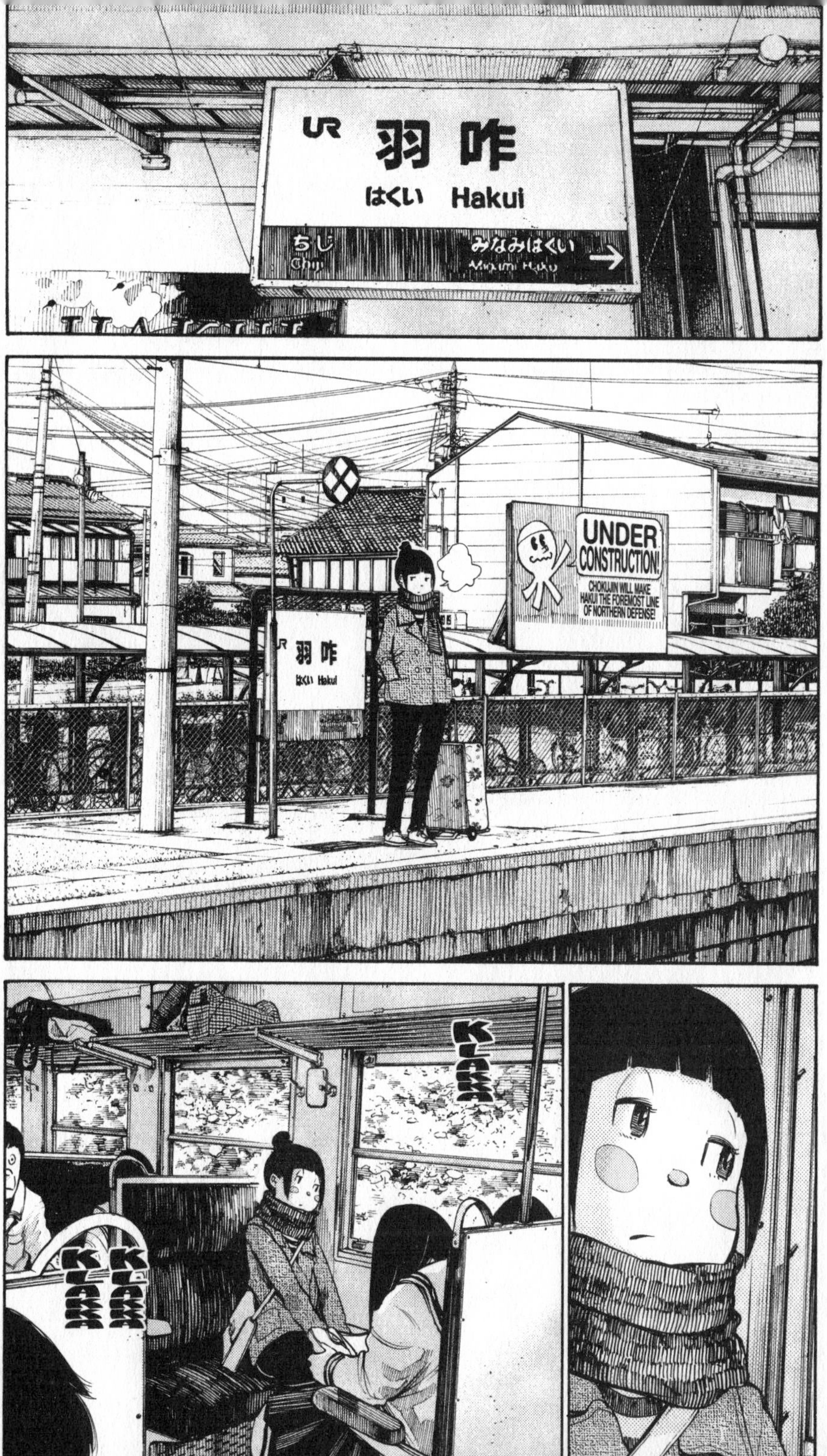
UR
羽咋
はくい Hakui
ちじ
みなみはくい
UR
羽咋
はくい Hakui
UNDER CONSTRUCTION!
CHOKUJIN WILL MAKE HAKUI THE FOREMOST LINE OF NORTHERN DEFENSE!
KLAKA
KLAKA
KLAKA

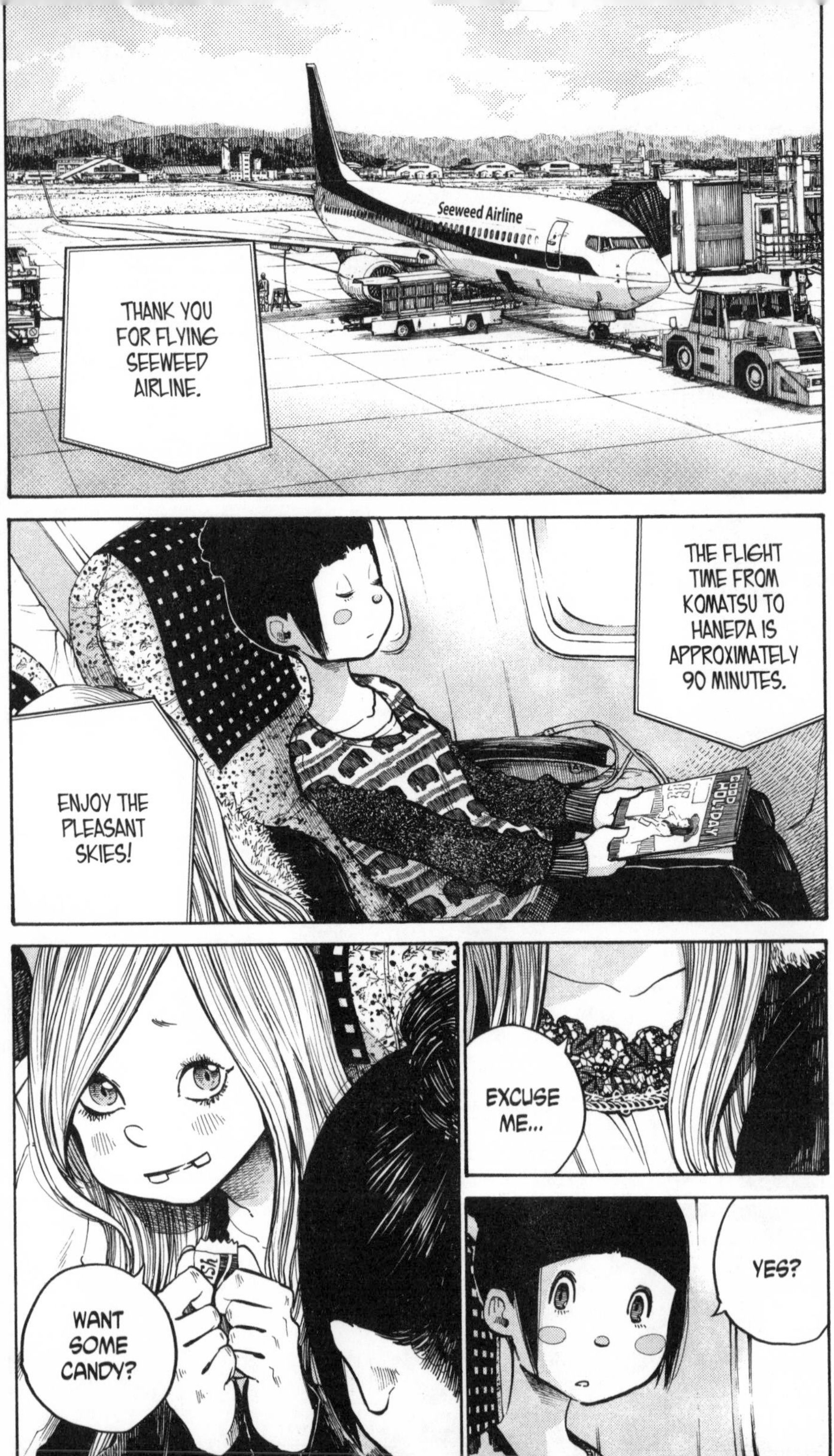
Seeweed Airline
THANK YOU FOR FLYING SEEWEED AIRLINE.
THE FLIGHT TIME FROM KOMATSU TO HANEDA IS APPROXIMATELY 90 MINUTES.
GOOD HOLIDAY
ENJOY THE PLEASANT SKIES!
EXCUSE ME...
YES?
WANT SOME CANDY?

MAKOTO?!
NO WAY...

UH, NO
THANK
Y—

YOU
FINALLY
NOTICED?

I KNOW IT'S
A SHOCK,
BUT DON'T
FREAK
OUT.

I DIDN'T
EXPECT OUR
SEATS TO
BE NEXT TO
EACH OTHER.

HUH?
HUH?
HUH?!

W-W-
WHAT
THE...?

WEIRD?
WELL...

...YOU'RE
WEARING
A *SKIRT*.

WHY
ARE
YOU...

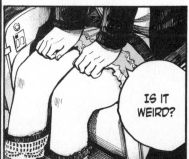

YEAH...

IS IT
WEIRD?

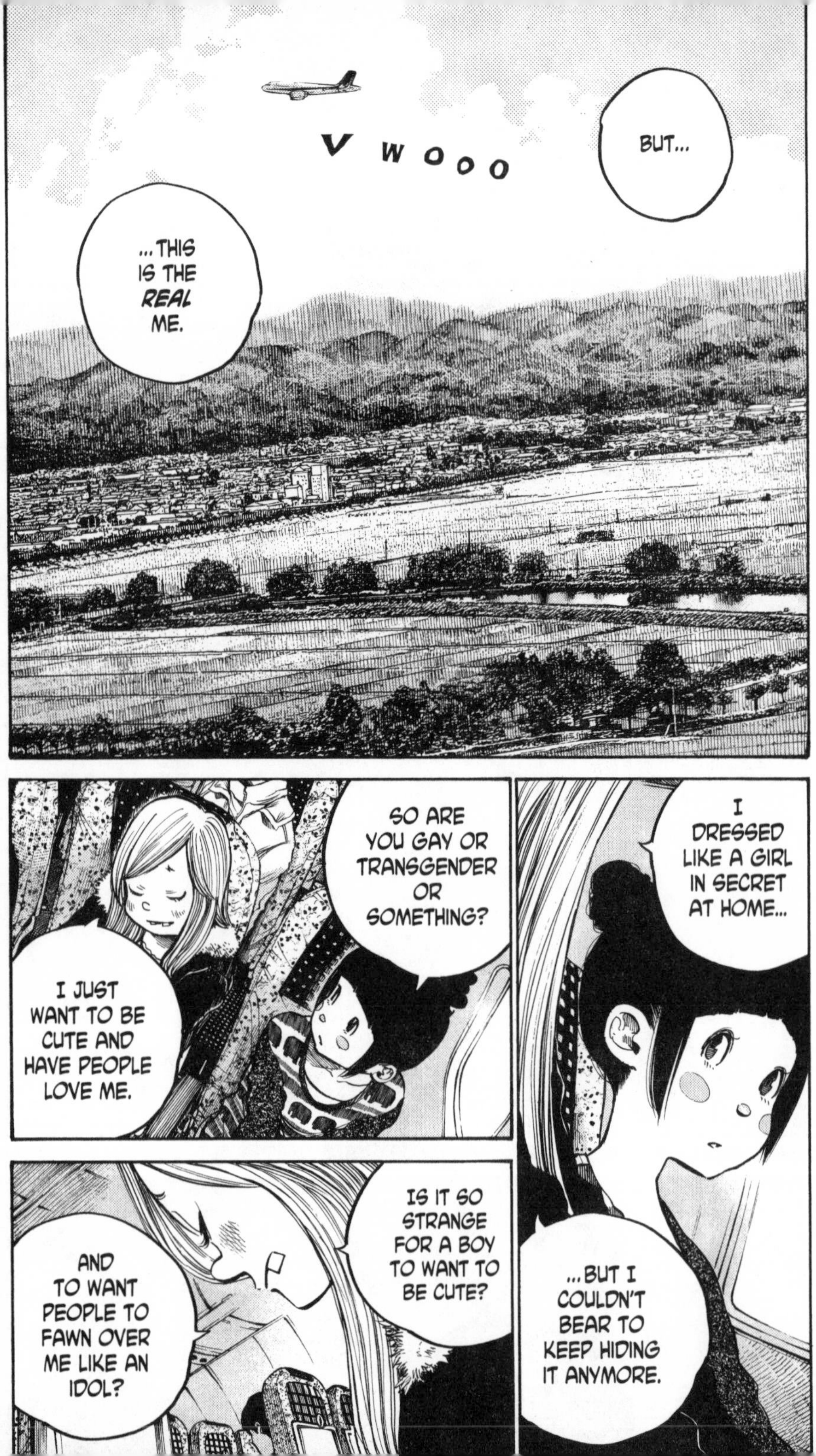
V WOOO
BUT...
...THIS IS THE *REAL* ME.
I DRESSED LIKE A GIRL IN SECRET AT HOME...
...BUT I COULDN'T BEAR TO KEEP HIDING IT ANYMORE.
SO ARE YOU GAY OR TRANSGENDER OR SOMETHING?
I JUST WANT TO BE CUTE AND HAVE PEOPLE LOVE ME.
IS IT SO STRANGE FOR A BOY TO WANT TO BE CUTE?
AND TO WANT PEOPLE TO FAWN OVER ME LIKE AN IDOL?

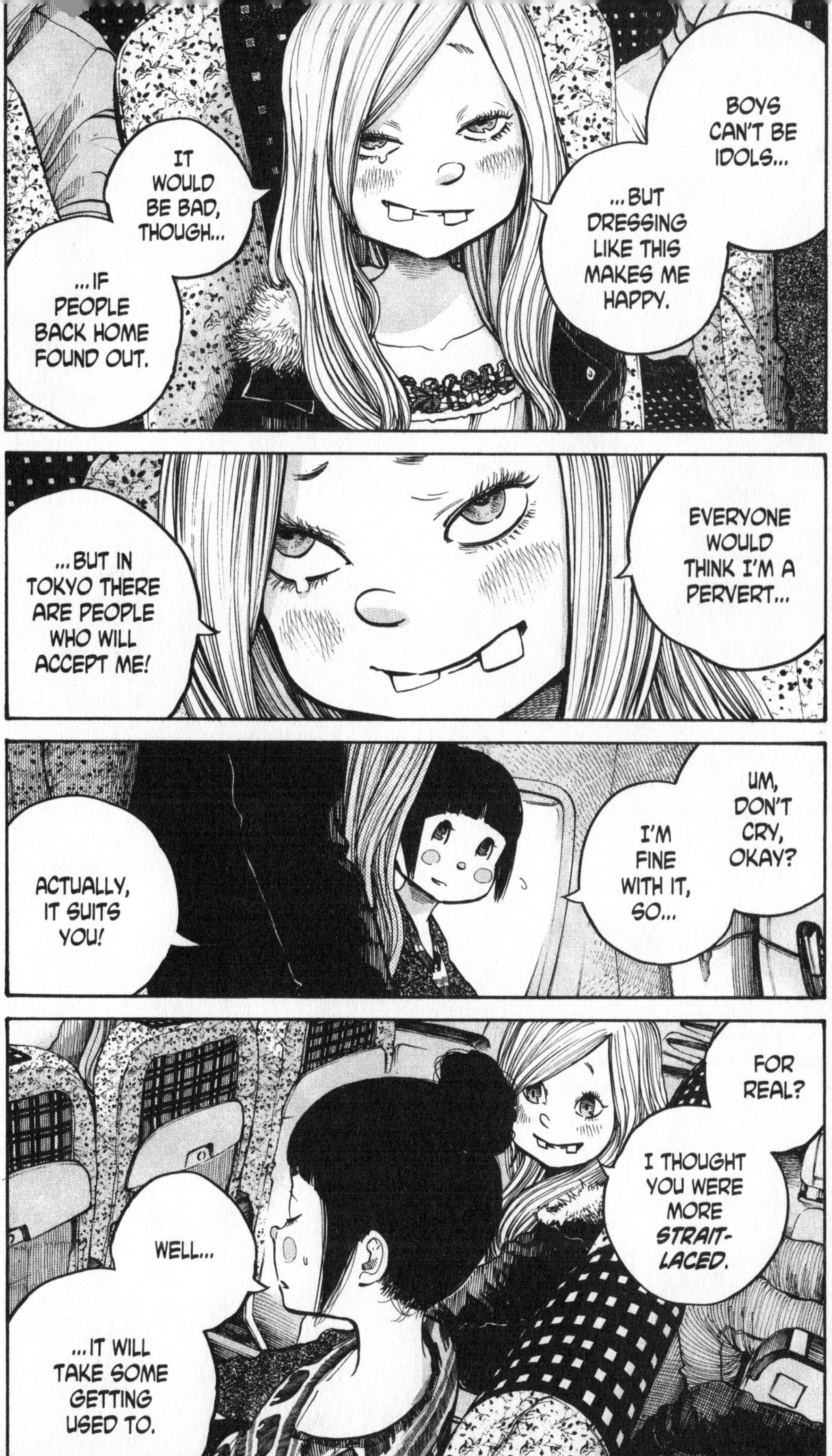
BOYS CAN'T BE IDOLS...
...BUT DRESSING LIKE THIS MAKES ME HAPPY.
IT WOULD BE BAD, THOUGH...
...IF PEOPLE BACK HOME FOUND OUT.
EVERYONE WOULD THINK I'M A PERVERT...
...BUT IN TOKYO THERE ARE PEOPLE WHO WILL ACCEPT ME!
UM, DON'T CRY, OKAY?
I'M FINE WITH IT, SO...
ACTUALLY, IT SUITS YOU!
FOR REAL?
I THOUGHT YOU WERE MORE *STRAIT-LACED*.
WELL...
...IT WILL TAKE SOME GETTING USED TO.

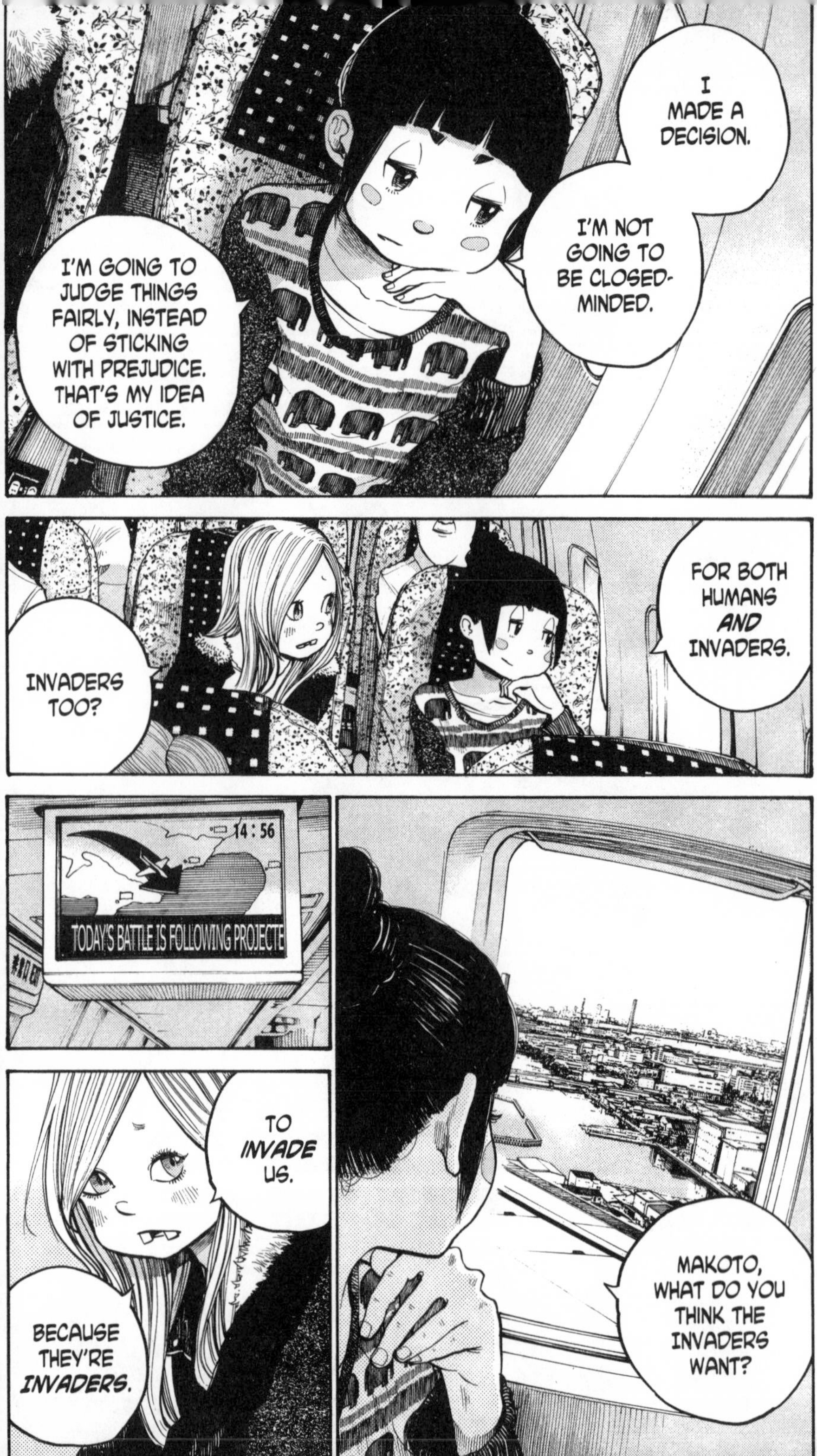
I MADE A DECISION.
I'M NOT GOING TO BE CLOSED-MINDED.
I'M GOING TO JUDGE THINGS FAIRLY, INSTEAD OF STICKING WITH PREJUDICE. THAT'S MY IDEA OF JUSTICE.
FOR BOTH HUMANS *AND* INVADERS.
INVADERS TOO?
MAKOTO, WHAT DO YOU THINK THE INVADERS WANT?
14:56
TODAY'S BATTLE IS FOLLOWING PROJECTE
TO *INVADE* US.
BECAUSE THEY'RE *INVADERS*.

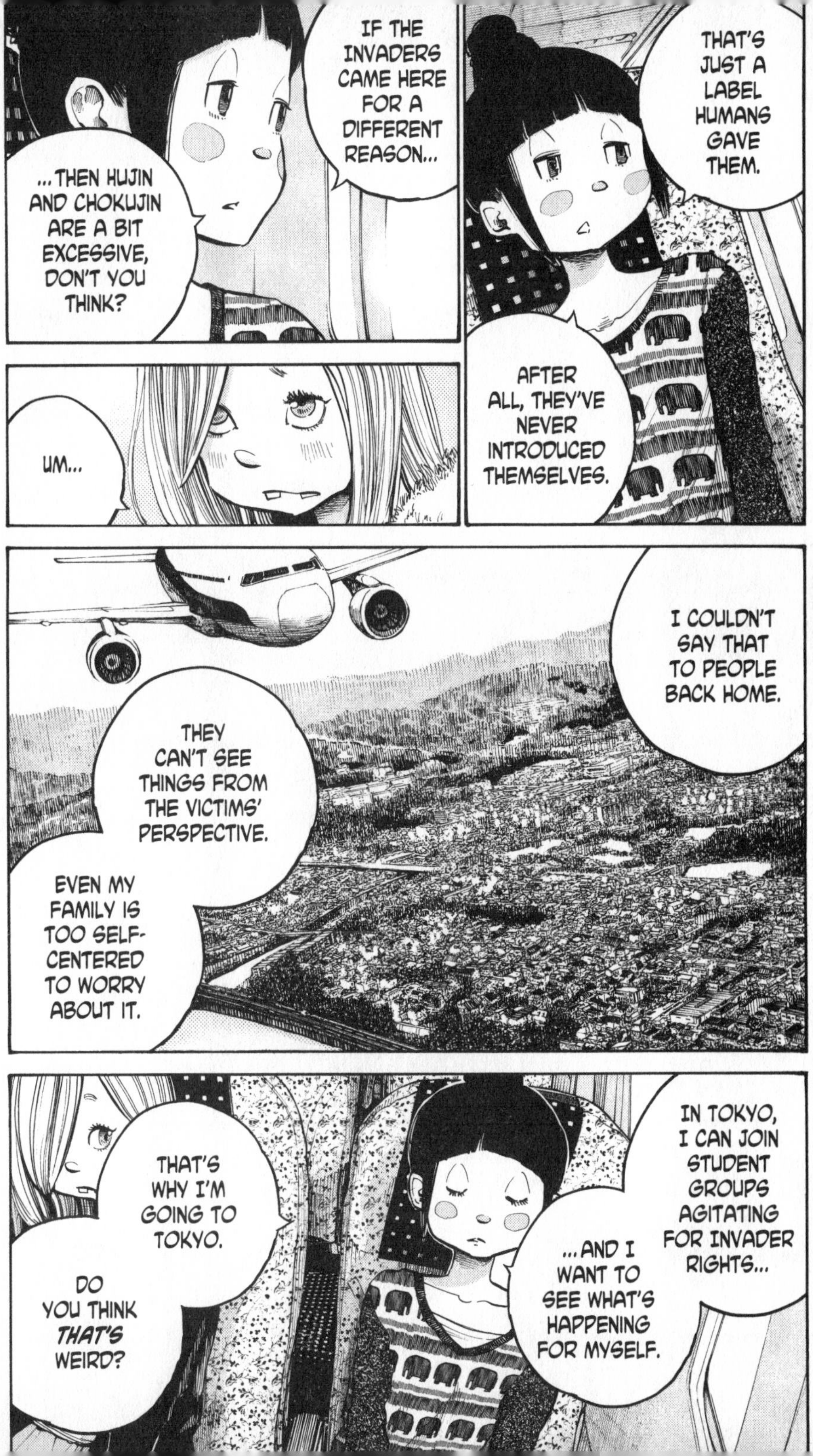
THAT'S JUST A LABEL HUMANS GAVE THEM.
AFTER ALL, THEY'VE NEVER INTRODUCED THEMSELVES.
IF THE INVADERS CAME HERE FOR A DIFFERENT REASON...
...THEN HUJIN AND CHOKUJIN ARE A BIT EXCESSIVE, DON'T YOU THINK?
UM...
I COULDN'T SAY THAT TO PEOPLE BACK HOME.
THEY CAN'T SEE THINGS FROM THE VICTIMS' PERSPECTIVE.
EVEN MY FAMILY IS TOO SELF-CENTERED TO WORRY ABOUT IT.
IN TOKYO, I CAN JOIN STUDENT GROUPS AGITATING FOR INVADER RIGHTS...
...AND I WANT TO SEE WHAT'S HAPPENING FOR MYSELF.
THAT'S WHY I'M GOING TO TOKYO.
DO YOU THINK *THAT'S* WEIRD?

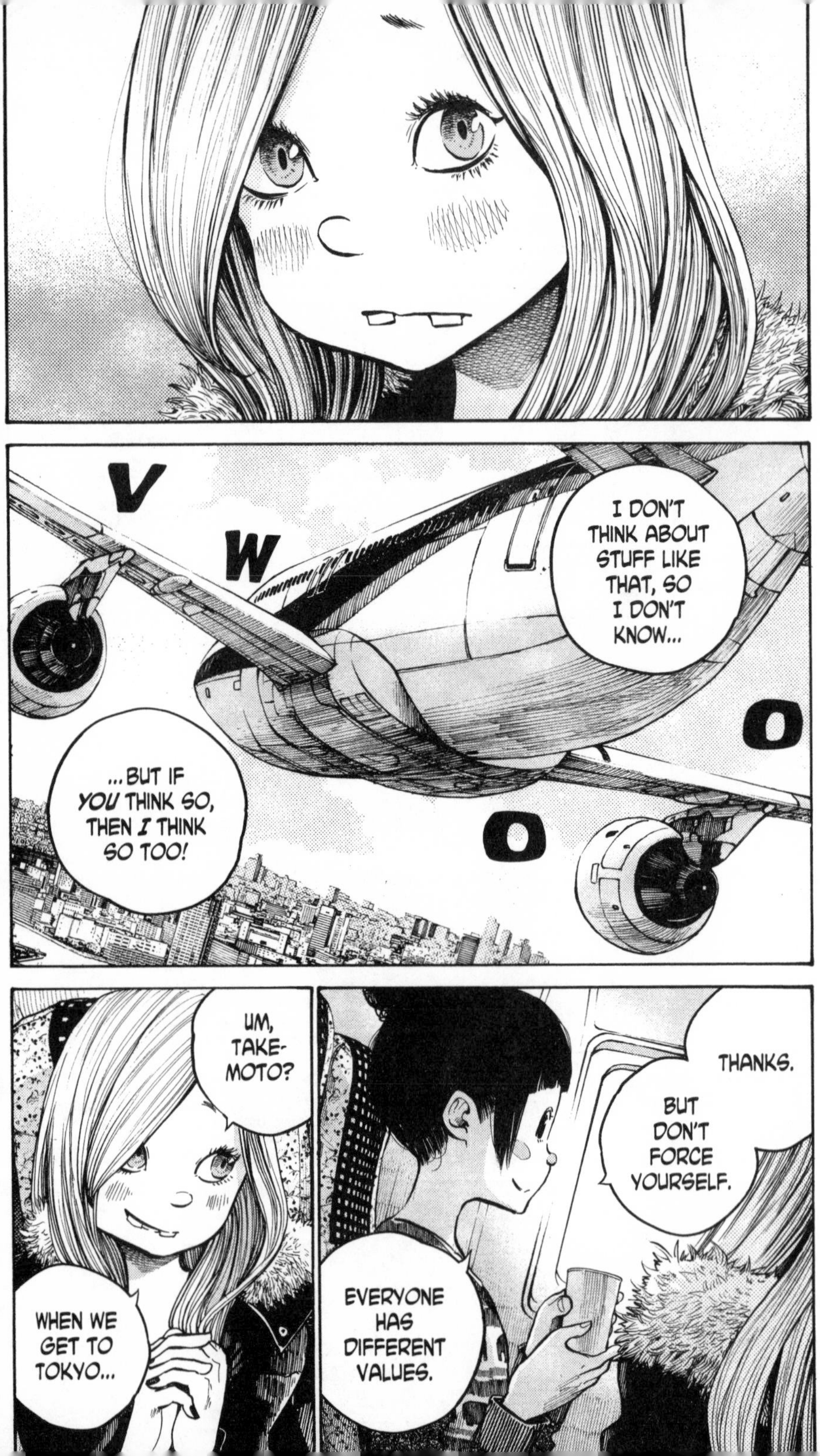
I DON'T THINK ABOUT STUFF LIKE THAT, SO I DON'T KNOW...
VWOO
...BUT IF *YOU* THINK SO, THEN *I* THINK SO TOO!
THANKS.
BUT DON'T FORCE YOURSELF.
EVERYONE HAS DIFFERENT VALUES.
UM, TAKE-MOTO?
WHEN WE GET TO TOKYO...

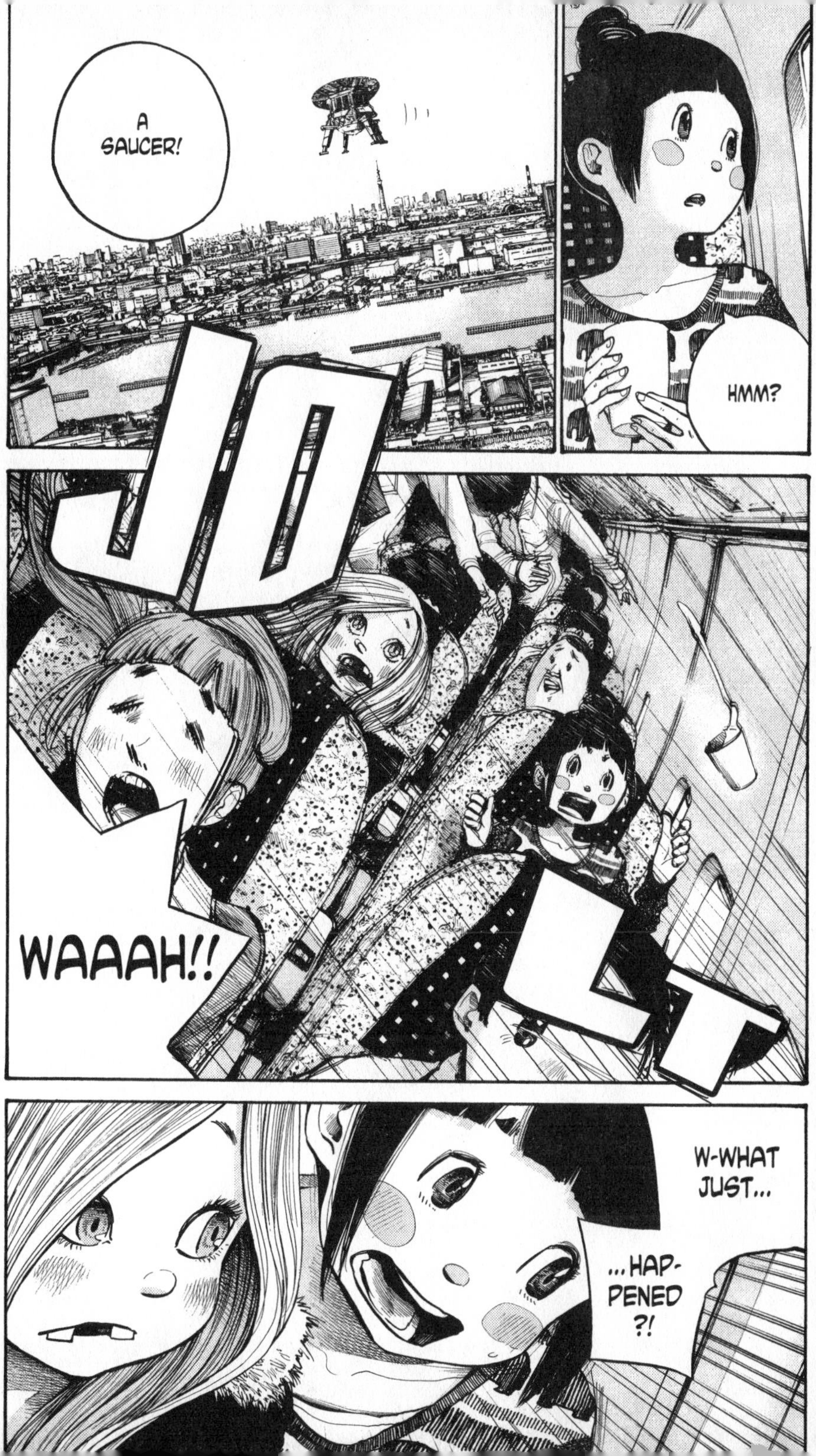
HMM?
A SAUCER!
JOLT
WAAAH!!
W-WHAT JUST...
...HAP-PENED ?!

MAY I HAVE YOUR ATTENTION PLEASE...

AIR TRAFFIC CONTROL HAS SENT AN EMERGENCY COURSE CORRECTION.

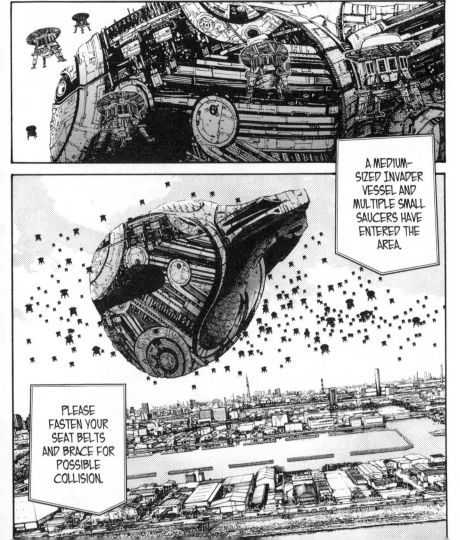

A MEDIUM-SIZED INVADER VESSEL AND MULTIPLE SMALL SAUCERS HAVE ENTERED THE AREA.

PLEASE FASTEN YOUR SEAT BELTS AND BRACE FOR POSSIBLE COLLISION.

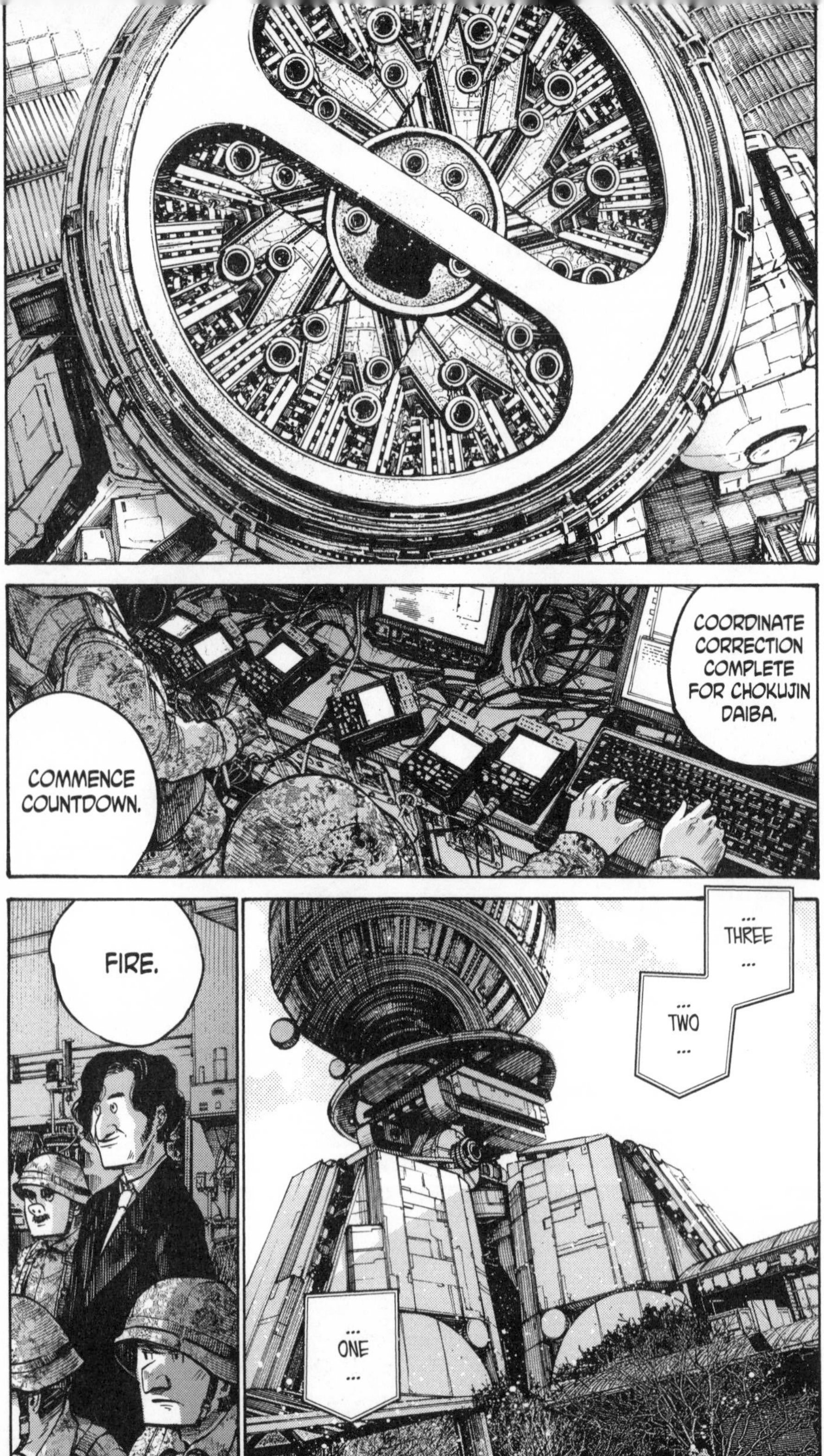
COORDINATE CORRECTION COMPLETE FOR CHOKUJIN DAIBA.
COMMENCE COUNTDOWN.
... THREE ...
... TWO ...
... ONE ...
FIRE.

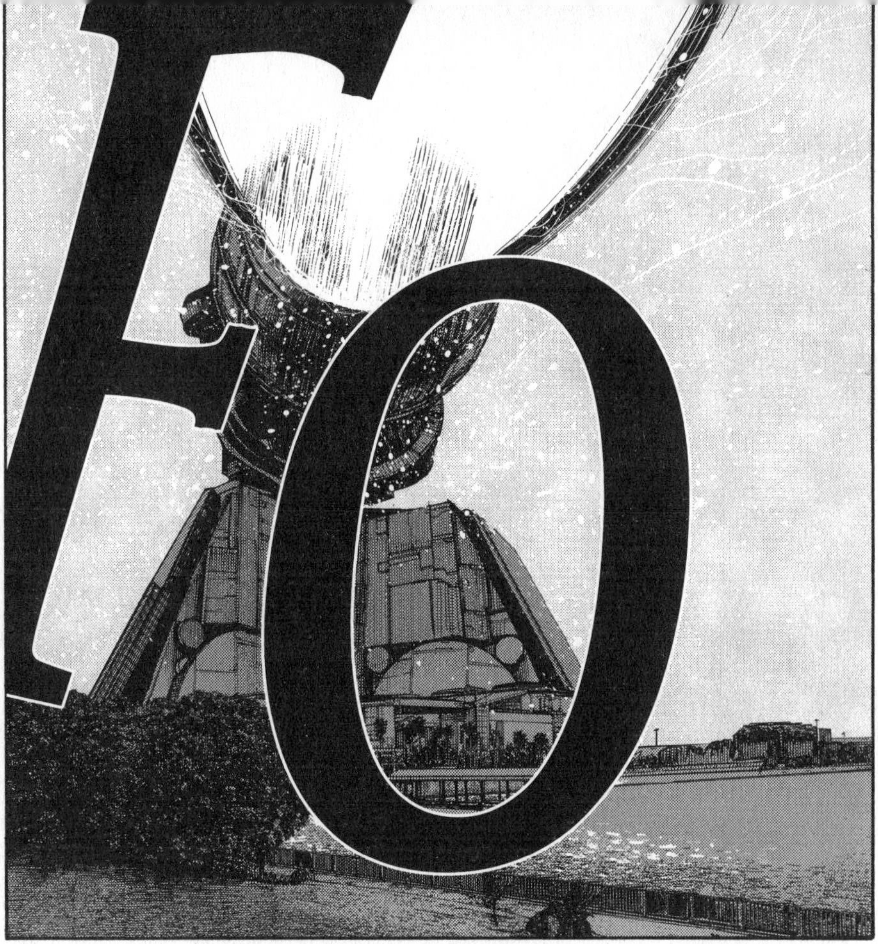
FO
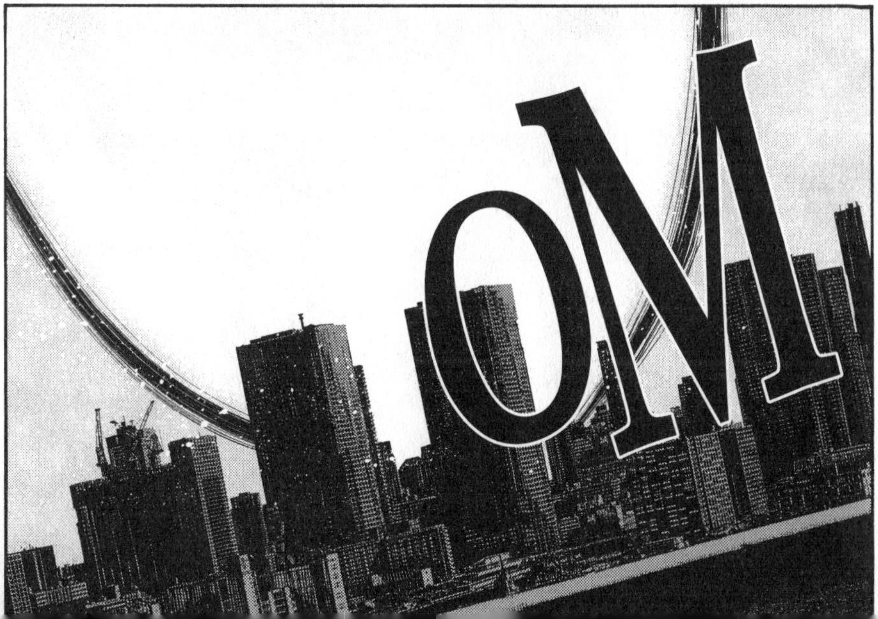
OM

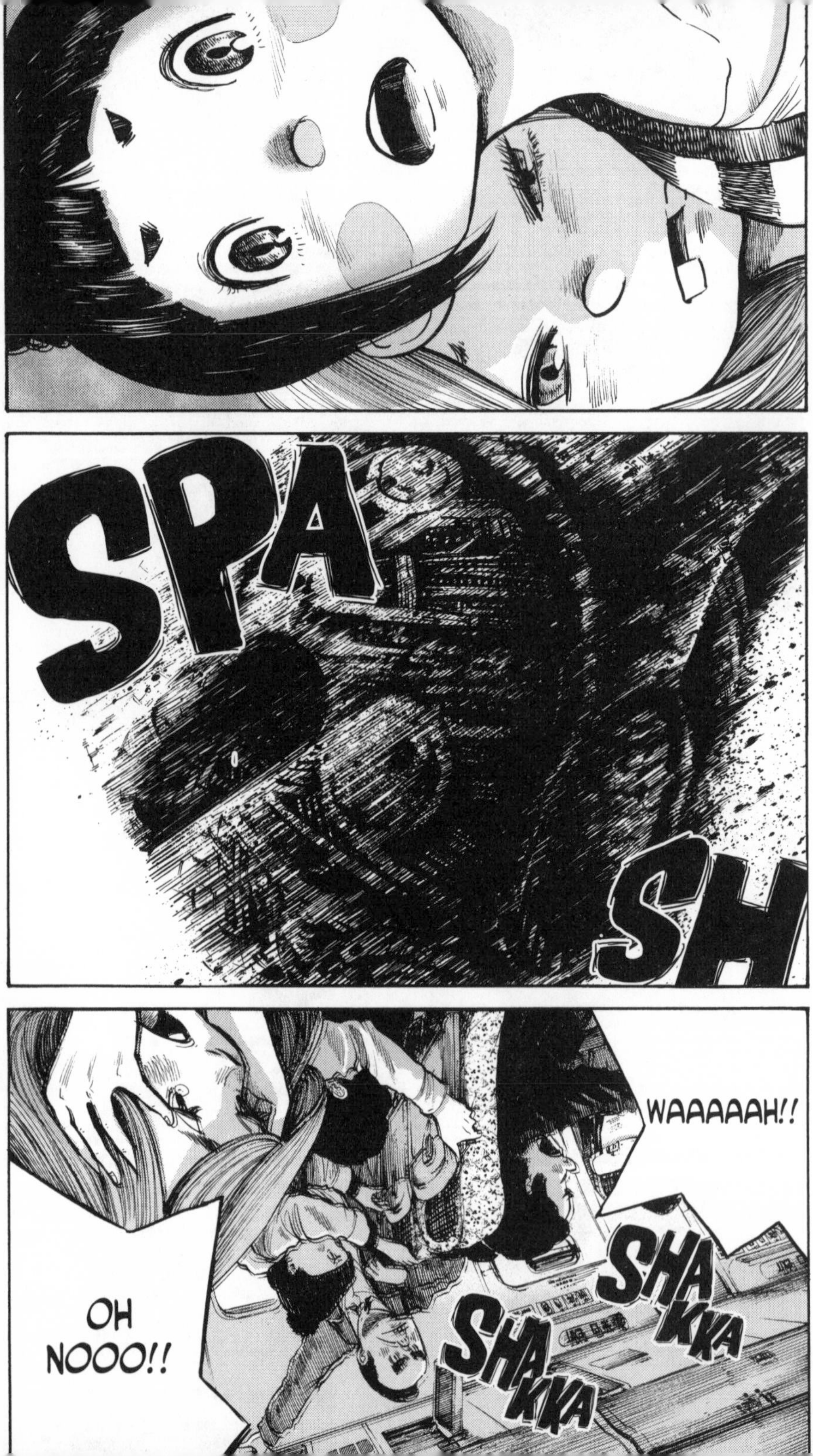
SPA
SH
WAAAAAH!!
SHAKKA
SHAKKA
OH NOOO!!

GWOOO
O...

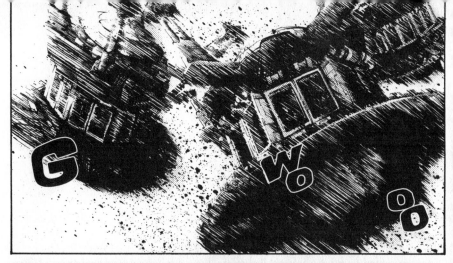

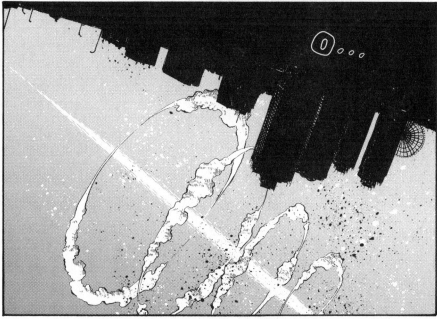

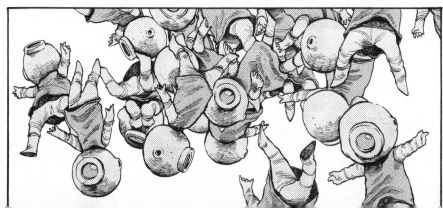

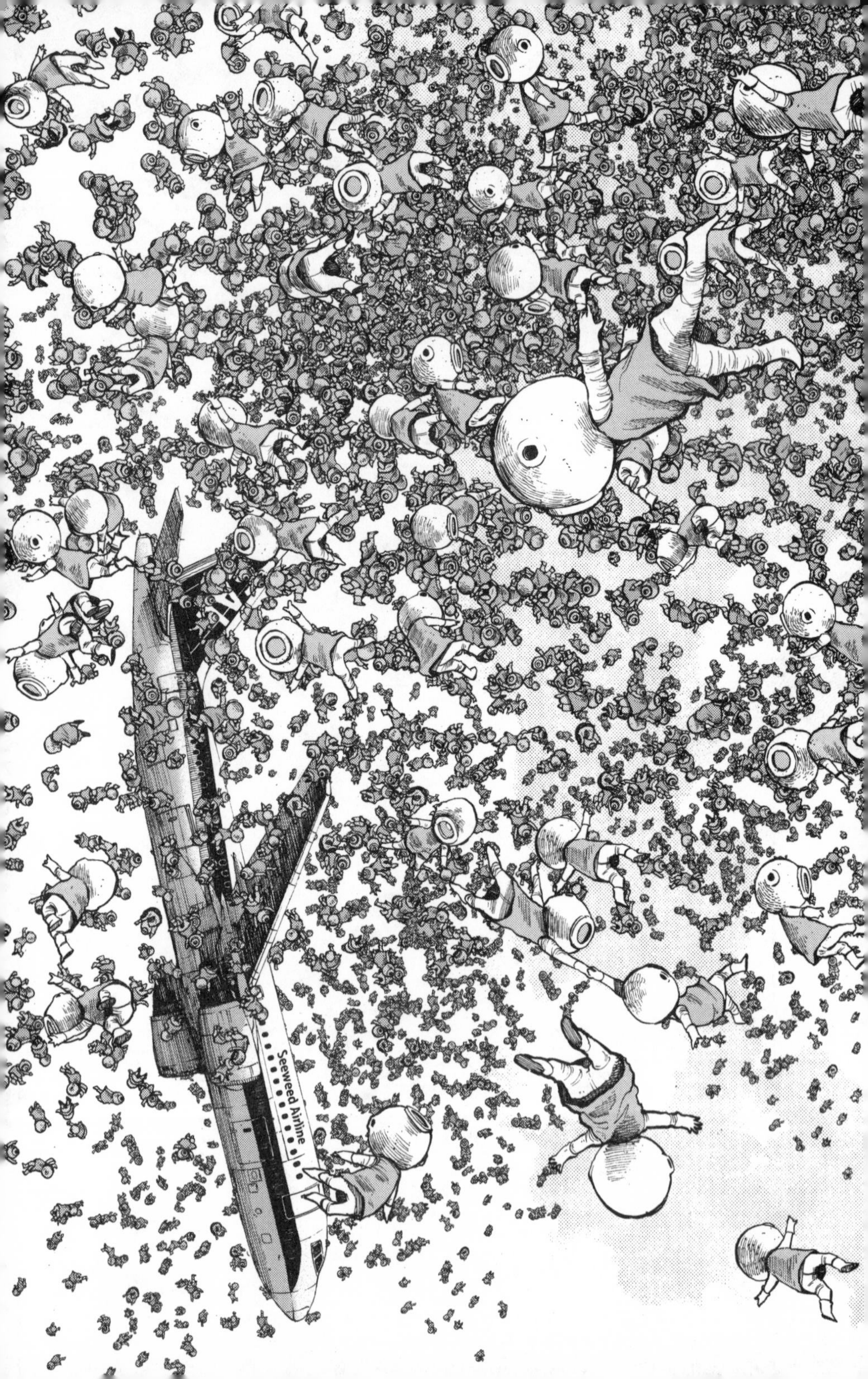
Seeweed Airline

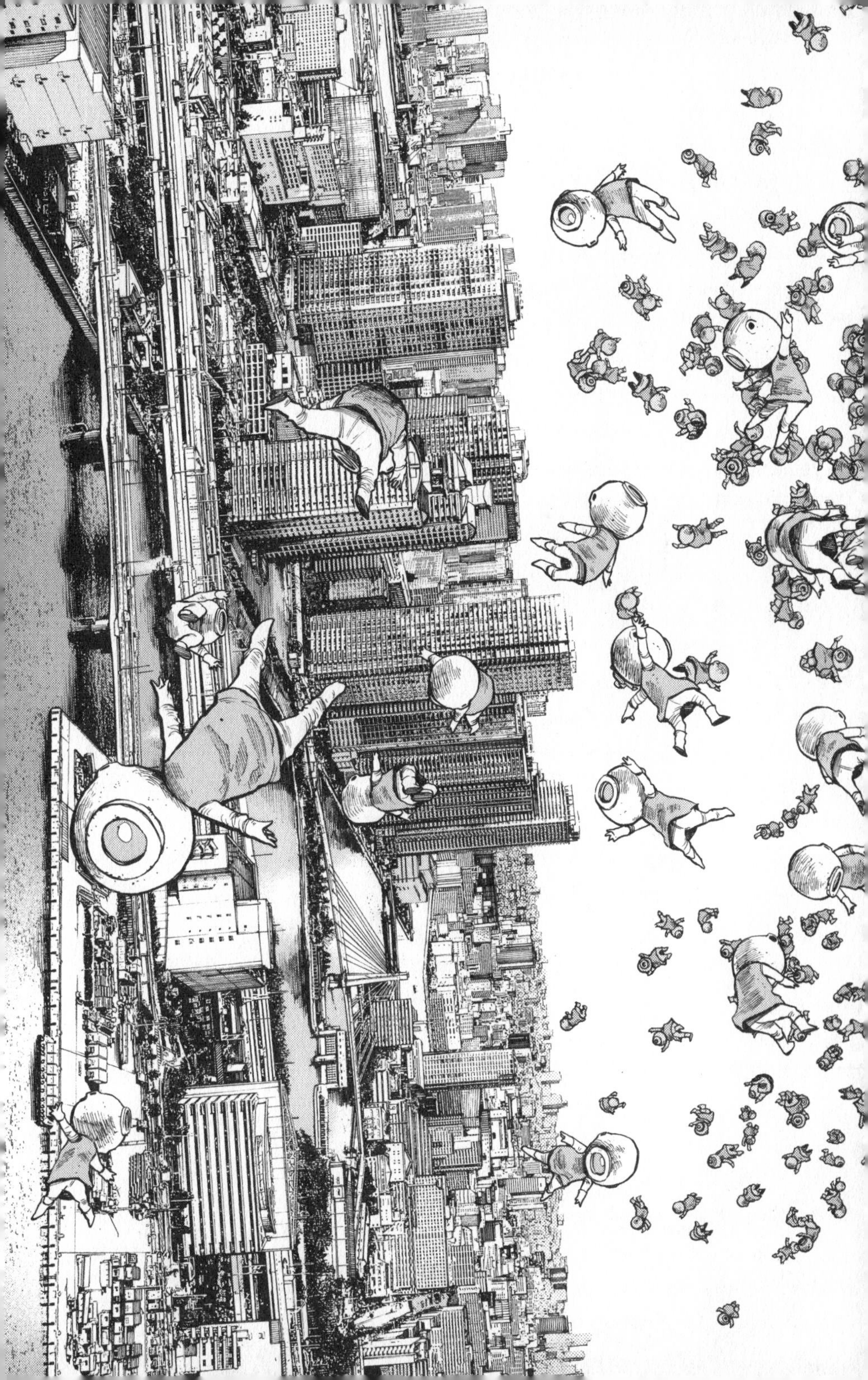

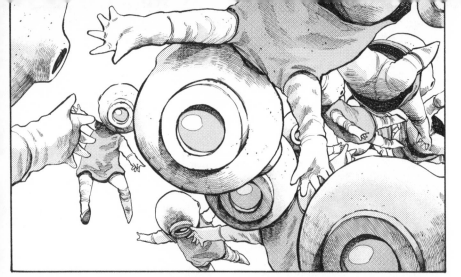

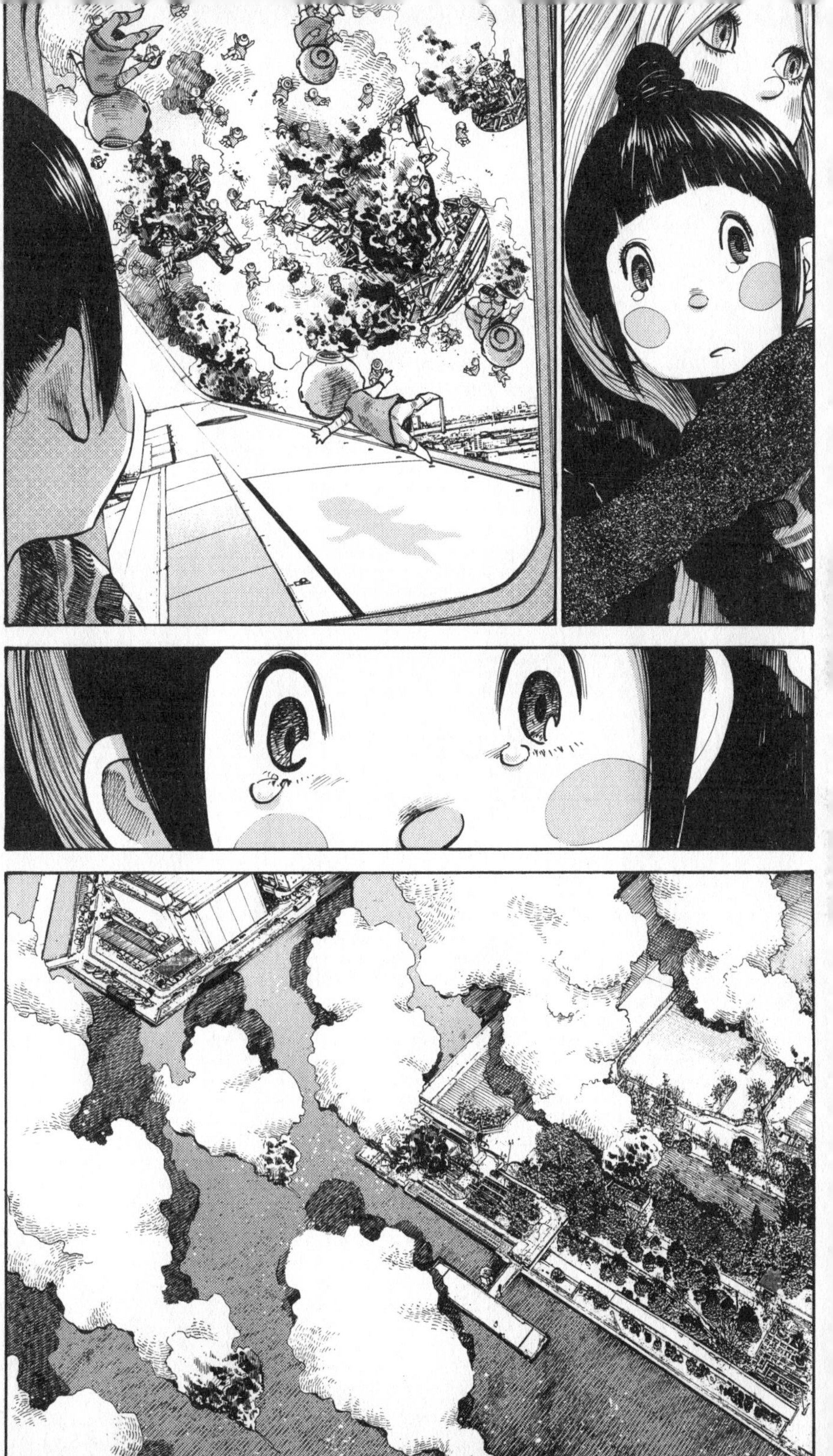

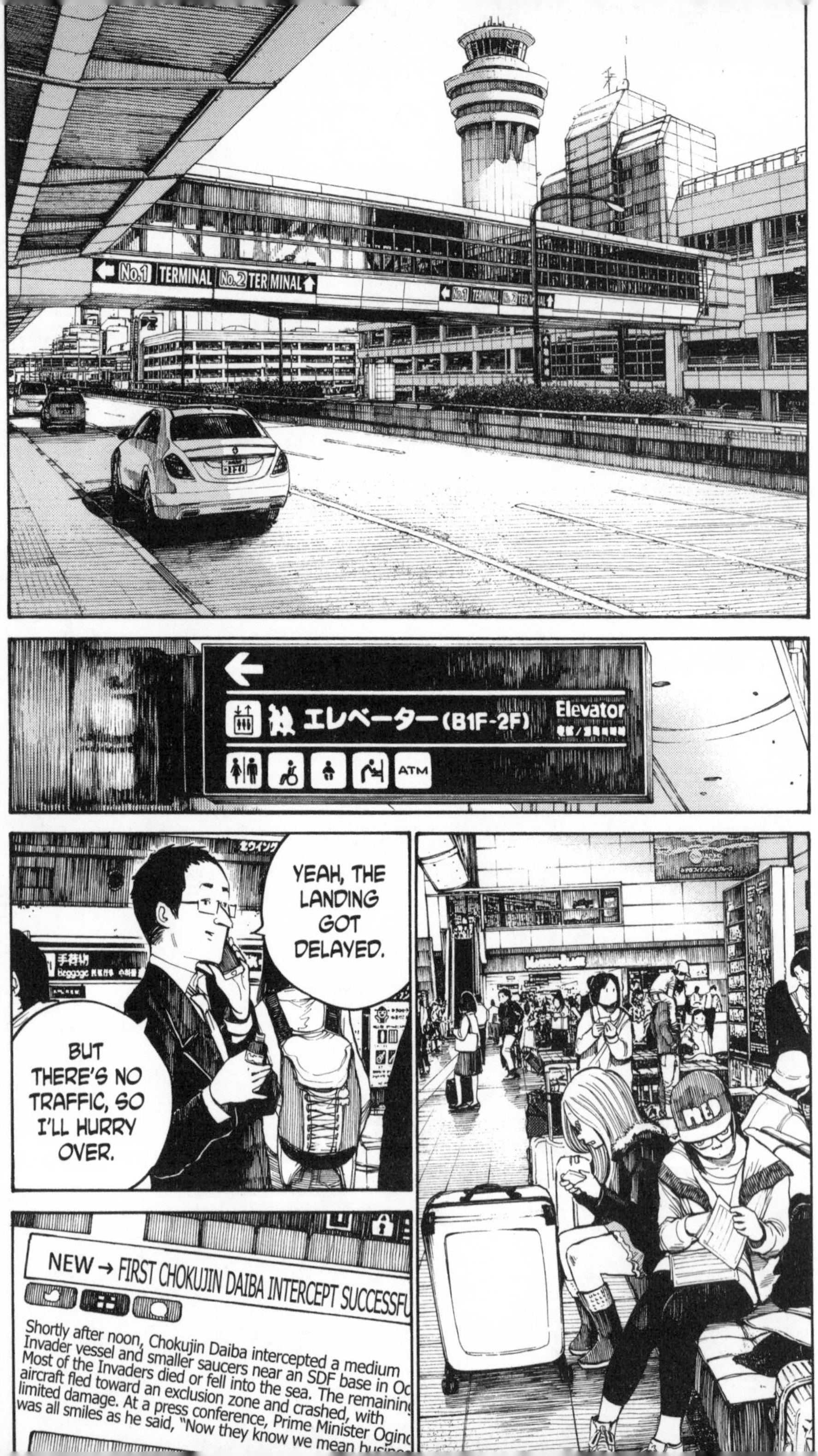
No.1 TERMINAL No.2 TERMINAL
No.1 TERMINAL No.2 TERMINAL
エレベーター (B1F-2F)
Elevator
ATM
YEAH, THE LANDING GOT DELAYED.
BUT THERE'S NO TRAFFIC, SO I'LL HURRY OVER.
NEW → FIRST CHOKUJIN DAIBA INTERCEPT SUCCESSFU
Shortly after noon, Chokujin Daiba intercepted a medium Invader vessel and smaller saucers near an SDF base in Oc Most of the Invaders died or fell into the sea. The remainin aircraft fled toward an exclusion zone and crashed, with limited damage. At a press conference, Prime Minister Oginc was all smiles as he said, "Now they know we mean busin

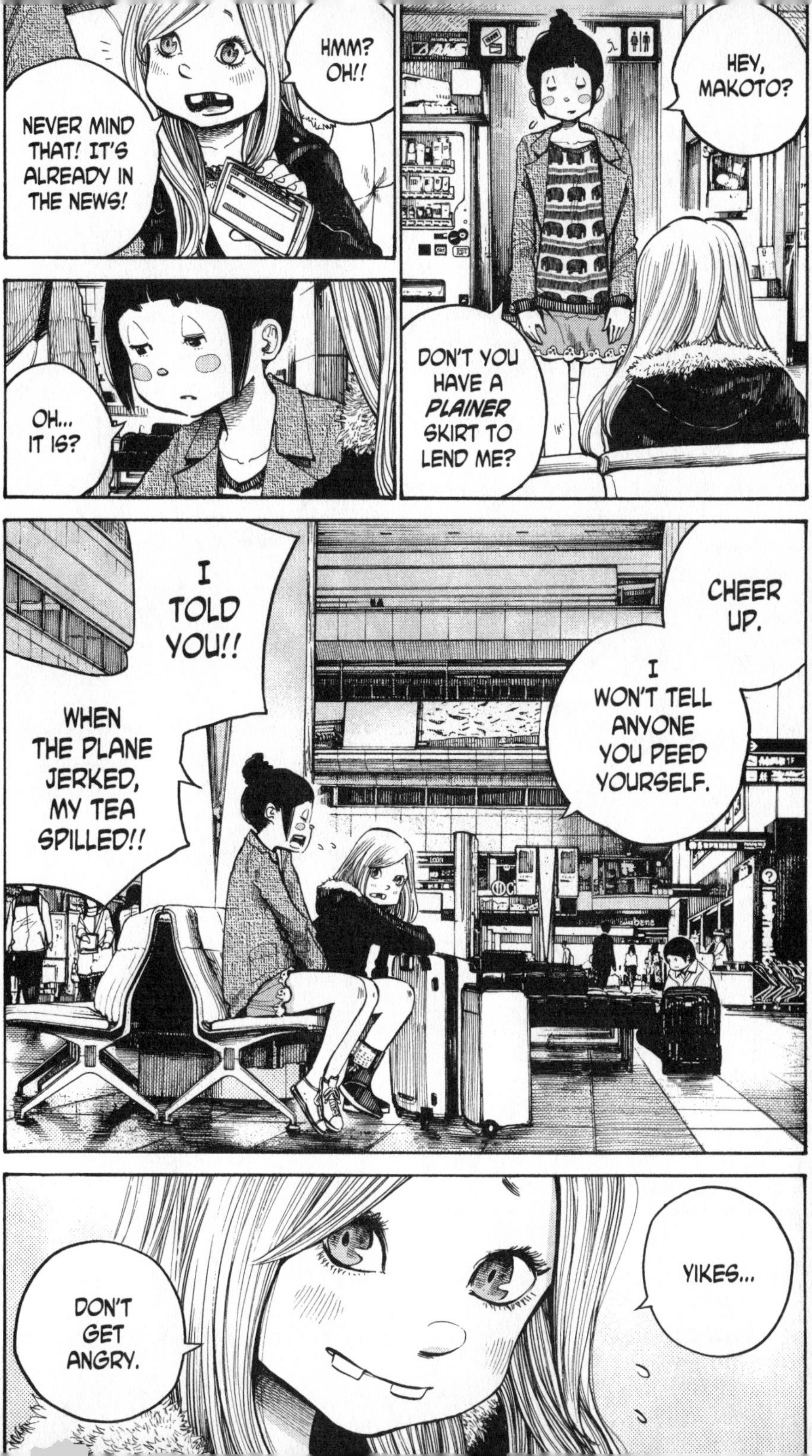
HEY, MAKOTO?
DON'T YOU HAVE A *PLAINER* SKIRT TO LEND ME?
HMM? OH!!
NEVER MIND THAT! IT'S ALREADY IN THE NEWS!
OH... IT IS?
CHEER UP.
I WON'T TELL ANYONE YOU PEED YOURSELF.
I TOLD YOU!!
WHEN THE PLANE JERKED, MY TEA SPILLED!!
YIKES...
DON'T GET ANGRY.

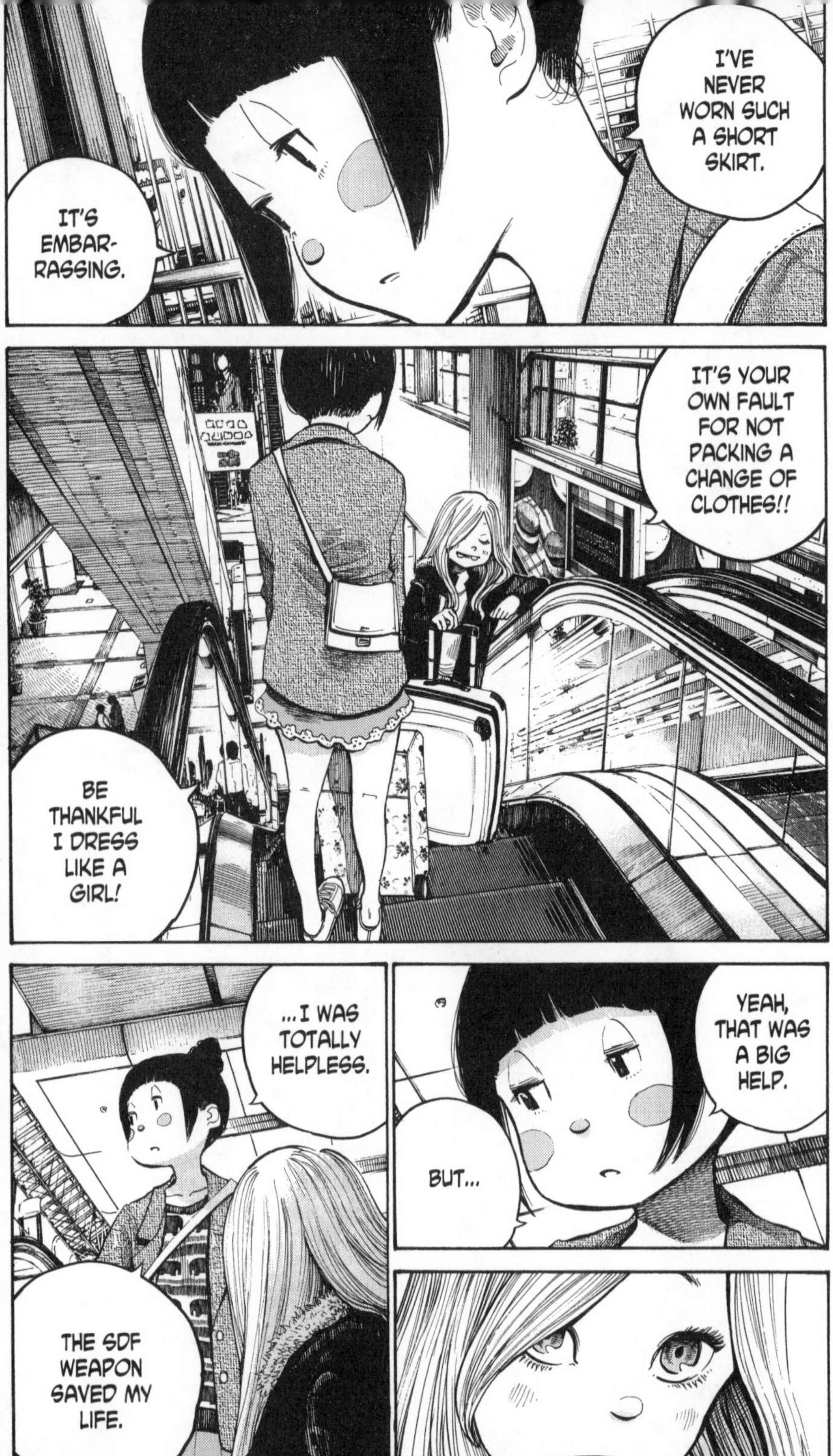
I'VE NEVER WORN SUCH A SHORT SKIRT.
IT'S EMBARRASSING.
IT'S YOUR OWN FAULT FOR NOT PACKING A CHANGE OF CLOTHES!!
BE THANKFUL I DRESS LIKE A GIRL!
YEAH, THAT WAS A BIG HELP.
BUT...
...I WAS TOTALLY HELPLESS.
THE SDF WEAPON SAVED MY LIFE.

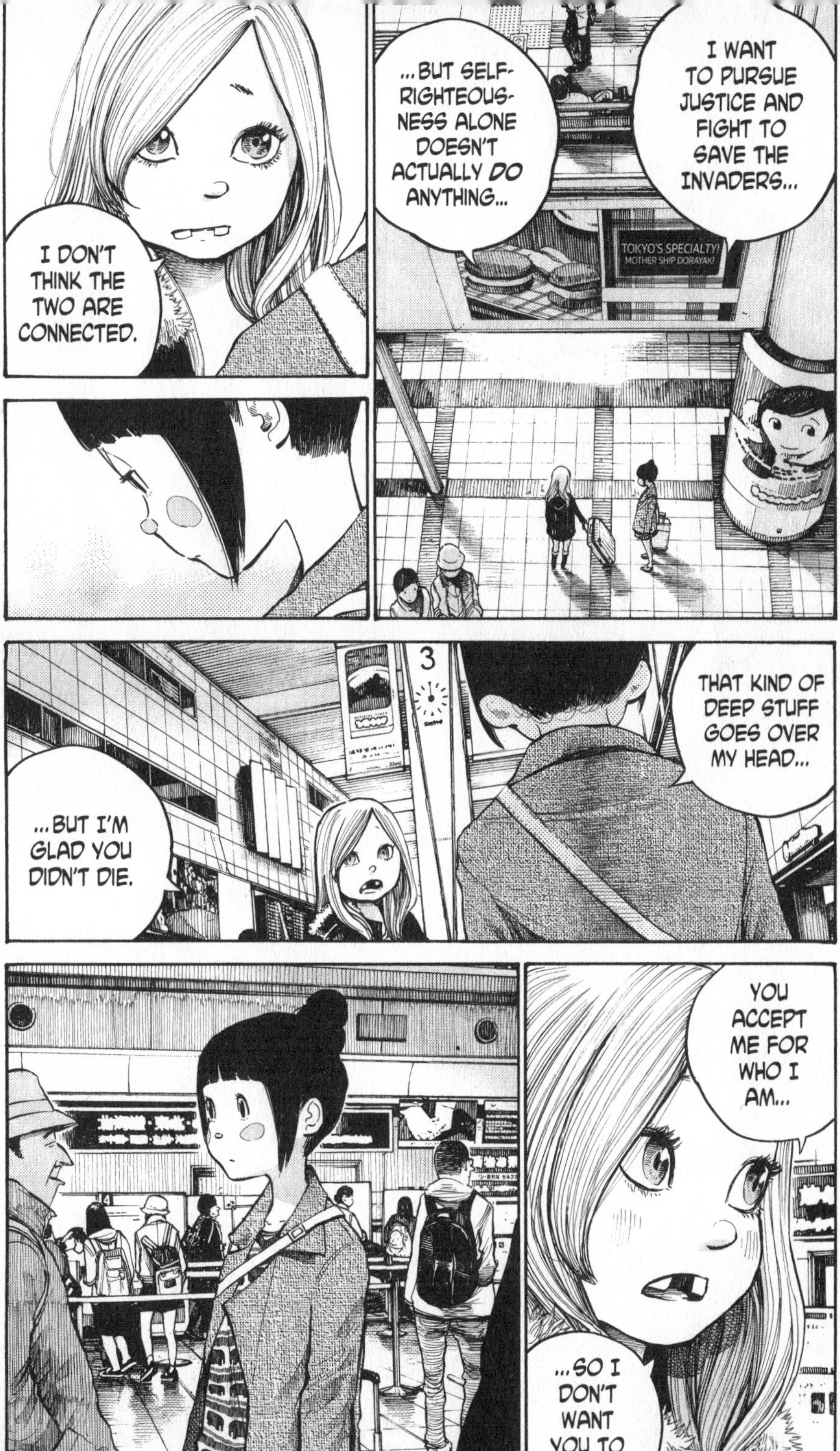
I WANT TO PURSUE JUSTICE AND FIGHT TO SAVE THE INVADERS...
...BUT SELF-RIGHTEOUSNESS ALONE DOESN'T ACTUALLY *DO* ANYTHING...
TOKYO'S SPECIALTY! MOTHER SHIP DORAYAKI!
I DON'T THINK THE TWO ARE CONNECTED.
THAT KIND OF DEEP STUFF GOES OVER MY HEAD...
...BUT I'M GLAD YOU DIDN'T DIE.
YOU ACCEPT ME FOR WHO I AM...
...SO I DON'T WANT YOU TO DIE.

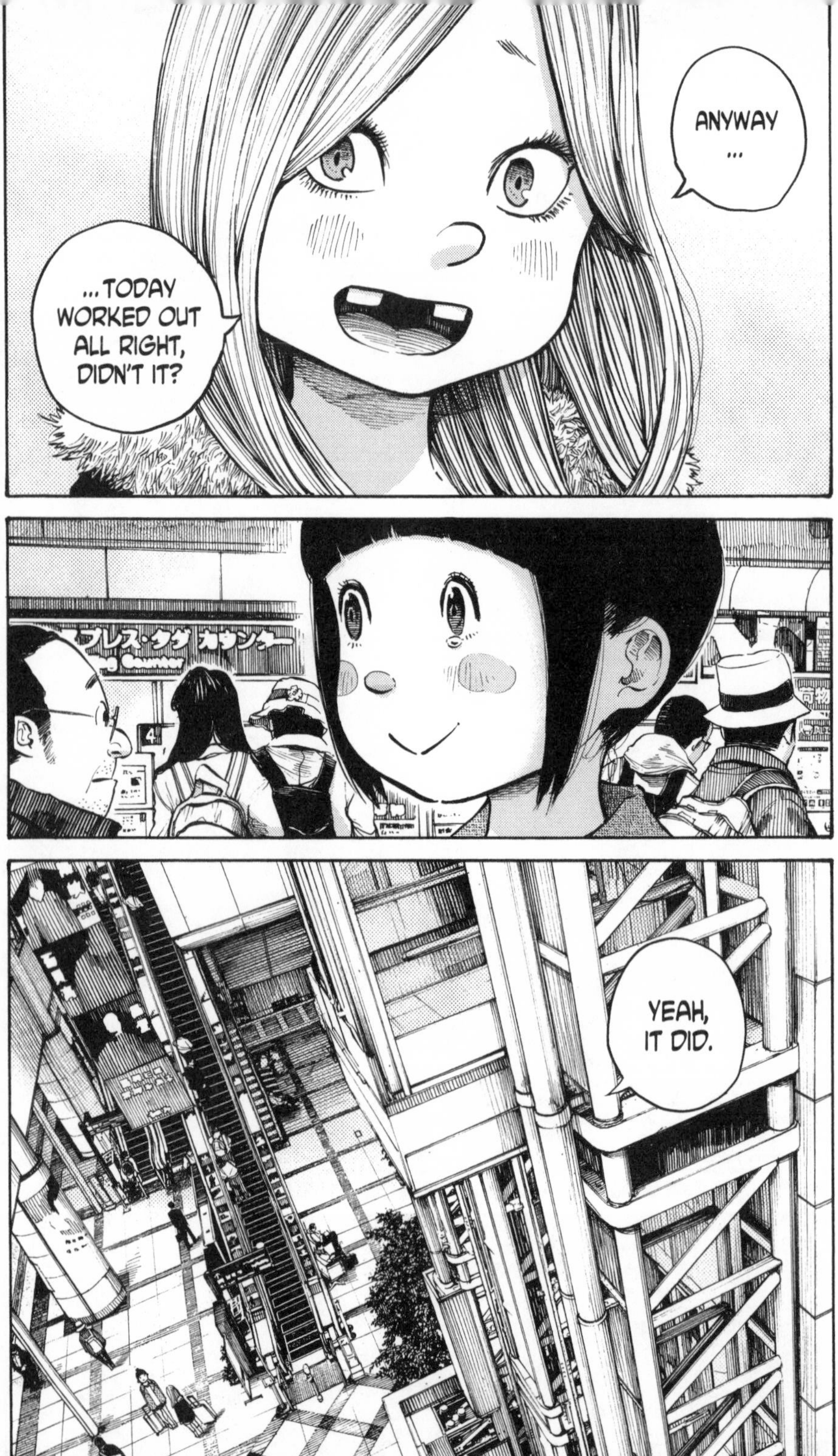
ANYWAY ...
...TODAY WORKED OUT ALL RIGHT, DIDN'T IT?
YEAH, IT DID.

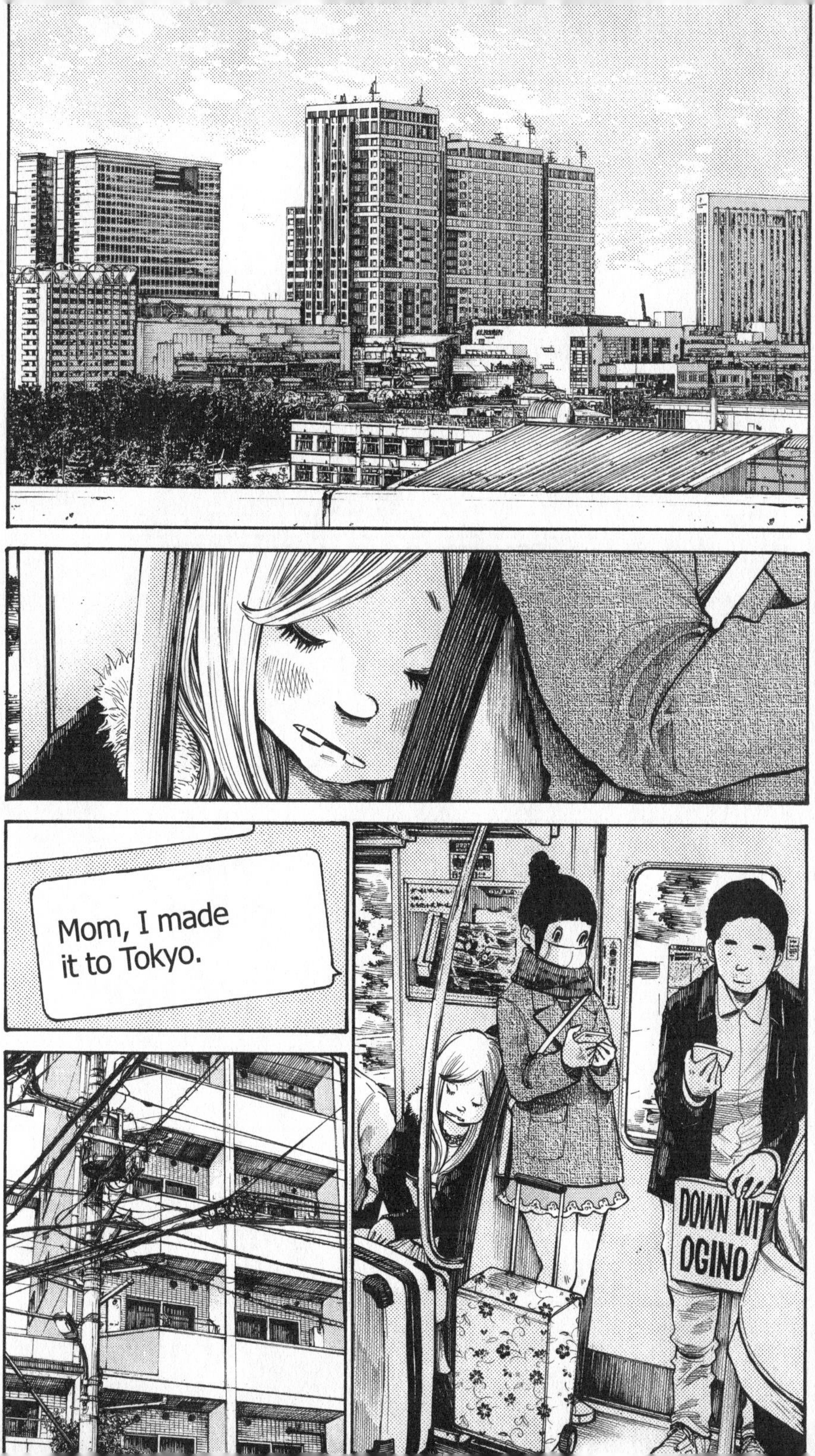
DOWN WIT
OGINO
Mom, I made it to Tokyo.

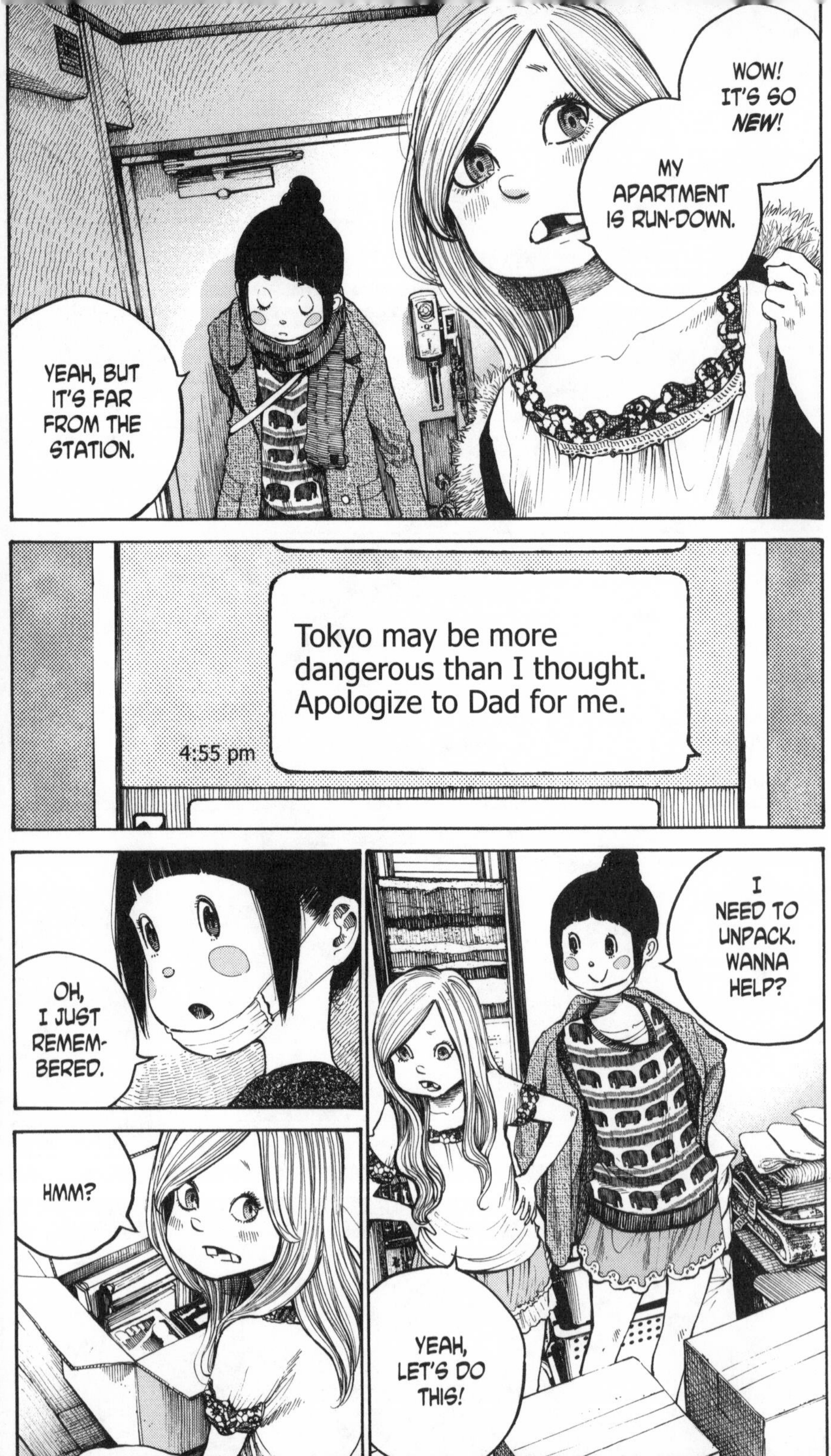
WOW! IT'S SO *NEW*!
MY APARTMENT IS RUN-DOWN.
YEAH, BUT IT'S FAR FROM THE STATION.
Tokyo may be more dangerous than I thought. Apologize to Dad for me.
4:55 pm
I NEED TO UNPACK. WANNA HELP?
YEAH, LET'S DO THIS!
OH, I JUST REMEM-BERED.
HMM?

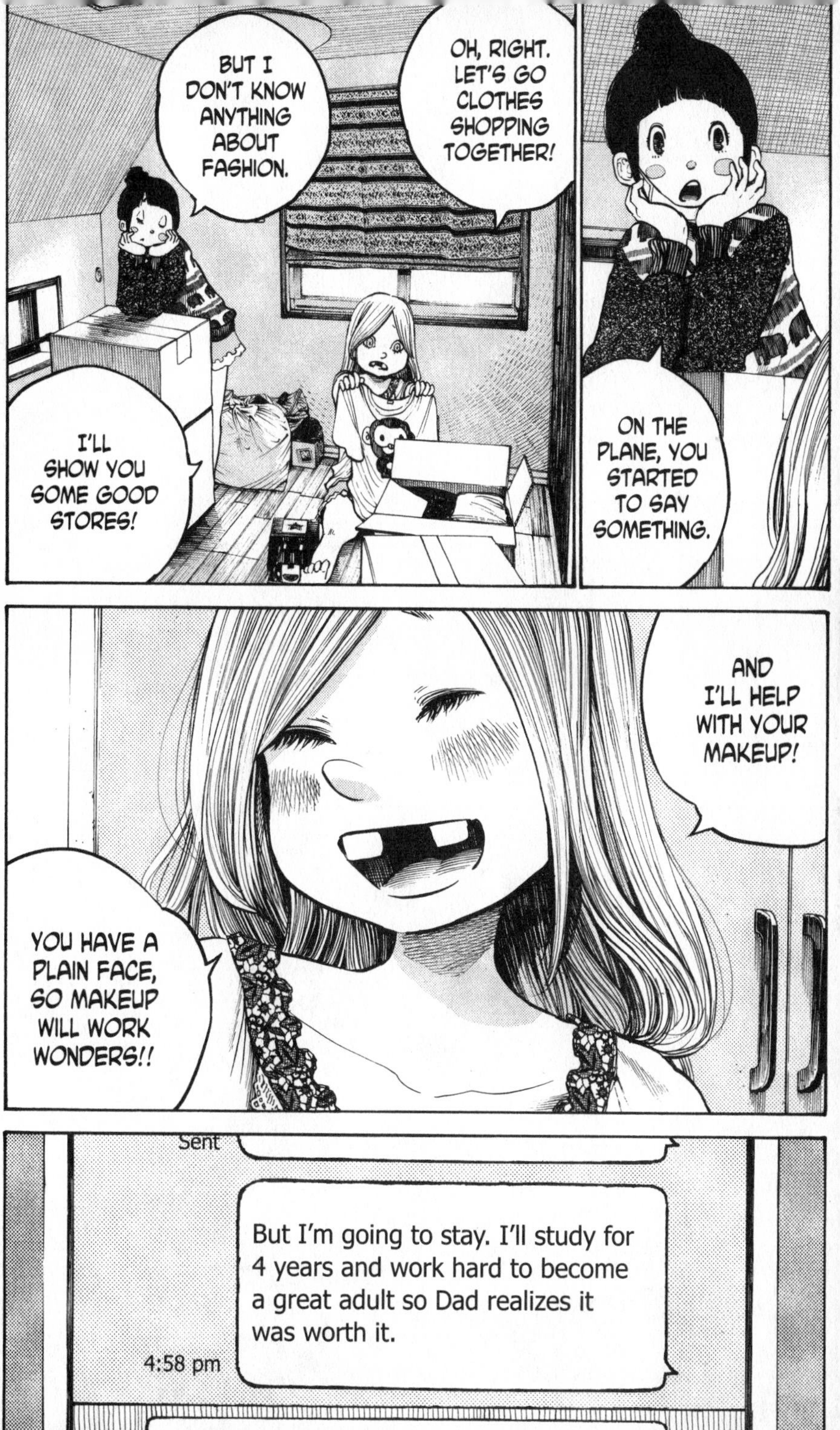
ON THE PLANE, YOU STARTED TO SAY SOMETHING.
OH, RIGHT. LET'S GO CLOTHES SHOPPING TOGETHER!
BUT I DON'T KNOW ANYTHING ABOUT FASHION.
I'LL SHOW YOU SOME GOOD STORES!
AND I'LL HELP WITH YOUR MAKEUP!
YOU HAVE A PLAIN FACE, SO MAKEUP WILL WORK WONDERS!!
Sent
But I'm going to stay. I'll study for 4 years and work hard to become a great adult so Dad realizes it was worth it.
4:58 pm

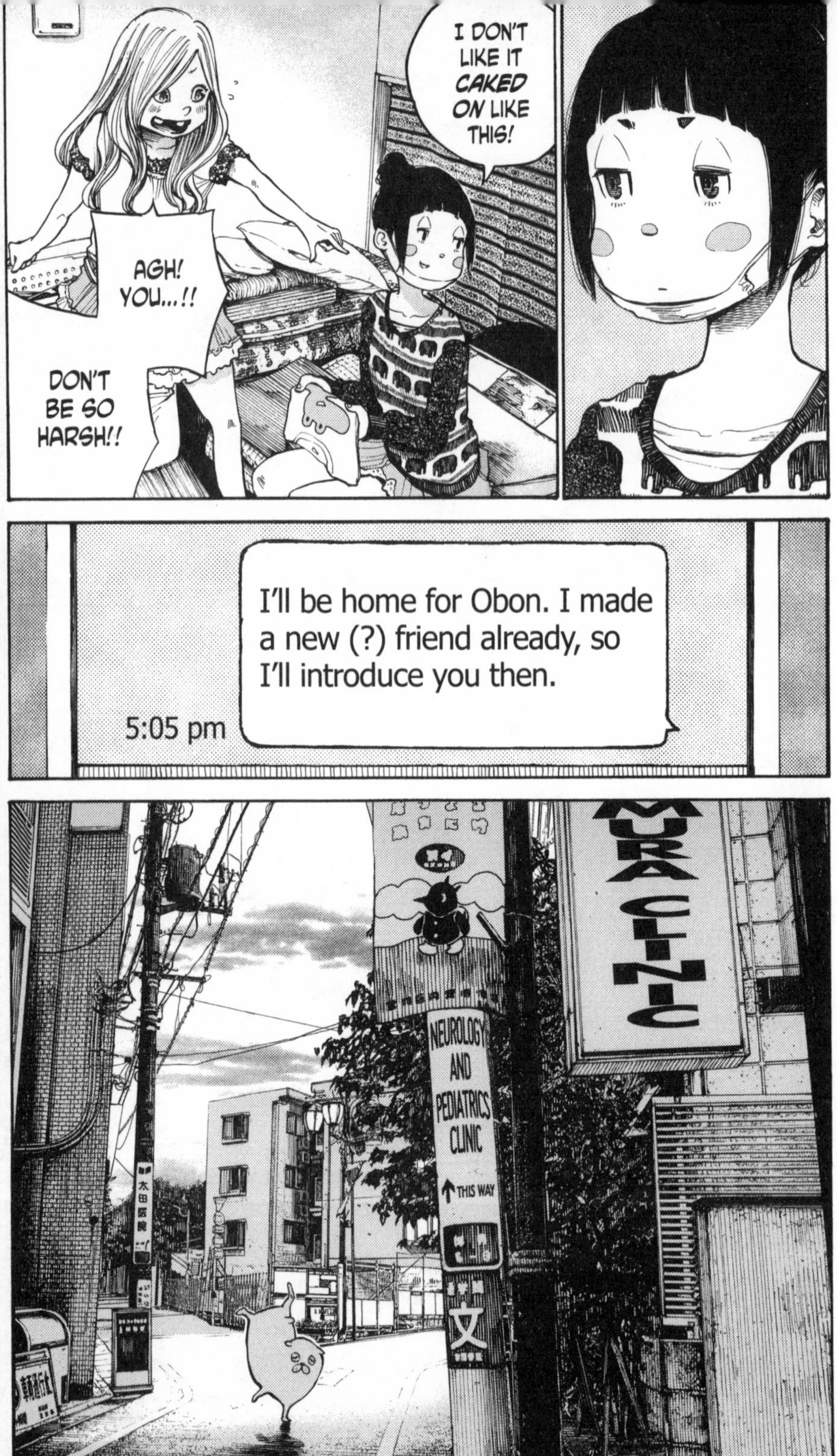
I DON'T LIKE IT CAKED ON LIKE THIS!
AGH! YOU...!!
DON'T BE SO HARSH!!
I'll be home for Obon. I made a new (?) friend already, so I'll introduce you then.
5:05 pm
MURA CLINIC
NEUROLOGY AND PEDIATRICS CLINIC
THIS WAY
文

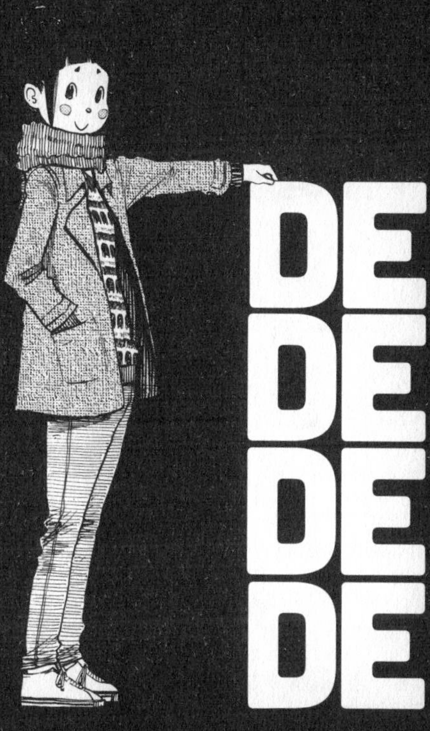
DE
DE
DE
DE

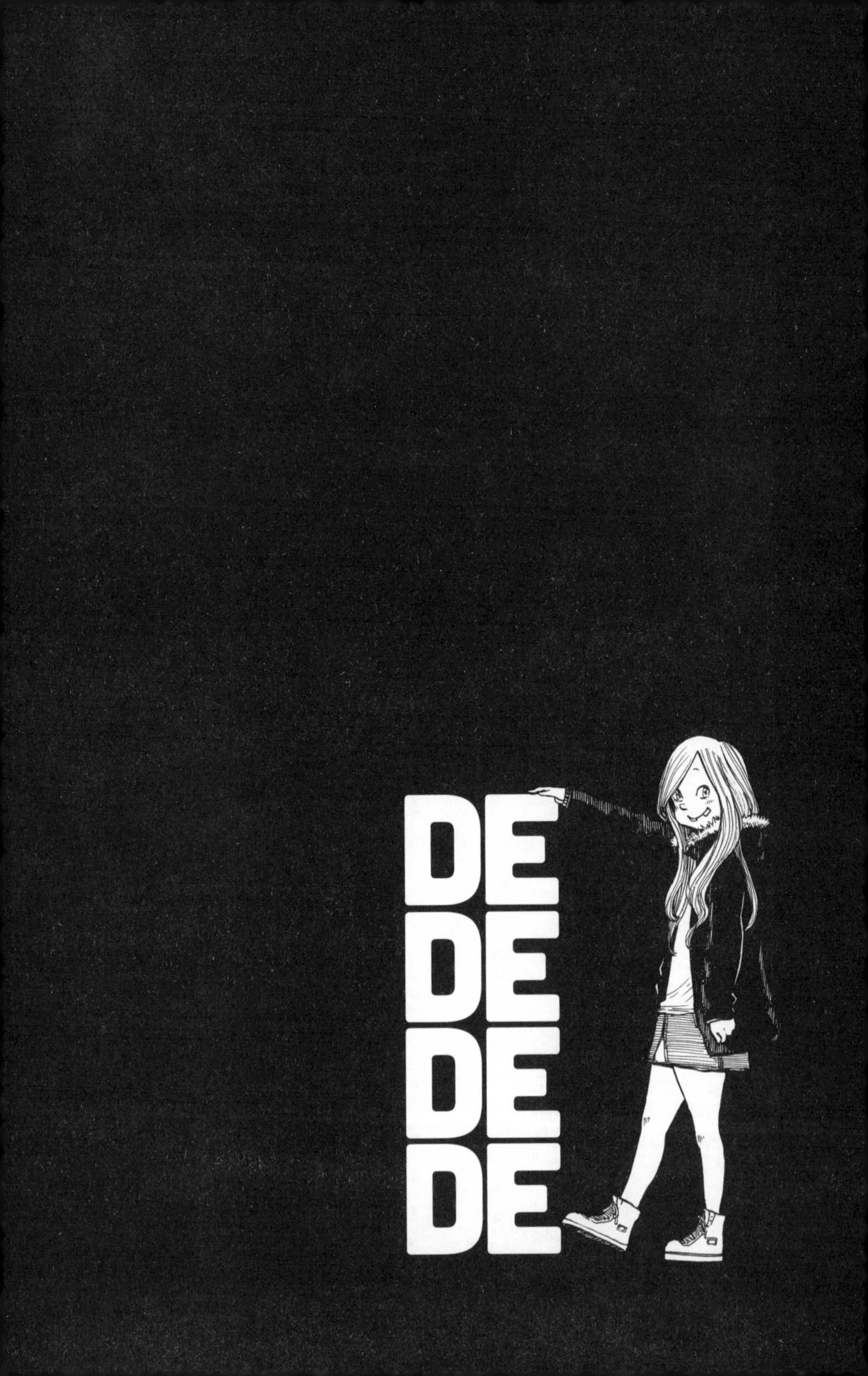
DE
DE
DE
DE

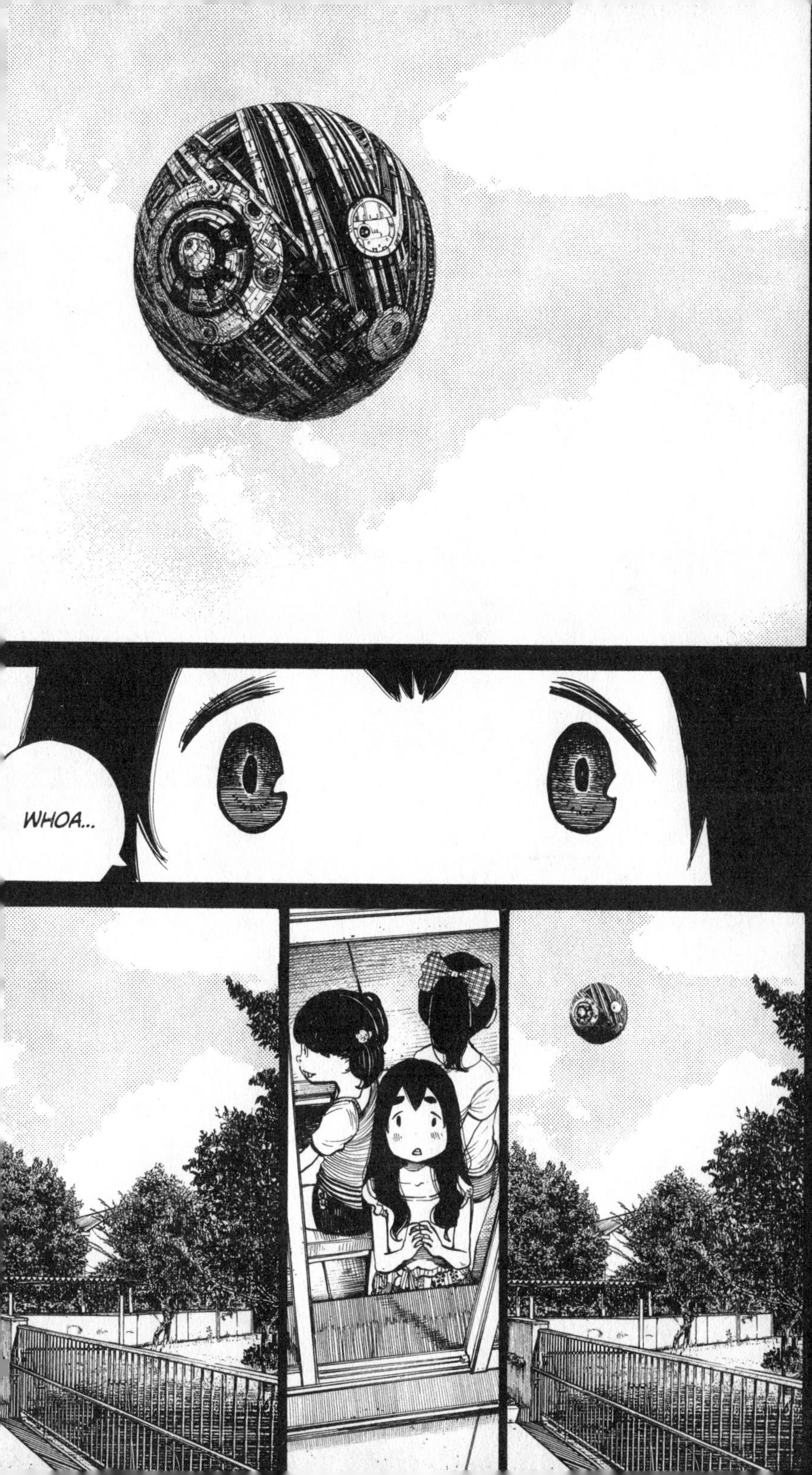
WHOA...

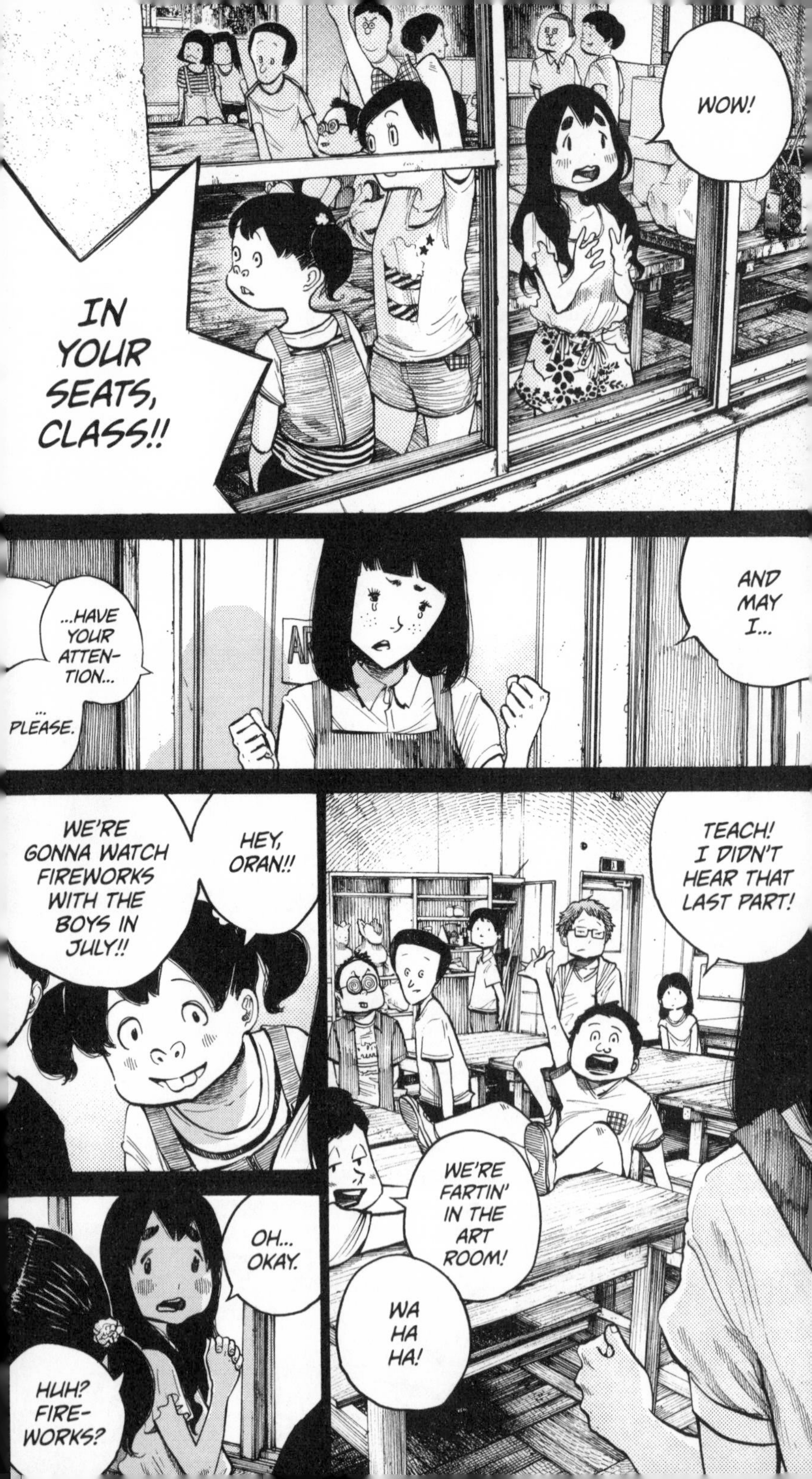
WOW!
IN YOUR SEATS, CLASS!!
AND MAY I...
...HAVE YOUR ATTEN-TION...
... PLEASE.
TEACH! I DIDN'T HEAR THAT LAST PART!
WE'RE FARTIN' IN THE ART ROOM!
WA HA HA!
HEY, ORAN!!
WE'RE GONNA WATCH FIREWORKS WITH THE BOYS IN JULY!!
OH... OKAY.
HUH? FIRE-WORKS?

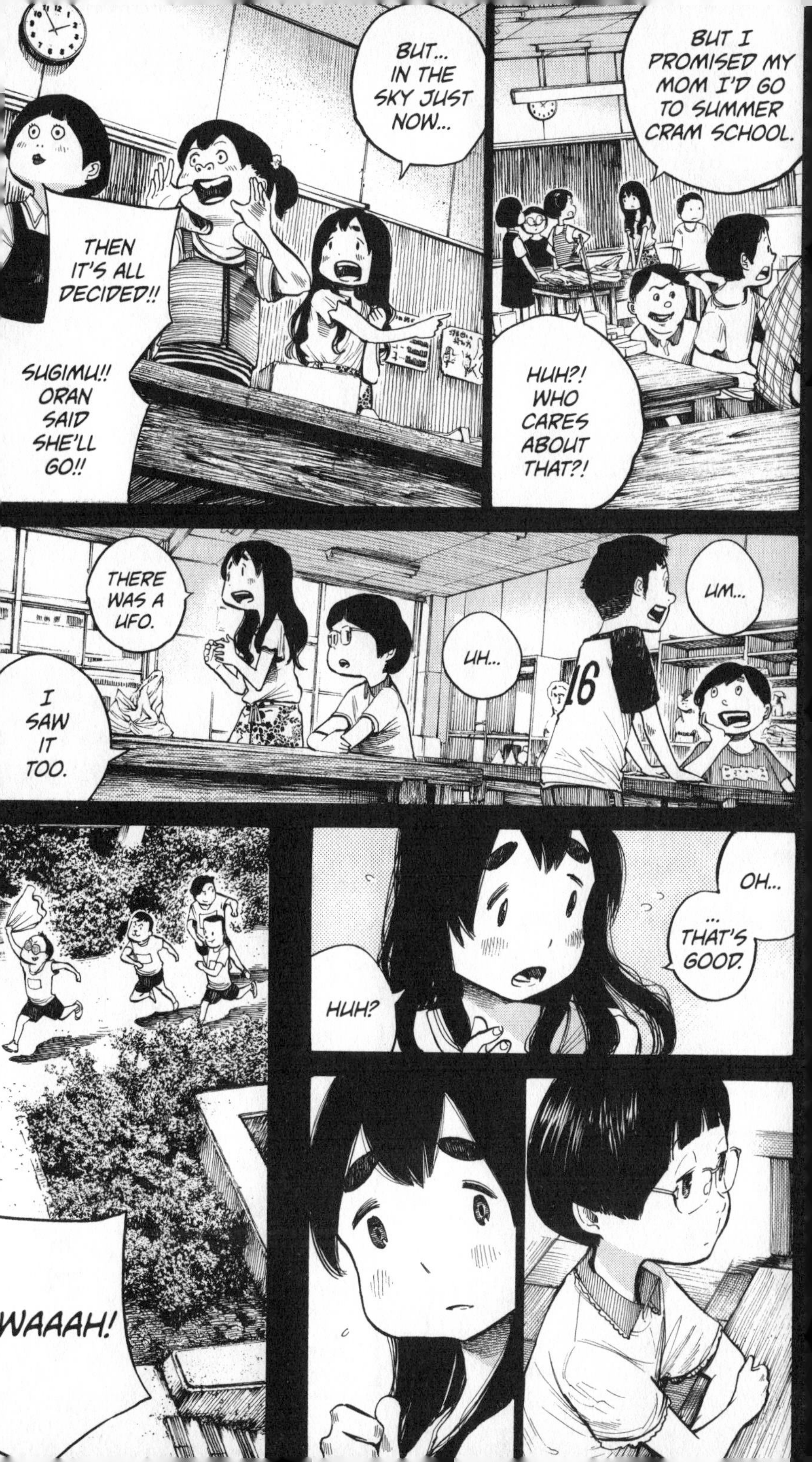
BUT I PROMISED MY MOM I'D GO TO SUMMER CRAM SCHOOL.
HUH?! WHO CARES ABOUT THAT?!
BUT... IN THE SKY JUST NOW...
THEN IT'S ALL DECIDED!!
SUGIMU!! ORAN SAID SHE'LL GO!!
UM...
UH...
THERE WAS A UFO.
I SAW IT TOO.
OH... ...THAT'S GOOD.
HUH?
WAAAH!

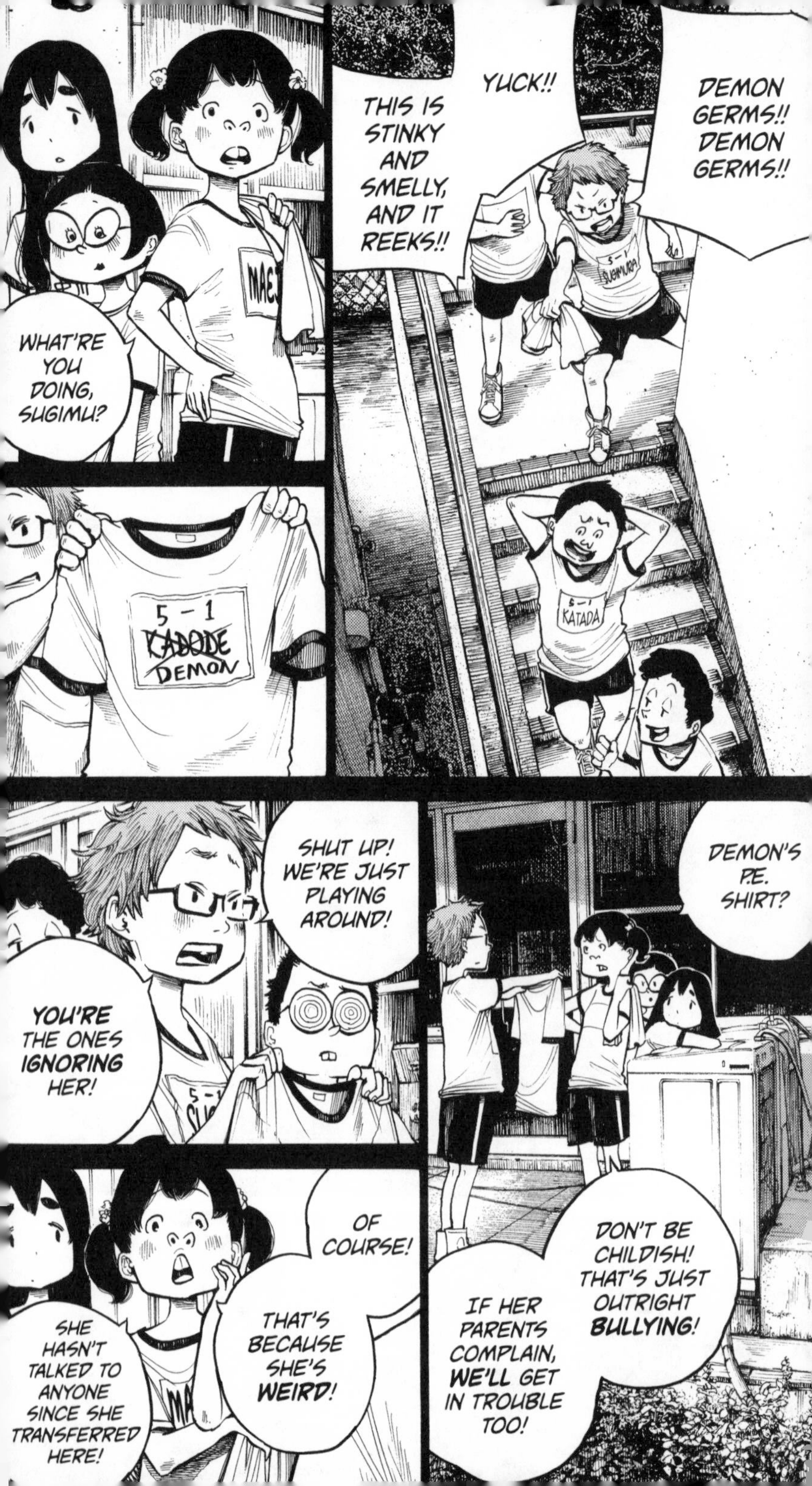
DEMON GERMS!! DEMON GERMS!!
YUCK!!
THIS IS STINKY AND SMELLY, AND IT REEKS!!
5-1 SUGIMURA
5-1 KATADA
WHAT'RE YOU DOING, SUGIMU?
5-1 KADODE DEMON
DEMON'S P.E. SHIRT?
DON'T BE CHILDISH! THAT'S JUST OUTRIGHT **BULLYING**!
IF HER PARENTS COMPLAIN, **WE'LL** GET IN TROUBLE TOO!
SHUT UP! WE'RE JUST PLAYING AROUND!
YOU'RE THE ONES **IGNORING** HER!
OF COURSE!
THAT'S BECAUSE SHE'S **WEIRD**!
SHE HASN'T TALKED TO ANYONE SINCE SHE TRANSFERRED HERE!

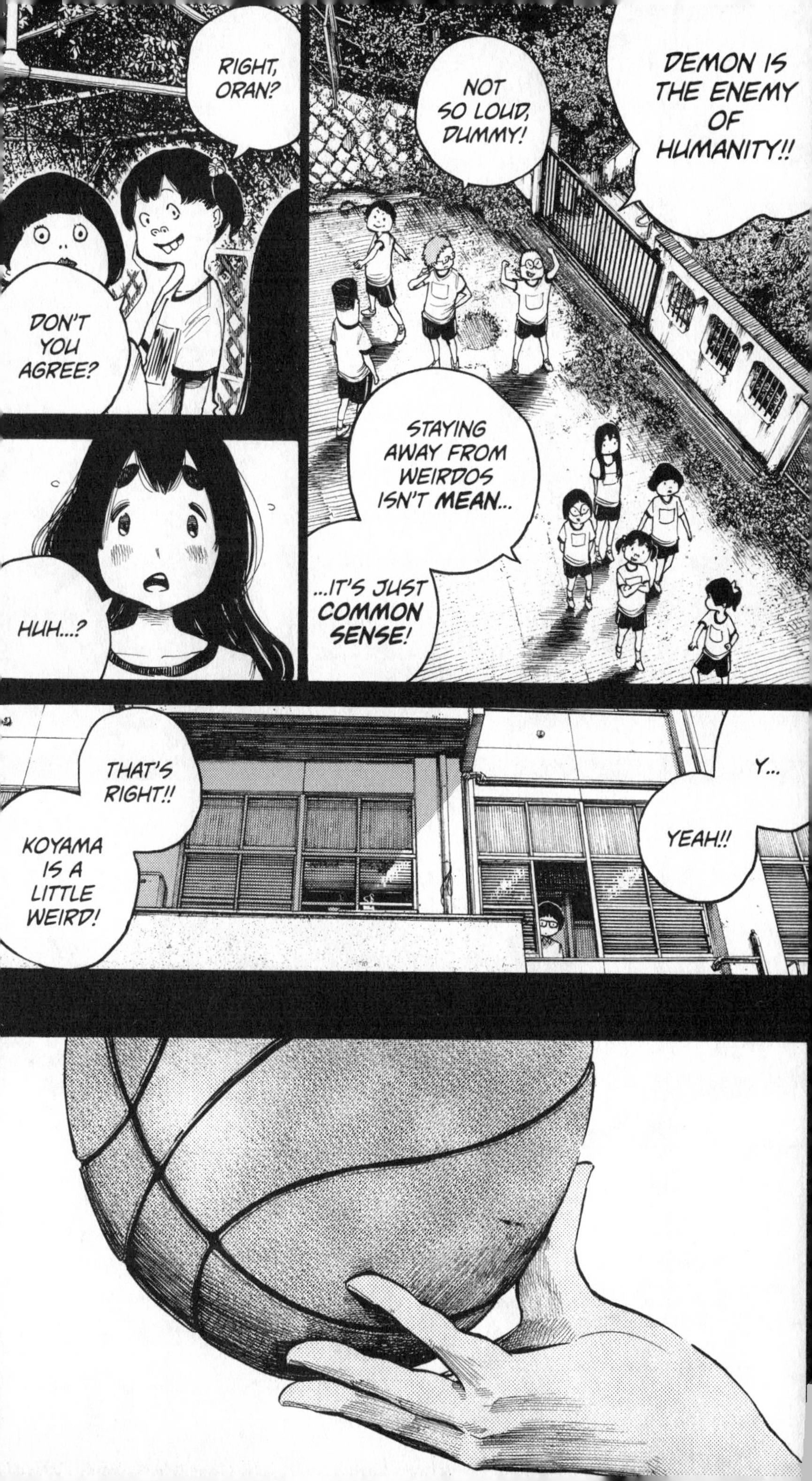
DEMON IS THE ENEMY OF HUMANITY!!
NOT SO LOUD, DUMMY!
STAYING AWAY FROM WEIRDOS ISN'T MEAN...
...IT'S JUST COMMON SENSE!
RIGHT, ORAN?
DON'T YOU AGREE?
HUH...?
Y...
YEAH!!
THAT'S RIGHT!!
KOYAMA IS A LITTLE WEIRD!

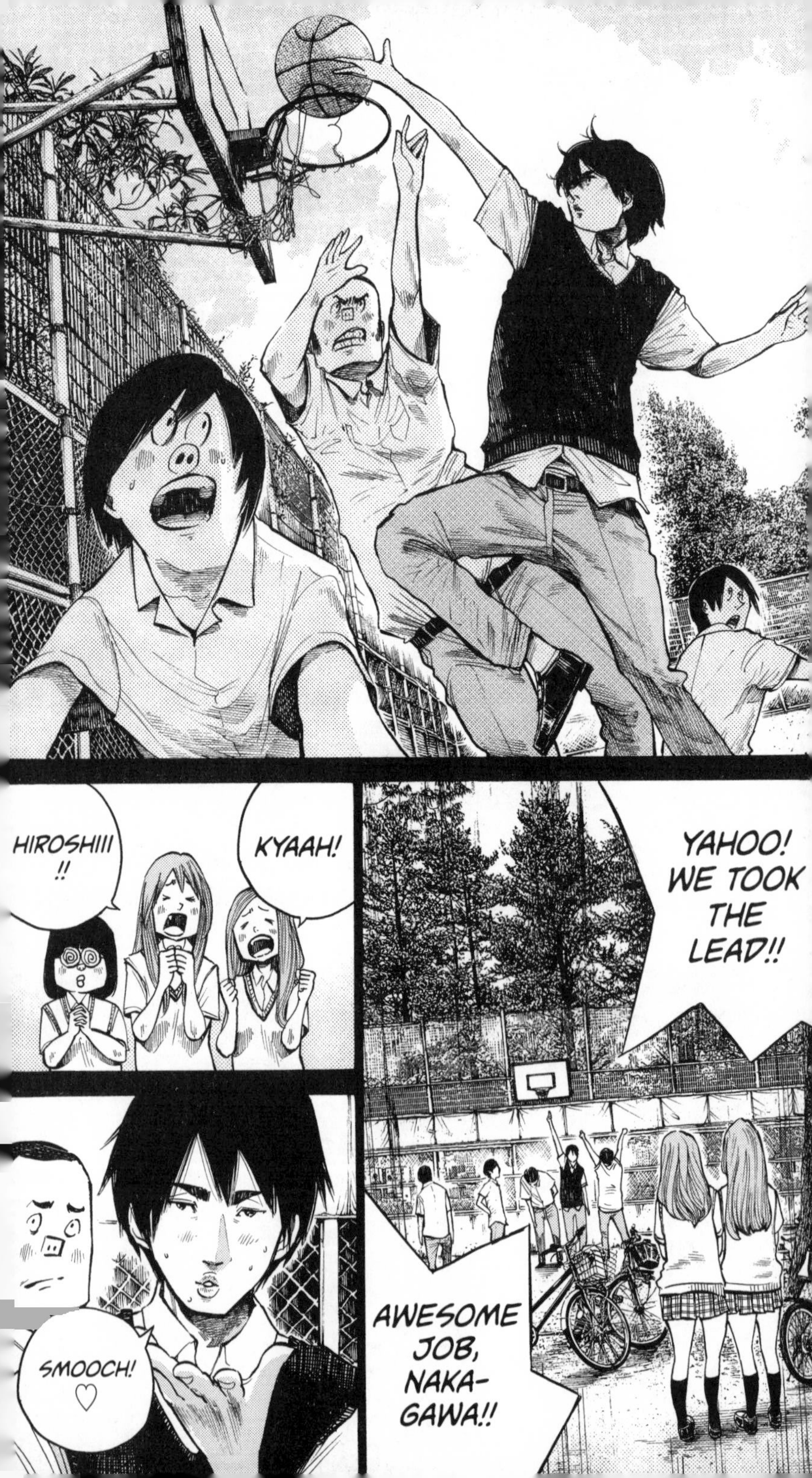
YAHOO! WE TOOK THE LEAD!!
AWESOME JOB, NAKA-GAWA!!
KYAAH!
HIROSHIII !!
SMOOCH! ♡

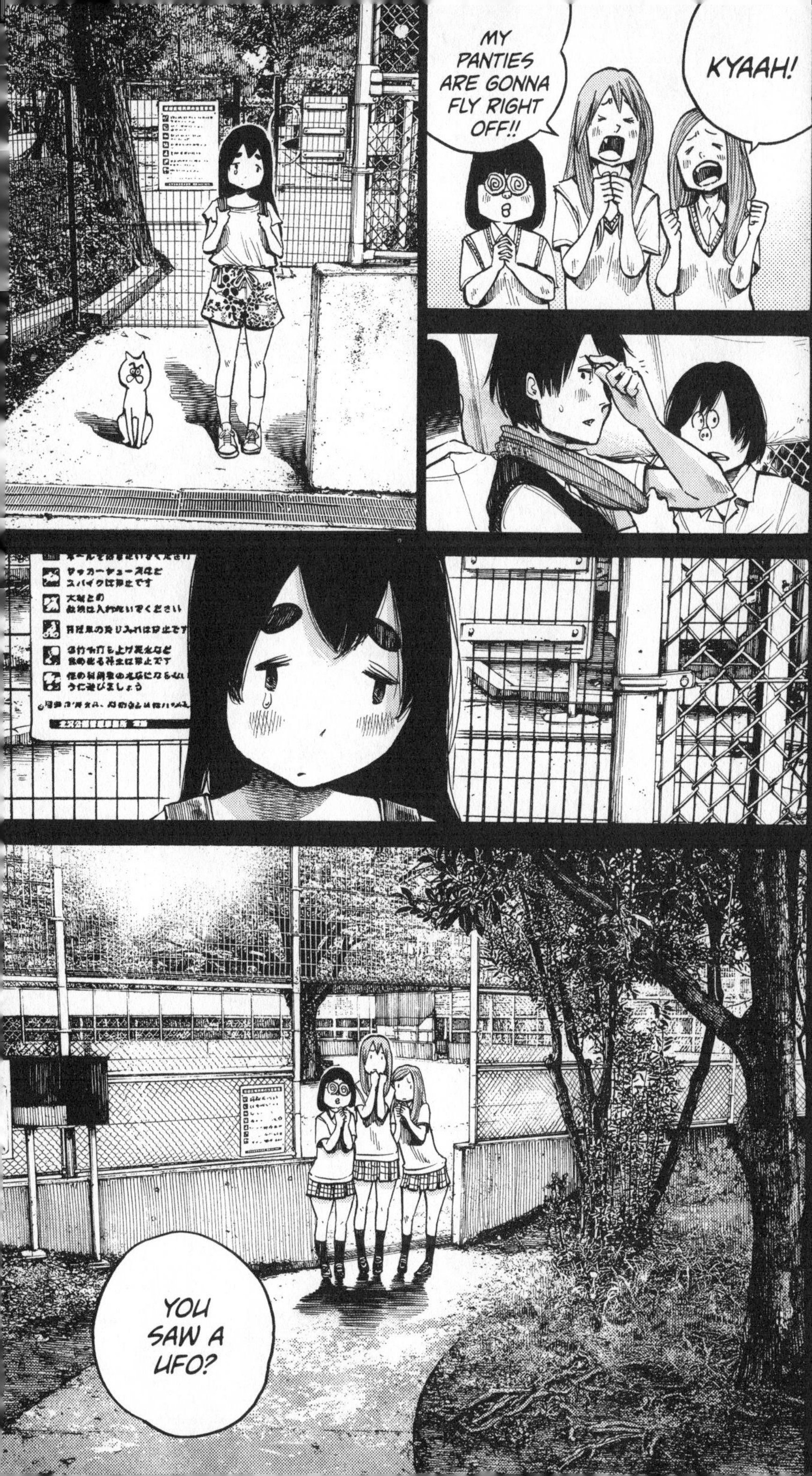
KYAAH!
MY PANTIES ARE GONNA FLY RIGHT OFF!!
YOU SAW A UFO?

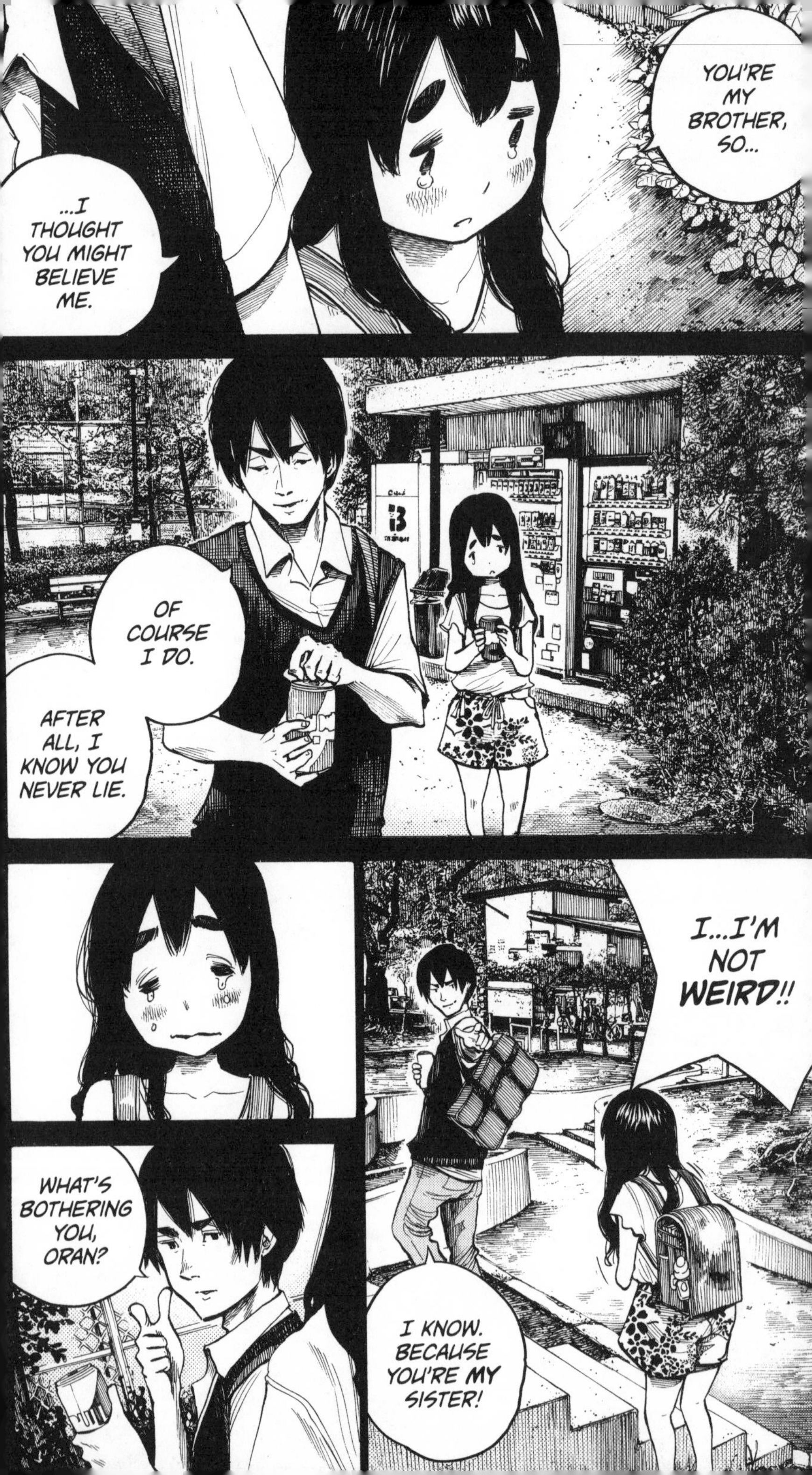
YOU'RE MY BROTHER, SO...
...I THOUGHT YOU MIGHT BELIEVE ME.
OF COURSE I DO.
AFTER ALL, I KNOW YOU NEVER LIE.
I...I'M NOT WEIRD!!
I KNOW. BECAUSE YOU'RE MY SISTER!
WHAT'S BOTHERING YOU, ORAN?

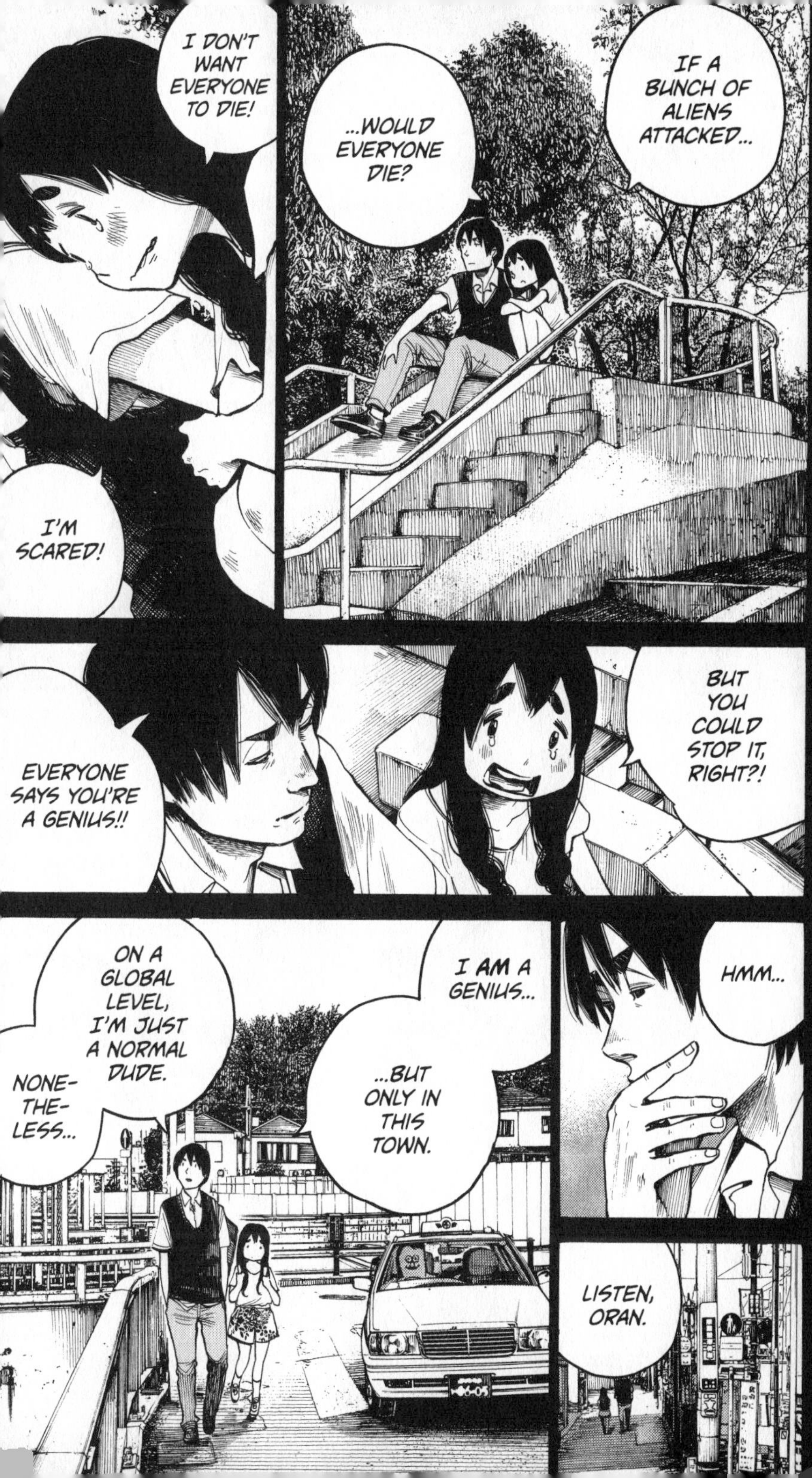
IF A BUNCH OF ALIENS ATTACKED...
...WOULD EVERYONE DIE?
I DON'T WANT EVERYONE TO DIE!
I'M SCARED!
BUT YOU COULD STOP IT, RIGHT?!
EVERYONE SAYS YOU'RE A GENIUS!!
HMM...
LISTEN, ORAN.
I AM A GENIUS...
...BUT ONLY IN THIS TOWN.
ON A GLOBAL LEVEL, I'M JUST A NORMAL DUDE.
NONE-THE-LESS...

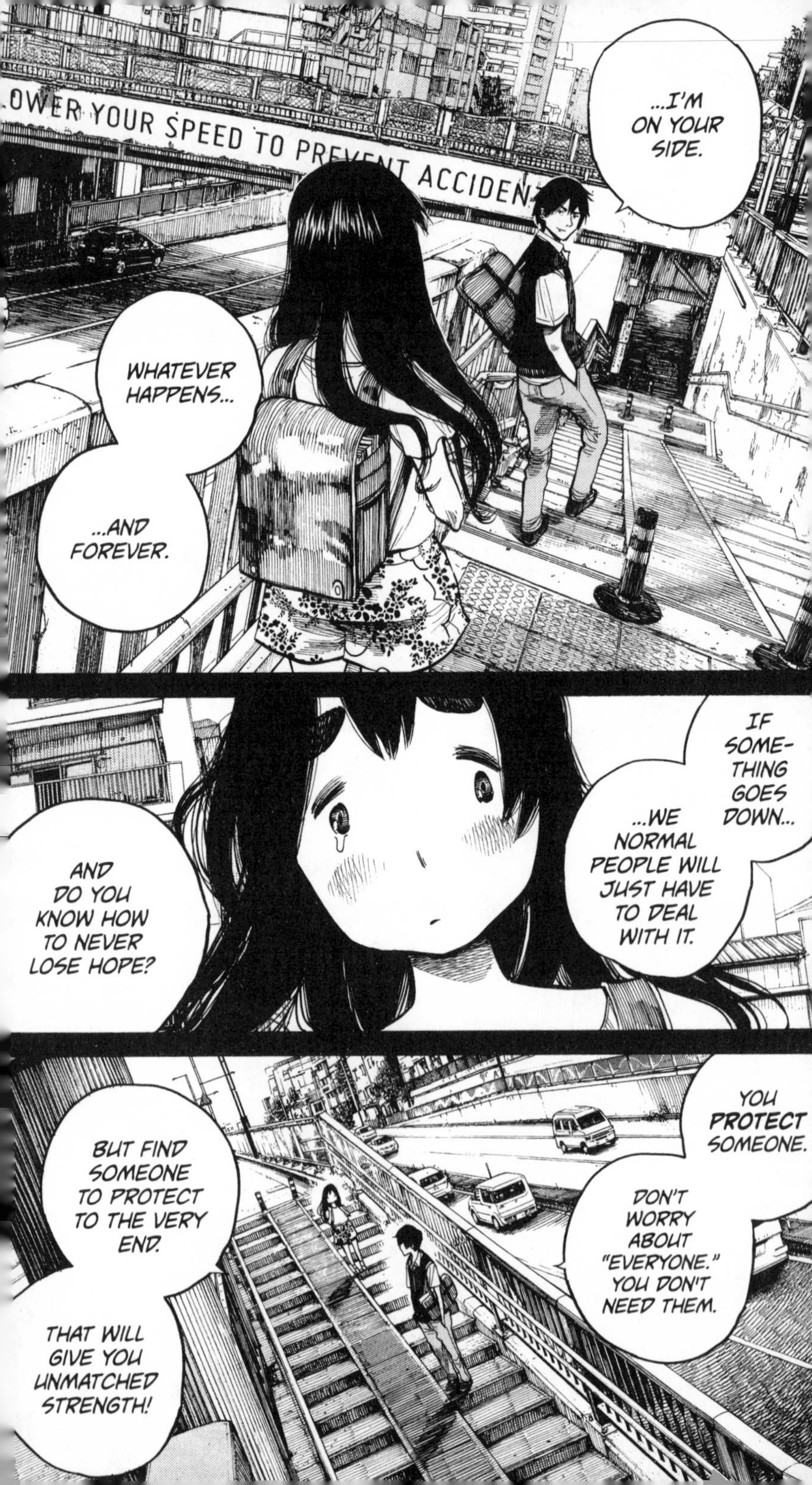
...I'M ON YOUR SIDE.
OWER YOUR SPEED TO PRE NT ACCIDEN
WHATEVER HAPPENS...
...AND FOREVER.
IF SOME-THING GOES DOWN...
...WE NORMAL PEOPLE WILL JUST HAVE TO DEAL WITH IT.
AND DO YOU KNOW HOW TO NEVER LOSE HOPE?
YOU **PROTECT** SOMEONE.
DON'T WORRY ABOUT "EVERYONE." YOU DON'T NEED THEM.
BUT FIND SOMEONE TO PROTECT TO THE VERY END.
THAT WILL GIVE YOU UNMATCHED STRENGTH!

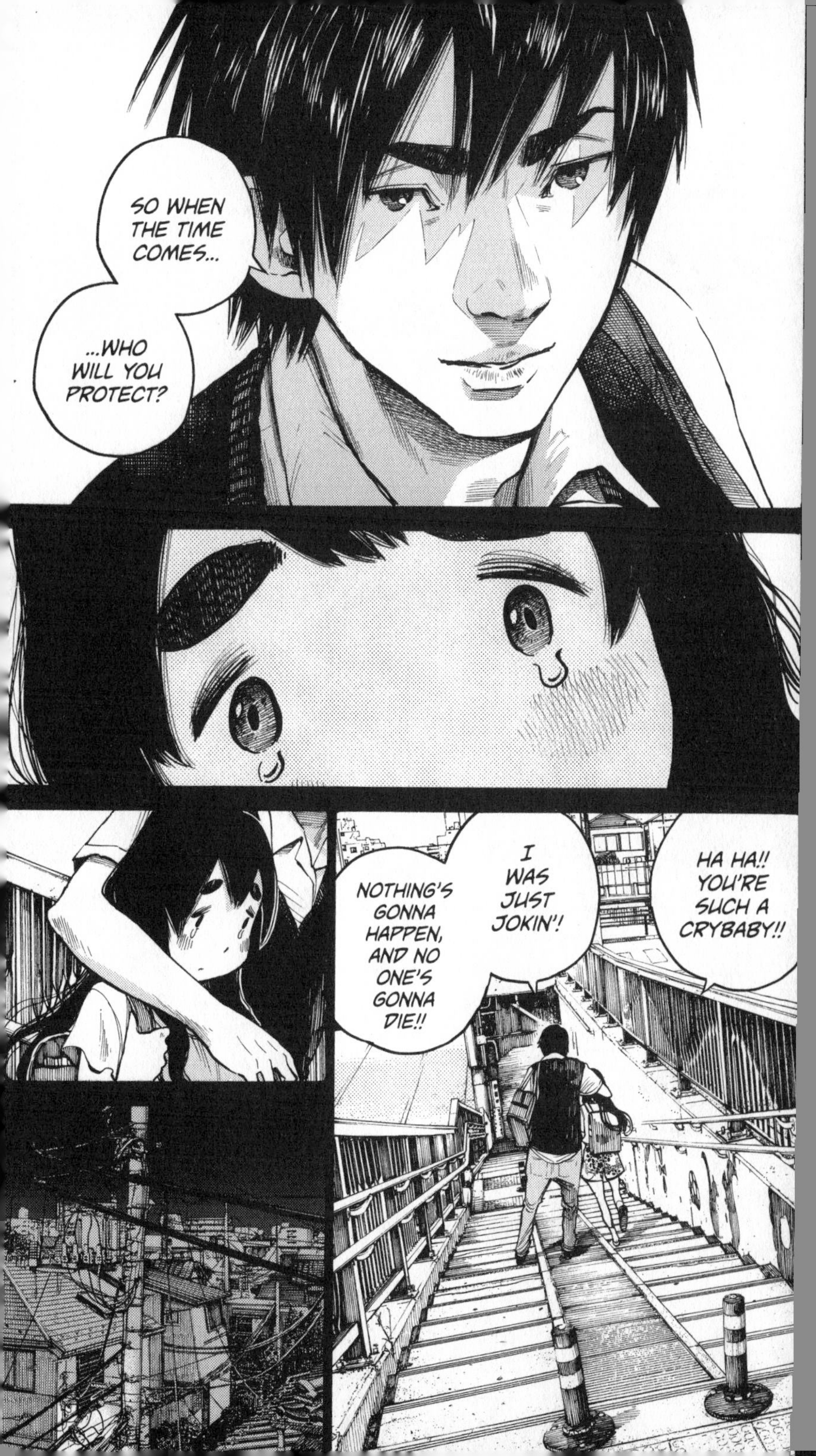
SO WHEN THE TIME COMES...
...WHO WILL YOU PROTECT?
HA HA!! YOU'RE SUCH A CRYBABY!!
I WAS JUST JOKIN'!
NOTHING'S GONNA HAPPEN, AND NO ONE'S GONNA DIE!!

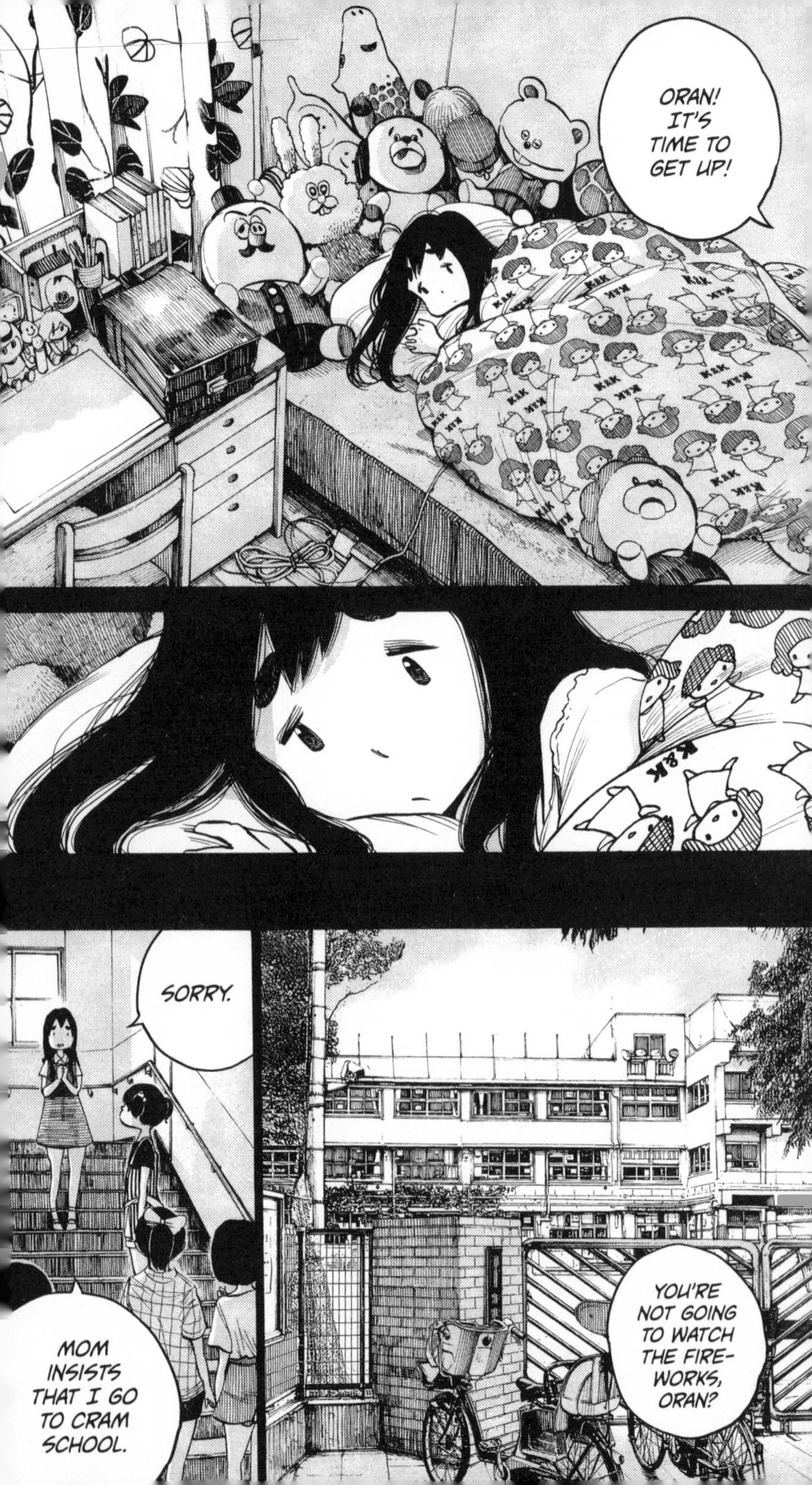
ORAN! IT'S TIME TO GET UP!
YOU'RE NOT GOING TO WATCH THE FIRE-WORKS, ORAN?
SORRY.
MOM INSISTS THAT I GO TO CRAM SCHOOL.

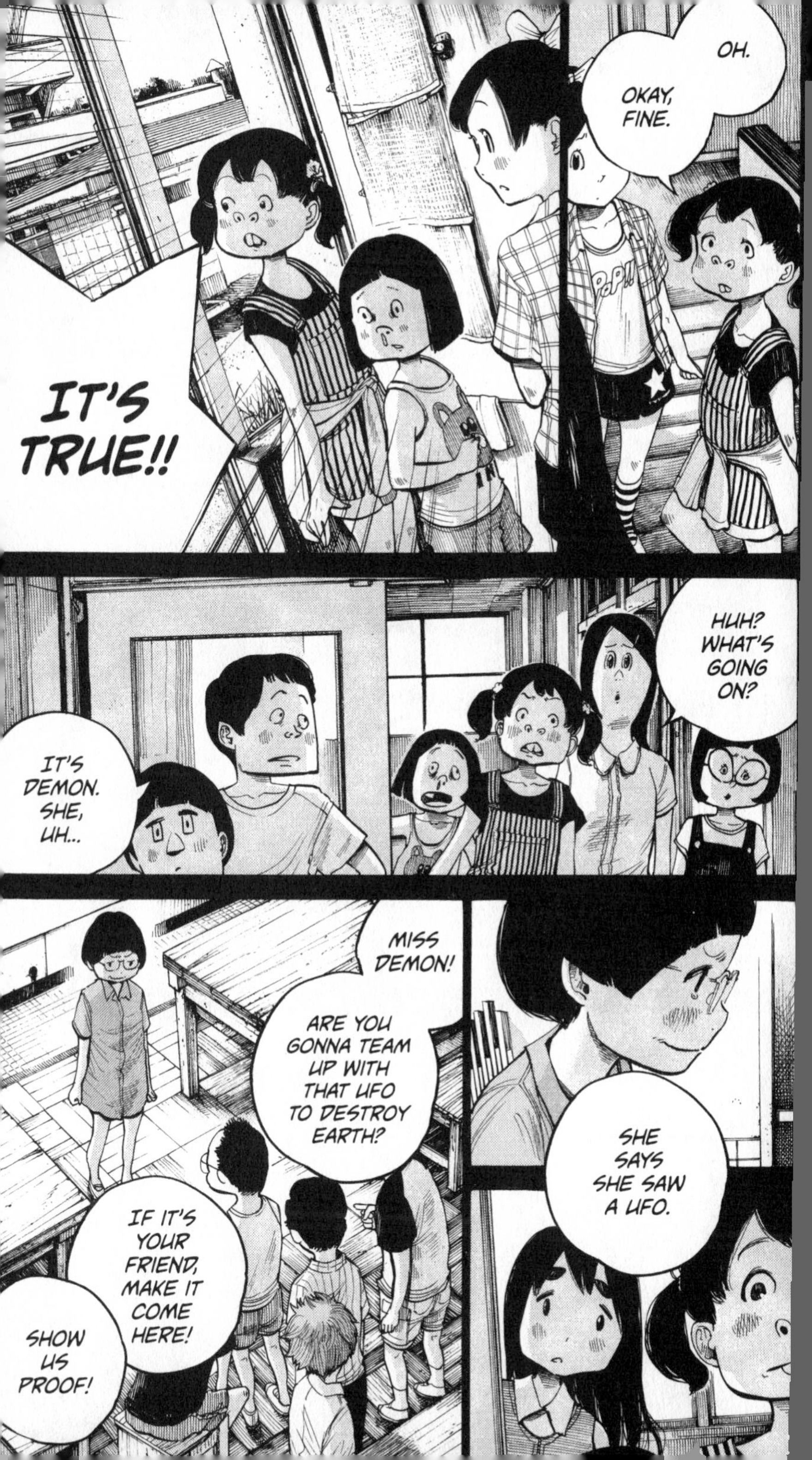
OH.
OKAY, FINE.
IT'S TRUE!!
HUH? WHAT'S GOING ON?
IT'S DEMON. SHE, UH...
SHE SAYS SHE SAW A UFO.
MISS DEMON!
ARE YOU GONNA TEAM UP WITH THAT UFO TO DESTROY EARTH?
IF IT'S YOUR FRIEND, MAKE IT COME HERE!
SHOW US PROOF!

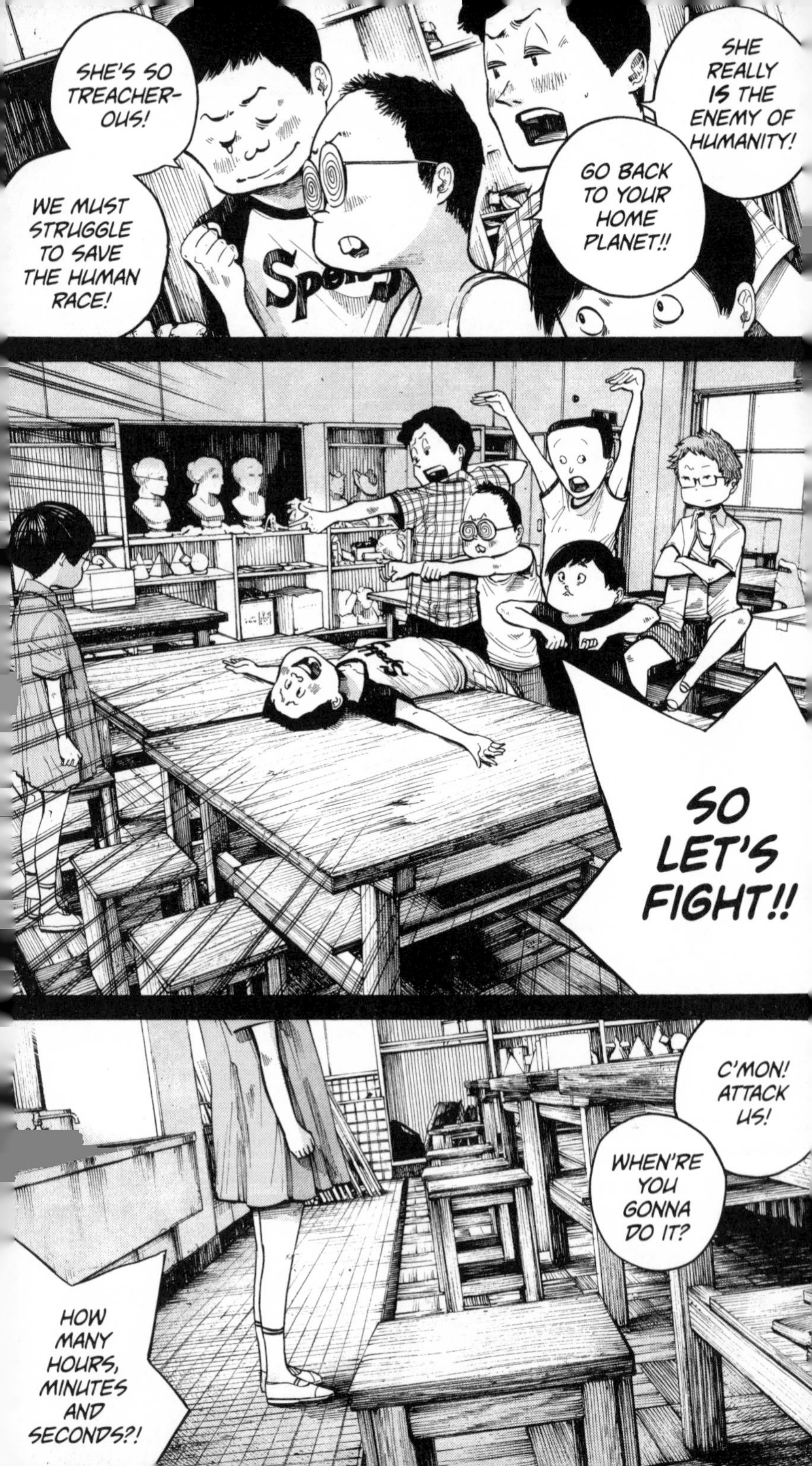
SHE REALLY IS THE ENEMY OF HUMANITY!
SHE'S SO TREACHEROUS!
GO BACK TO YOUR HOME PLANET!!
WE MUST STRUGGLE TO SAVE THE HUMAN RACE!
SO LET'S FIGHT!!
C'MON! ATTACK US!
WHEN'RE YOU GONNA DO IT?
HOW MANY HOURS, MINUTES AND SECONDS?!

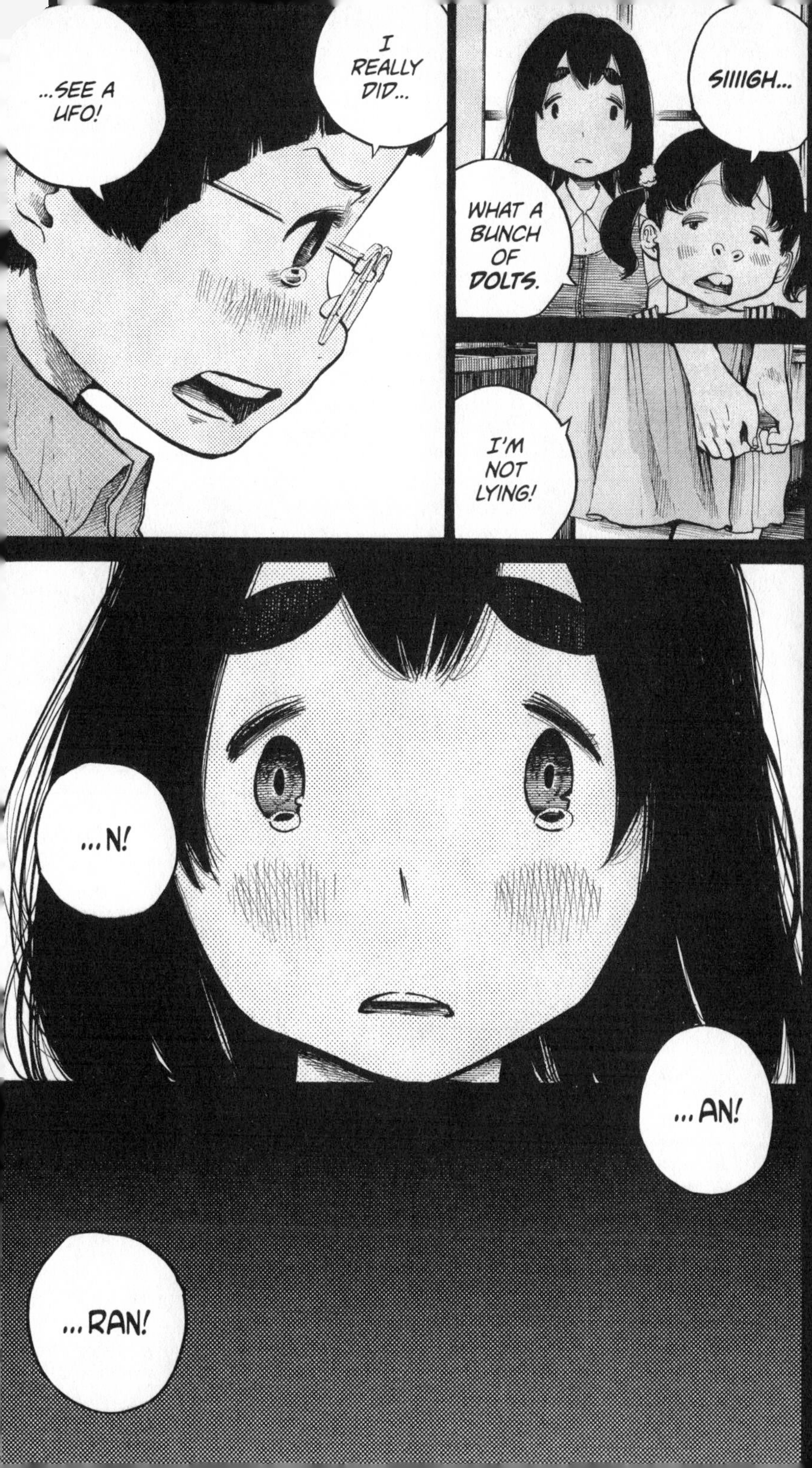
SIIIGH...
WHAT A BUNCH OF DOLTS.
I'M NOT LYING!
I REALLY DID...
...SEE A UFO!
...N!
...AN!
...RAN!

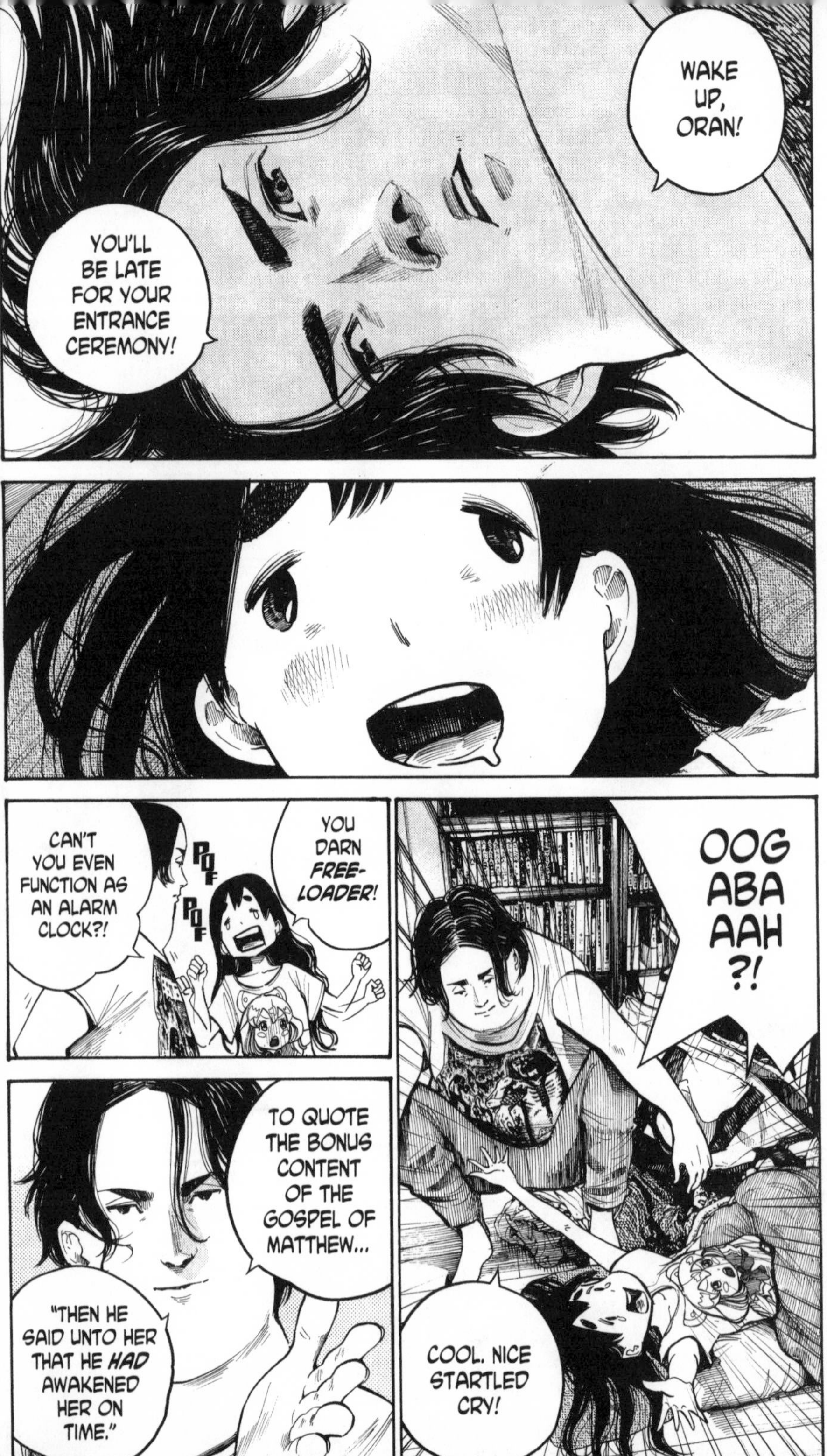
WAKE UP, ORAN!
YOU'LL BE LATE FOR YOUR ENTRANCE CEREMONY!
OOG ABA AAH ?!
COOL. NICE STARTLED CRY!
YOU DARN *FREE-LOADER*!
POF
POF
CAN'T YOU EVEN FUNCTION AS AN ALARM CLOCK?!
TO QUOTE THE BONUS CONTENT OF THE GOSPEL OF MATTHEW...
"THEN HE SAID UNTO HER THAT HE *HAD* AWAKENED HER ON TIME."

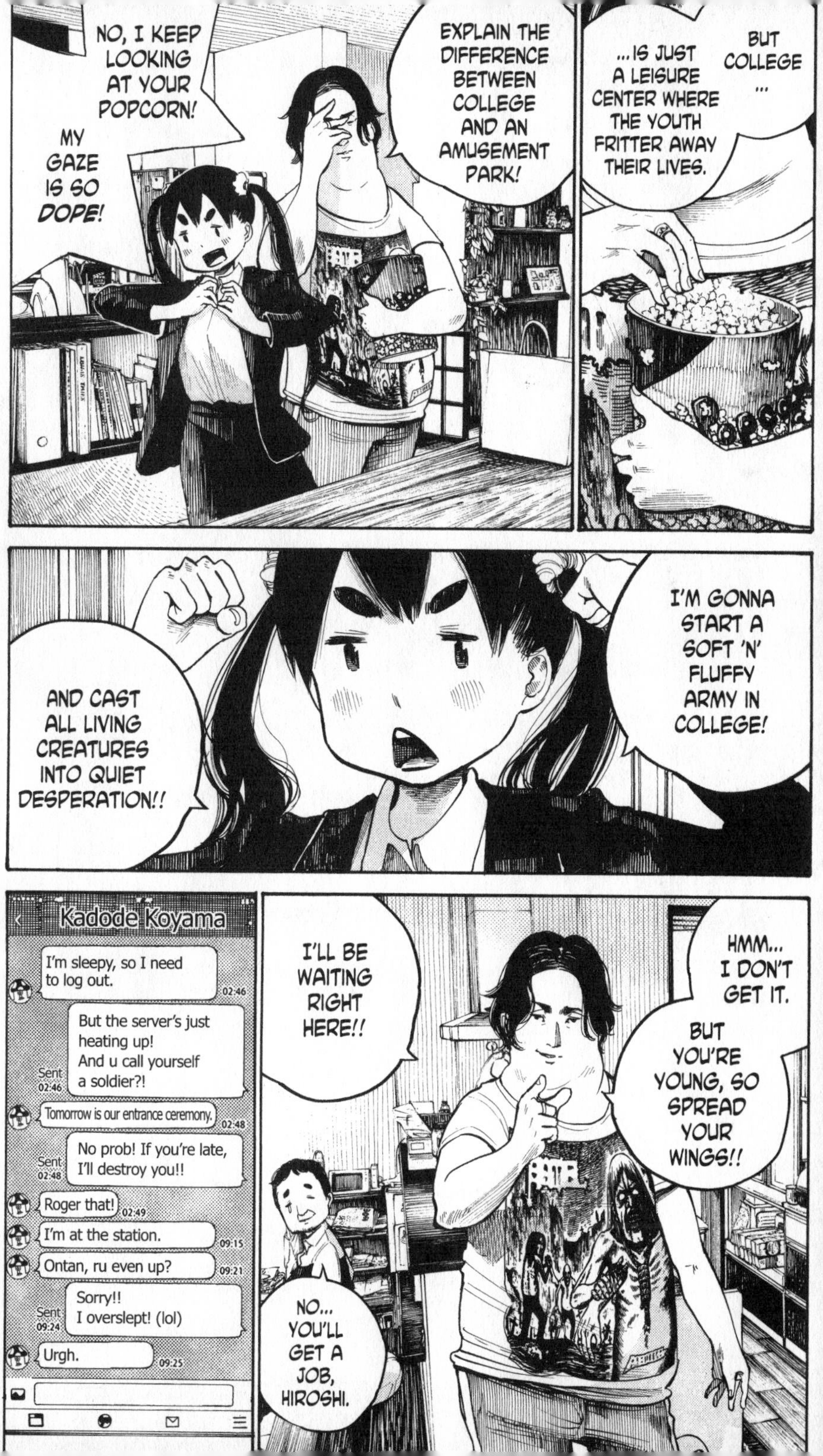
BUT COLLEGE ...
...IS JUST A LEISURE CENTER WHERE THE YOUTH FRITTER AWAY THEIR LIVES.
EXPLAIN THE DIFFERENCE BETWEEN COLLEGE AND AN AMUSEMENT PARK!
NO, I KEEP LOOKING AT YOUR POPCORN!
MY GAZE IS SO *DOPE*!
I'M GONNA START A SOFT 'N' FLUFFY ARMY IN COLLEGE!
AND CAST ALL LIVING CREATURES INTO QUIET DESPERATION!!
HMM... I DON'T GET IT.
BUT YOU'RE YOUNG, SO SPREAD YOUR WINGS!!
I'LL BE WAITING RIGHT HERE!!
NO... YOU'LL GET A JOB, HIROSHI.
Kadode Koyama
I'm sleepy, so I need to log out. 02:46
Sent 02:46 But the server's just heating up! And u call yourself a soldier?!
Tomorrow is our entrance ceremony. 02:48
Sent 02:48 No prob! If you're late, I'll destroy you!!
Roger that! 02:49
I'm at the station. 09:15
Ontan, ru even up? 09:21
Sent 09:24 Sorry!! I overslept! (lol)
Urgh. 09:25

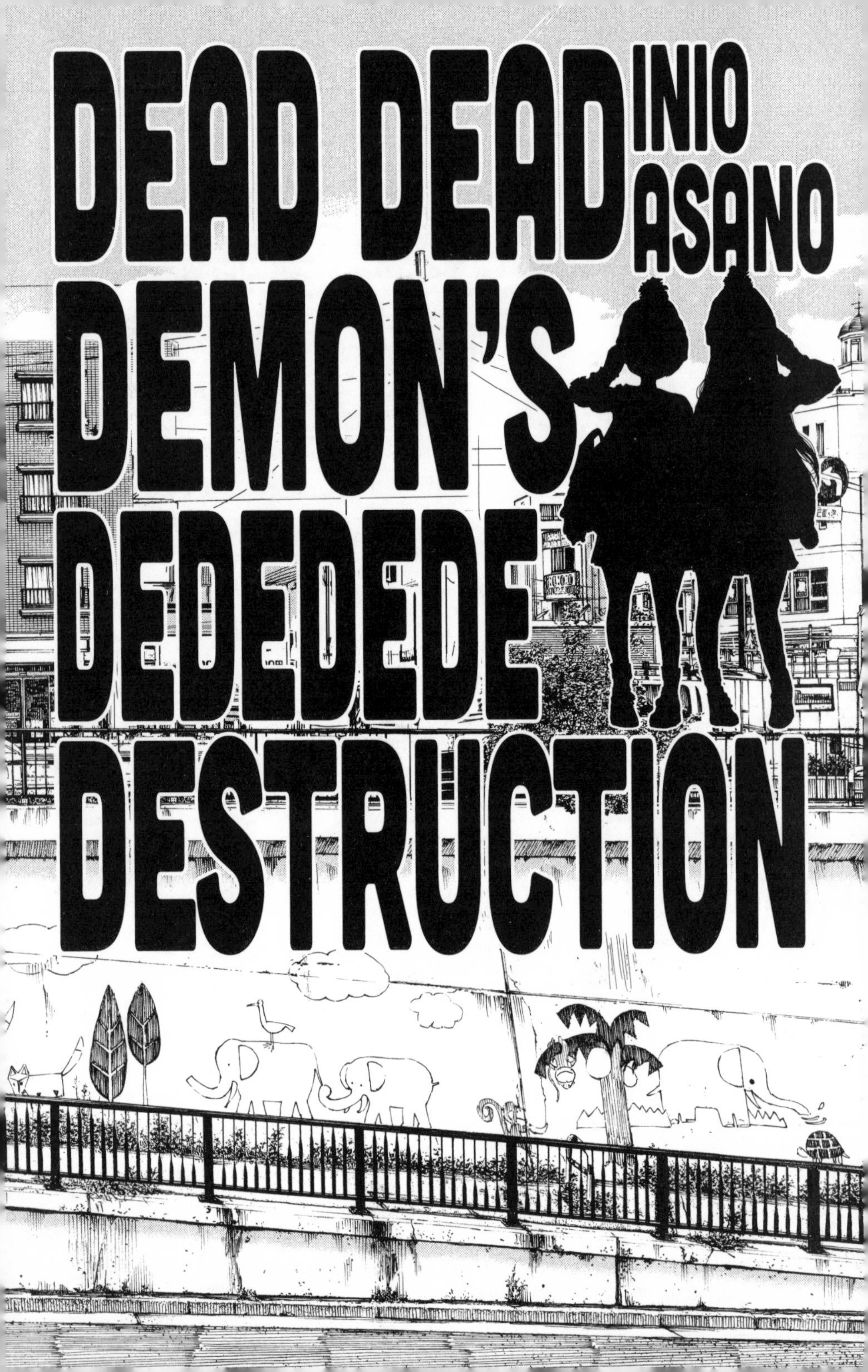
DEAD DEAD
DEMON'S
DEDEDEDE
DESTRUCTION
INIO
ASANO

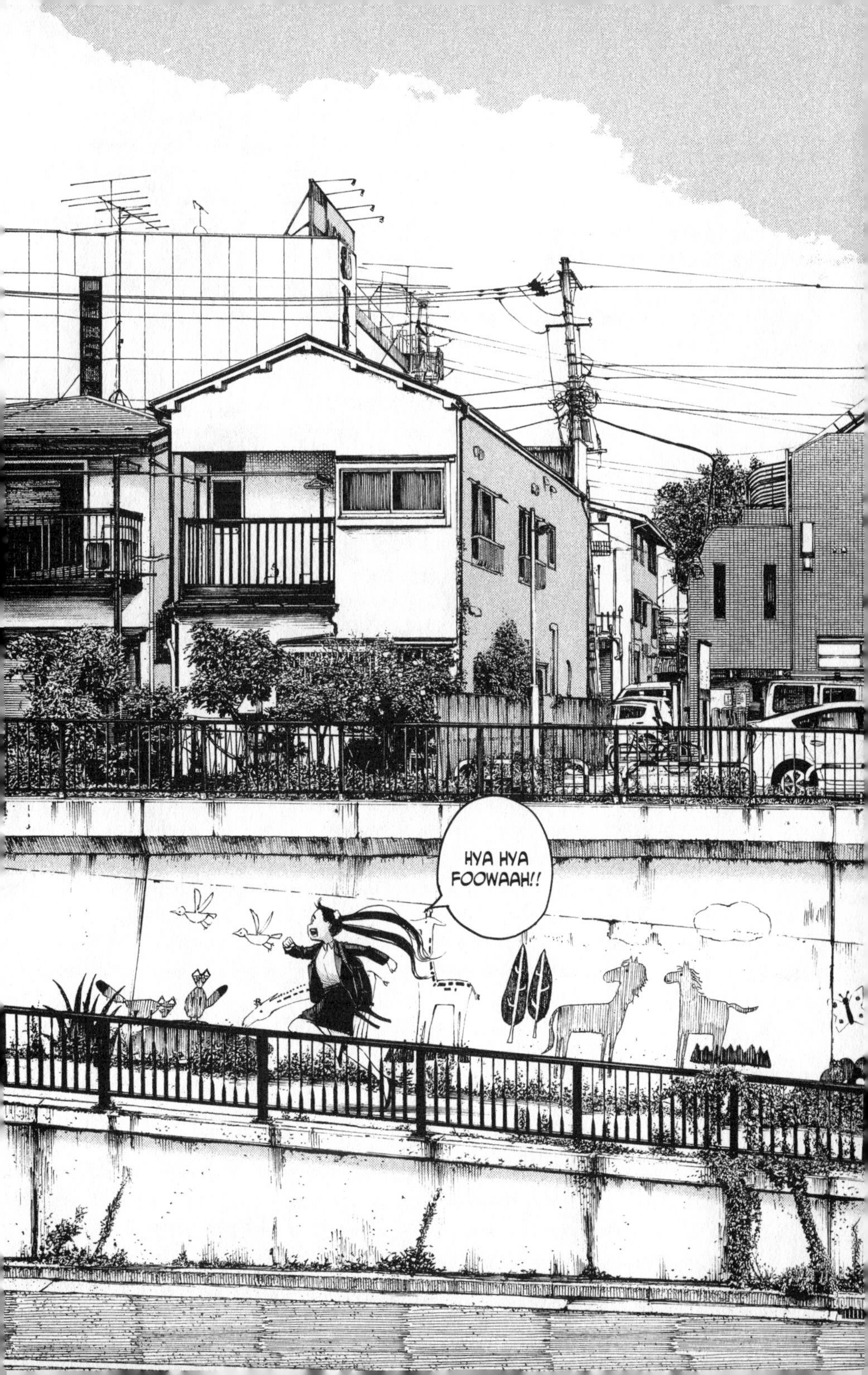
HYA HYA FOOWAAH!!

D
DEDE

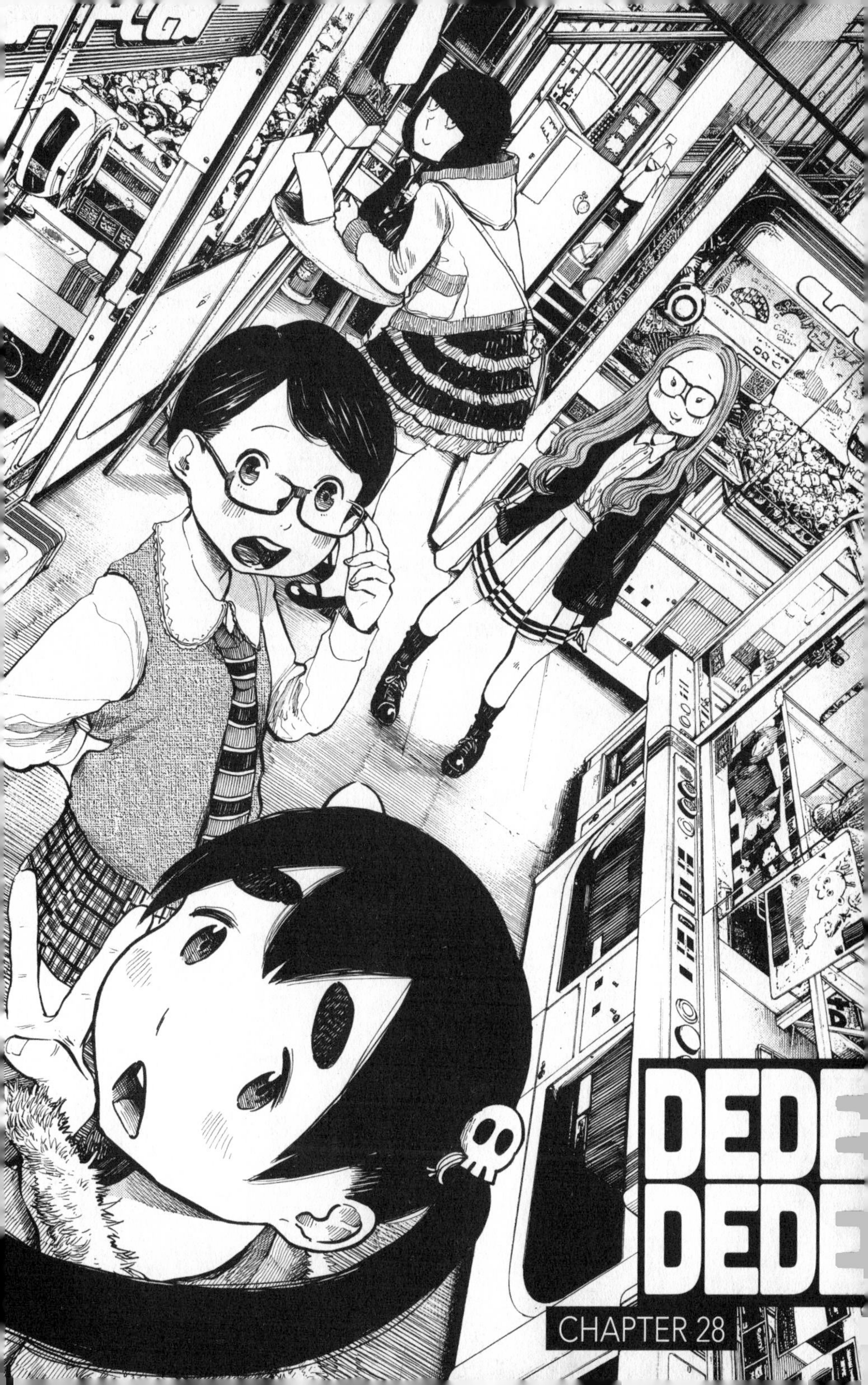
DEDE DEDE
CHAPTER 28

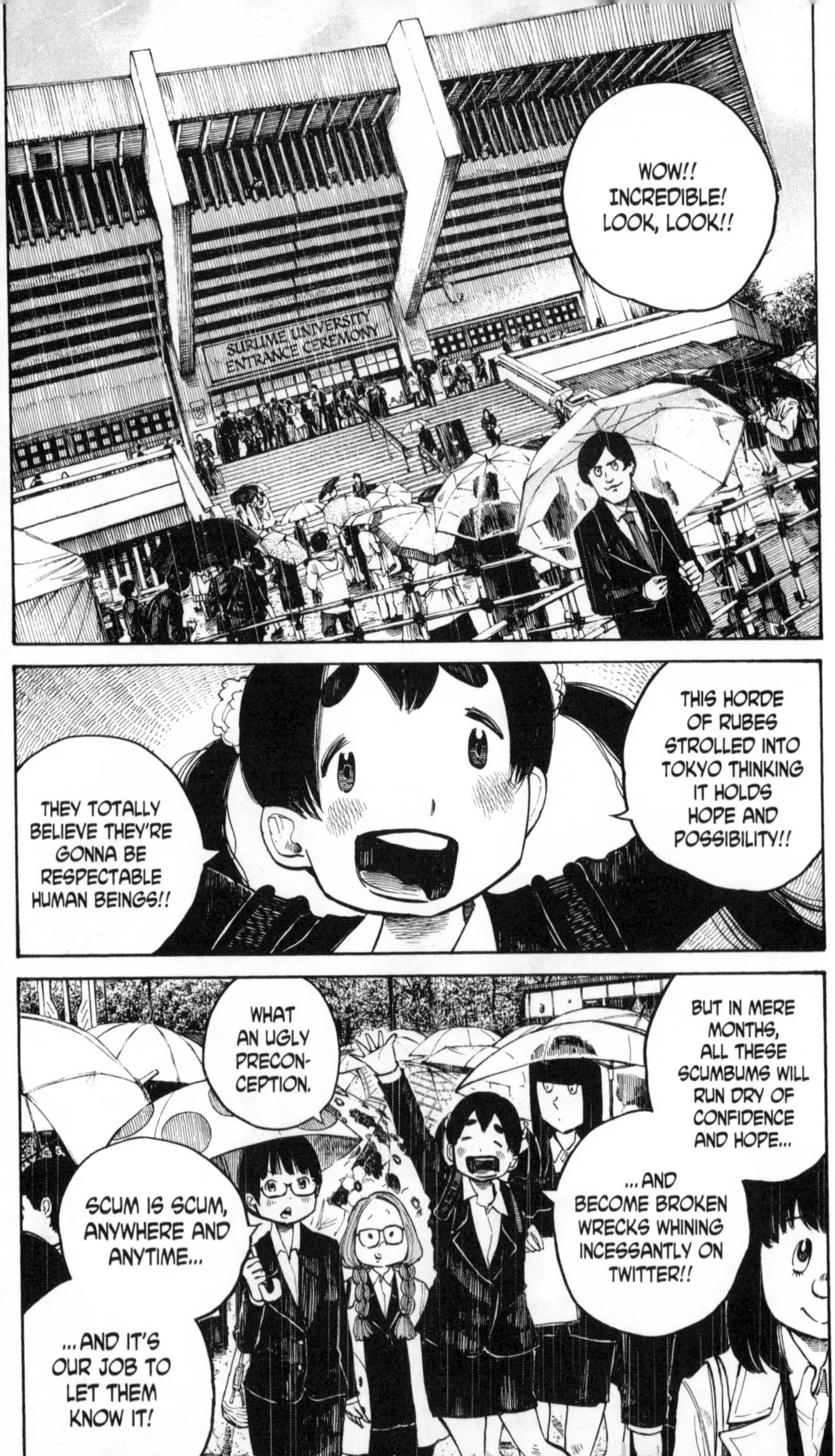
WOW!! INCREDIBLE! LOOK, LOOK!!
SURUME UNIVERSITY ENTRANCE CEREMONY
THIS HORDE OF RUBES STROLLED INTO TOKYO THINKING IT HOLDS HOPE AND POSSIBILITY!!
THEY TOTALLY BELIEVE THEY'RE GONNA BE RESPECTABLE HUMAN BEINGS!!
BUT IN MERE MONTHS, ALL THESE SCUMBUMS WILL RUN DRY OF CONFIDENCE AND HOPE...
...AND BECOME BROKEN WRECKS WHINING INCESSANTLY ON TWITTER!!
WHAT AN UGLY PRECONCEPTION.
SCUM IS SCUM, ANYWHERE AND ANYTIME...
...AND IT'S OUR JOB TO LET THEM KNOW IT!

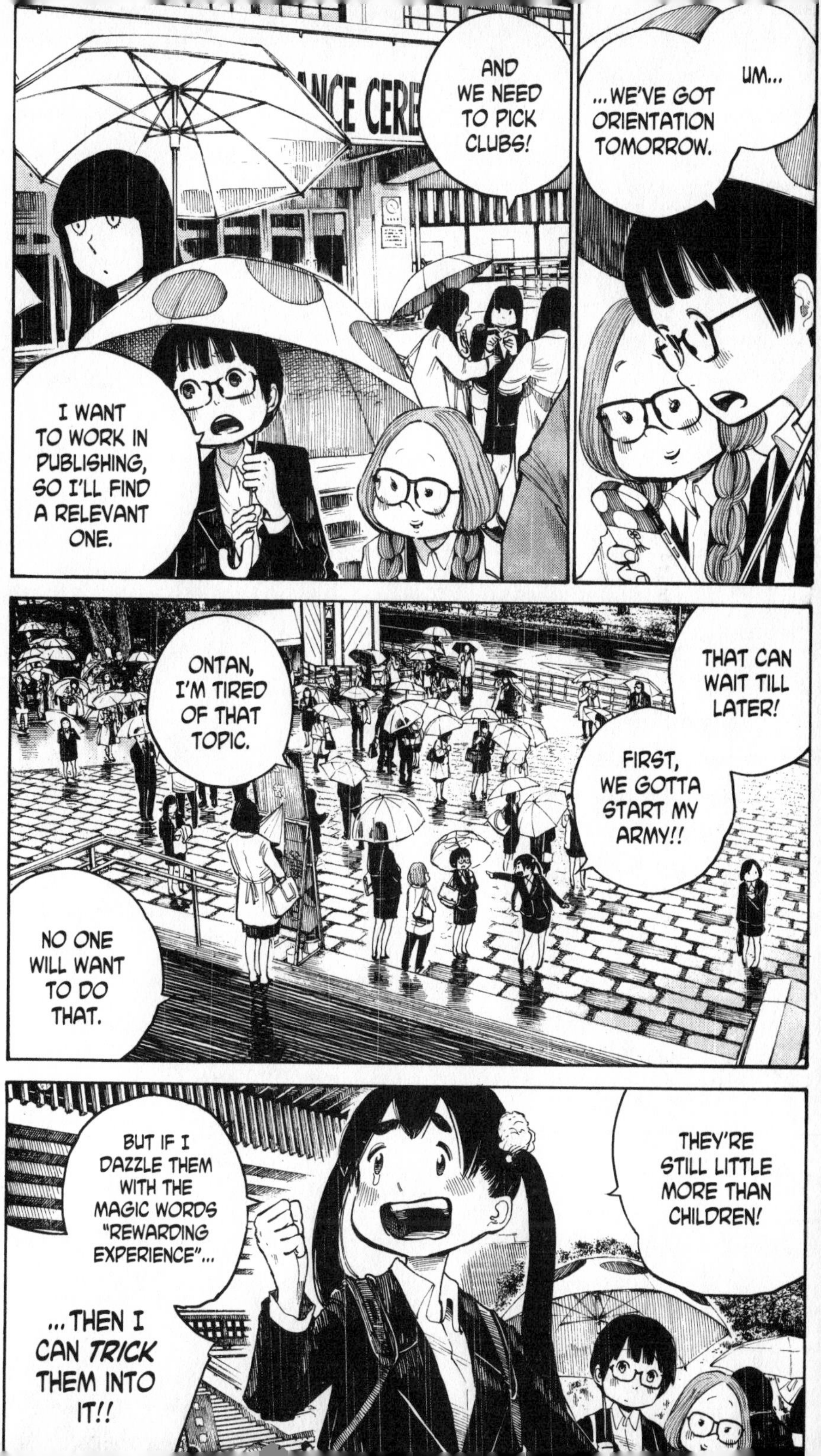
UM...
...WE'VE GOT ORIENTATION TOMORROW.
ANCE CERE
AND WE NEED TO PICK CLUBS!
I WANT TO WORK IN PUBLISHING, SO I'LL FIND A RELEVANT ONE.
THAT CAN WAIT TILL LATER!
FIRST, WE GOTTA START MY ARMY!!
ONTAN, I'M TIRED OF THAT TOPIC.
NO ONE WILL WANT TO DO THAT.
THEY'RE STILL LITTLE MORE THAN CHILDREN!
BUT IF I DAZZLE THEM WITH THE MAGIC WORDS "REWARDING EXPERIENCE"...
...THEN I CAN *TRICK* THEM INTO IT!!

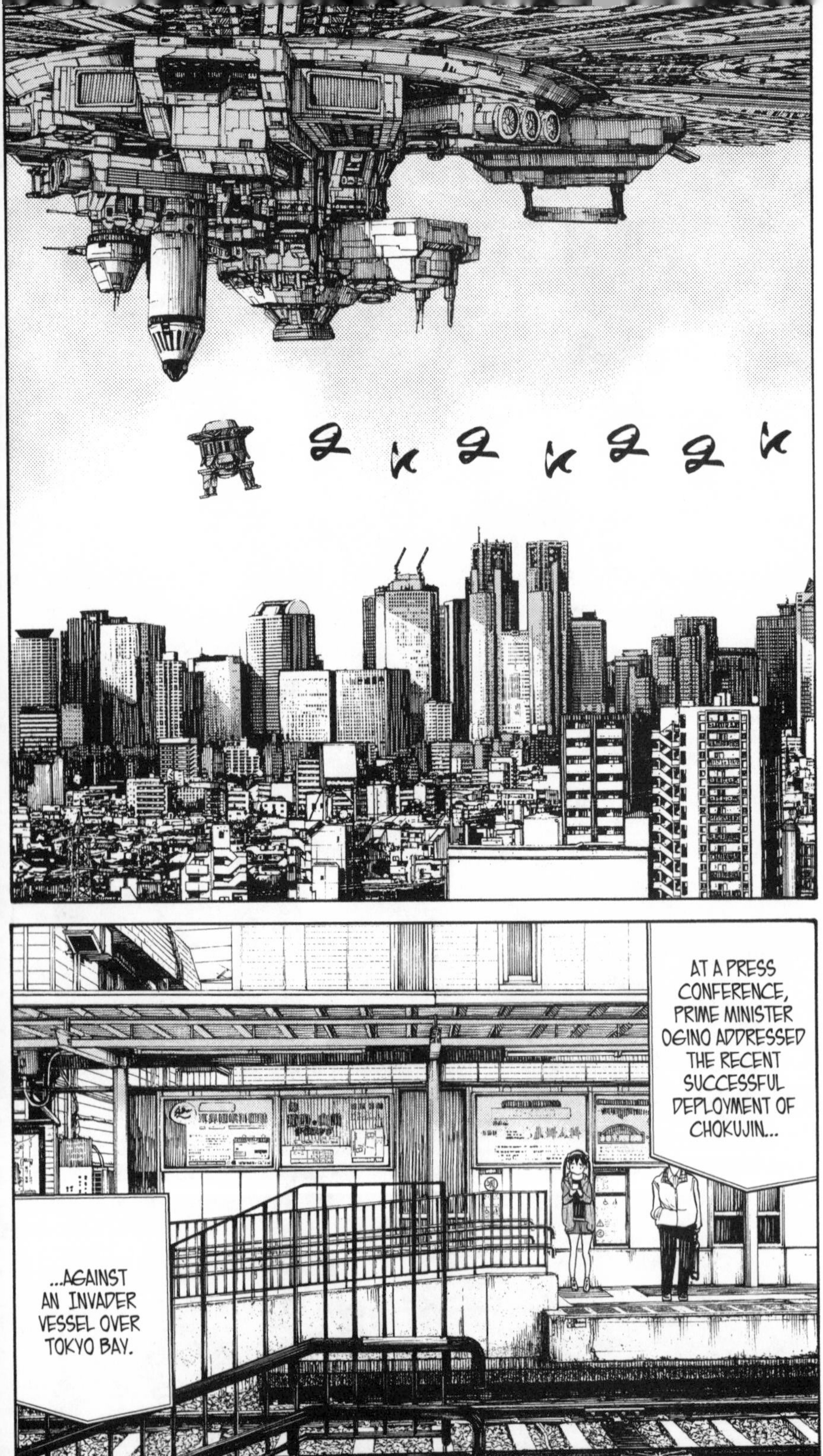
AT A PRESS CONFERENCE, PRIME MINISTER OGINO ADDRESSED THE RECENT SUCCESSFUL DEPLOYMENT OF CHOKUJIN...
...AGAINST AN INVADER VESSEL OVER TOKYO BAY.

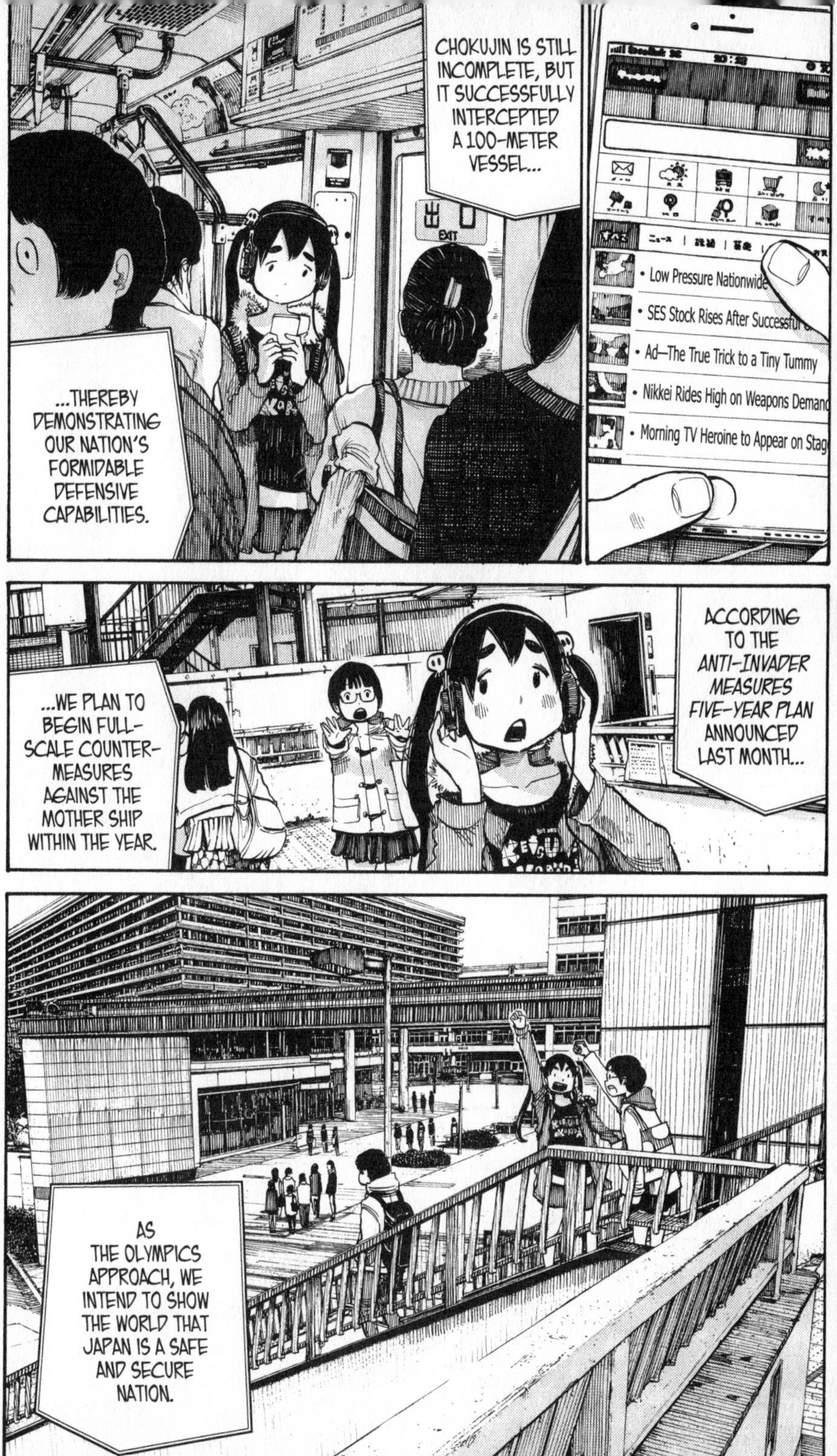
• Low Pressure Nationwide
• SES Stock Rises After Successful
• Ad—The True Trick to a Tiny Tummy
• Nikkei Rides High on Weapons Deman
• Morning TV Heroine to Appear on Stag
CHOKUJIN IS STILL INCOMPLETE, BUT IT SUCCESSFULLY INTERCEPTED A 100-METER VESSEL...
EXIT
...THEREBY DEMONSTRATING OUR NATION'S FORMIDABLE DEFENSIVE CAPABILITIES.
ACCORDING TO THE ANTI-INVADER MEASURES FIVE-YEAR PLAN ANNOUNCED LAST MONTH...
...WE PLAN TO BEGIN FULL-SCALE COUNTER-MEASURES AGAINST THE MOTHER SHIP WITHIN THE YEAR.
AS THE OLYMPICS APPROACH, WE INTEND TO SHOW THE WORLD THAT JAPAN IS A SAFE AND SECURE NATION.

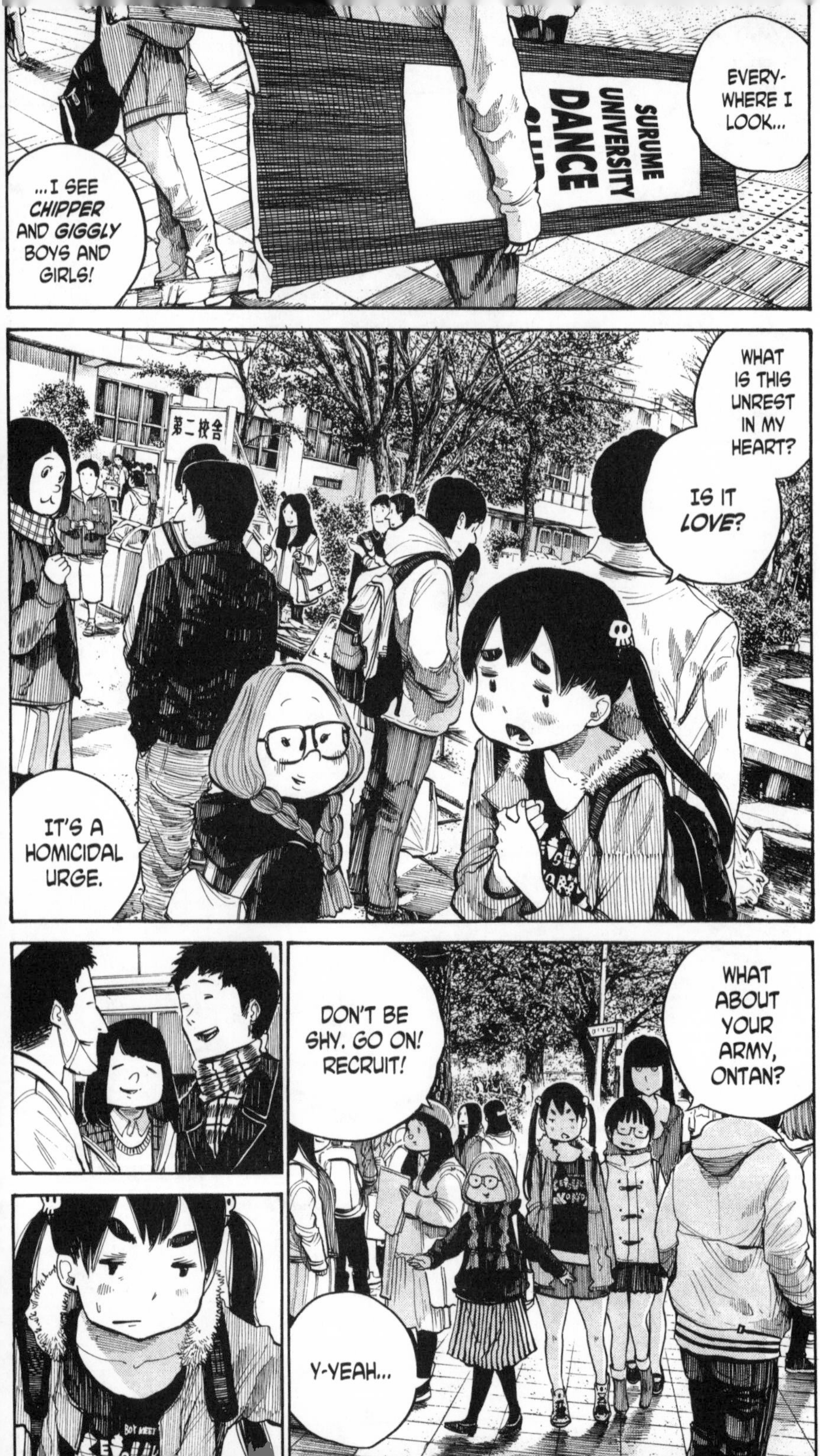
EVERY-WHERE I LOOK...
SURUME UNIVERSITY DANCE
...I SEE *CHIPPER* AND *GIGGLY* BOYS AND GIRLS!
WHAT IS THIS UNREST IN MY HEART?
IS IT *LOVE*?
第二校舎
IT'S A HOMICIDAL URGE.
WHAT ABOUT YOUR ARMY, ONTAN?
DON'T BE SHY. GO ON! RECRUIT!
Y-YEAH...

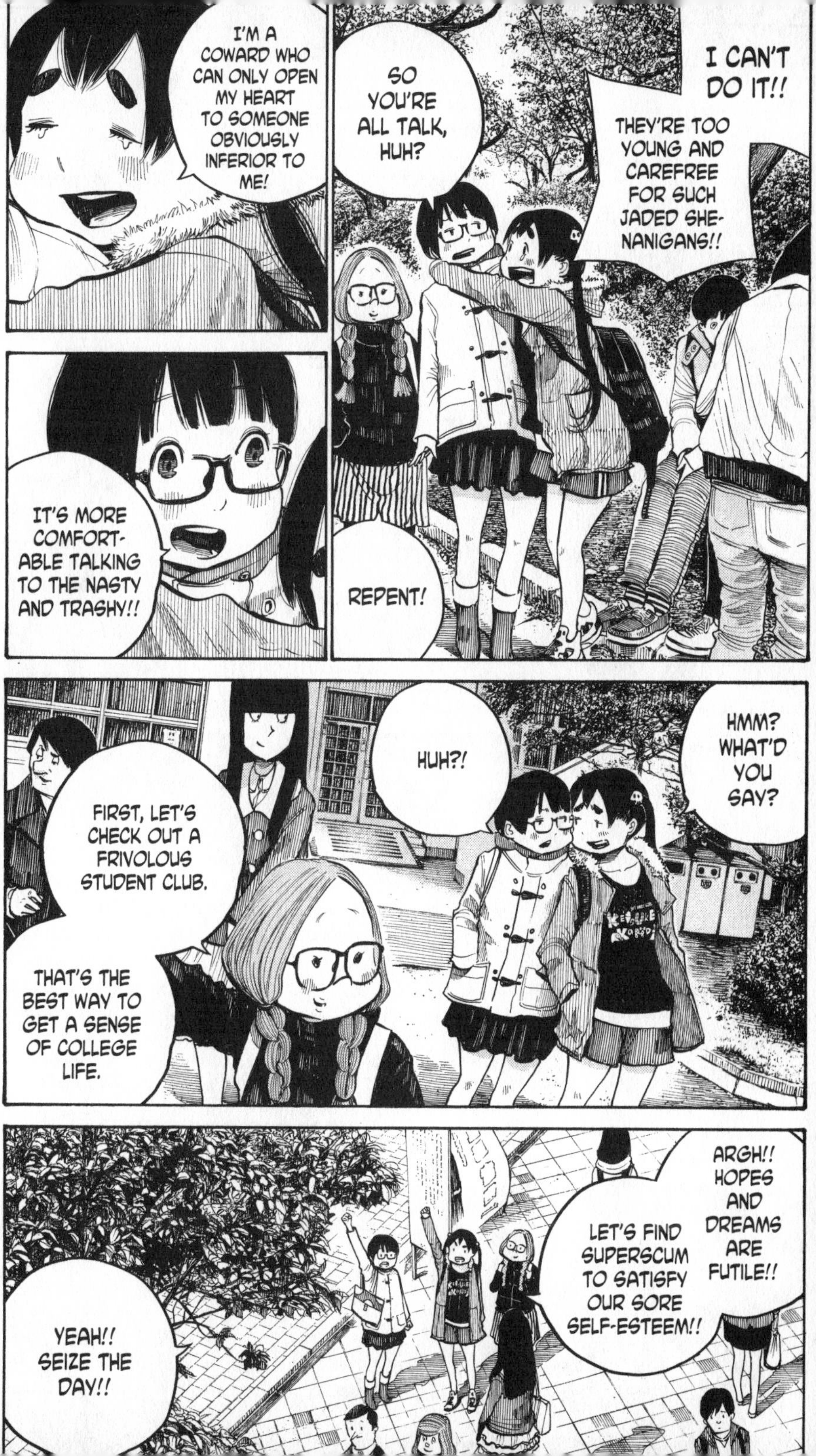
I CAN'T DO IT!!
THEY'RE TOO YOUNG AND CAREFREE FOR SUCH JADED SHE-NANIGANS!!
SO YOU'RE ALL TALK, HUH?
REPENT!
I'M A COWARD WHO CAN ONLY OPEN MY HEART TO SOMEONE OBVIOUSLY INFERIOR TO ME!
IT'S MORE COMFORT-ABLE TALKING TO THE NASTY AND TRASHY!!
HMM? WHAT'D YOU SAY?
HUH?!
FIRST, LET'S CHECK OUT A FRIVOLOUS STUDENT CLUB.
THAT'S THE BEST WAY TO GET A SENSE OF COLLEGE LIFE.
ARGH!! HOPES AND DREAMS ARE FUTILE!!
LET'S FIND SUPERSCUM TO SATISFY OUR SORE SELF-ESTEEM!!
YEAH!! SEIZE THE DAY!!

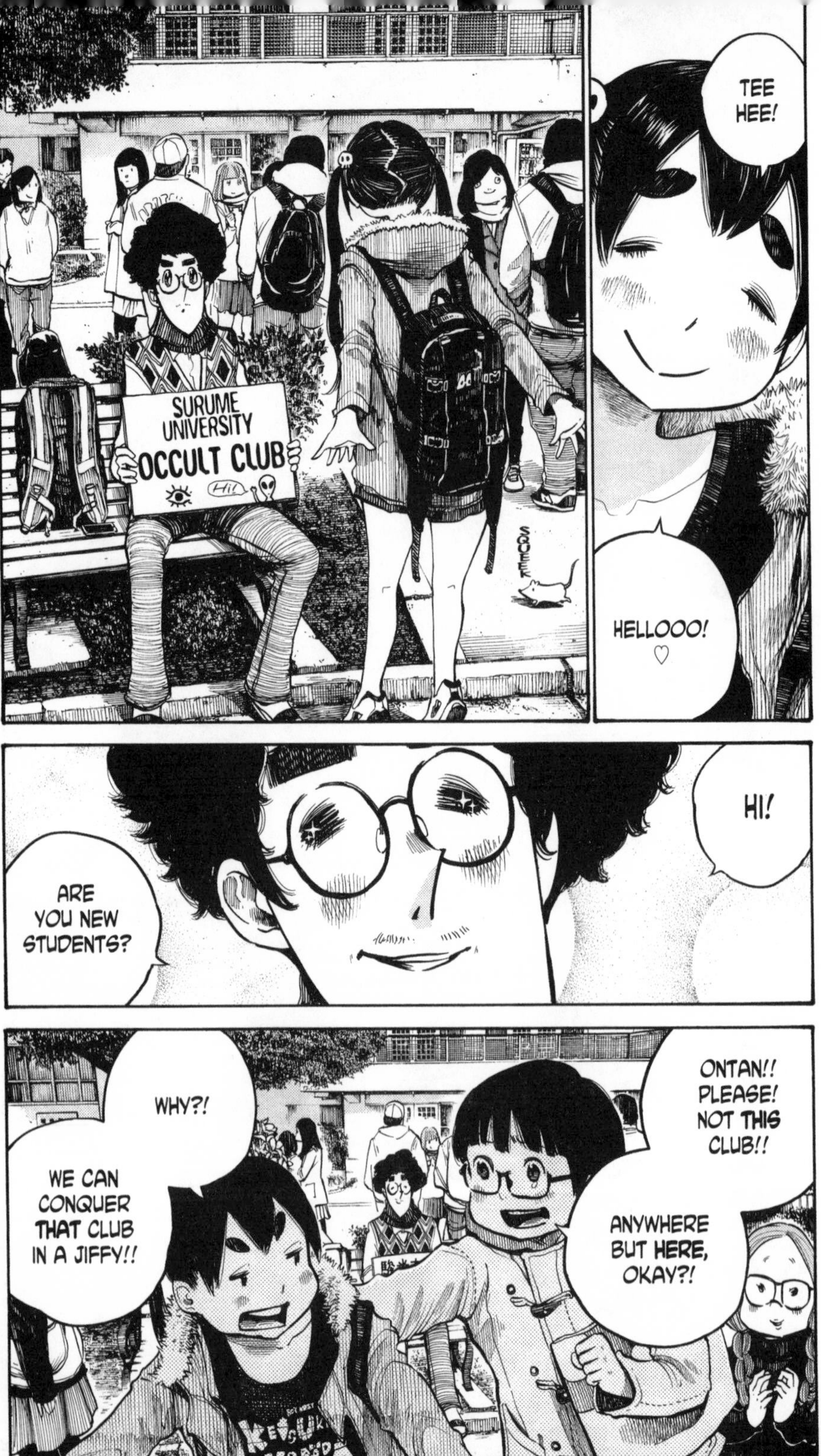
TEE HEE!
HELLOOO! ♡
SURUME UNIVERSITY
OCCULT CLUB
Hi!
SQUEEK
HI!
ARE YOU NEW STUDENTS?
ONTAN!! PLEASE! NOT THIS CLUB!!
ANYWHERE BUT HERE, OKAY?!
WHY?!
WE CAN CONQUER THAT CLUB IN A JIFFY!!

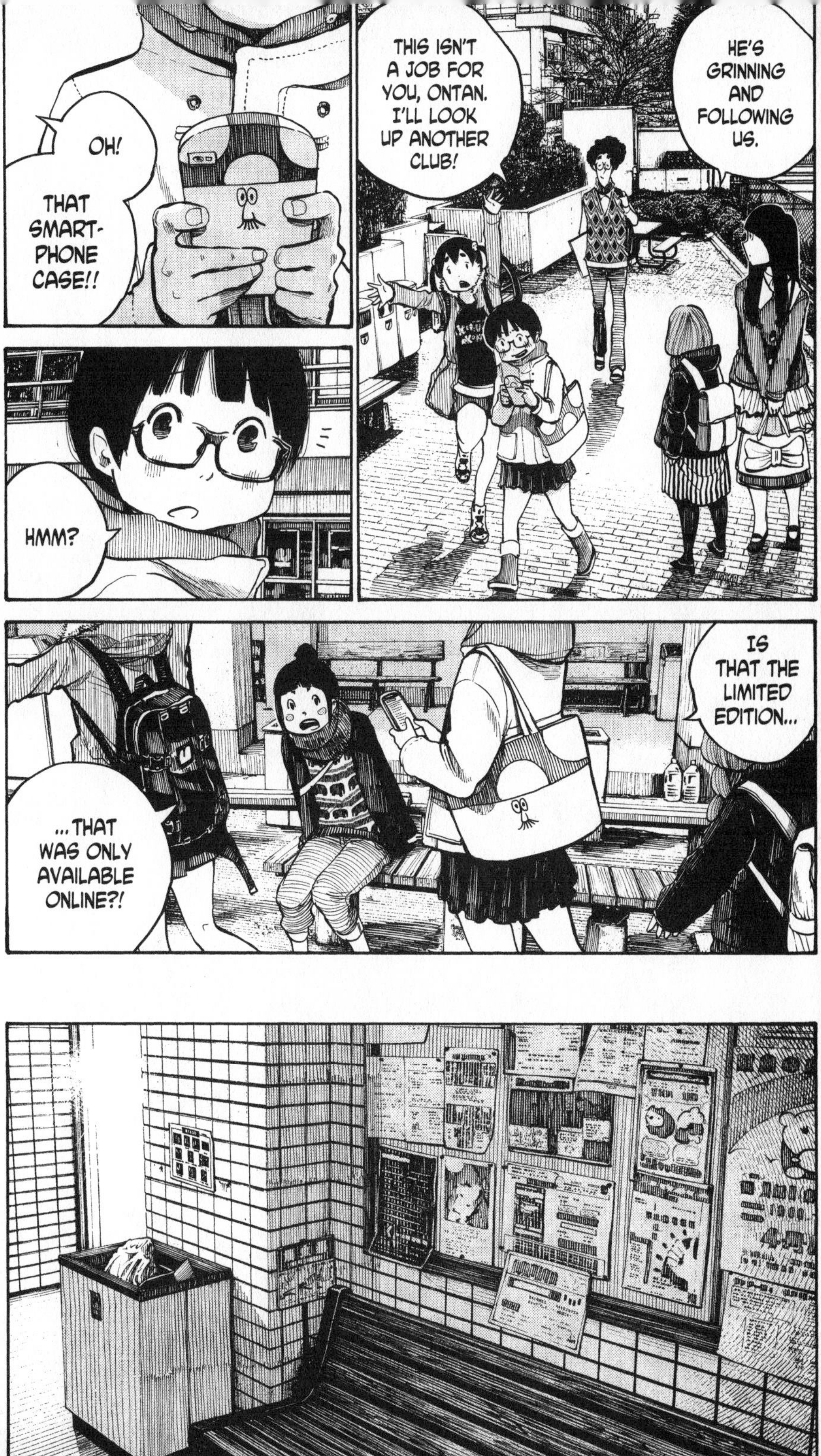
HE'S GRINNING AND FOLLOWING US.
THIS ISN'T A JOB FOR YOU, ONTAN. I'LL LOOK UP ANOTHER CLUB!
OH!
THAT SMART-PHONE CASE!!
HMM?
IS THAT THE LIMITED EDITION...
...THAT WAS ONLY AVAILABLE ONLINE?!

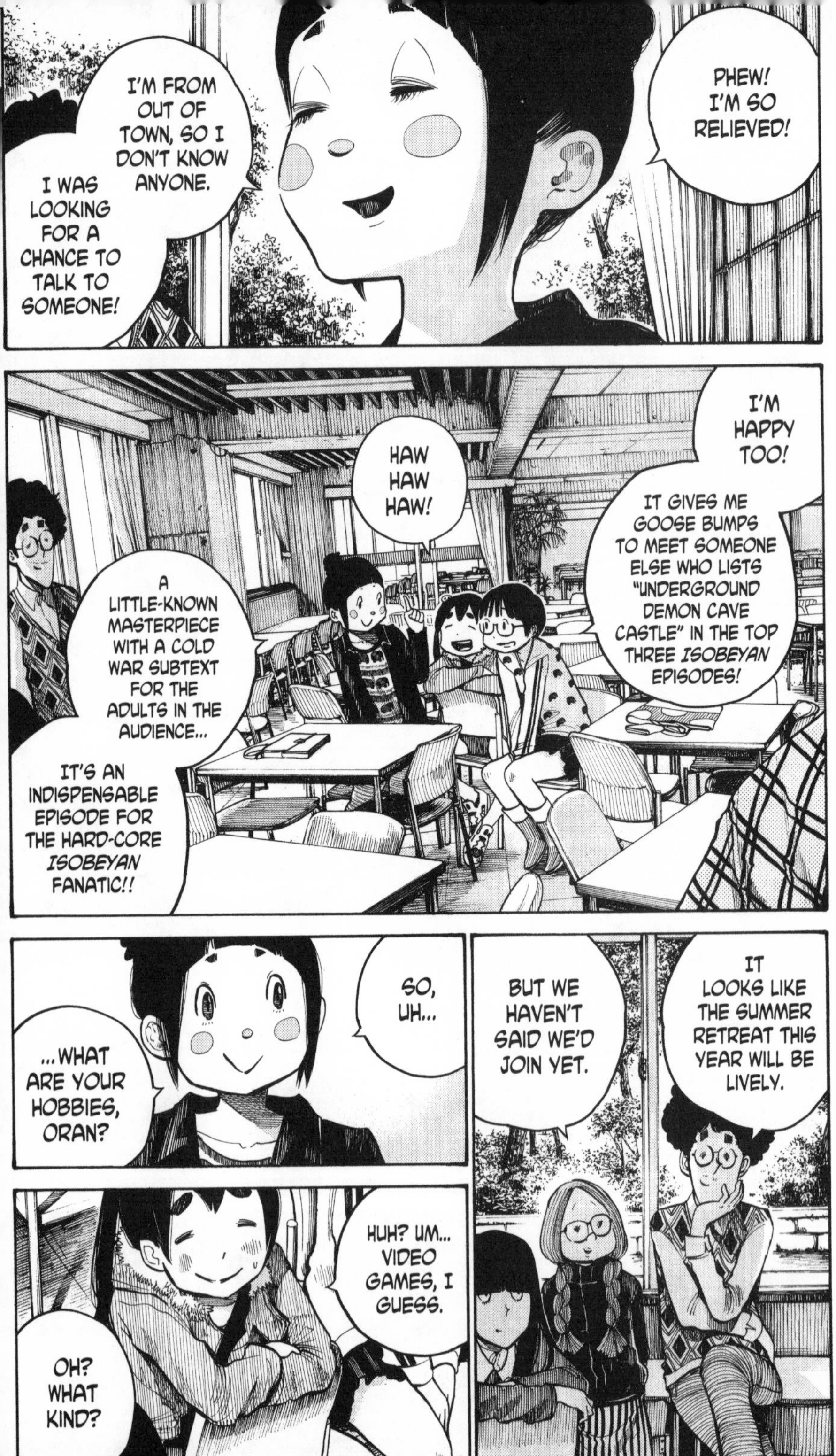
PHEW! I'M SO RELIEVED!
I'M FROM OUT OF TOWN, SO I DON'T KNOW ANYONE.
I WAS LOOKING FOR A CHANCE TO TALK TO SOMEONE!
I'M HAPPY TOO!
IT GIVES ME GOOSE BUMPS TO MEET SOMEONE ELSE WHO LISTS "UNDERGROUND DEMON CAVE CASTLE" IN THE TOP THREE *ISOBEYAN* EPISODES!
HAW HAW HAW!
A LITTLE-KNOWN MASTERPIECE WITH A COLD WAR SUBTEXT FOR THE ADULTS IN THE AUDIENCE...
IT'S AN INDISPENSABLE EPISODE FOR THE HARD-CORE *ISOBEYAN* FANATIC!!
IT LOOKS LIKE THE SUMMER RETREAT THIS YEAR WILL BE LIVELY.
BUT WE HAVEN'T SAID WE'D JOIN YET.
SO, UH...
...WHAT ARE YOUR HOBBIES, ORAN?
HUH? UM... VIDEO GAMES, I GUESS.
OH? WHAT KIND?

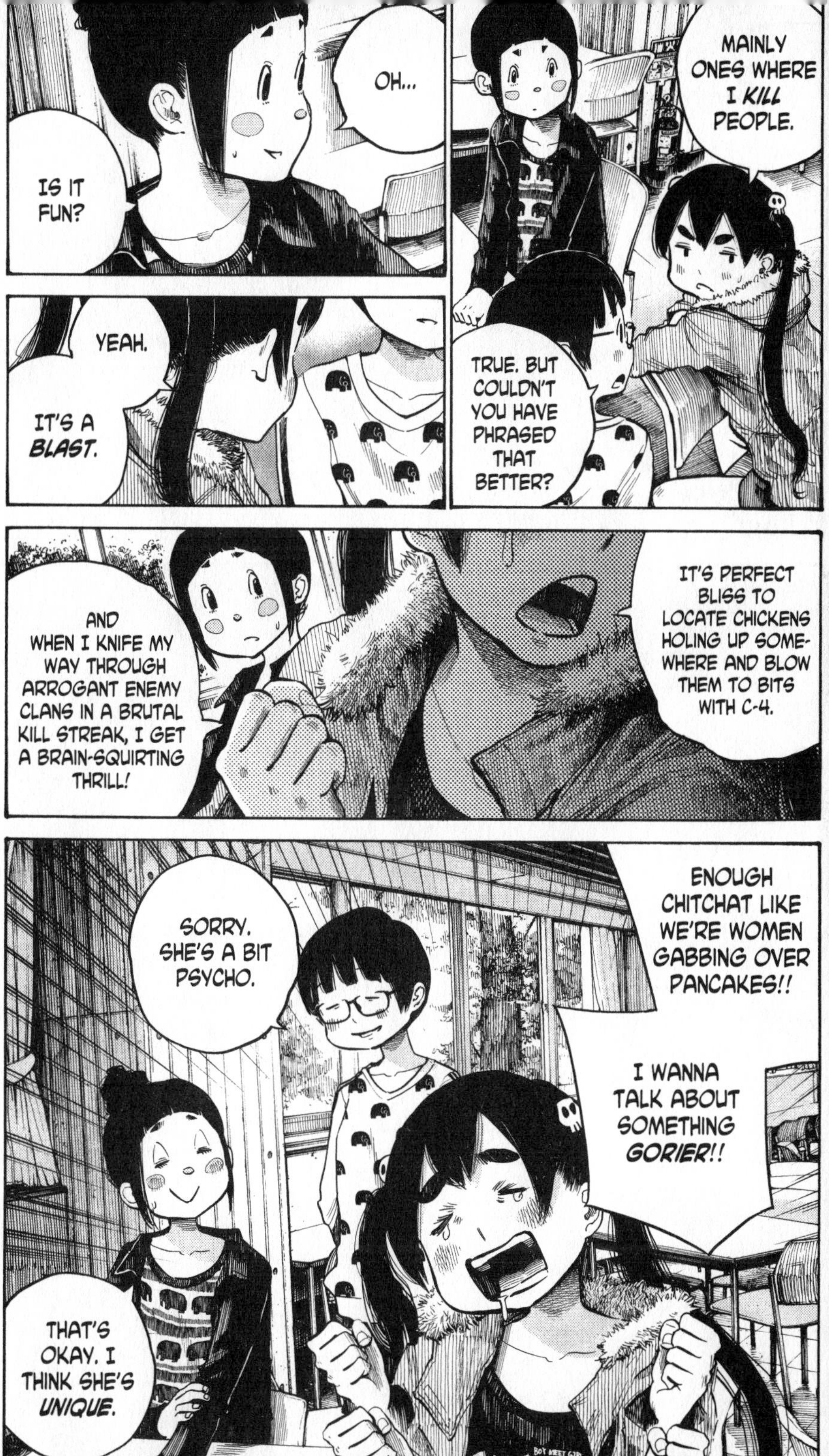
MAINLY ONES WHERE I *KILL* PEOPLE.
TRUE. BUT COULDN'T YOU HAVE PHRASED THAT BETTER?
OH...
IS IT FUN?
YEAH.
IT'S A *BLAST*.
IT'S PERFECT BLISS TO LOCATE CHICKENS HOLING UP SOME-WHERE AND BLOW THEM TO BITS WITH C-4.
AND WHEN I KNIFE MY WAY THROUGH ARROGANT ENEMY CLANS IN A BRUTAL KILL STREAK, I GET A BRAIN-SQUIRTING THRILL!
ENOUGH CHITCHAT LIKE WE'RE WOMEN GABBING OVER PANCAKES!!
I WANNA TALK ABOUT SOMETHING *GORIER*!!
SORRY. SHE'S A BIT PSYCHO.
THAT'S OKAY. I THINK SHE'S *UNIQUE*.

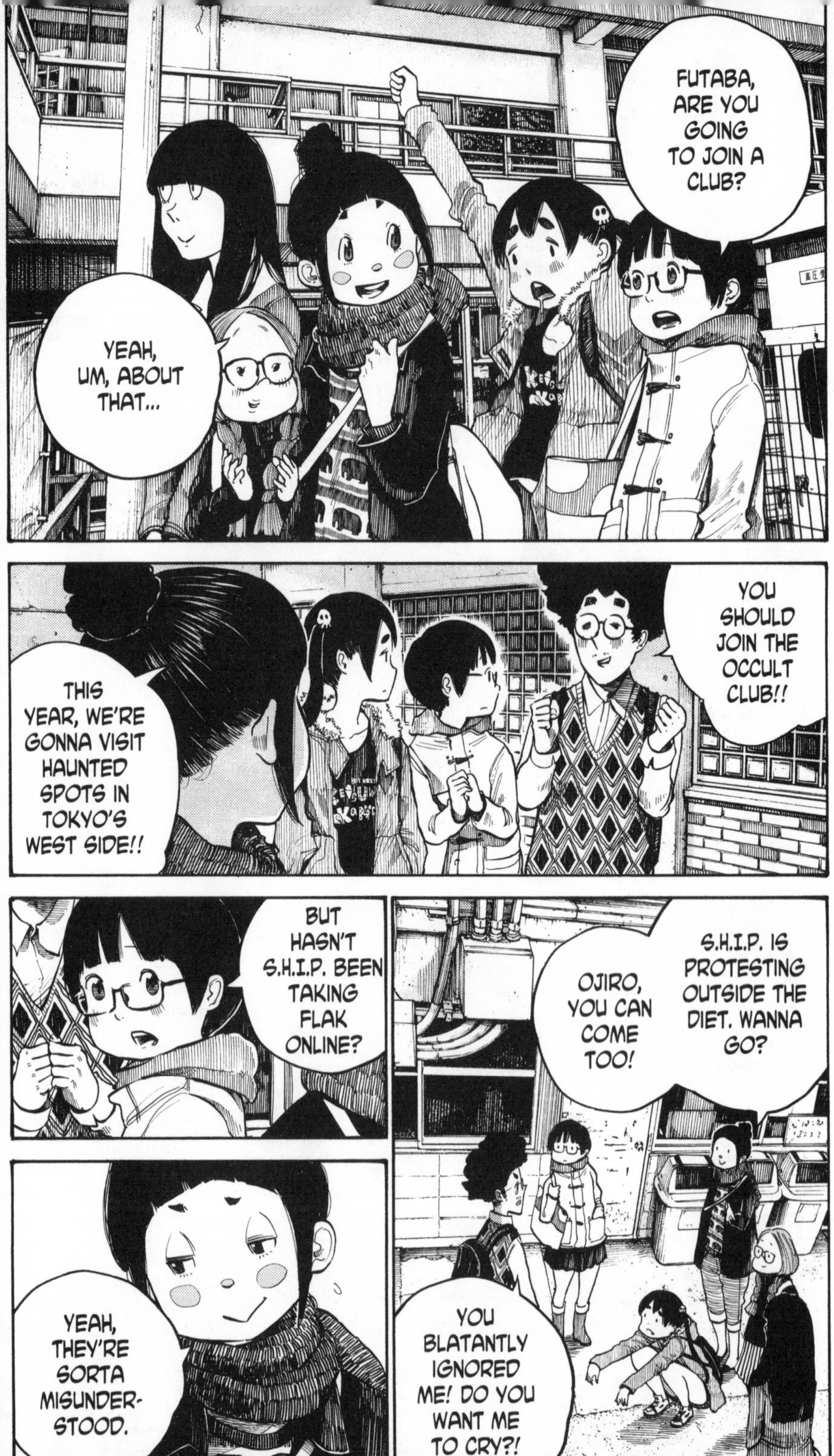
FUTABA, ARE YOU GOING TO JOIN A CLUB?
YEAH, UM, ABOUT THAT...
YOU SHOULD JOIN THE OCCULT CLUB!!
THIS YEAR, WE'RE GONNA VISIT HAUNTED SPOTS IN TOKYO'S WEST SIDE!!
S.H.I.P. IS PROTESTING OUTSIDE THE DIET. WANNA GO?
OJIRO, YOU CAN COME TOO!
YOU BLATANTLY IGNORED ME! DO YOU WANT ME TO CRY?!
BUT HASN'T S.H.I.P. BEEN TAKING FLAK ONLINE?
YEAH, THEY'RE SORTA MISUNDERSTOOD.

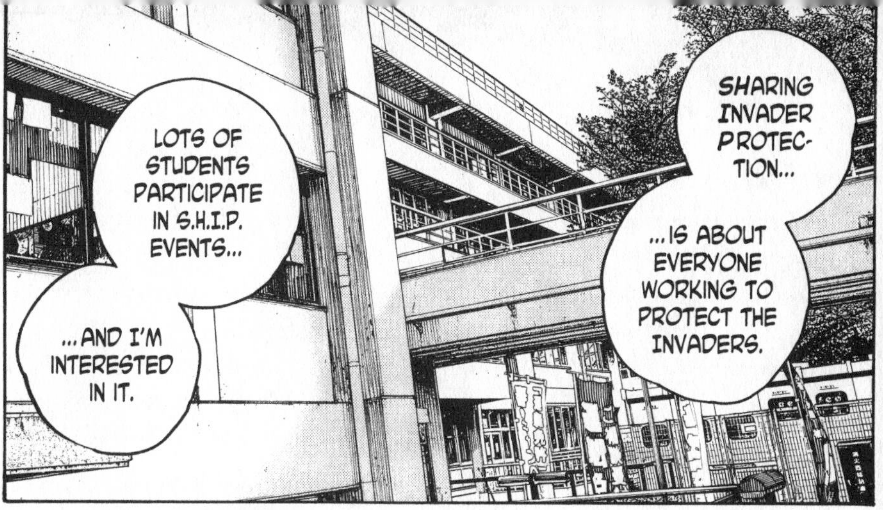
SHARING INVADER PROTECTION...
...IS ABOUT EVERYONE WORKING TO PROTECT THE INVADERS.
LOTS OF STUDENTS PARTICIPATE IN S.H.I.P. EVENTS...
...AND I'M INTERESTED IN IT.
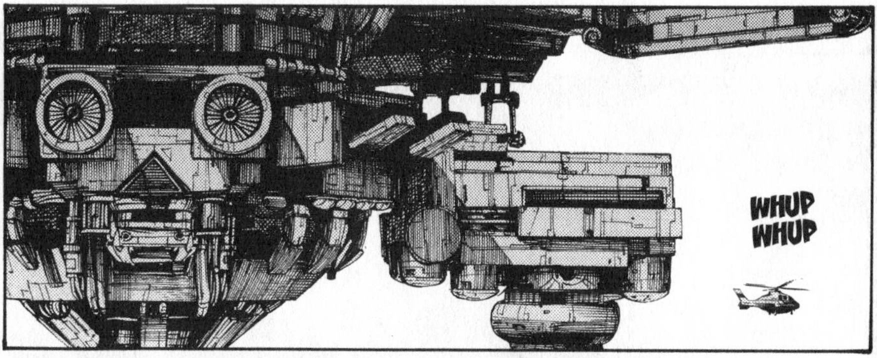
WHUP WHUP
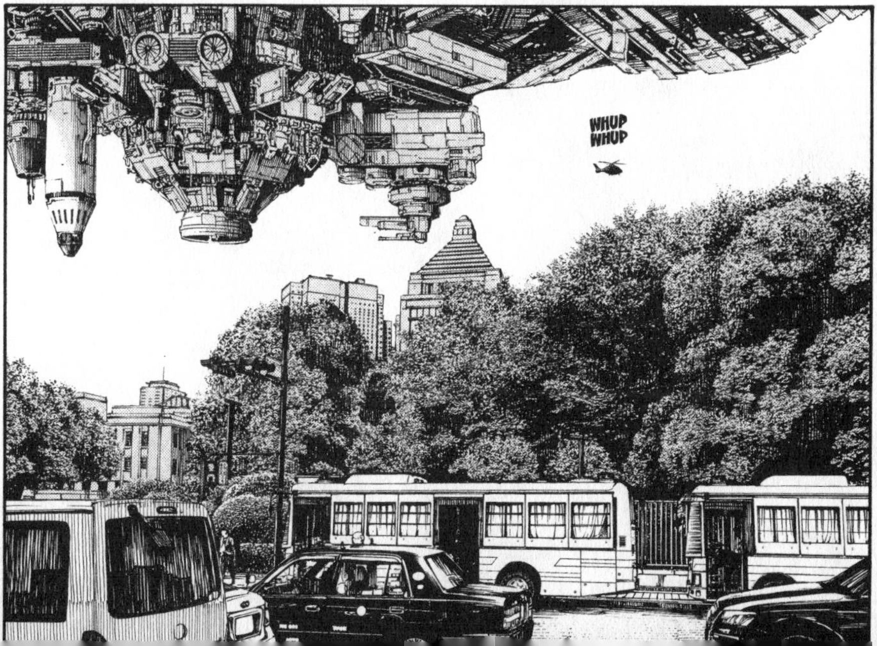
WHUP WHUP

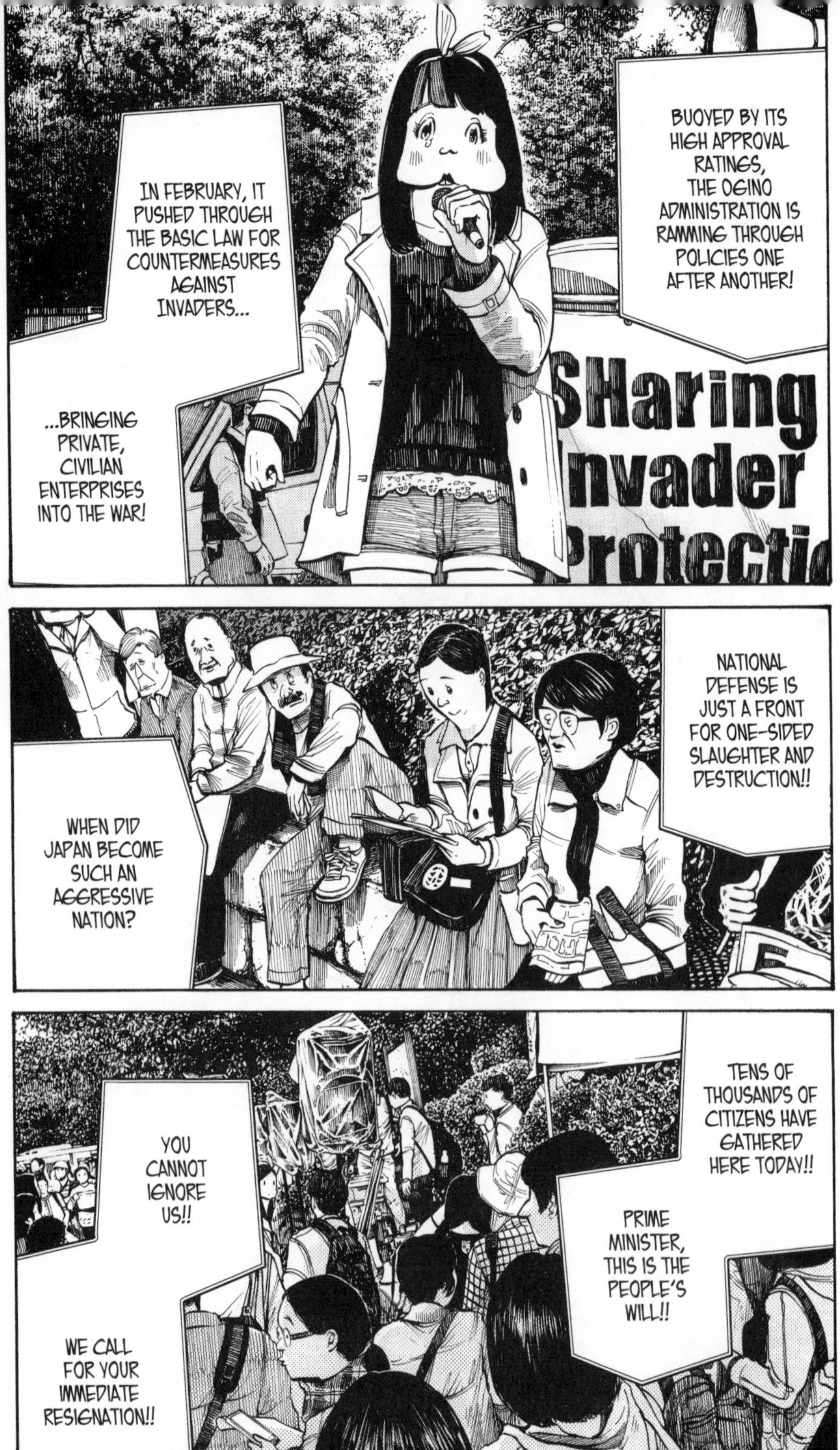
BUOYED BY ITS HIGH APPROVAL RATINGS, THE OGINO ADMINISTRATION IS RAMMING THROUGH POLICIES ONE AFTER ANOTHER!
IN FEBRUARY, IT PUSHED THROUGH THE BASIC LAW FOR COUNTERMEASURES AGAINST INVADERS...
...BRINGING PRIVATE, CIVILIAN ENTERPRISES INTO THE WAR!
SHaring
Invader
Protecti
NATIONAL DEFENSE IS JUST A FRONT FOR ONE-SIDED SLAUGHTER AND DESTRUCTION!!
WHEN DID JAPAN BECOME SUCH AN AGGRESSIVE NATION?
TENS OF THOUSANDS OF CITIZENS HAVE GATHERED HERE TODAY!!
PRIME MINISTER, THIS IS THE PEOPLE'S WILL!!
YOU CANNOT IGNORE US!!
WE CALL FOR YOUR IMMEDIATE RESIGNATION!!

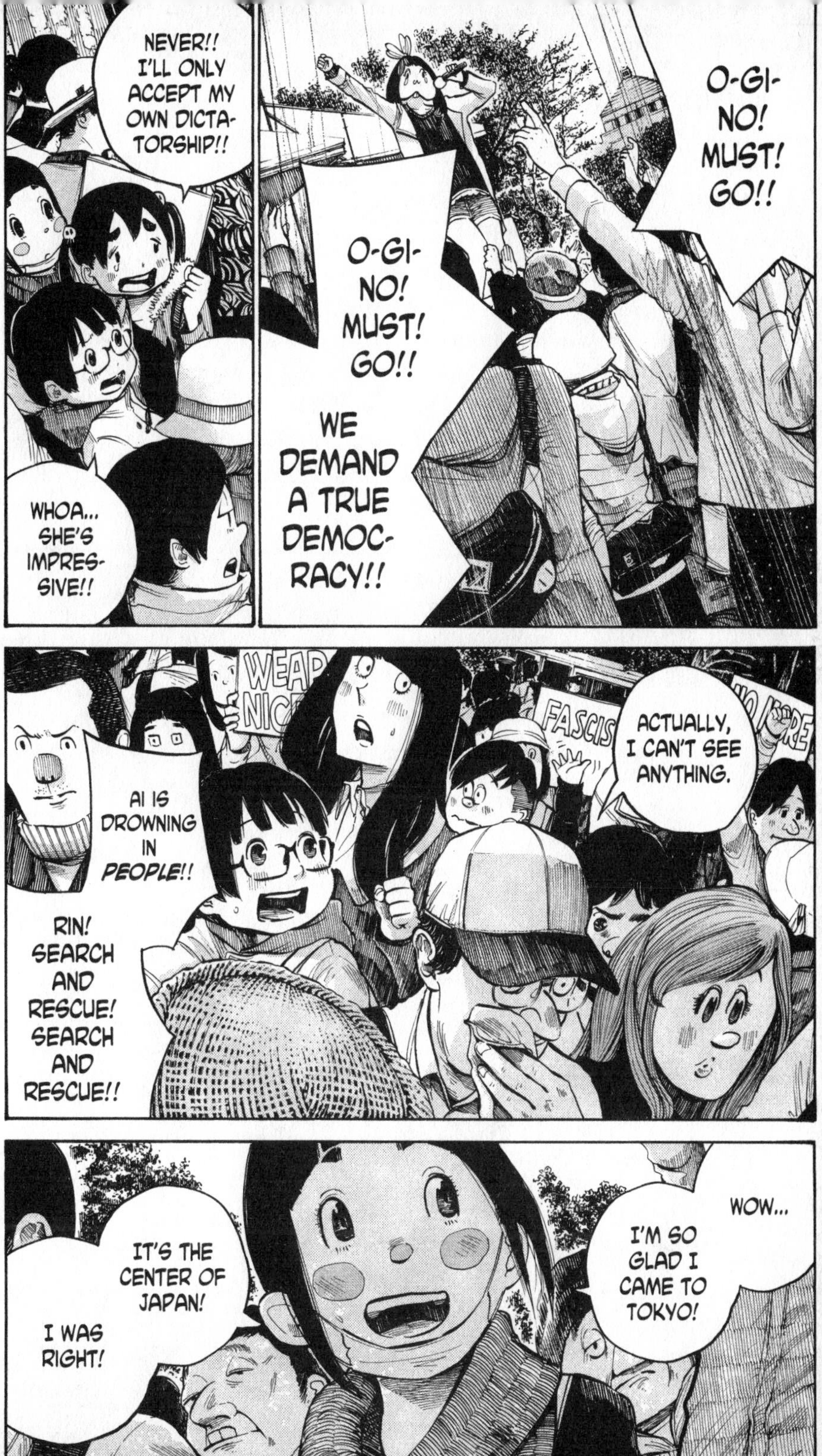
O-GI-NO! MUST! GO!!
O-GI-NO! MUST! GO!!
WE DEMAND A TRUE DEMOCRACY!!
NEVER!! I'LL ONLY ACCEPT MY OWN DICTATORSHIP!!
WHOA... SHE'S IMPRESSIVE!!
ACTUALLY, I CAN'T SEE ANYTHING.
AI IS DROWNING IN *PEOPLE*!!
RIN! SEARCH AND RESCUE! SEARCH AND RESCUE!!
WOW...
I'M SO GLAD I CAME TO TOKYO!
IT'S THE CENTER OF JAPAN!
I WAS RIGHT!

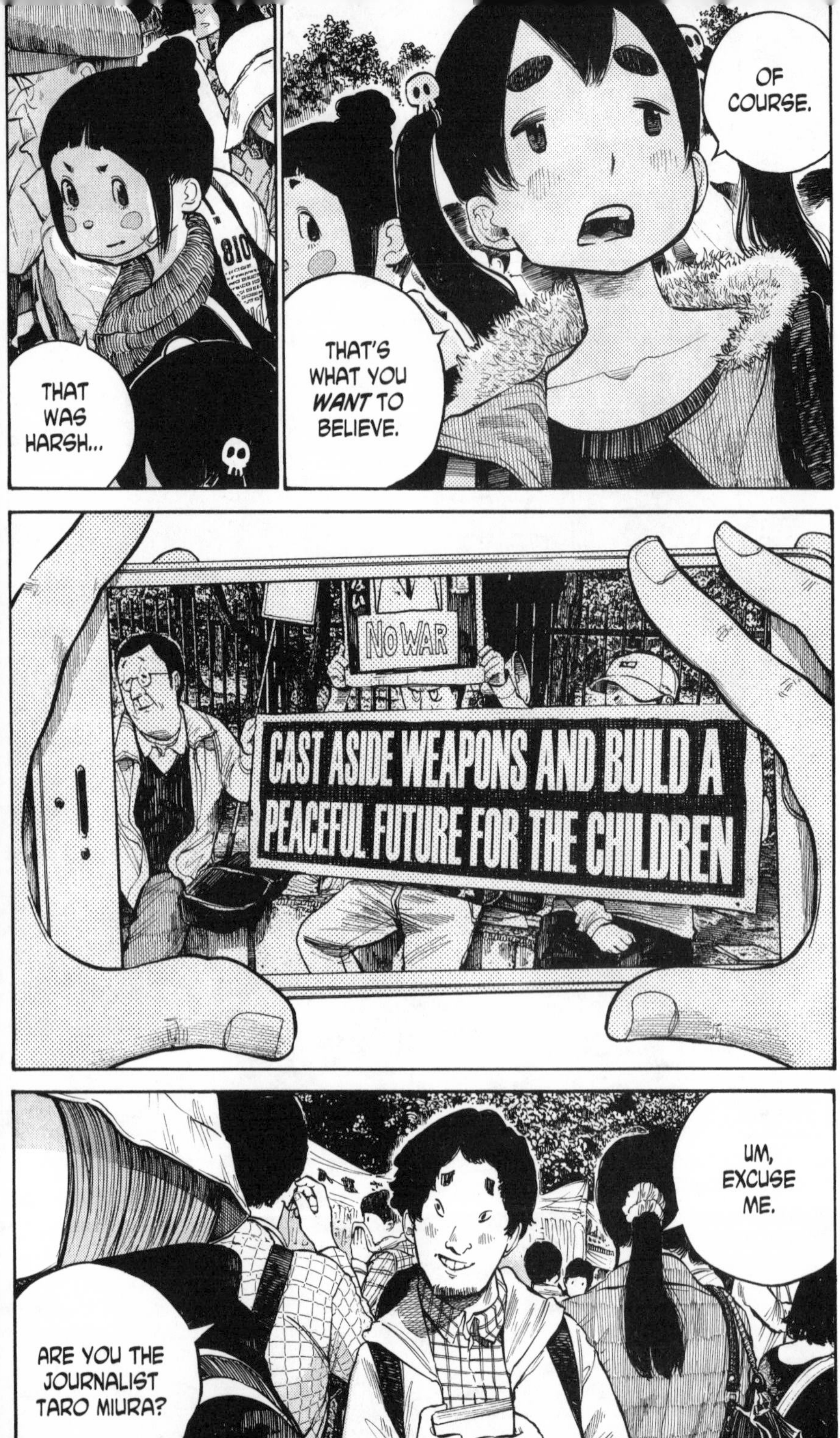
OF COURSE.
THAT'S WHAT YOU *WANT* TO BELIEVE.
THAT WAS HARSH...
NO WAR
CAST ASIDE WEAPONS AND BUILD A PEACEFUL FUTURE FOR THE CHILDREN
UM, EXCUSE ME.
ARE YOU THE JOURNALIST TARO MIURA?

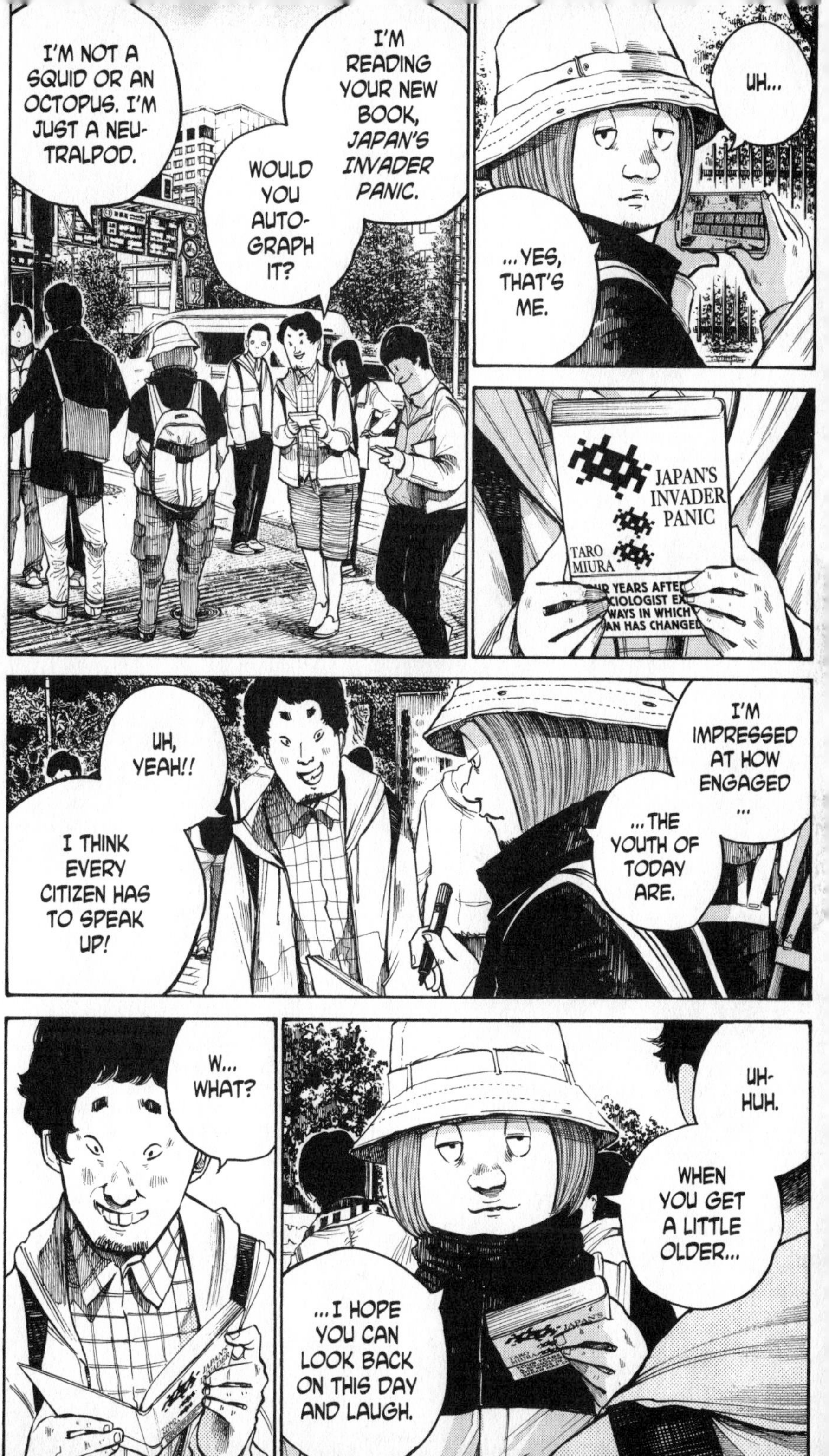
UH...
...YES, THAT'S ME.
JAPAN'S INVADER PANIC
TARO MIURA
I'M READING YOUR NEW BOOK, JAPAN'S INVADER PANIC.
WOULD YOU AUTOGRAPH IT?
I'M NOT A SQUID OR AN OCTOPUS. I'M JUST A NEUTRALPOD.
I'M IMPRESSED AT HOW ENGAGED...
...THE YOUTH OF TODAY ARE.
UH, YEAH!!
I THINK EVERY CITIZEN HAS TO SPEAK UP!
UH-HUH.
WHEN YOU GET A LITTLE OLDER...
...I HOPE YOU CAN LOOK BACK ON THIS DAY AND LAUGH.
W... WHAT?

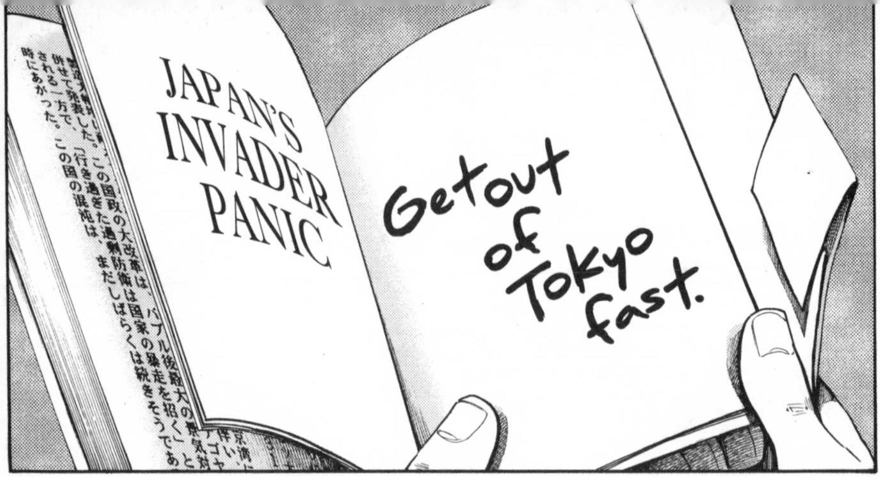
JAPAN'S
INVADER
PANIC
Get out
of
Tokyo
fast.
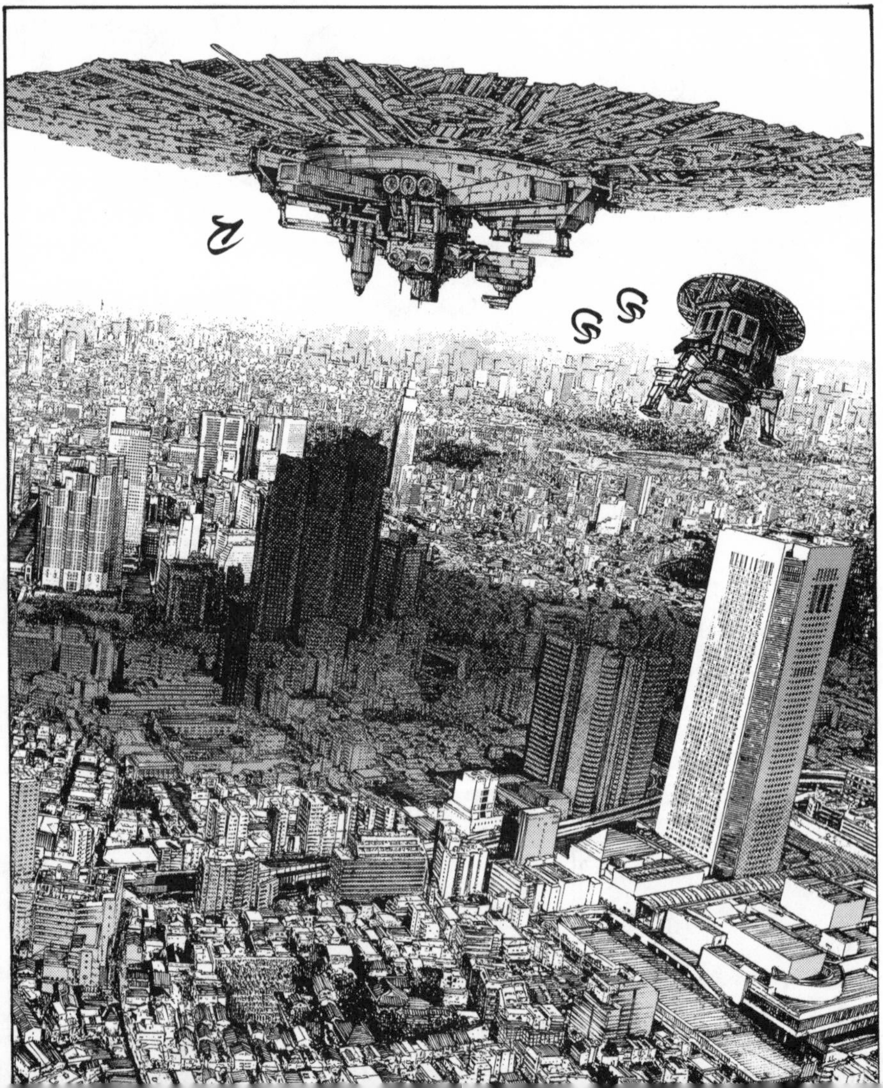

CHAPTER 29

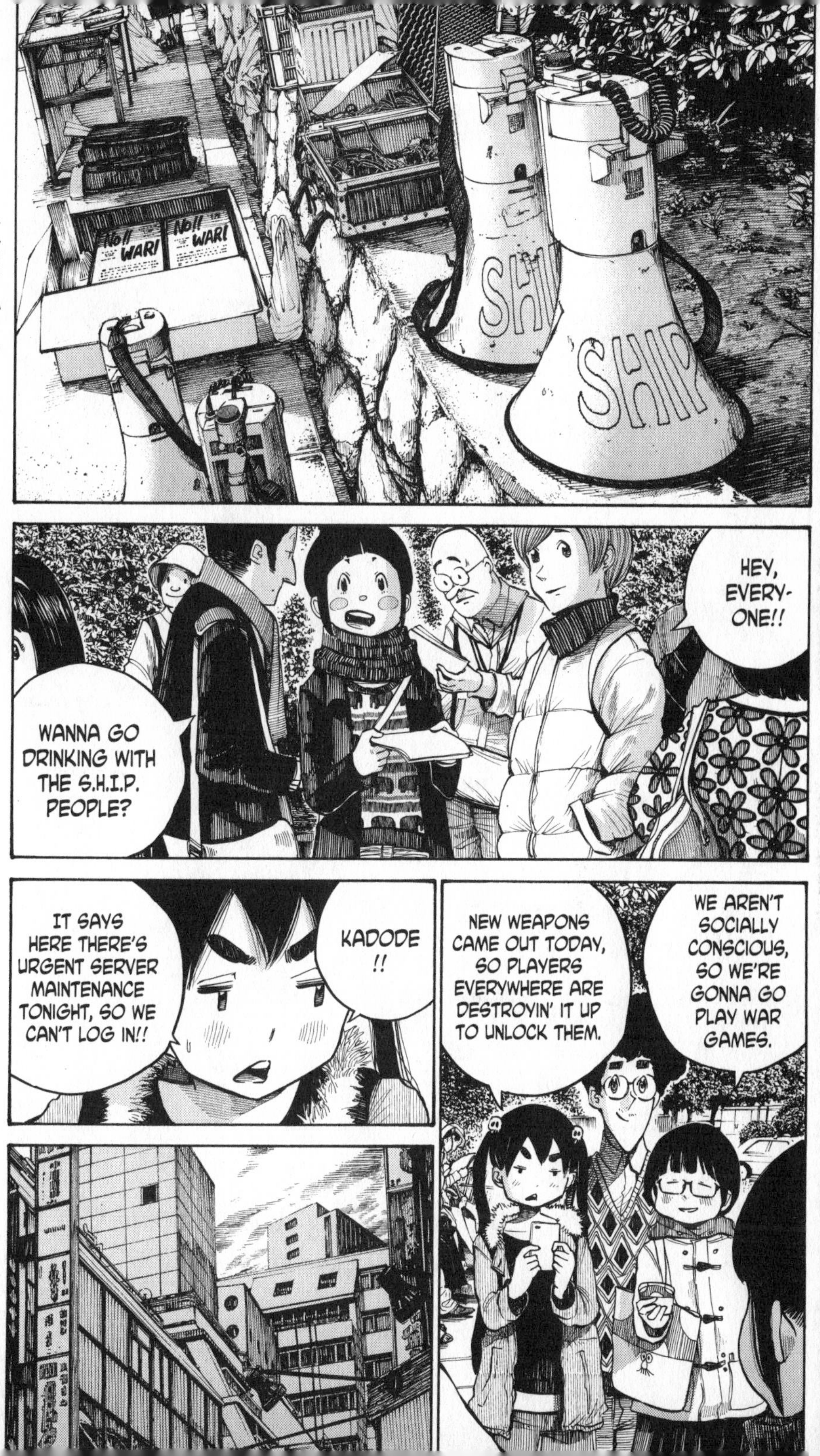
No!! WAR!
No!! WAR!
SHIP
SHIP
HEY, EVERY-ONE!!
WANNA GO DRINKING WITH THE S.H.I.P. PEOPLE?
WE AREN'T SOCIALLY CONSCIOUS, SO WE'RE GONNA GO PLAY WAR GAMES.
NEW WEAPONS CAME OUT TODAY, SO PLAYERS EVERYWHERE ARE DESTROYIN' IT UP TO UNLOCK THEM.
KADODE !!
IT SAYS HERE THERE'S URGENT SERVER MAINTENANCE TONIGHT, SO WE CAN'T LOG IN!!

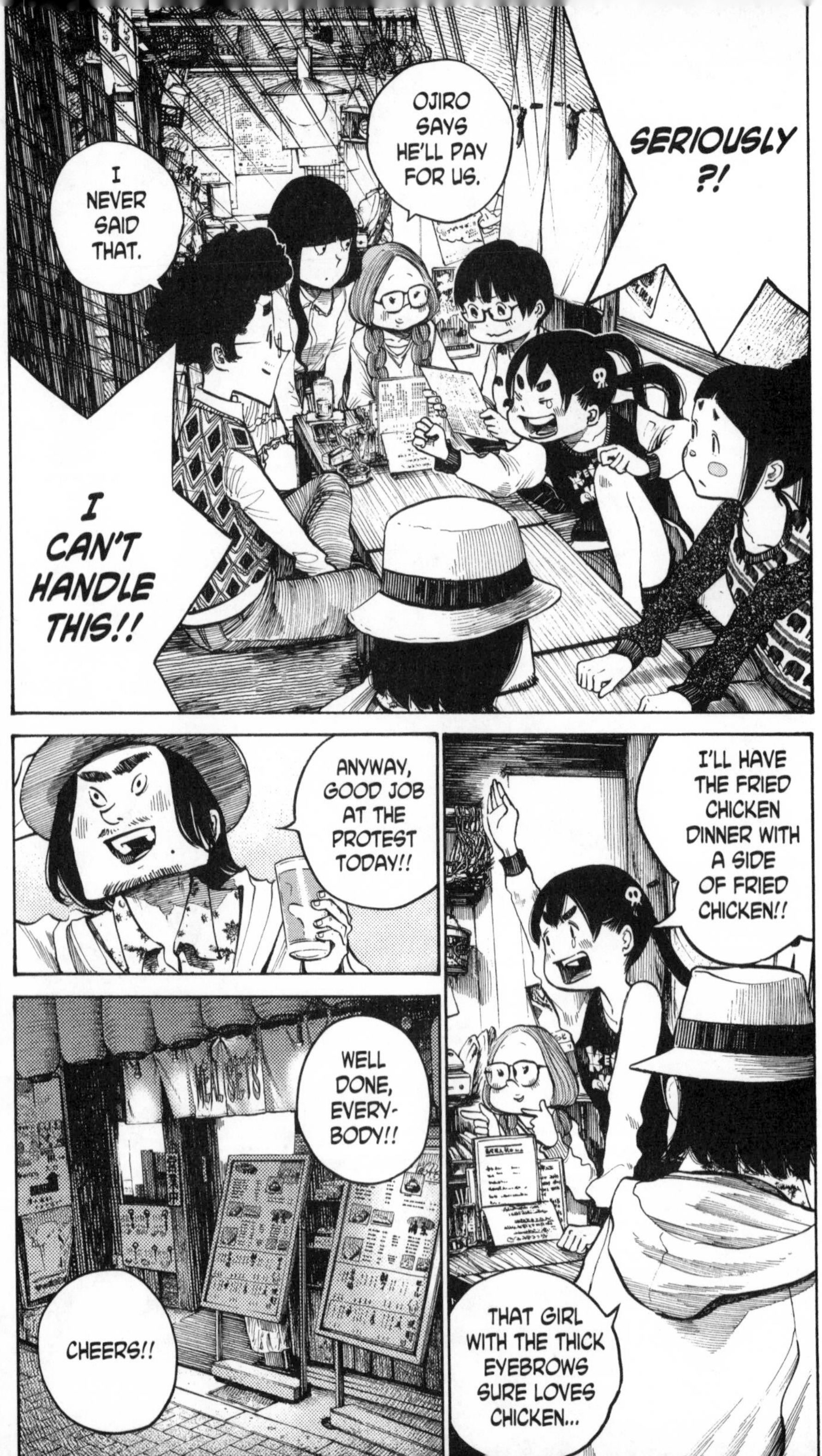
OJIRO SAYS HE'LL PAY FOR US.
SERIOUSLY ?!
I NEVER SAID THAT.
I CAN'T HANDLE THIS!!
I'LL HAVE THE FRIED CHICKEN DINNER WITH A SIDE OF FRIED CHICKEN!!
THAT GIRL WITH THE THICK EYEBROWS SURE LOVES CHICKEN...
ANYWAY, GOOD JOB AT THE PROTEST TODAY!!
MEAL SETS
WELL DONE, EVERY-BODY!!
CHEERS!!

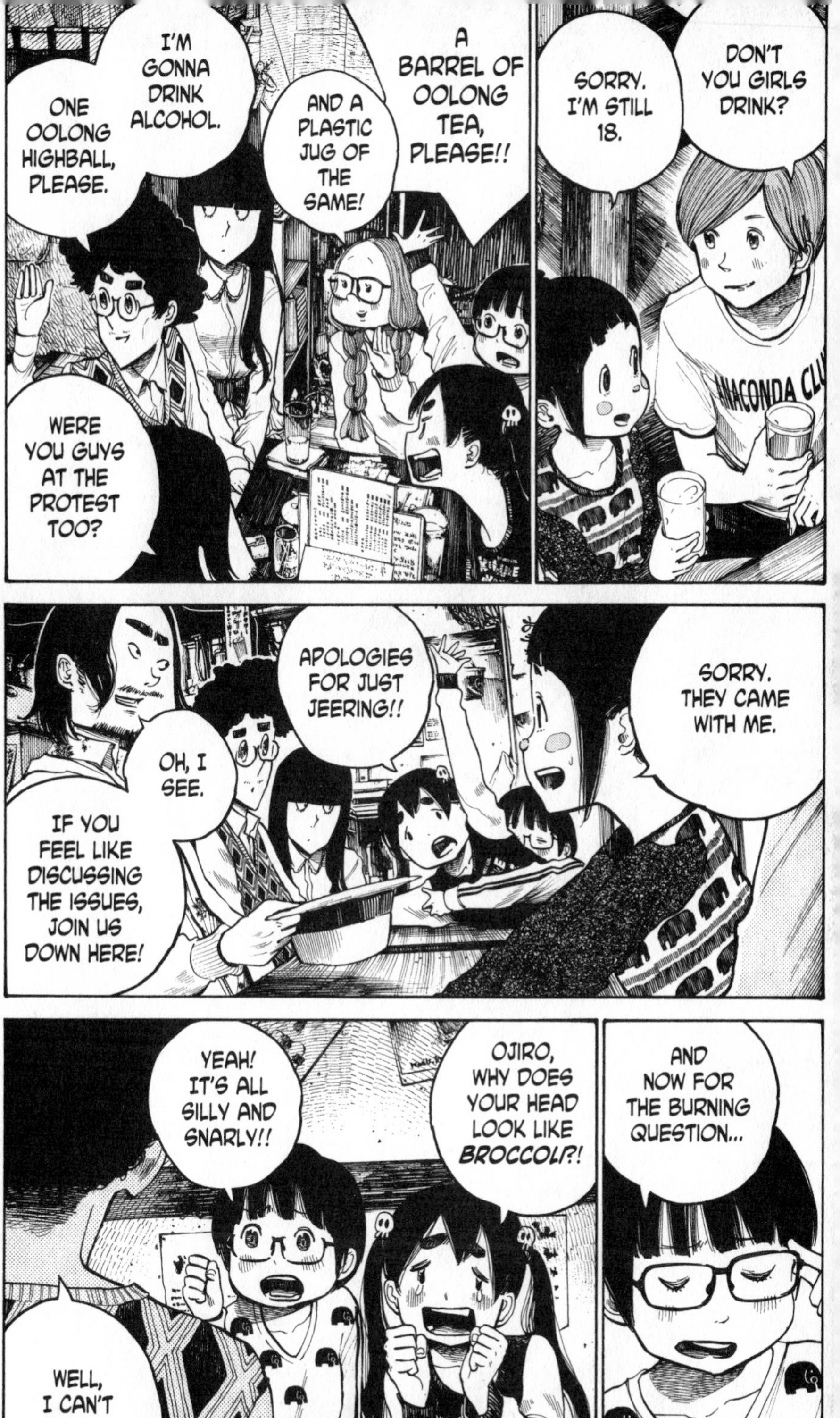
DON'T YOU GIRLS DRINK?
SORRY. I'M STILL 18.
A BARREL OF OOLONG TEA, PLEASE!!
AND A PLASTIC JUG OF THE SAME!
I'M GONNA DRINK ALCOHOL.
ONE OOLONG HIGHBALL, PLEASE.
WERE YOU GUYS AT THE PROTEST TOO?
SORRY. THEY CAME WITH ME.
APOLOGIES FOR JUST JEERING!!
OH, I SEE.
IF YOU FEEL LIKE DISCUSSING THE ISSUES, JOIN US DOWN HERE!
AND NOW FOR THE BURNING QUESTION...
OJIRO, WHY DOES YOUR HEAD LOOK LIKE *BROCCOLI*?!
YEAH! IT'S ALL SILLY AND SNARLY!!
WELL, I CAN'T HELP IT.

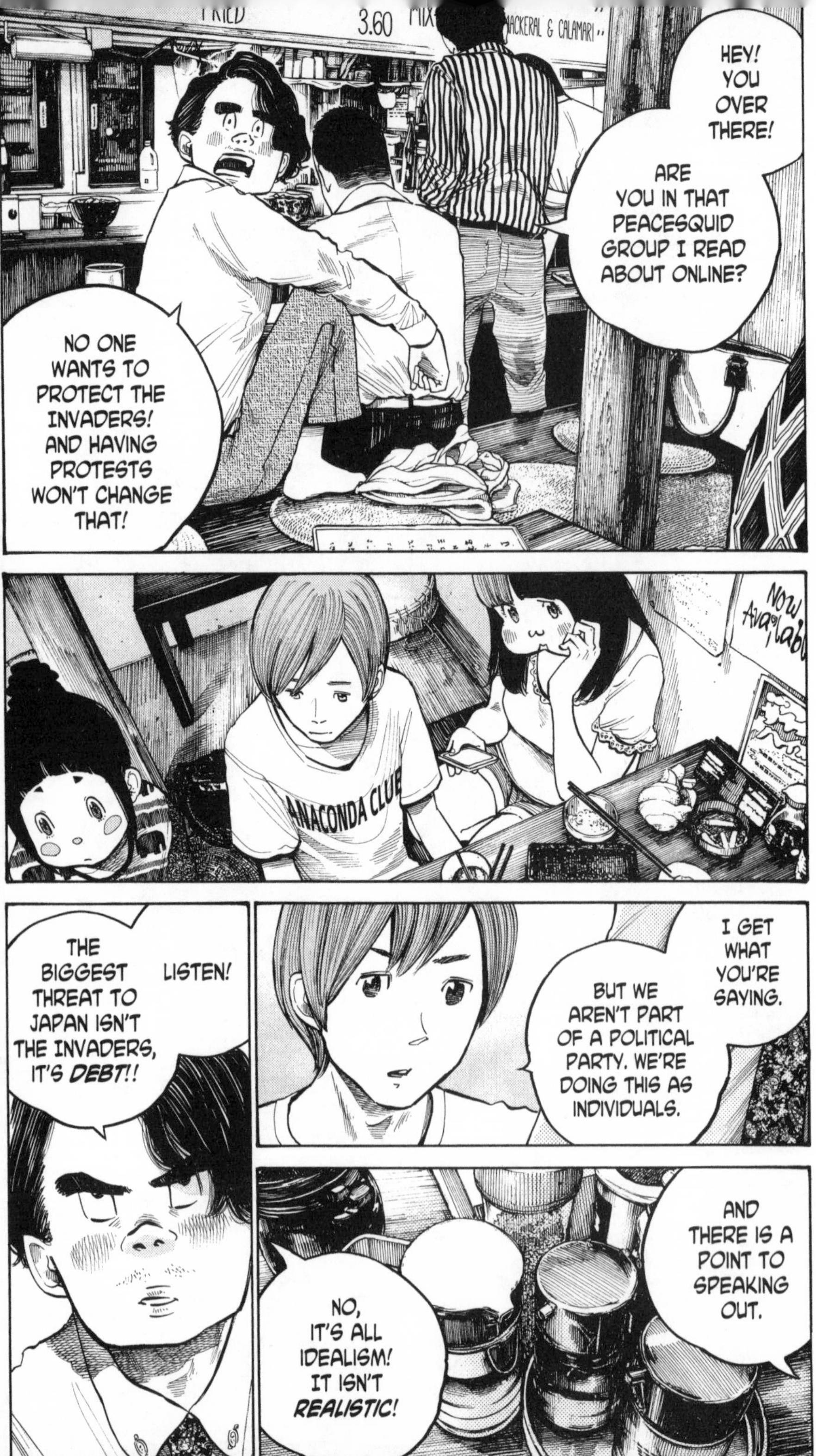
3.60
MACKERAL & CALAMARI
HEY! YOU OVER THERE!
ARE YOU IN THAT PEACESQUID GROUP I READ ABOUT ONLINE?
NO ONE WANTS TO PROTECT THE INVADERS! AND HAVING PROTESTS WON'T CHANGE THAT!
I GET WHAT YOU'RE SAYING.
BUT WE AREN'T PART OF A POLITICAL PARTY. WE'RE DOING THIS AS INDIVIDUALS.
AND THERE IS A POINT TO SPEAKING OUT.
NO, IT'S ALL IDEALISM! IT ISN'T *REALISTIC*!
LISTEN!
THE BIGGEST THREAT TO JAPAN ISN'T THE INVADERS, IT'S *DEBT*!!

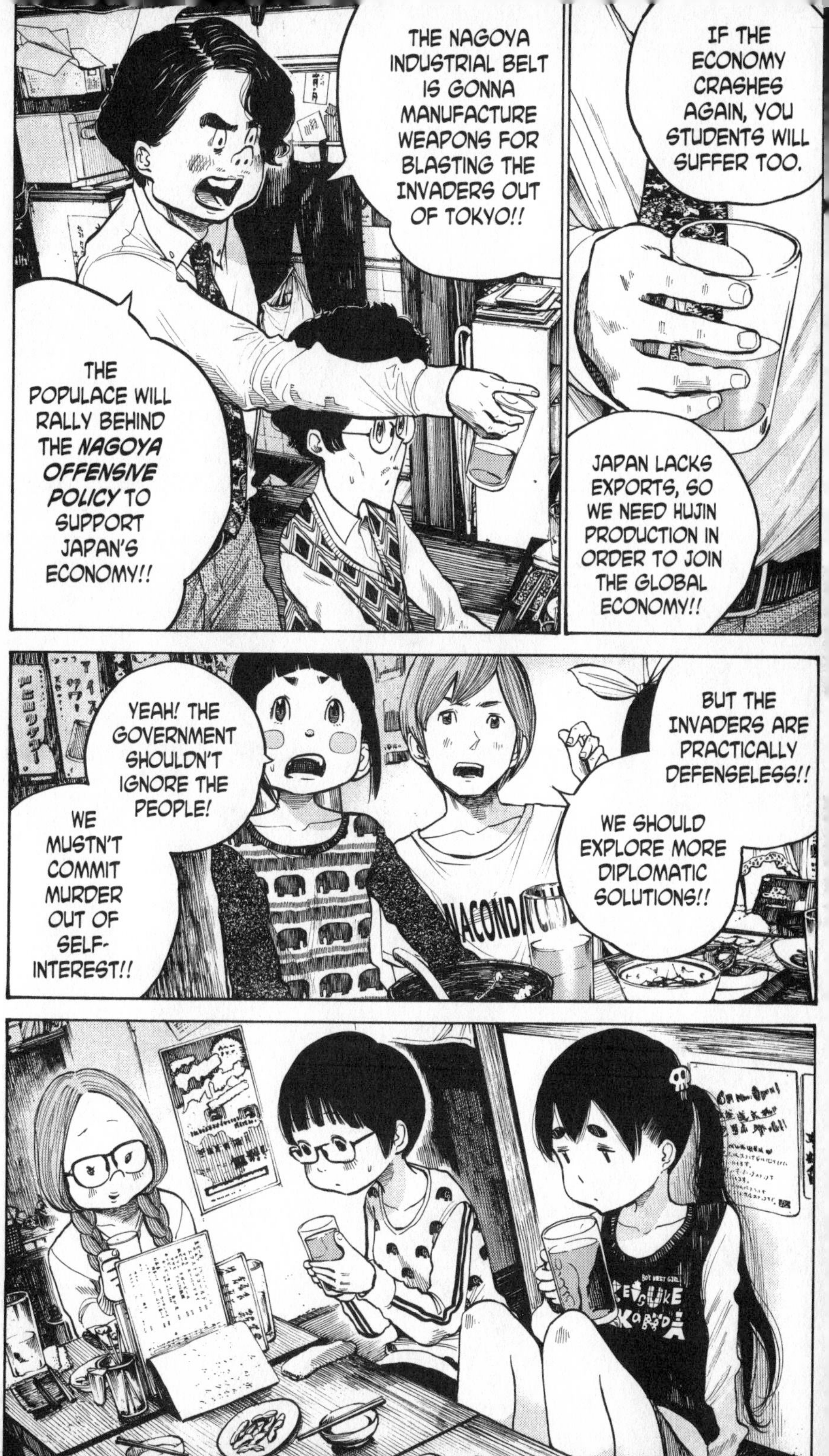
IF THE ECONOMY CRASHES AGAIN, YOU STUDENTS WILL SUFFER TOO.
JAPAN LACKS EXPORTS, SO WE NEED HUJIN PRODUCTION IN ORDER TO JOIN THE GLOBAL ECONOMY!!
THE NAGOYA INDUSTRIAL BELT IS GONNA MANUFACTURE WEAPONS FOR BLASTING THE INVADERS OUT OF TOKYO!!
THE POPULACE WILL RALLY BEHIND THE *NAGOYA OFFENSIVE POLICY* TO SUPPORT JAPAN'S ECONOMY!!
BUT THE INVADERS ARE PRACTICALLY DEFENSELESS!!
WE SHOULD EXPLORE MORE DIPLOMATIC SOLUTIONS!!
YEAH! THE GOVERNMENT SHOULDN'T IGNORE THE PEOPLE!
WE MUSTN'T COMMIT MURDER OUT OF SELF-INTEREST!!

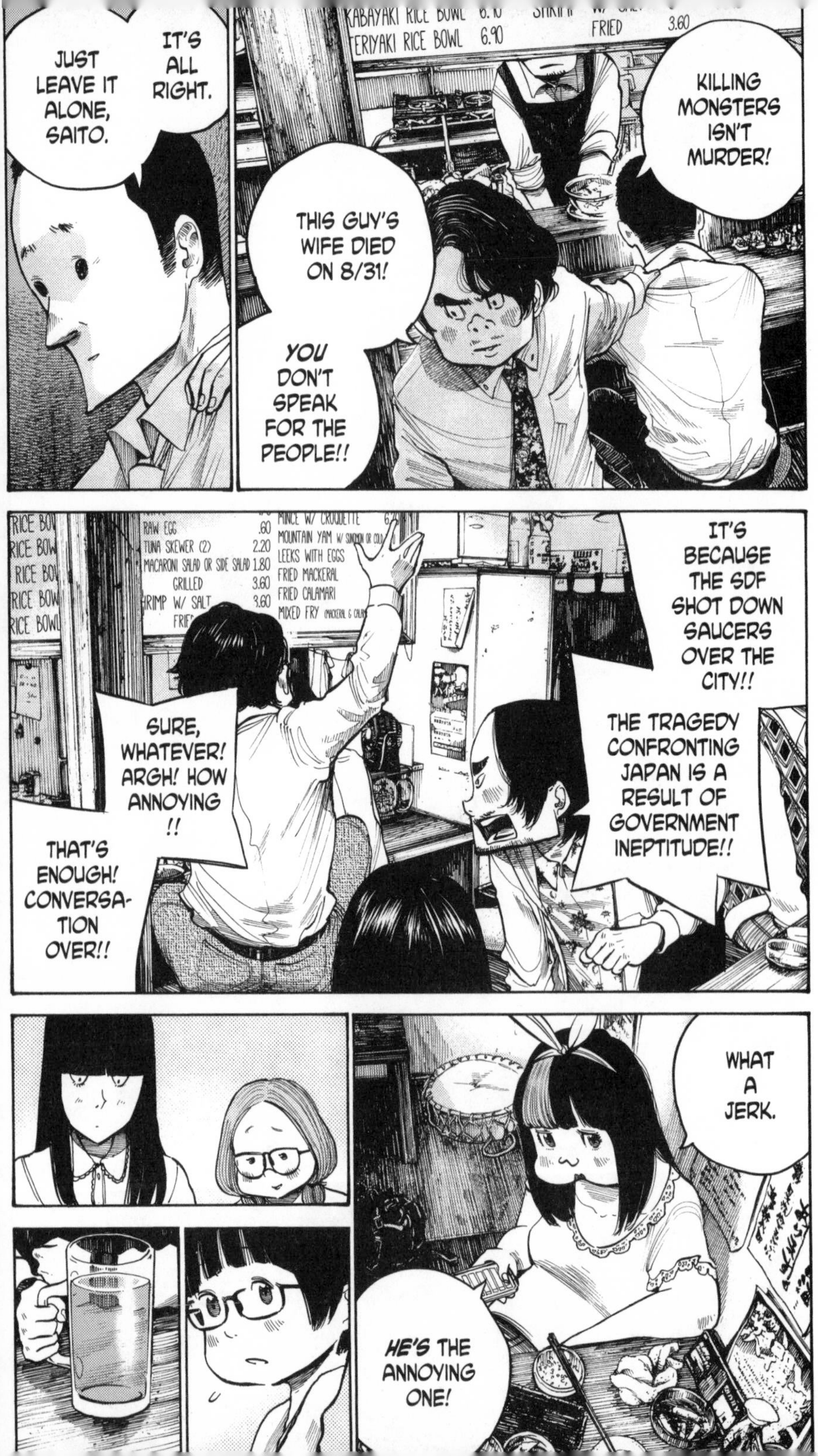
KABAYAKI RICE BOWL 6.10
TERIYAKI RICE BOWL 6.90
FRIED 3.60
KILLING MONSTERS ISN'T MURDER!
THIS GUY'S WIFE DIED ON 8/31!
YOU DON'T SPEAK FOR THE PEOPLE!!
IT'S ALL RIGHT.
JUST LEAVE IT ALONE, SAITO.
RAW EGG .60
TUNA SKEWER (2) 2.20
MACARONI SALAD OR SIDE SALAD 1.80
GRILLED 3.60
FRIED MACKEREL
FRIED CALAMARI
LEEKS WITH EGGS
MIXED FRY
IT'S BECAUSE THE SDF SHOT DOWN SAUCERS OVER THE CITY!!
THE TRAGEDY CONFRONTING JAPAN IS A RESULT OF GOVERNMENT INEPTITUDE!!
SURE, WHATEVER! ARGH! HOW ANNOYING!!
THAT'S ENOUGH! CONVERSATION OVER!!
WHAT A JERK.
HE'S THE ANNOYING ONE!

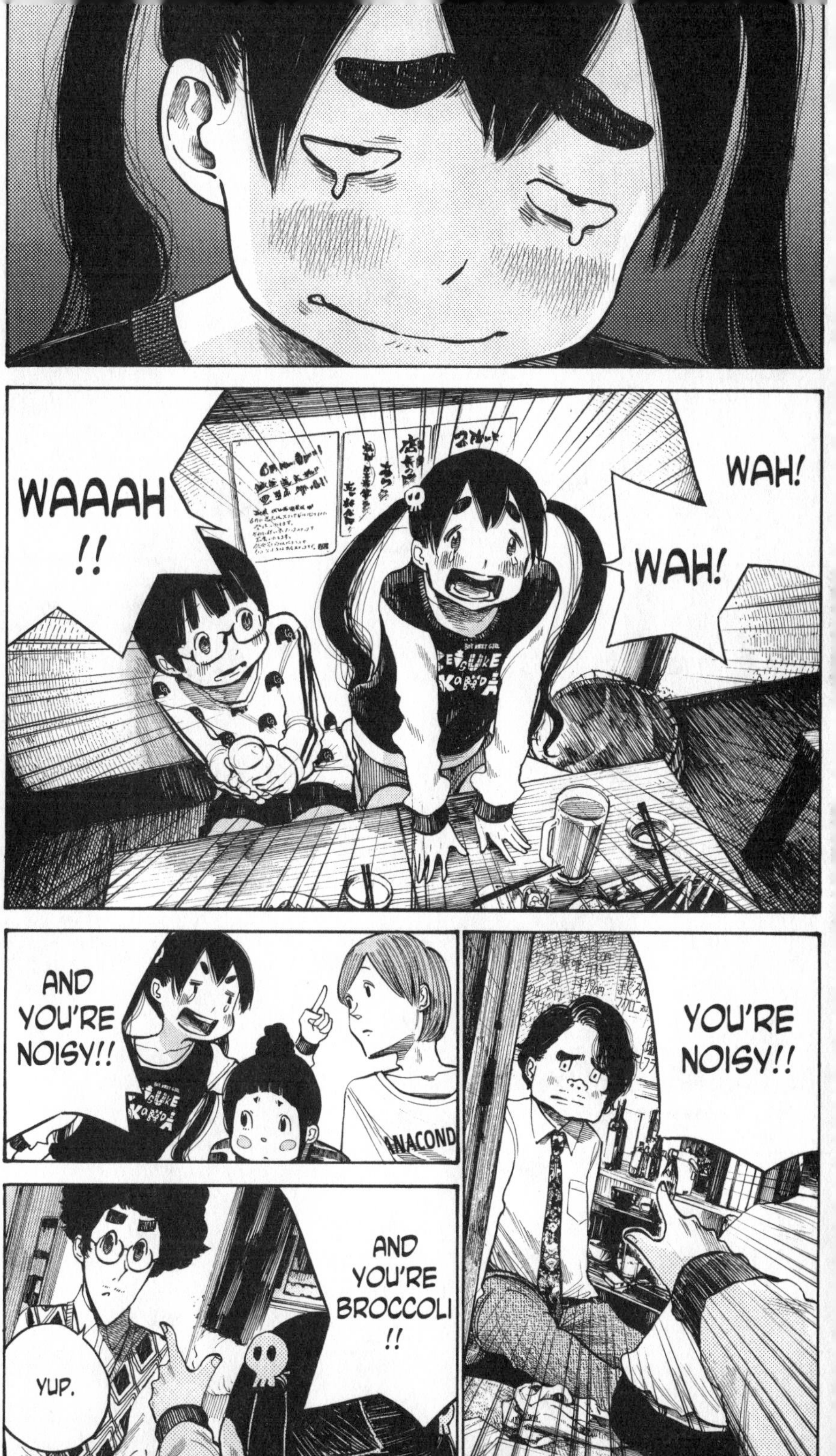
WAH!
WAH!
WAAAH !!
YOU'RE NOISY!!
AND YOU'RE NOISY!!
AND YOU'RE BROCCOLI !!
YUP.

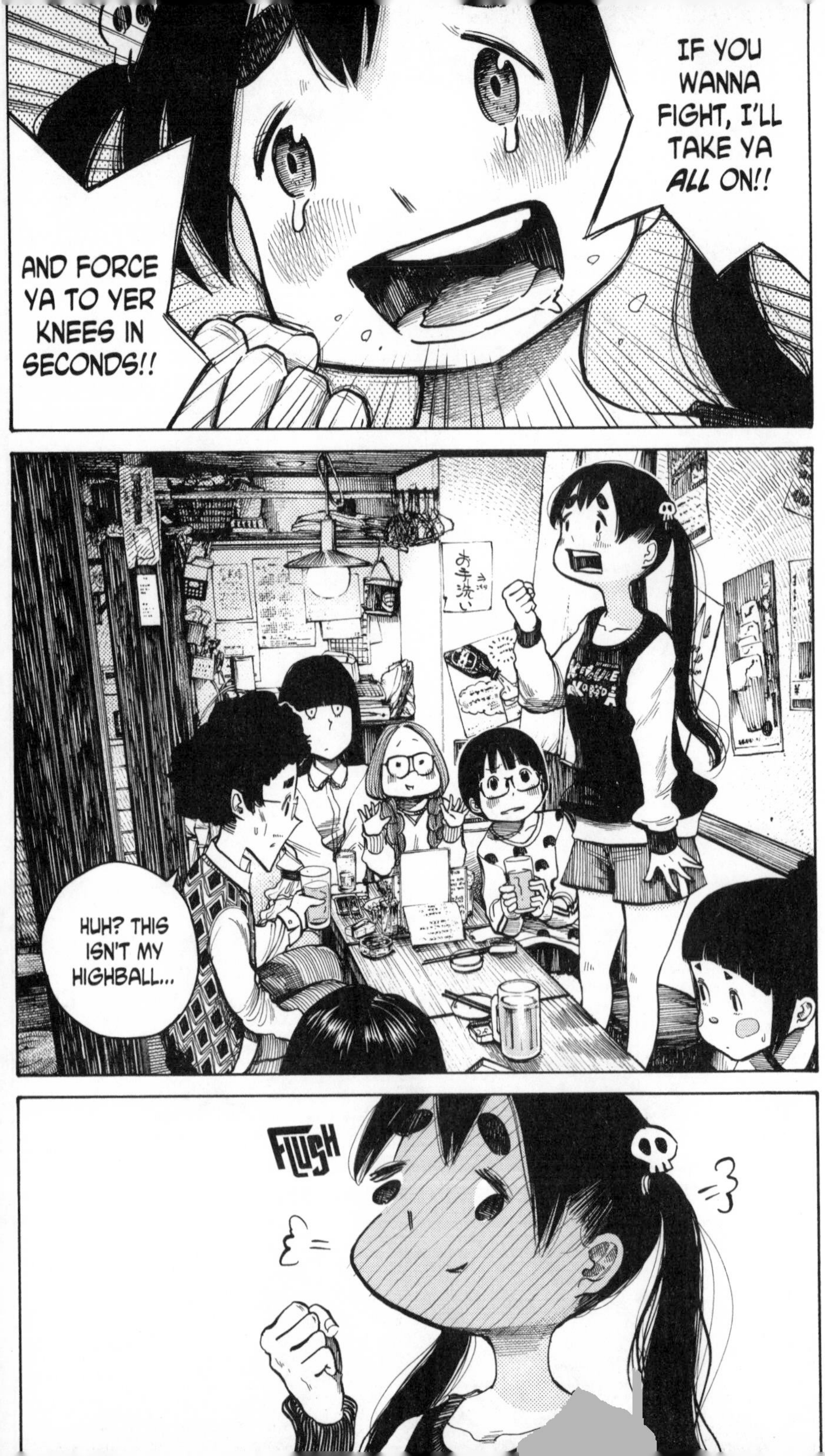
IF YOU WANNA FIGHT, I'LL TAKE YA ALL ON!!
AND FORCE YA TO YER KNEES IN SECONDS!!
お手洗い
HUH? THIS ISN'T MY HIGHBALL...
FLUSH

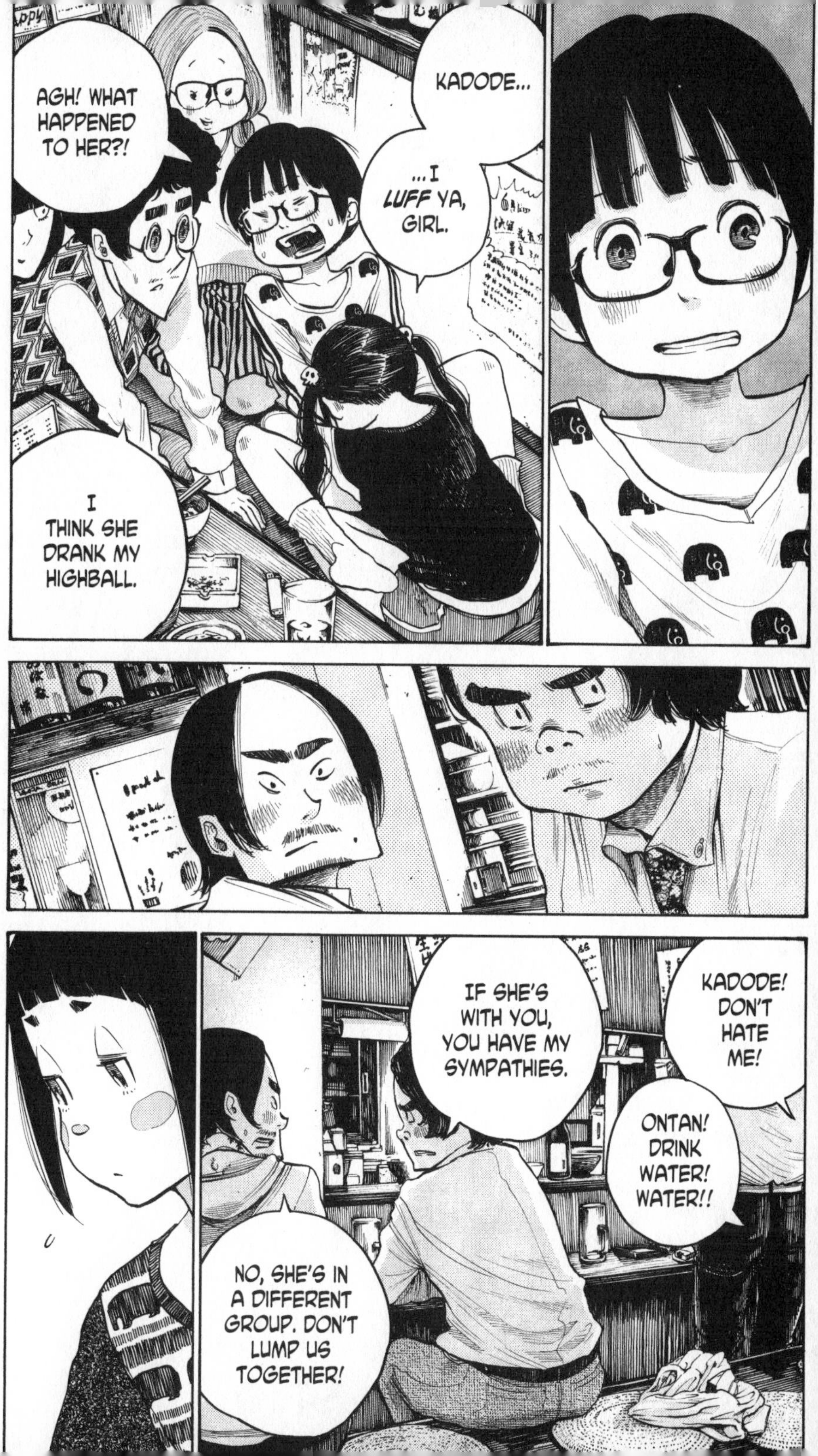
KADODE...
...I LUFF YA, GIRL.
AGH! WHAT HAPPENED TO HER?!
I THINK SHE DRANK MY HIGHBALL.
KADODE! DON'T HATE ME!
IF SHE'S WITH YOU, YOU HAVE MY SYMPATHIES.
ONTAN! DRINK WATER! WATER!!
NO, SHE'S IN A DIFFERENT GROUP. DON'T LUMP US TOGETHER!

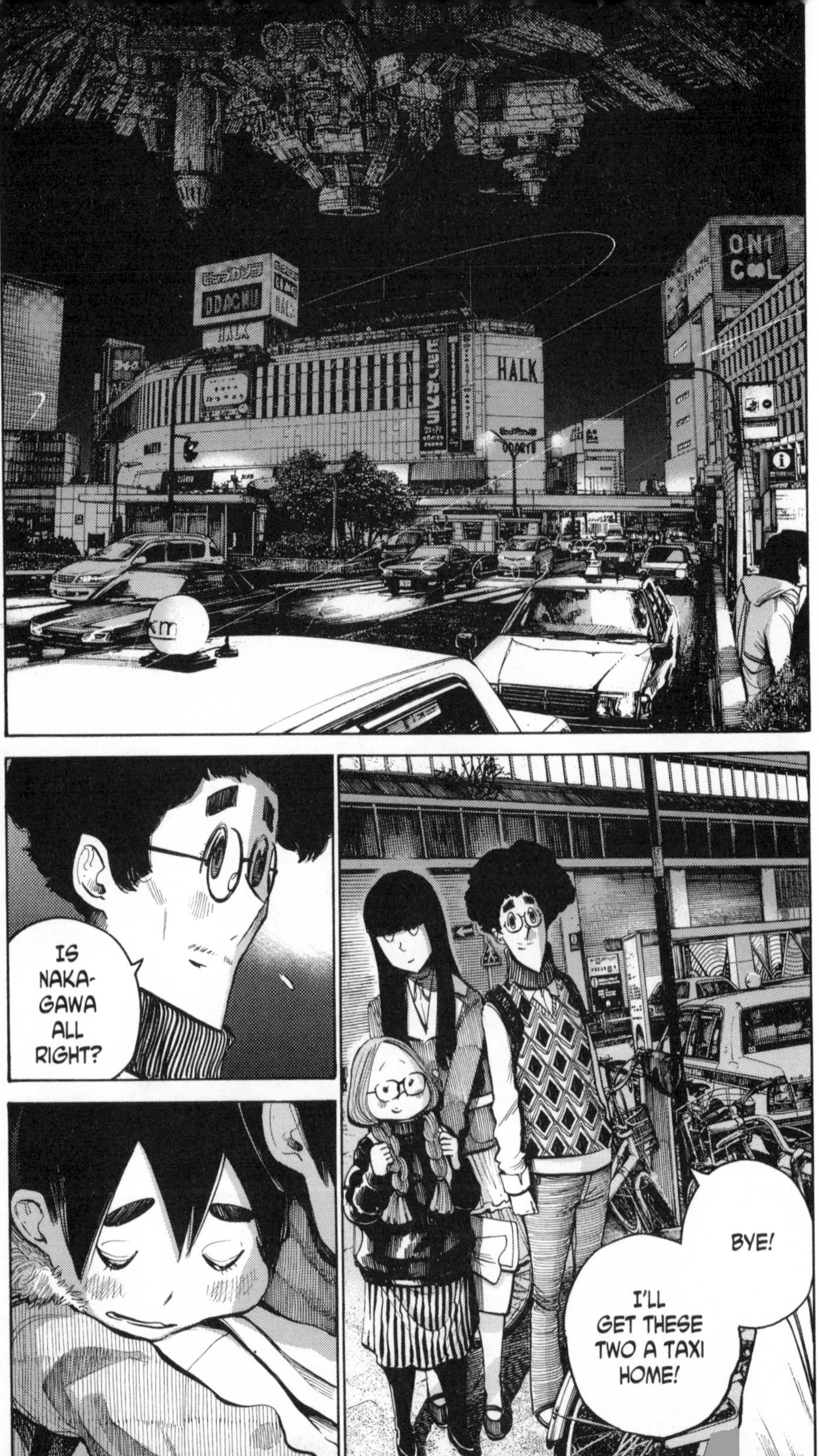
HALK
BYE!
I'LL GET THESE TWO A TAXI HOME!
IS NAKA-GAWA ALL RIGHT?

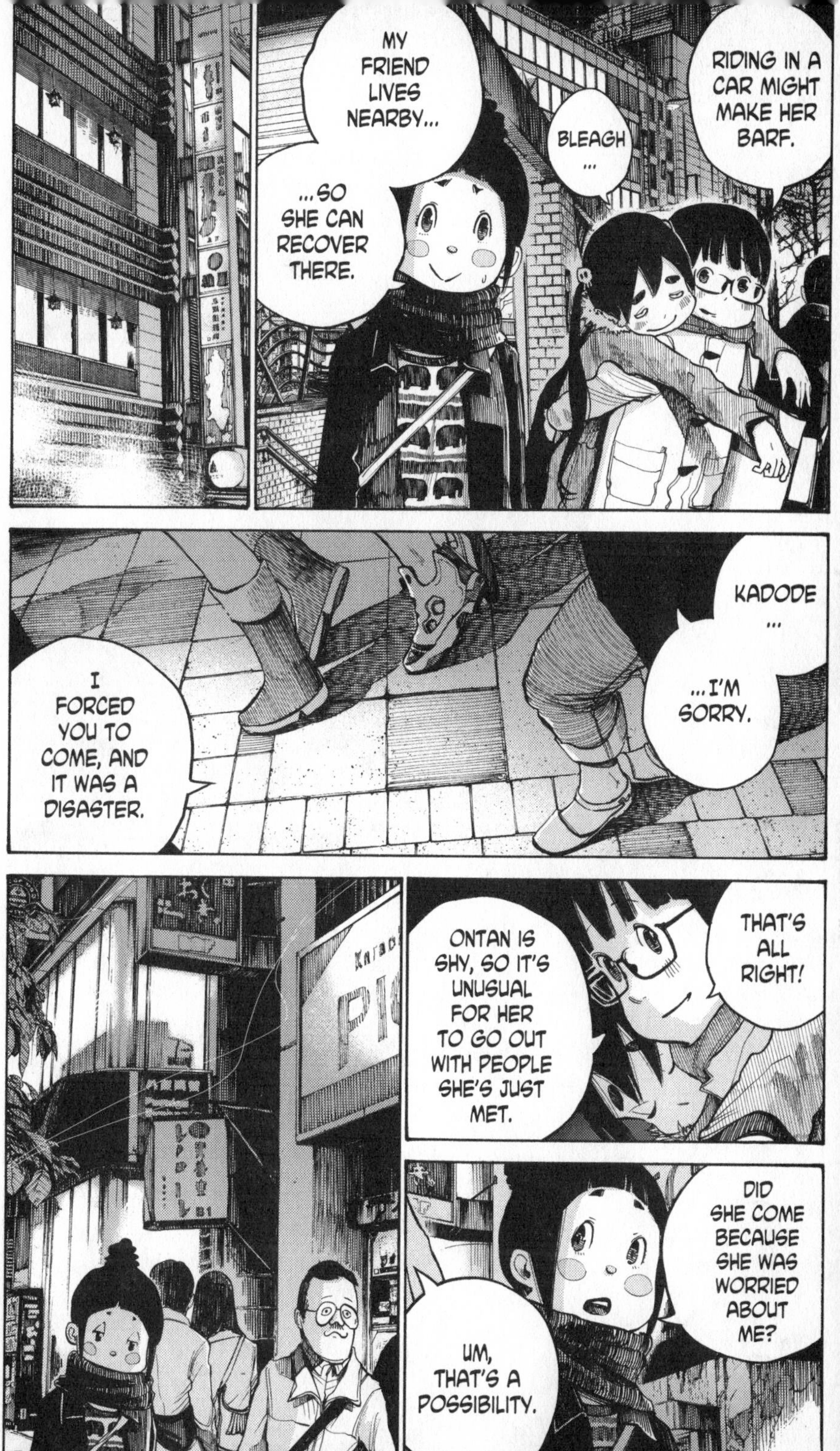
RIDING IN A CAR MIGHT MAKE HER BARF.
BLEAGH ...
MY FRIEND LIVES NEARBY...
...SO SHE CAN RECOVER THERE.
KADODE ...
...I'M SORRY.
I FORCED YOU TO COME, AND IT WAS A DISASTER.
THAT'S ALL RIGHT!
ONTAN IS SHY, SO IT'S UNUSUAL FOR HER TO GO OUT WITH PEOPLE SHE'S JUST MET.
DID SHE COME BECAUSE SHE WAS WORRIED ABOUT ME?
UM, THAT'S A POSSIBILITY.

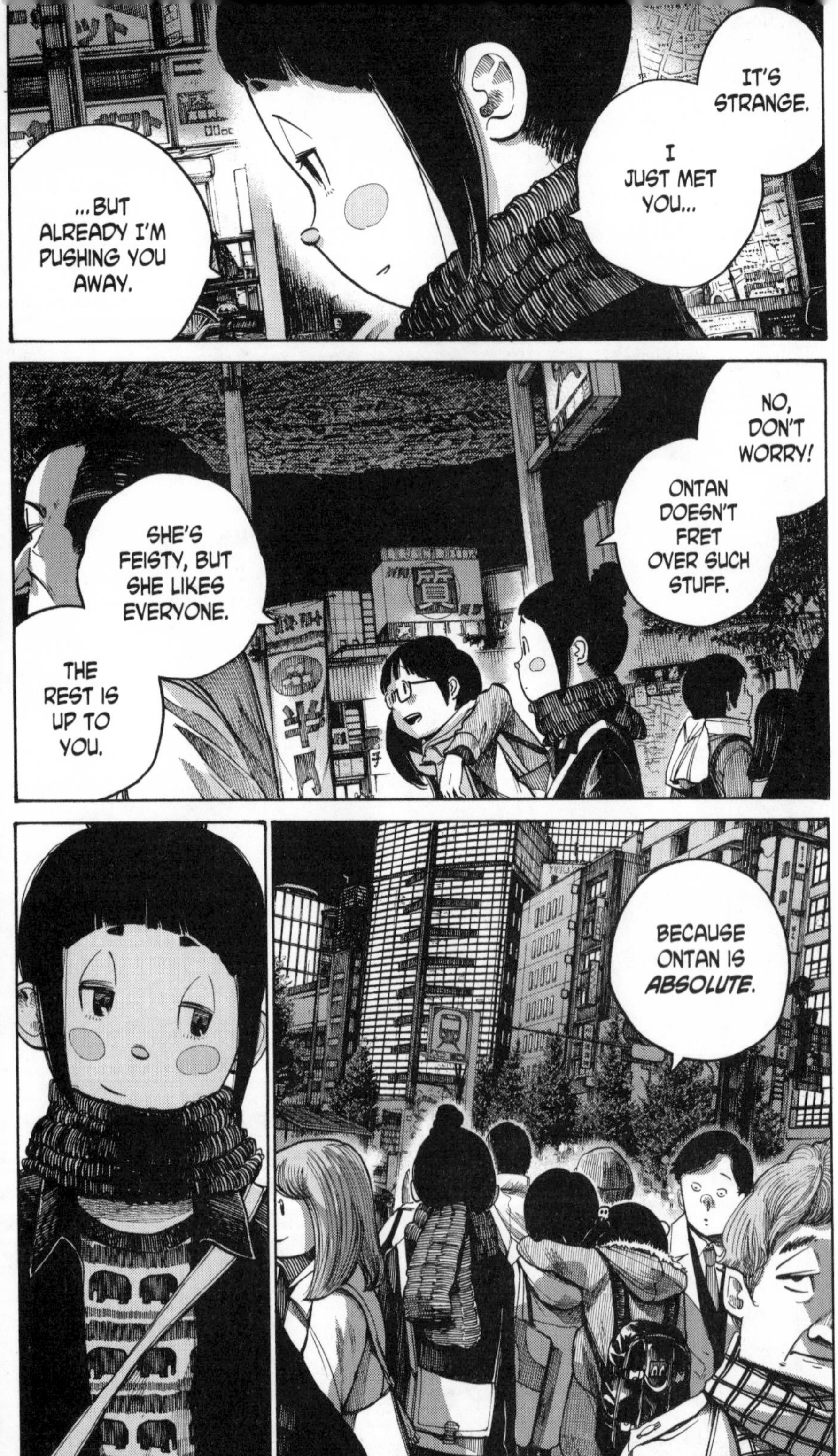
IT'S STRANGE.
I JUST MET YOU...
...BUT ALREADY I'M PUSHING YOU AWAY.
NO, DON'T WORRY!
ONTAN DOESN'T FRET OVER SUCH STUFF.
SHE'S FEISTY, BUT SHE LIKES EVERYONE.
THE REST IS UP TO YOU.
BECAUSE ONTAN IS *ABSOLUTE*.

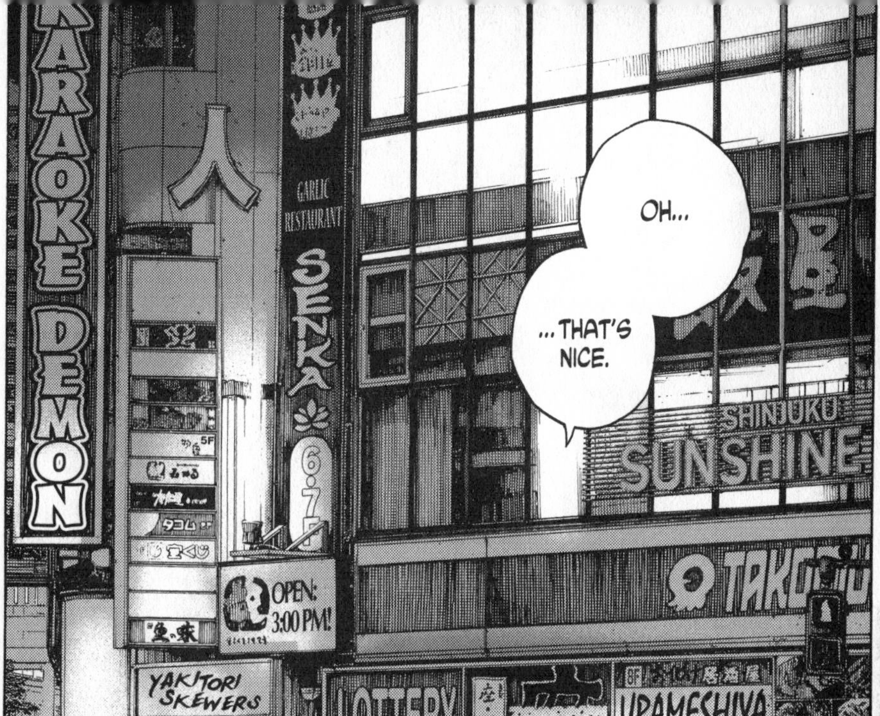
OH...
...THAT'S NICE.
SHINJUKU SUNSHINE
GARLIC RESTAURANT
SENKA
KARAOKE DEMON
OPEN: 3:00 PM!
URAMESHIYA
LOTTERY
YAKITORI SKEWERS

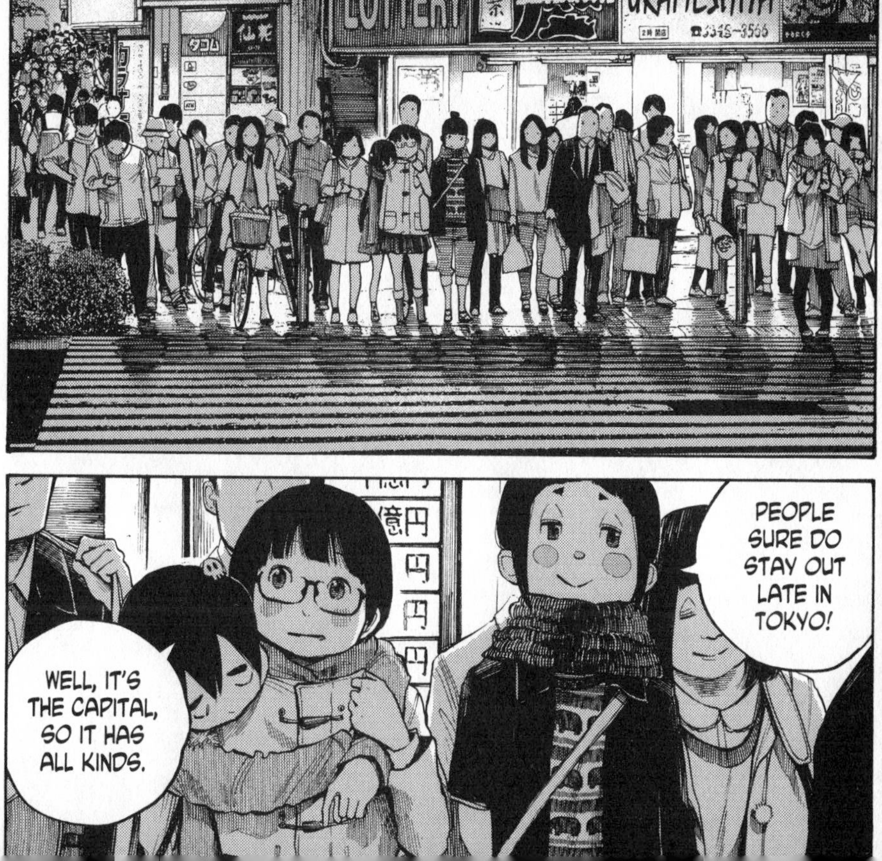
PEOPLE SURE DO STAY OUT LATE IN TOKYO!
WELL, IT'S THE CAPITAL, SO IT HAS ALL KINDS.

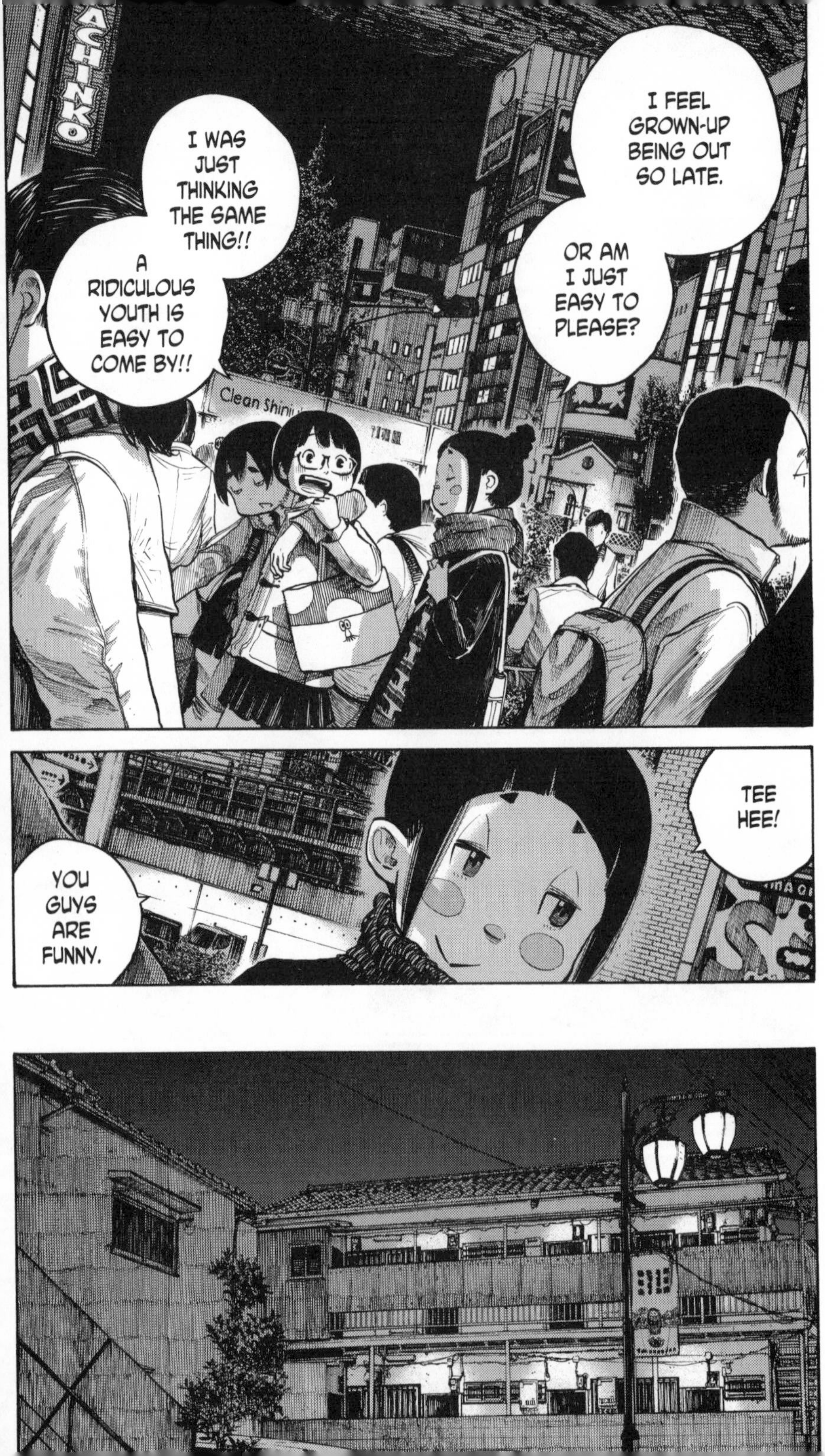
I FEEL GROWN-UP BEING OUT SO LATE.
OR AM I JUST EASY TO PLEASE?
I WAS JUST THINKING THE SAME THING!!
A RIDICULOUS YOUTH IS EASY TO COME BY!!
TEE HEE!
YOU GUYS ARE FUNNY.

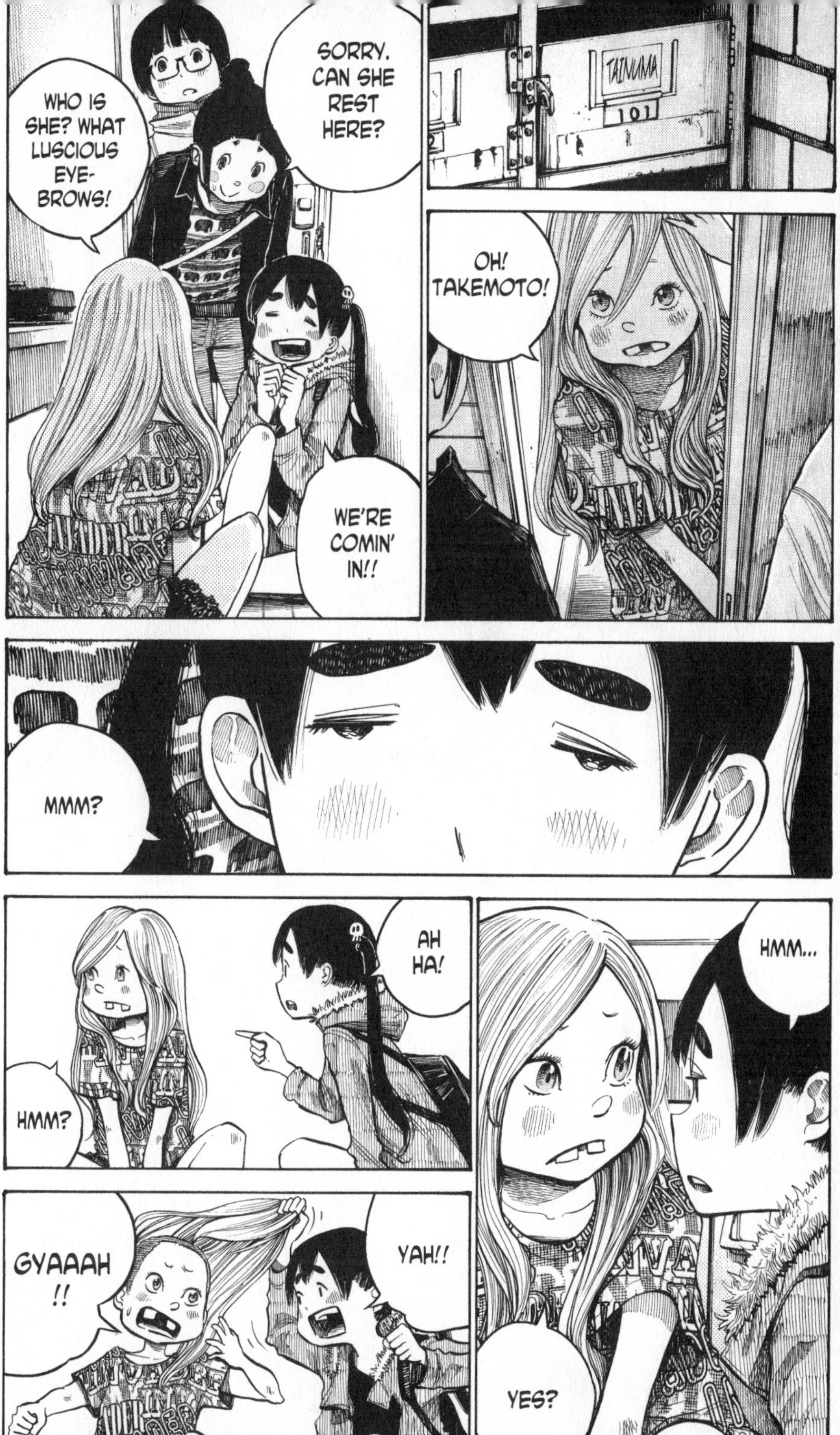
TAINUMA
101
OH! TAKEMOTO!
SORRY. CAN SHE REST HERE?
WHO IS SHE? WHAT LUSCIOUS EYE-BROWS!
WE'RE COMIN' IN!!
MMM?
HMM...
YES?
AH HA!
HMM?
YAH!!
GYAAAH!!

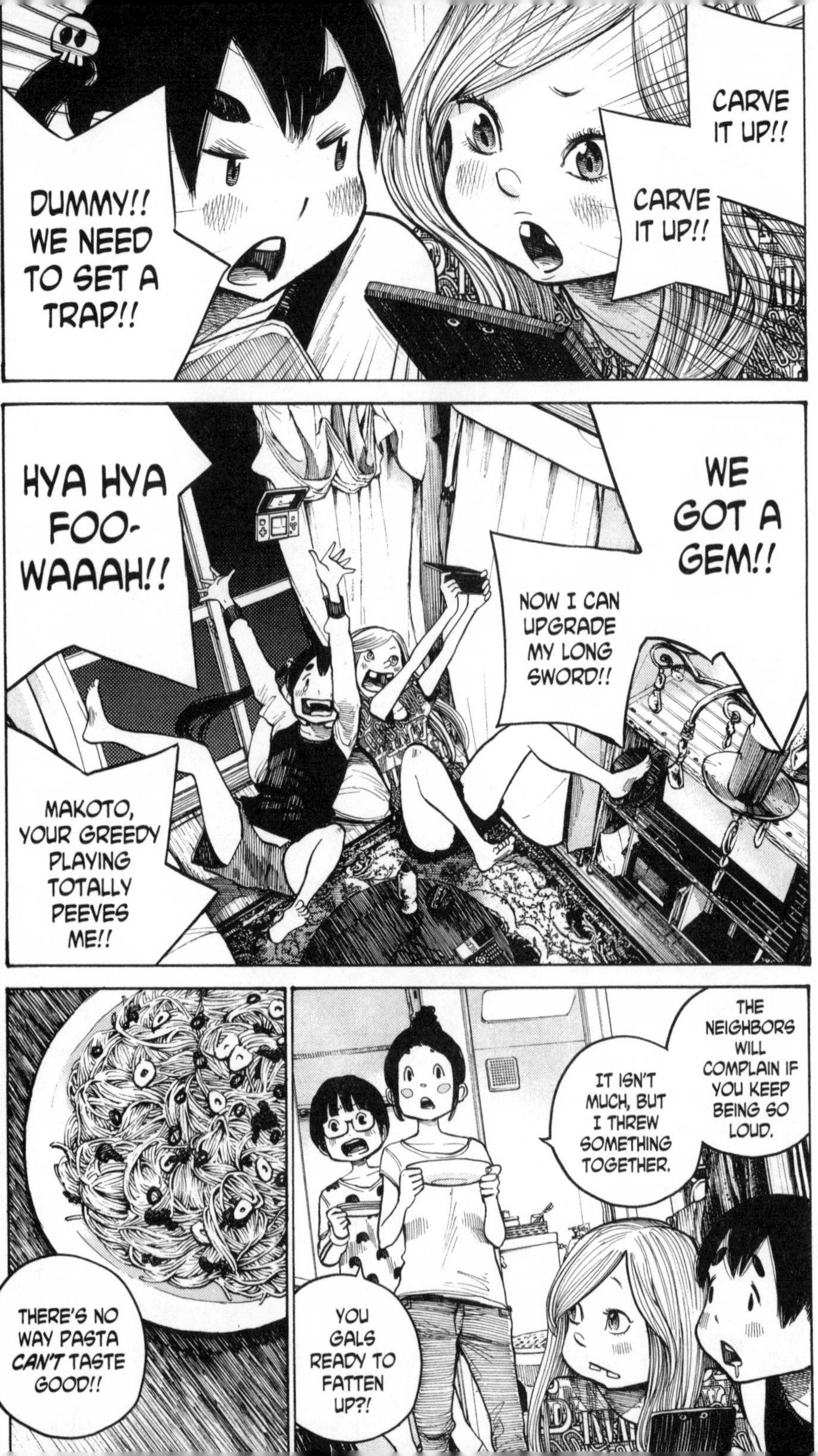
CARVE IT UP!!
CARVE IT UP!!
DUMMY!! WE NEED TO SET A TRAP!!
WE GOT A GEM!!
NOW I CAN UPGRADE MY LONG SWORD!!
HYA HYA FOO-WAAAH!!
MAKOTO, YOUR GREEDY PLAYING TOTALLY PEEVES ME!!
THE NEIGHBORS WILL COMPLAIN IF YOU KEEP BEING SO LOUD.
IT ISN'T MUCH, BUT I THREW SOMETHING TOGETHER.
YOU GALS READY TO FATTEN UP?!
THERE'S NO WAY PASTA *CAN'T* TASTE GOOD!!

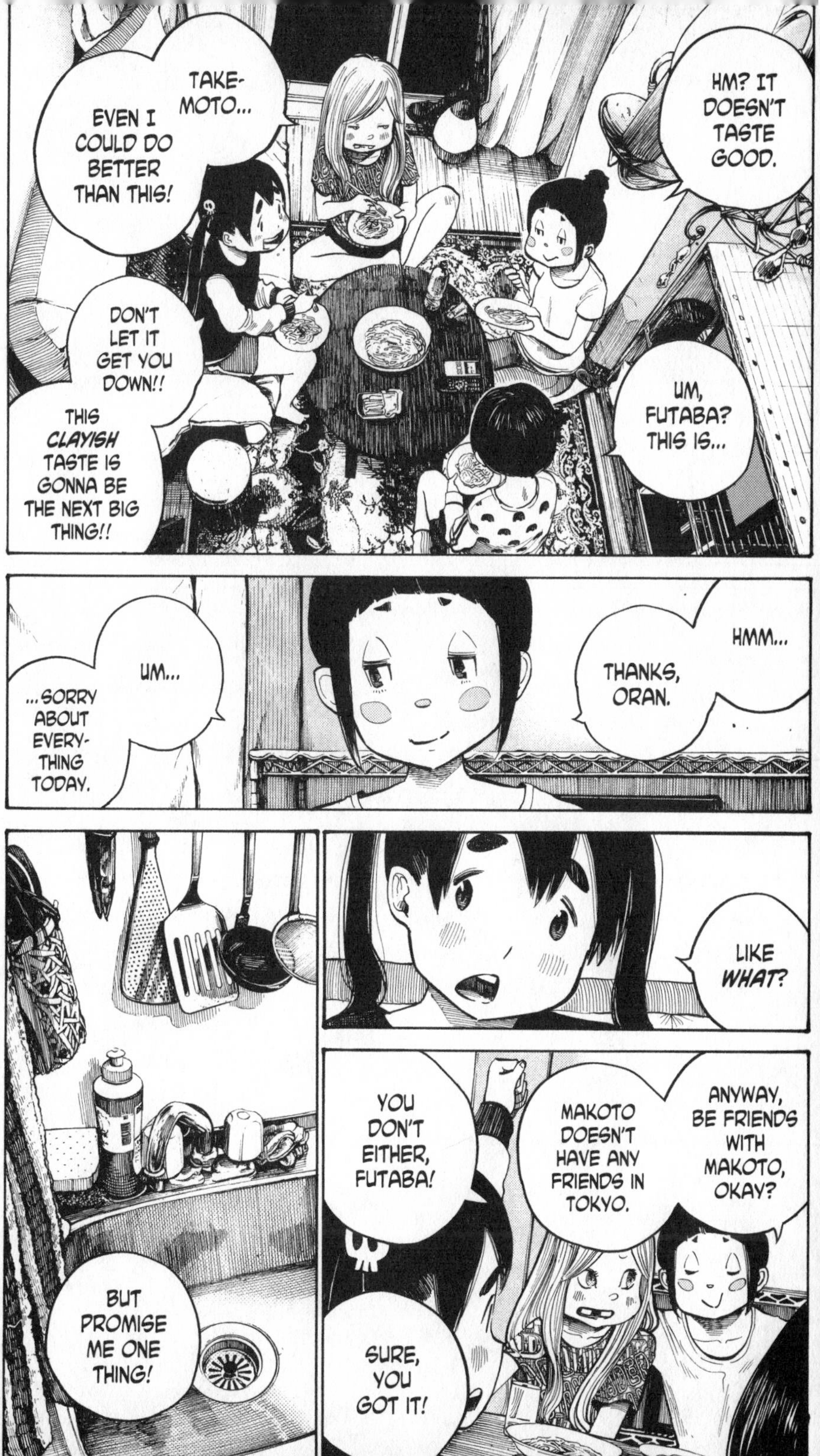
HM? IT DOESN'T TASTE GOOD.
UM, FUTABA? THIS IS...
TAKE-MOTO...
EVEN I COULD DO BETTER THAN THIS!
DON'T LET IT GET YOU DOWN!!
THIS *CLAYISH* TASTE IS GONNA BE THE NEXT BIG THING!!
HMM...
THANKS, ORAN.
UM...
...SORRY ABOUT EVERY-THING TODAY.
LIKE *WHAT?*
ANYWAY, BE FRIENDS WITH MAKOTO, OKAY?
MAKOTO DOESN'T HAVE ANY FRIENDS IN TOKYO.
YOU DON'T EITHER, FUTABA!
SURE, YOU GOT IT!
BUT PROMISE ME ONE THING!

HUH?

DON'T SUDDENLY DISAPPEAR.

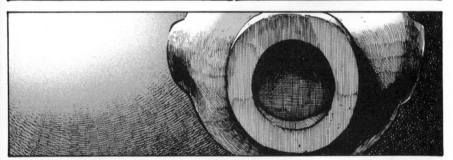

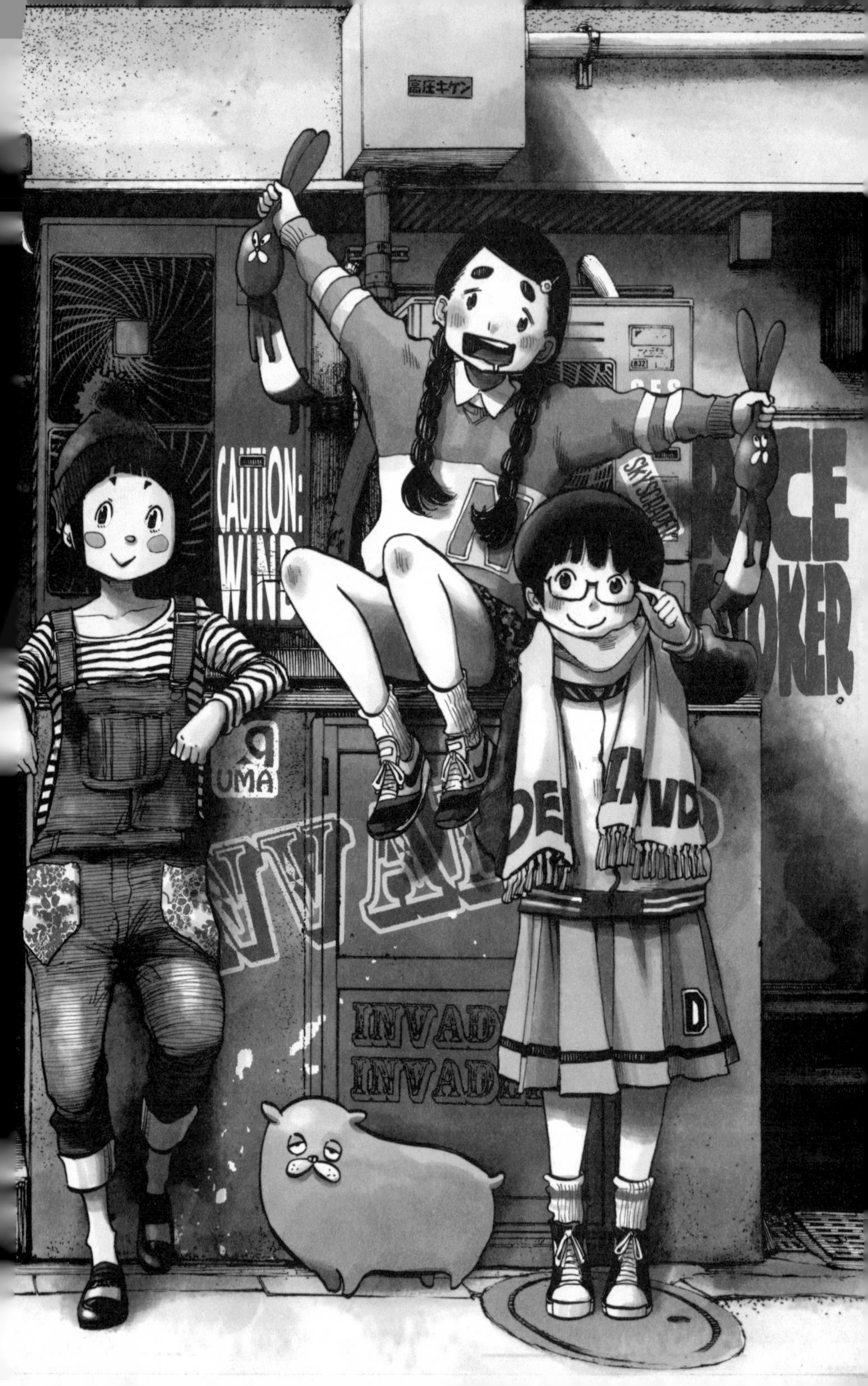

高圧キケン
CAUTION:
SKYSCRAPER
UMA

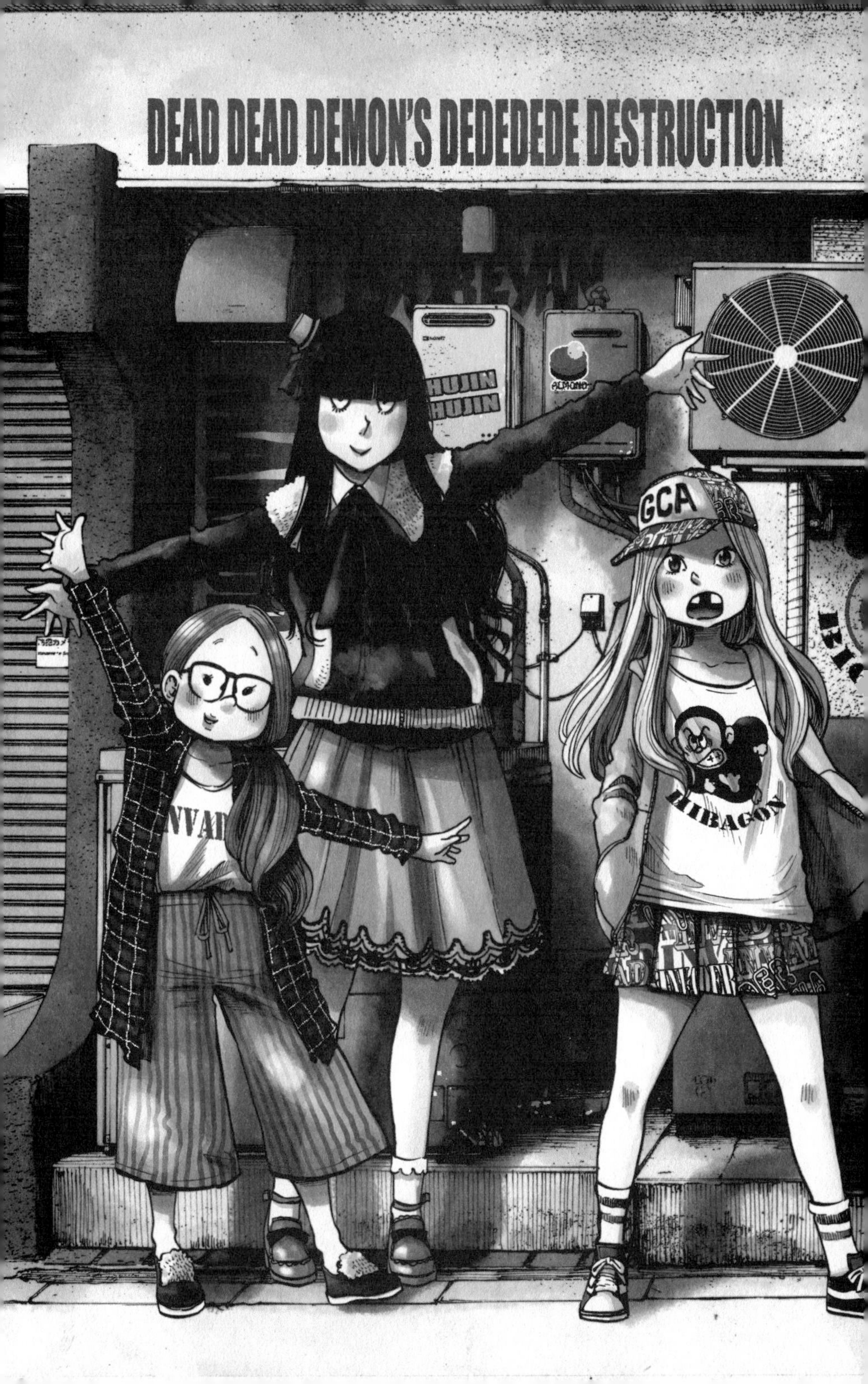
DEAD DEAD DEMON'S DEDEDEDE DESTRUCTION
GCA
HIBAGON

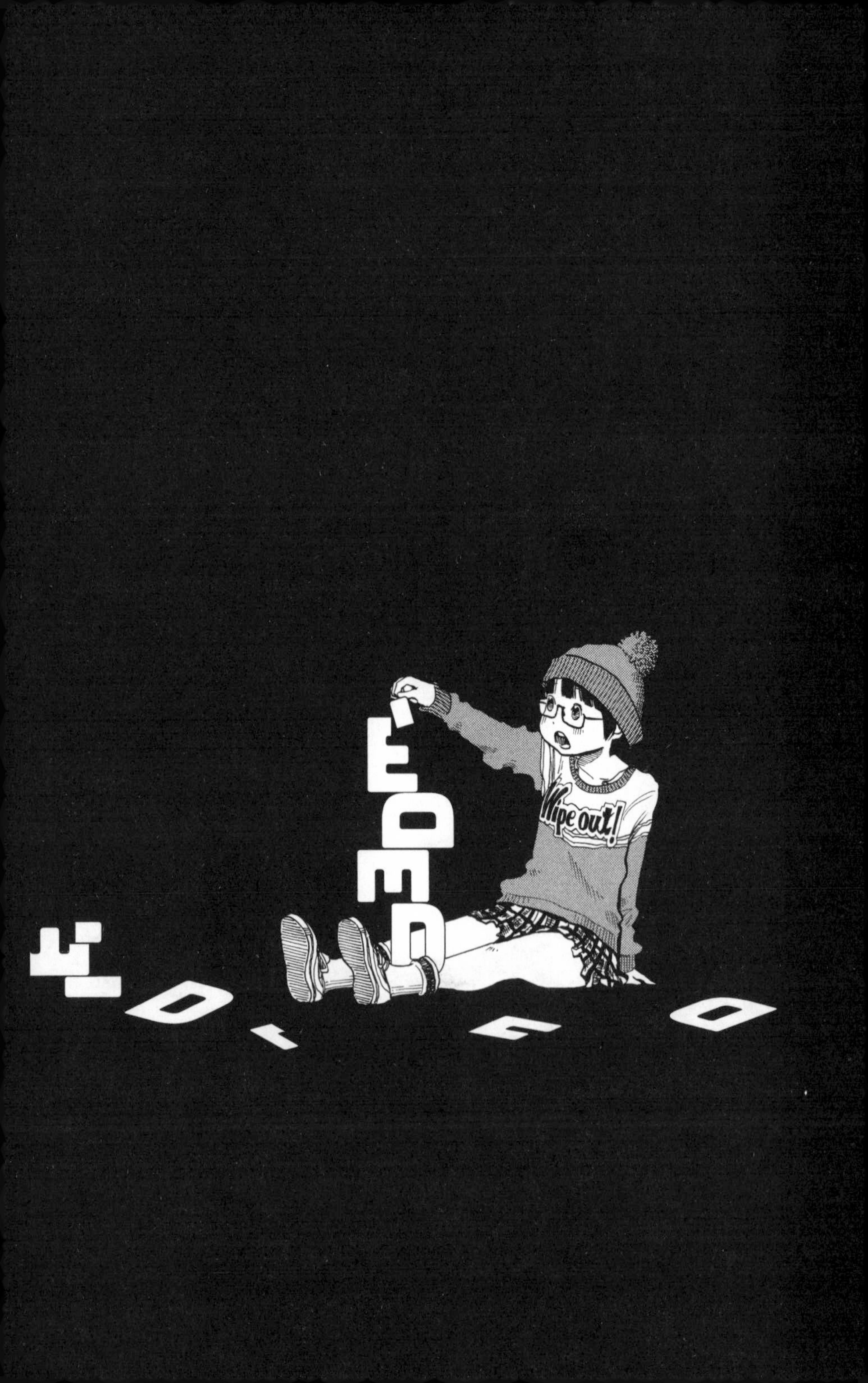
Wipe out!

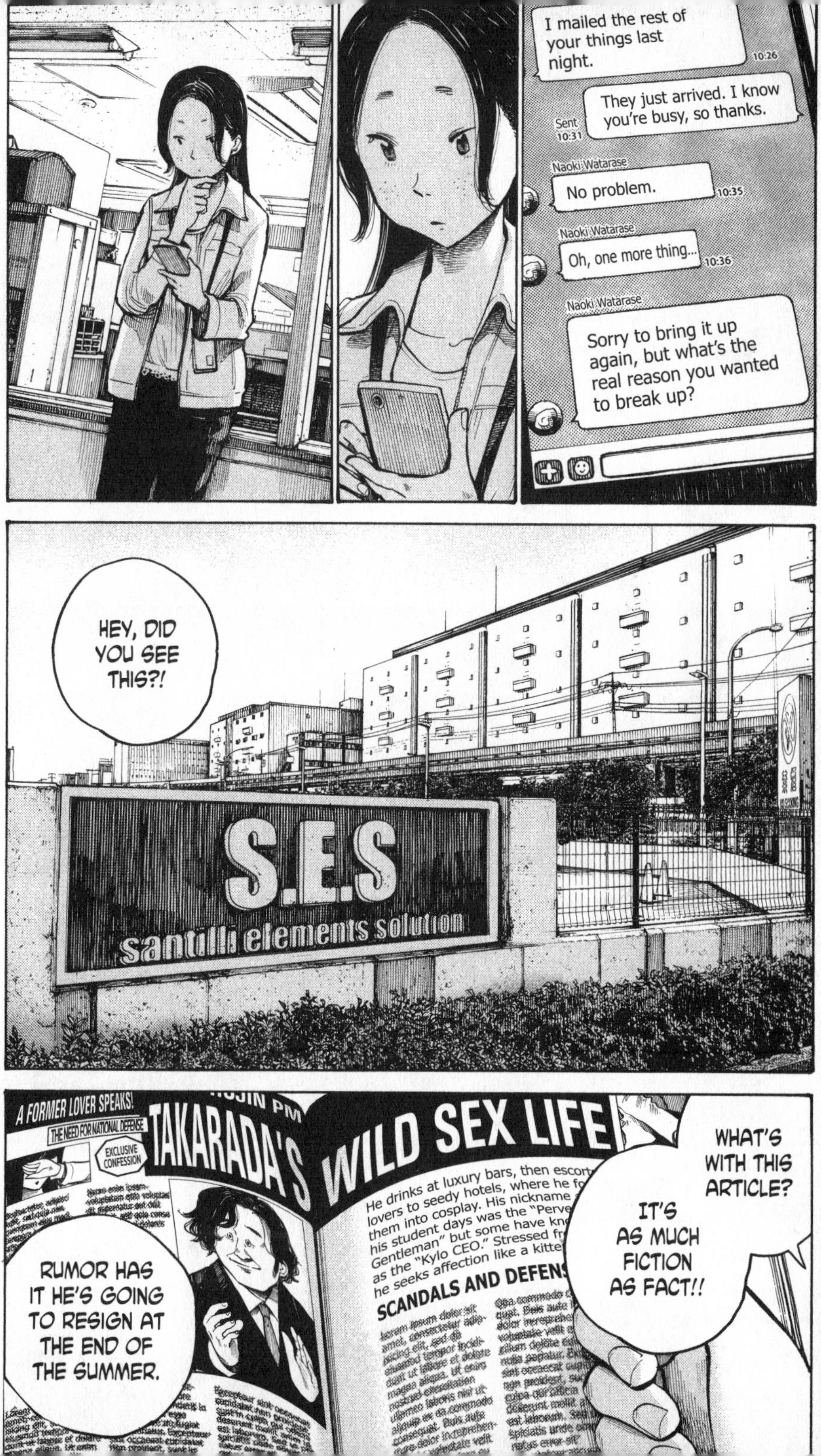
I mailed the rest of your things last night.
10:26
They just arrived. I know you're busy, so thanks.
Sent 10:31
Naoki Watarase
No problem.
10:35
Naoki Watarase
Oh, one more thing...
10:36
Naoki Watarase
Sorry to bring it up again, but what's the real reason you wanted to break up?
HEY, DID YOU SEE THIS?!
S.E.S
santilli elements solution
WHAT'S WITH THIS ARTICLE?
IT'S AS MUCH FICTION AS FACT!!
A FORMER LOVER SPEAKS!
THE NEED FOR NATIONAL DEFENSE
EXCLUSIVE CONFESSION
TAKARADA'S WILD SEX LIFE
RUMOR HAS IT HE'S GOING TO RESIGN AT THE END OF THE SUMMER.

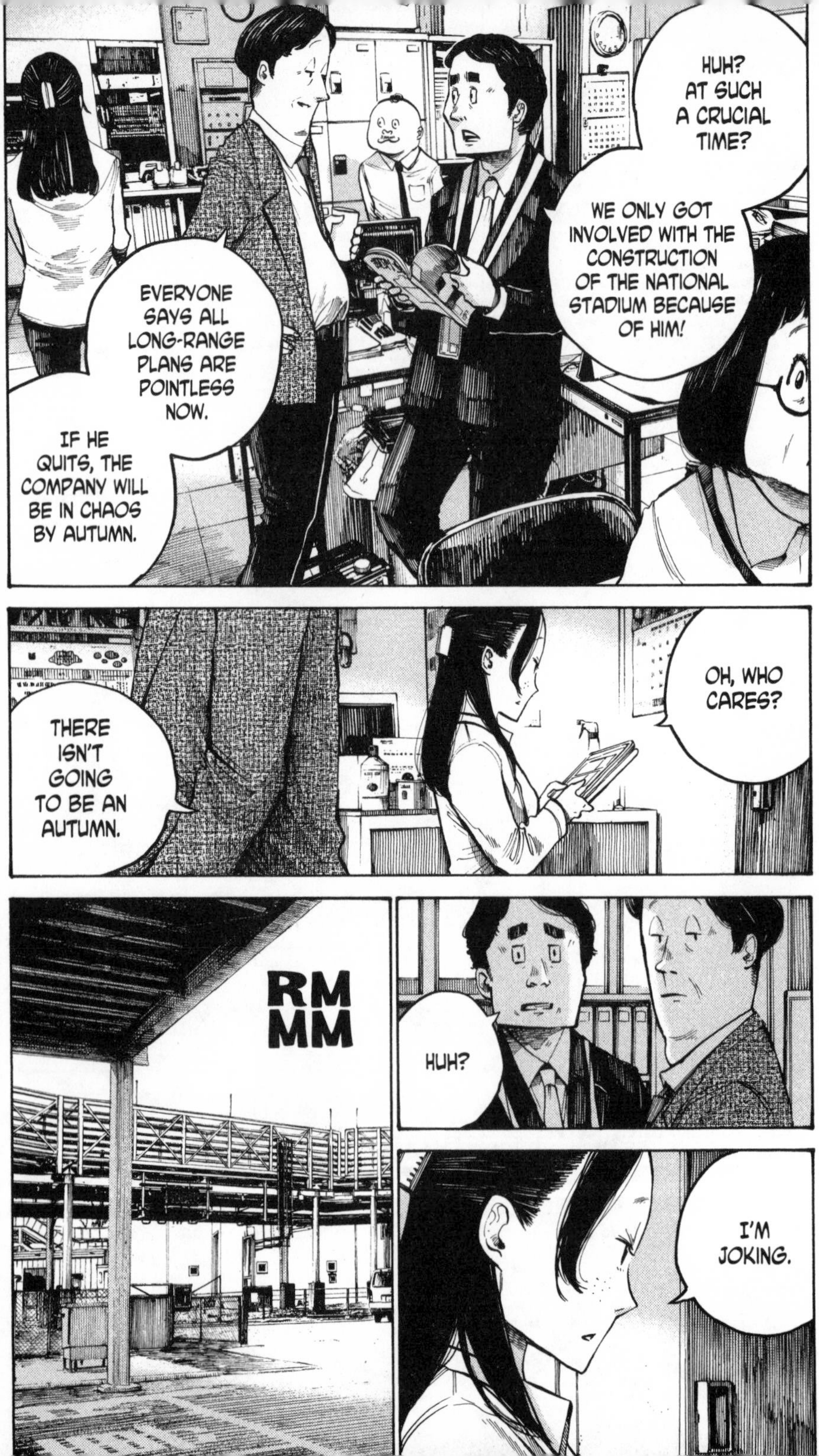
HUH? AT SUCH A CRUCIAL TIME?
WE ONLY GOT INVOLVED WITH THE CONSTRUCTION OF THE NATIONAL STADIUM BECAUSE OF HIM!
EVERYONE SAYS ALL LONG-RANGE PLANS ARE POINTLESS NOW.
IF HE QUITS, THE COMPANY WILL BE IN CHAOS BY AUTUMN.
OH, WHO CARES?
THERE ISN'T GOING TO BE AN AUTUMN.
HUH?
I'M JOKING.
RMMM

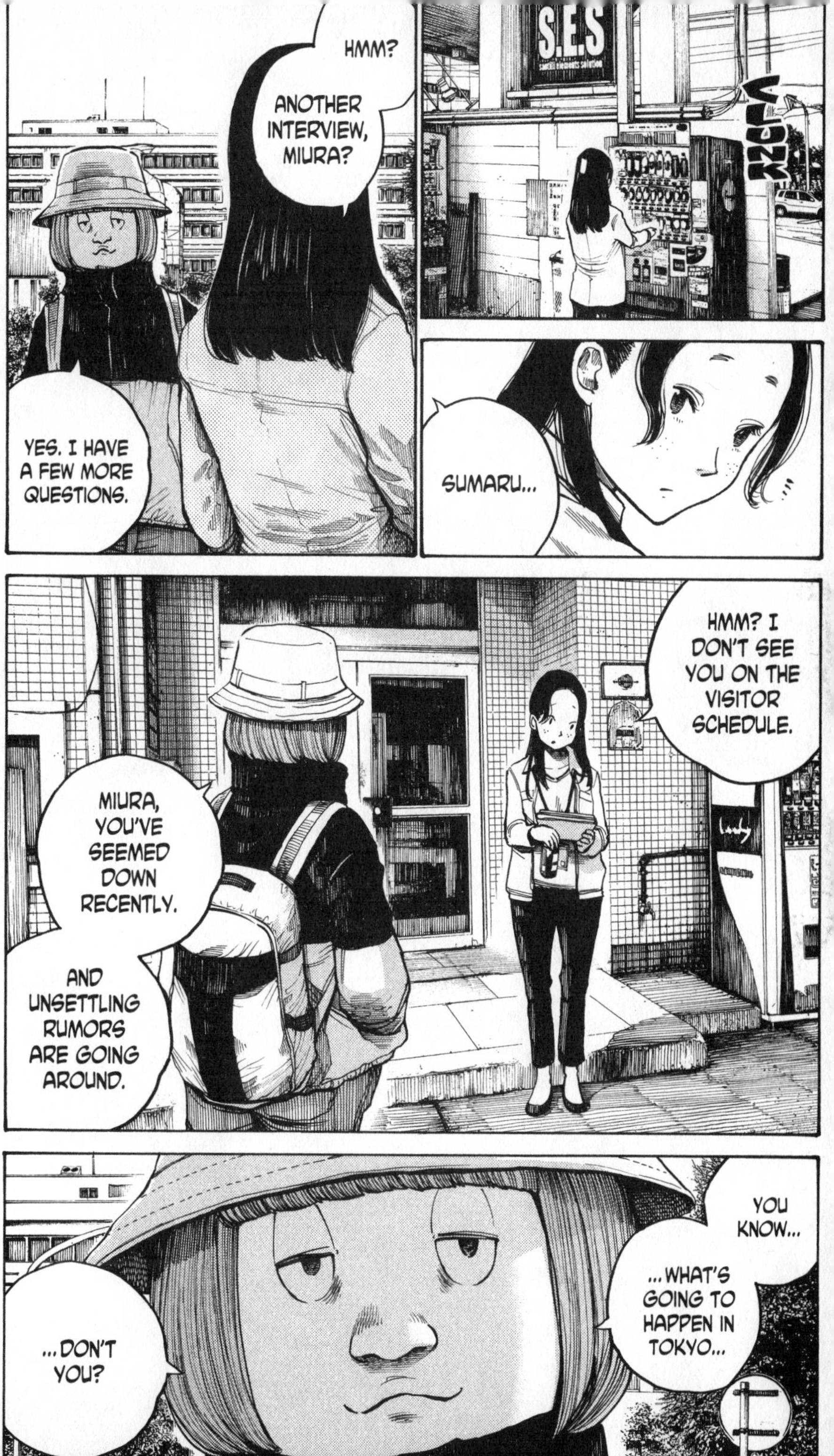
S.E.S
CLUNK
SUMARU...
HMM?
ANOTHER INTERVIEW, MIURA?
YES. I HAVE A FEW MORE QUESTIONS.
HMM? I DON'T SEE YOU ON THE VISITOR SCHEDULE.
MIURA, YOU'VE SEEMED DOWN RECENTLY.
AND UNSETTLING RUMORS ARE GOING AROUND.
YOU KNOW...
...WHAT'S GOING TO HAPPEN IN TOKYO...
...DON'T YOU?

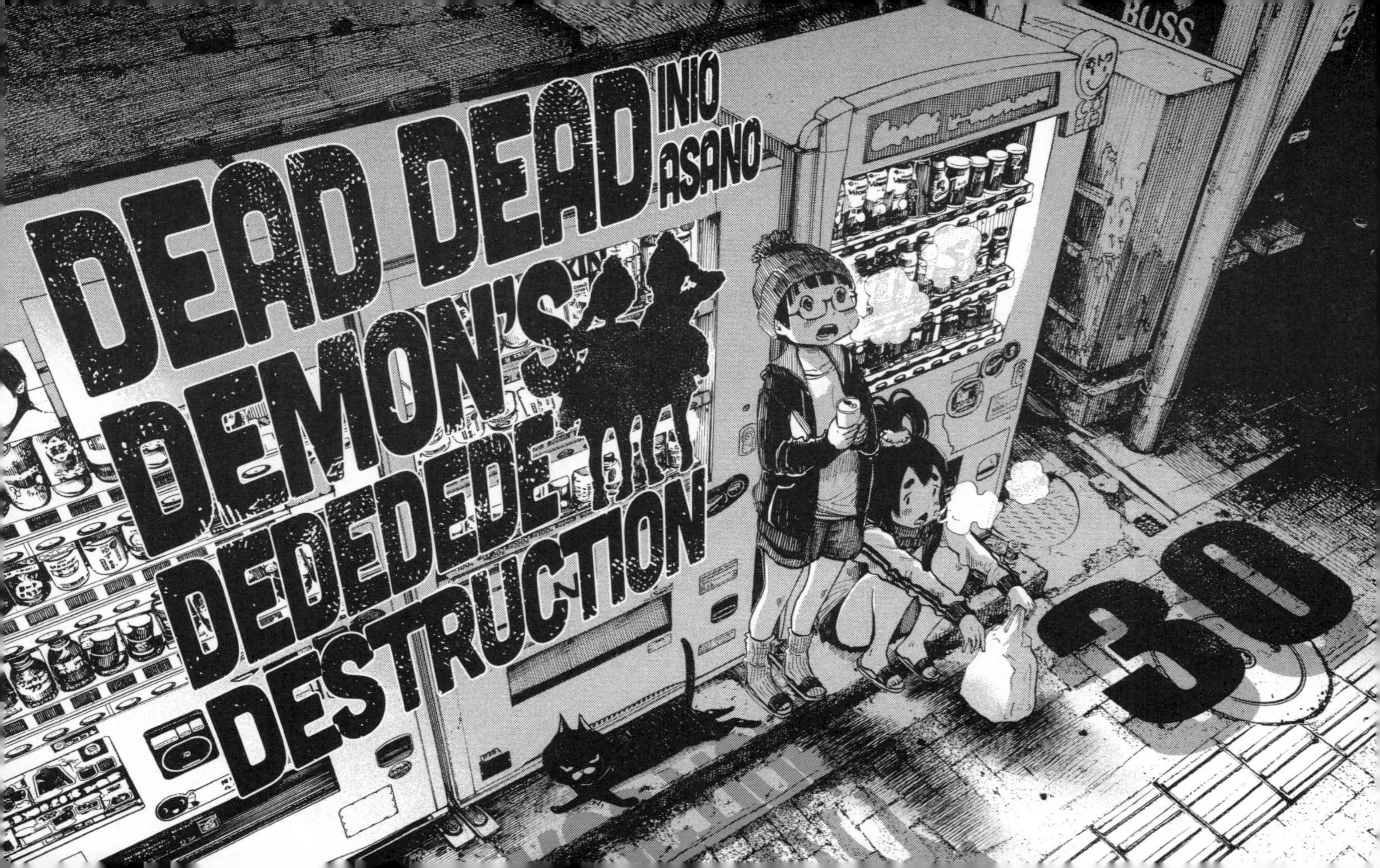
DEAD DEAD DEMON'S DEDEDEDE DESTRUCTION
INIÓ ASANO
30
BOSS

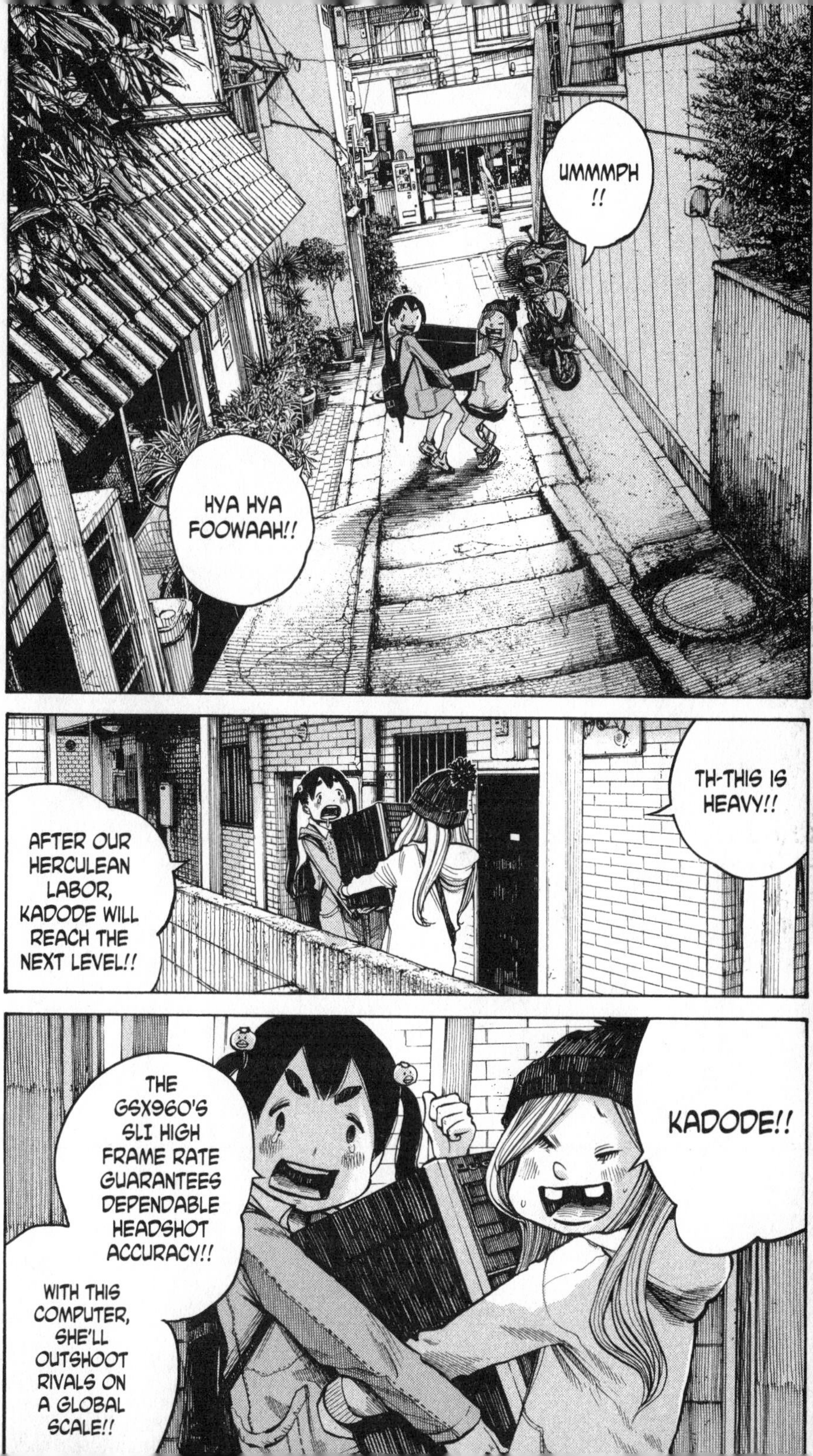
UMMMPH !!
HYA HYA FOOWAAH!!
TH-THIS IS HEAVY!!
AFTER OUR HERCULEAN LABOR, KADODE WILL REACH THE NEXT LEVEL!!
KADODE!!
THE GSX960'S SLI HIGH FRAME RATE GUARANTEES DEPENDABLE HEADSHOT ACCURACY!!
WITH THIS COMPUTER, SHE'LL OUTSHOOT RIVALS ON A GLOBAL SCALE!!

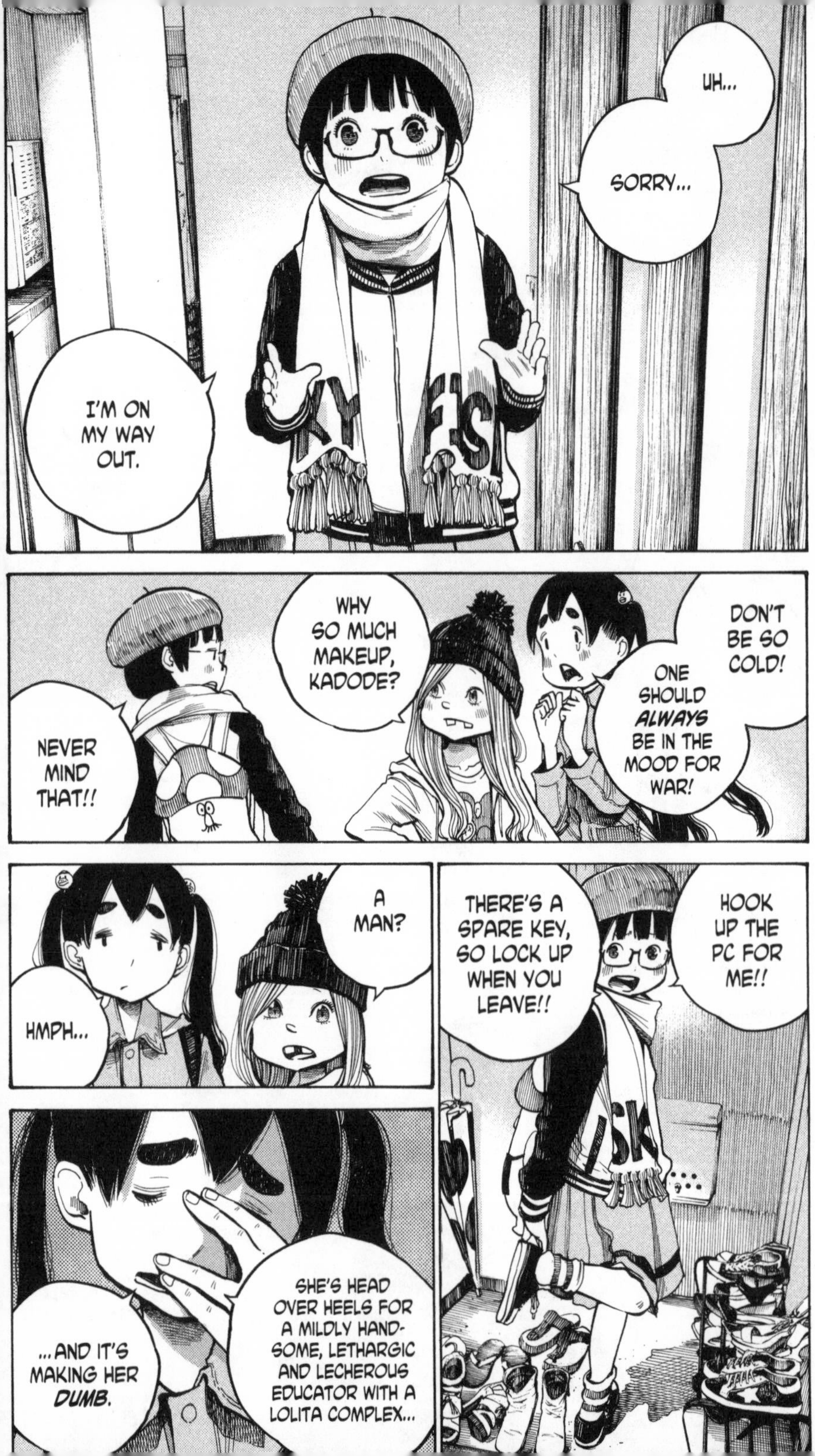
UH...
SORRY...
I'M ON MY WAY OUT.
DON'T BE SO COLD!
ONE SHOULD *ALWAYS* BE IN THE MOOD FOR WAR!
WHY SO MUCH MAKEUP, KADODE?
NEVER MIND THAT!!
HOOK UP THE PC FOR ME!!
THERE'S A SPARE KEY, SO LOCK UP WHEN YOU LEAVE!!
A MAN?
HMPH...
SHE'S HEAD OVER HEELS FOR A MILDLY HAND-SOME, LETHARGIC AND LECHEROUS EDUCATOR WITH A LOLITA COMPLEX...
...AND IT'S MAKING HER *DUMB*.

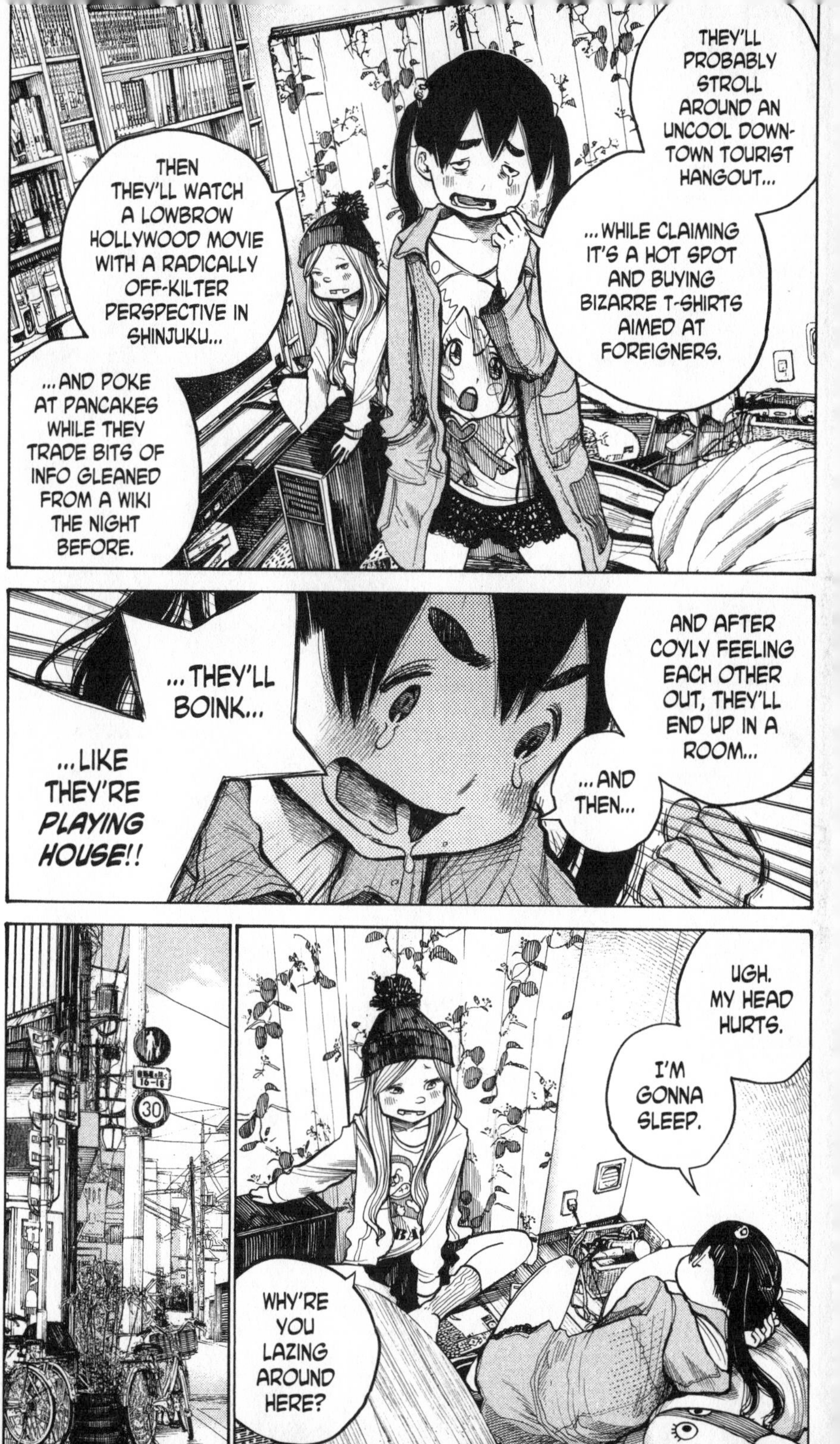
THEY'LL PROBABLY STROLL AROUND AN UNCOOL DOWNTOWN TOURIST HANGOUT...
...WHILE CLAIMING IT'S A HOT SPOT AND BUYING BIZARRE T-SHIRTS AIMED AT FOREIGNERS.
THEN THEY'LL WATCH A LOWBROW HOLLYWOOD MOVIE WITH A RADICALLY OFF-KILTER PERSPECTIVE IN SHINJUKU...
...AND POKE AT PANCAKES WHILE THEY TRADE BITS OF INFO GLEANED FROM A WIKI THE NIGHT BEFORE.
AND AFTER COYLY FEELING EACH OTHER OUT, THEY'LL END UP IN A ROOM...
...AND THEN...
...THEY'LL BOINK...
...LIKE THEY'RE *PLAYING HOUSE*!!
UGH. MY HEAD HURTS.
I'M GONNA SLEEP.
WHY'RE YOU LAZING AROUND HERE?
30

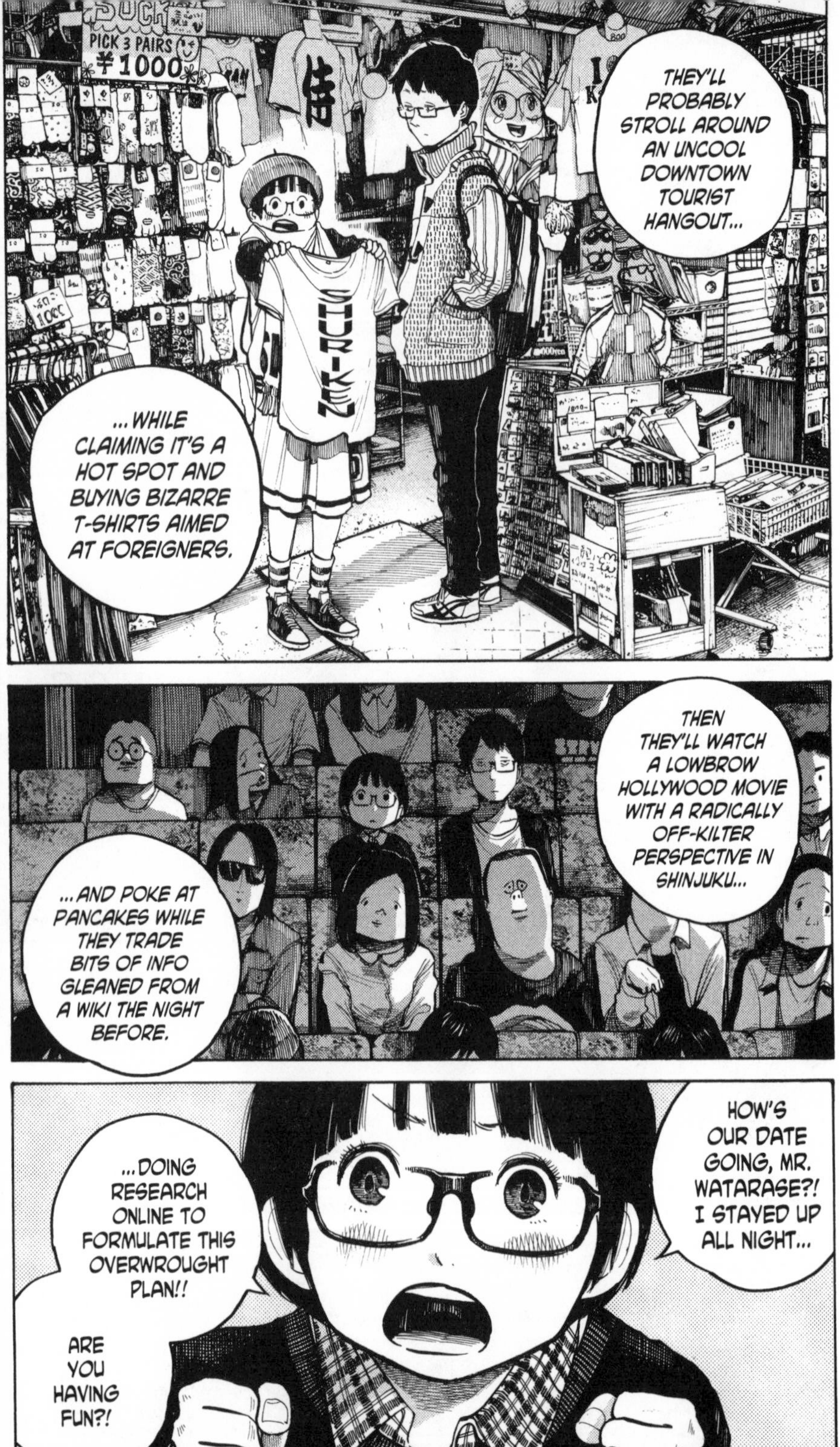
PICK 3 PAIRS
¥1000
THEY'LL PROBABLY STROLL AROUND AN UNCOOL DOWNTOWN TOURIST HANGOUT...
SHURIKEN
...WHILE CLAIMING IT'S A HOT SPOT AND BUYING BIZARRE T-SHIRTS AIMED AT FOREIGNERS.
THEN THEY'LL WATCH A LOWBROW HOLLYWOOD MOVIE WITH A RADICALLY OFF-KILTER PERSPECTIVE IN SHINJUKU...
...AND POKE AT PANCAKES WHILE THEY TRADE BITS OF INFO GLEANED FROM A WIKI THE NIGHT BEFORE.
HOW'S OUR DATE GOING, MR. WATARASE?! I STAYED UP ALL NIGHT...
...DOING RESEARCH ONLINE TO FORMULATE THIS OVERWROUGHT PLAN!!
ARE YOU HAVING FUN?!

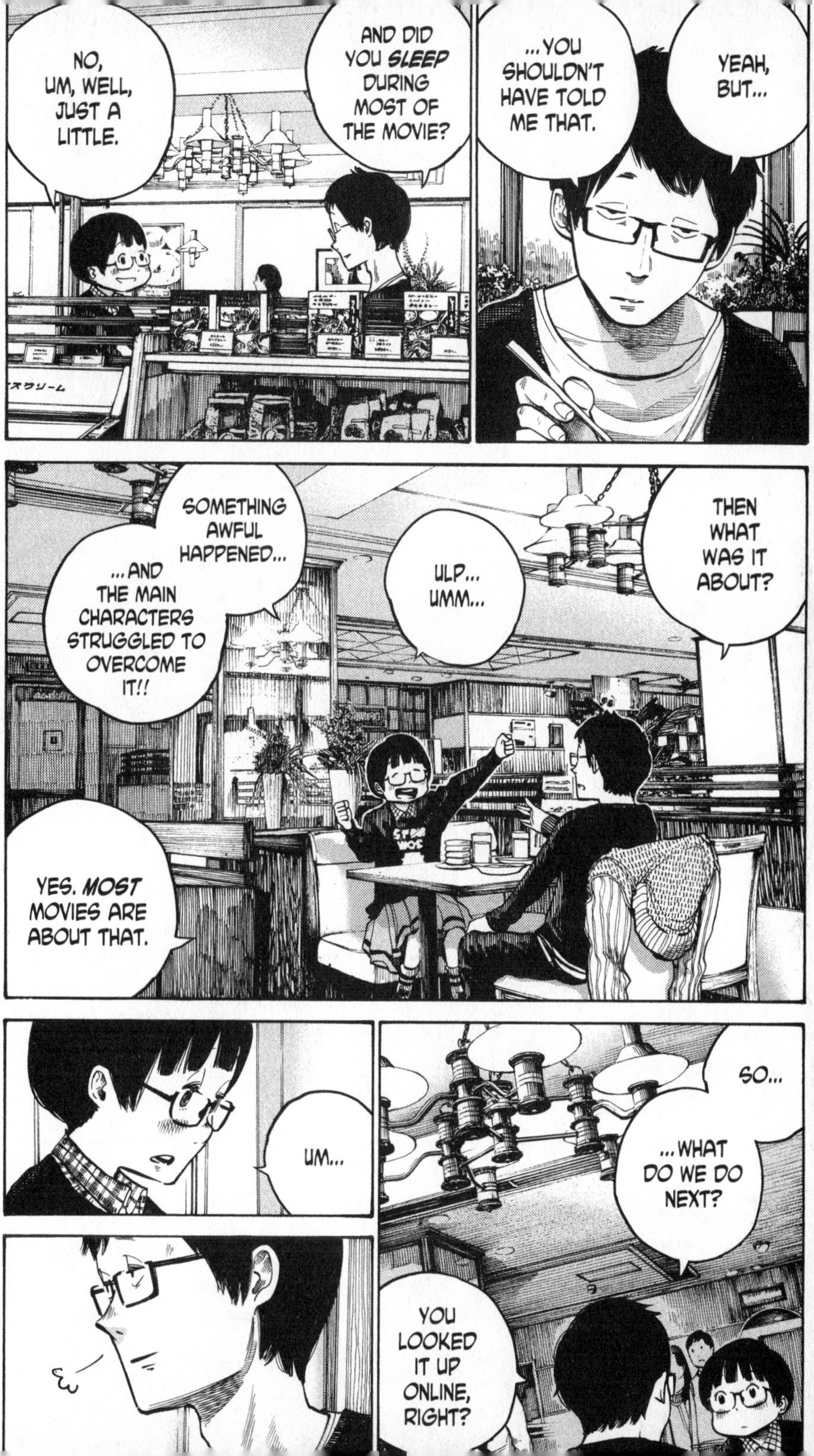
YEAH, BUT...
...YOU SHOULDN'T HAVE TOLD ME THAT.
AND DID YOU *SLEEP* DURING MOST OF THE MOVIE?
NO, UM, WELL, JUST A LITTLE.
THEN WHAT WAS IT ABOUT?
ULP... UMM...
SOMETHING AWFUL HAPPENED...
...AND THE MAIN CHARACTERS STRUGGLED TO OVERCOME IT!!
YES. *MOST* MOVIES ARE ABOUT THAT.
SO...
...WHAT DO WE DO NEXT?
YOU LOOKED IT UP ONLINE, RIGHT?
UM...

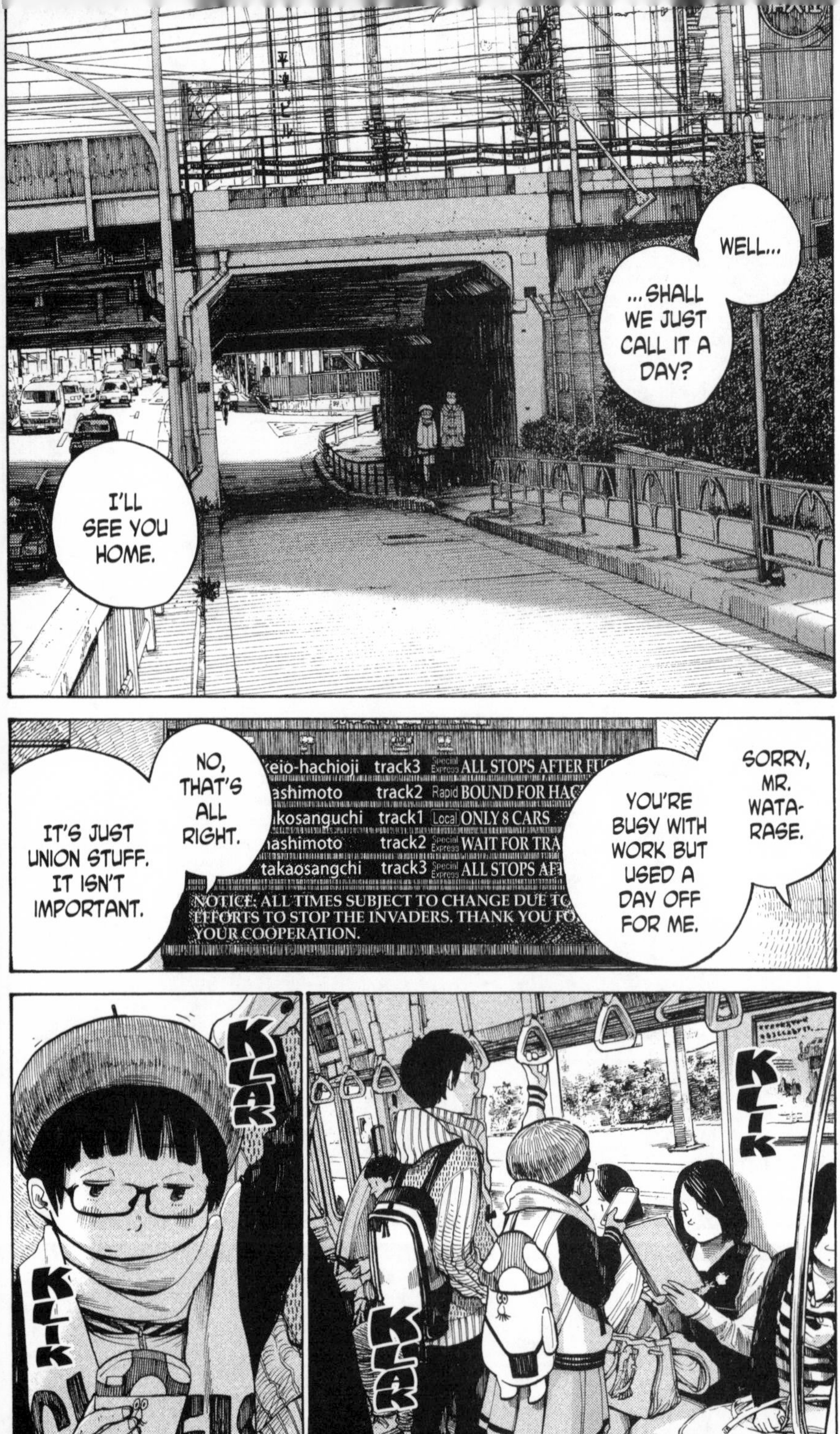
WELL...
...SHALL WE JUST CALL IT A DAY?
I'LL SEE YOU HOME.
SORRY, MR. WATA-RASE.
YOU'RE BUSY WITH WORK BUT USED A DAY OFF FOR ME.
NO, THAT'S ALL RIGHT.
IT'S JUST UNION STUFF. IT ISN'T IMPORTANT.
keio-hachioji track3 Special Express ALL STOPS AFTER FU
ashimoto track2 Rapid BOUND FOR HAC
kosanguchi track1 Local ONLY 8 CARS
ashimoto track2 Express WAIT FOR TRA
takaosanguchi track3 Special Express ALL STOPS AF
NOTICE: ALL TIMES SUBJECT TO CHANGE DUE TO EFFORTS TO STOP THE INVADERS. THANK YOU FO YOUR COOPERATION.
KLIK
KLAK
KLAK
KLIK

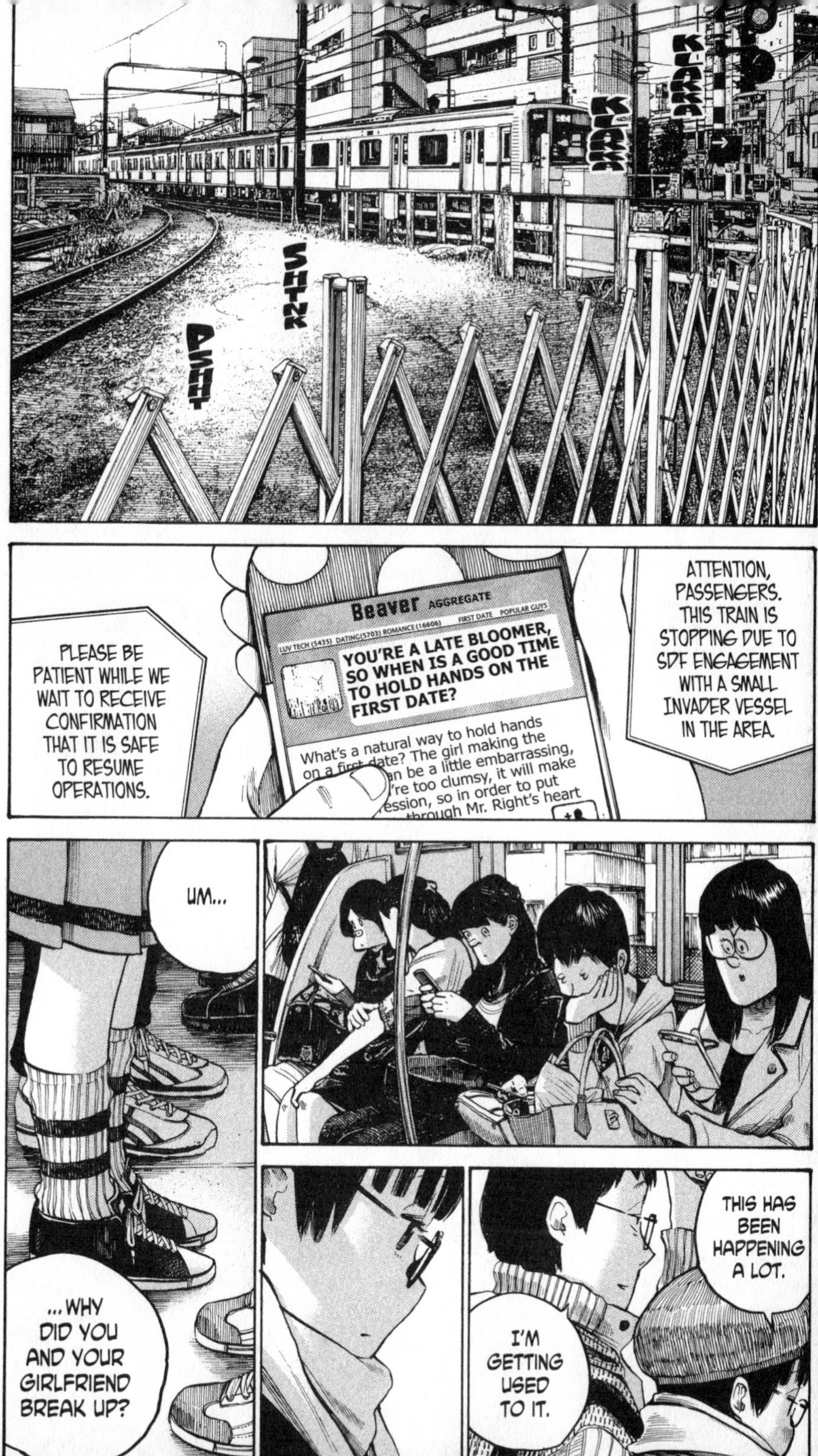
KLAKA
KLAKA
SHTNK
PSHT
ATTENTION, PASSENGERS. THIS TRAIN IS STOPPING DUE TO SDF ENGAGEMENT WITH A SMALL INVADER VESSEL IN THE AREA.
Beaver AGGREGATE
FIRST DATE POPULAR GUYS
LUV TECH (5435) DATING(5703) ROMANCE (16606)
YOU'RE A LATE BLOOMER, SO WHEN IS A GOOD TIME TO HOLD HANDS ON THE FIRST DATE?
What's a natural way to hold hands
PLEASE BE PATIENT WHILE WE WAIT TO RECEIVE CONFIRMATION THAT IT IS SAFE TO RESUME OPERATIONS.
THIS HAS BEEN HAPPENING A LOT.
I'M GETTING USED TO IT.
UM...
...WHY DID YOU AND YOUR GIRLFRIEND BREAK UP?

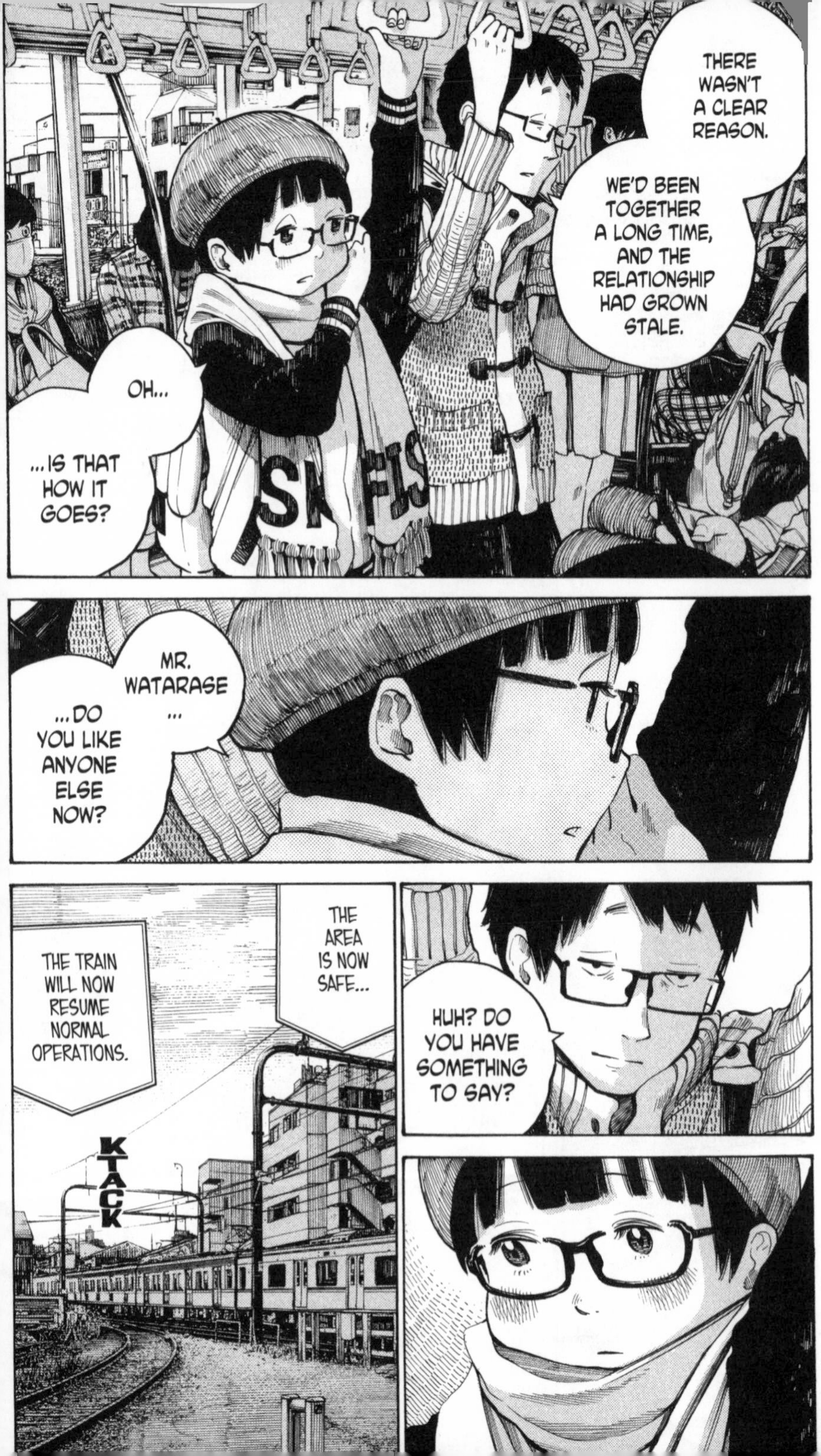
THERE WASN'T A CLEAR REASON.
WE'D BEEN TOGETHER A LONG TIME, AND THE RELATIONSHIP HAD GROWN STALE.
OH...
...IS THAT HOW IT GOES?
MR. WATARASE ...
...DO YOU LIKE ANYONE ELSE NOW?
HUH? DO YOU HAVE SOMETHING TO SAY?
THE AREA IS NOW SAFE...
THE TRAIN WILL NOW RESUME NORMAL OPERATIONS.
KTACK

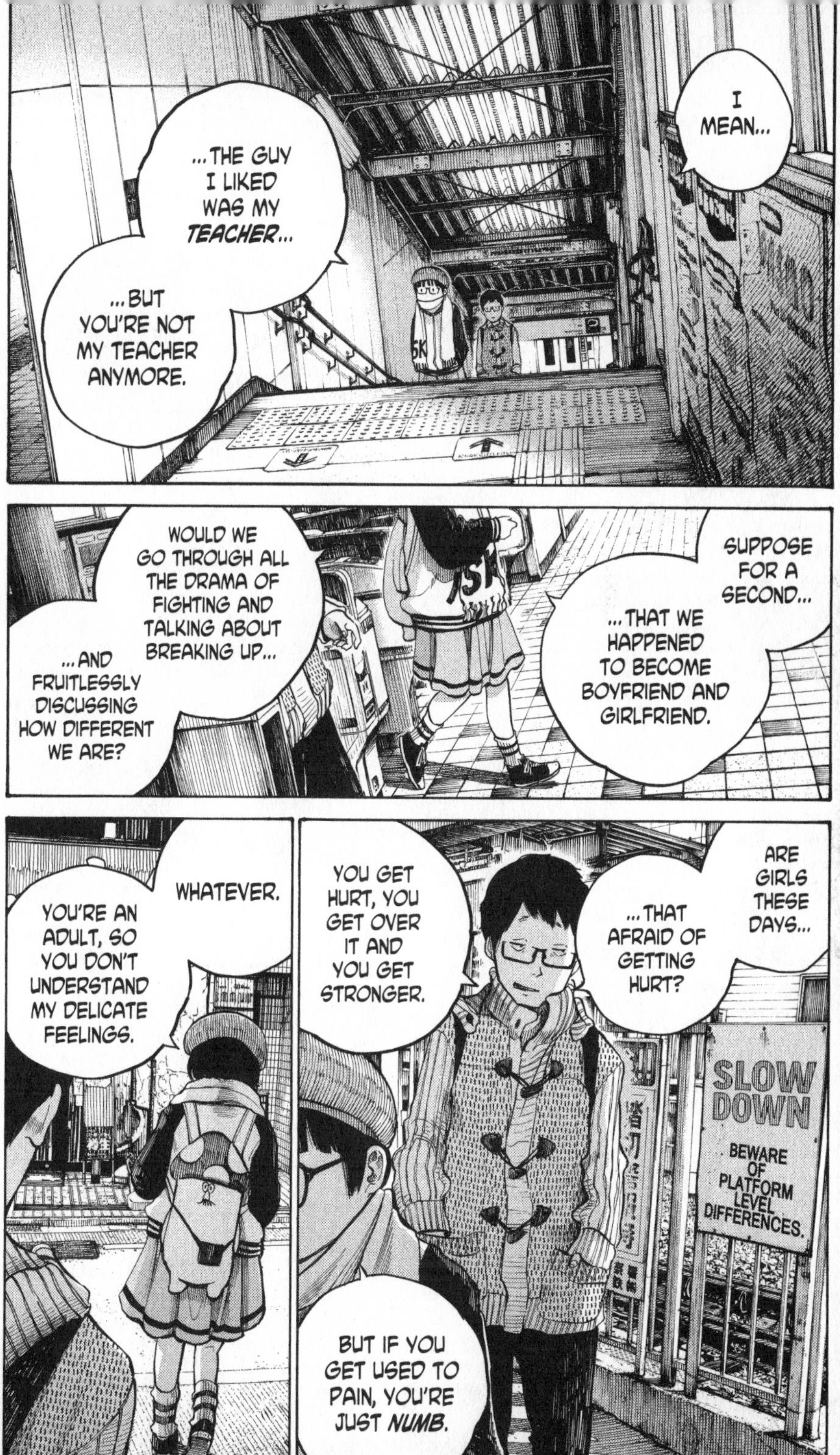
I MEAN...
...THE GUY I LIKED WAS MY *TEACHER*...
...BUT YOU'RE NOT MY TEACHER ANYMORE.
SUPPOSE FOR A SECOND...
...THAT WE HAPPENED TO BECOME BOYFRIEND AND GIRLFRIEND.
WOULD WE GO THROUGH ALL THE DRAMA OF FIGHTING AND TALKING ABOUT BREAKING UP...
...AND FRUITLESSLY DISCUSSING HOW DIFFERENT WE ARE?
ARE GIRLS THESE DAYS...
...THAT AFRAID OF GETTING HURT?
YOU GET HURT, YOU GET OVER IT AND YOU GET STRONGER.
SLOW DOWN
BEWARE OF PLATFORM LEVEL DIFFERENCES.
BUT IF YOU GET USED TO PAIN, YOU'RE JUST *NUMB*.
WHATEVER.
YOU'RE AN ADULT, SO YOU DON'T UNDERSTAND MY DELICATE FEELINGS.

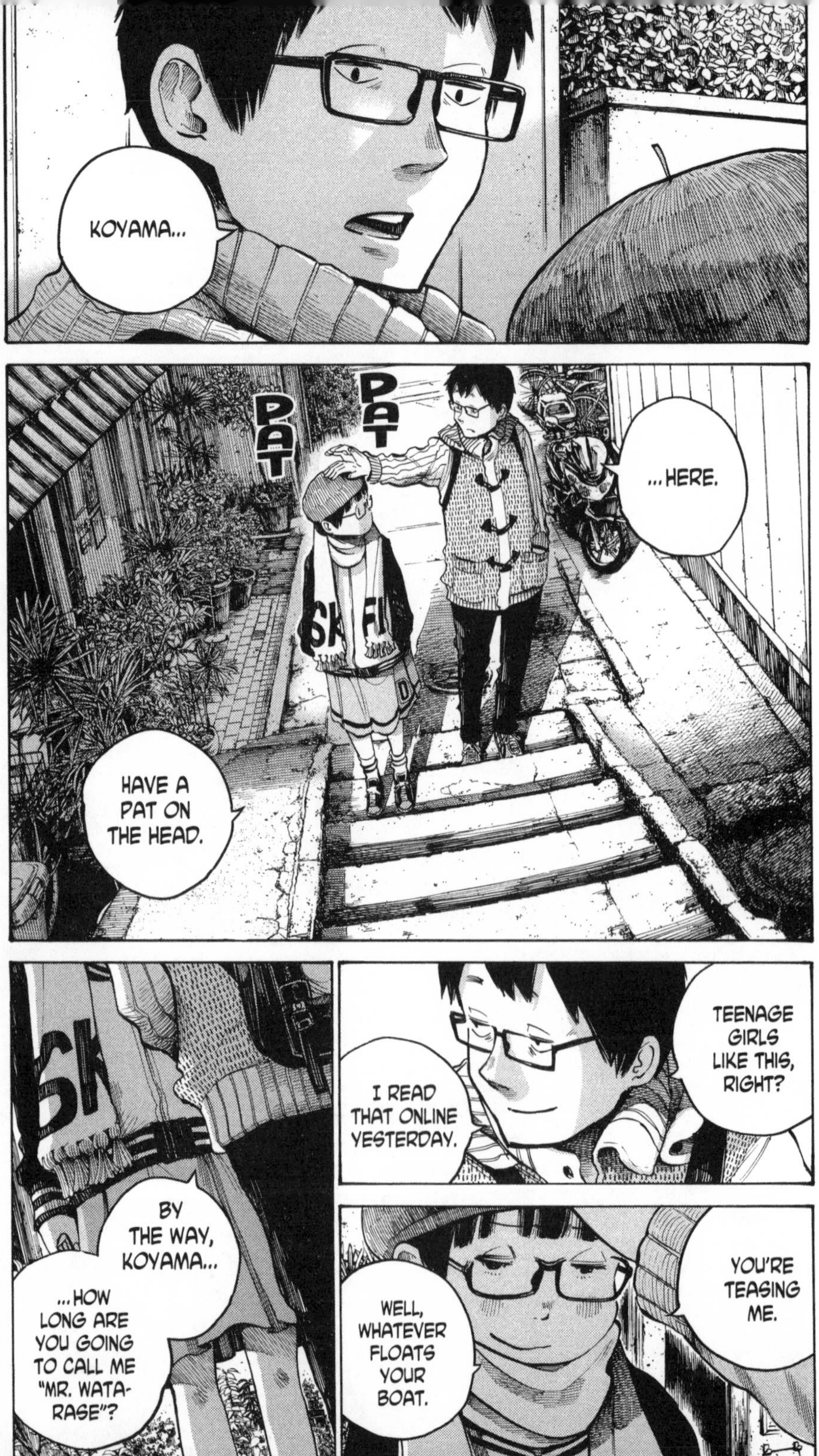
KOYAMA...
PAT
PAT
...HERE.
HAVE A PAT ON THE HEAD.
TEENAGE GIRLS LIKE THIS, RIGHT?
I READ THAT ONLINE YESTERDAY.
YOU'RE TEASING ME.
WELL, WHATEVER FLOATS YOUR BOAT.
BY THE WAY, KOYAMA...
...HOW LONG ARE YOU GOING TO CALL ME "MR. WATA-RASE"?

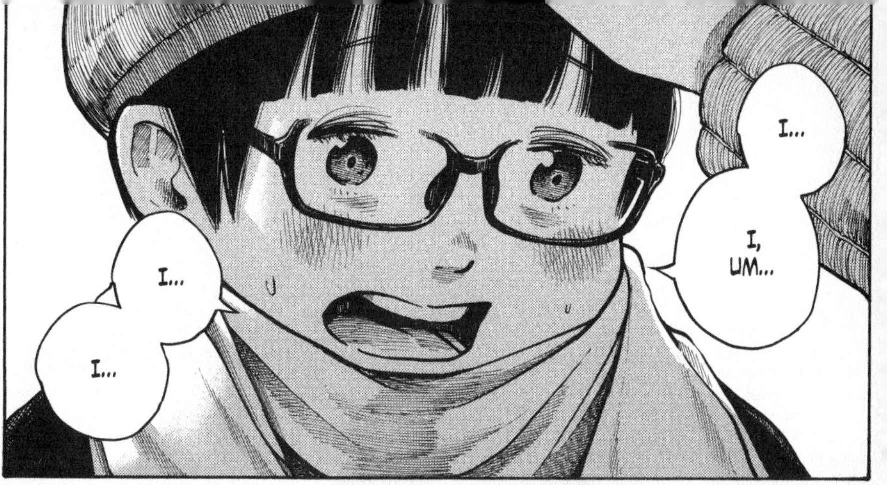
I...
I, UM...
I...
I...

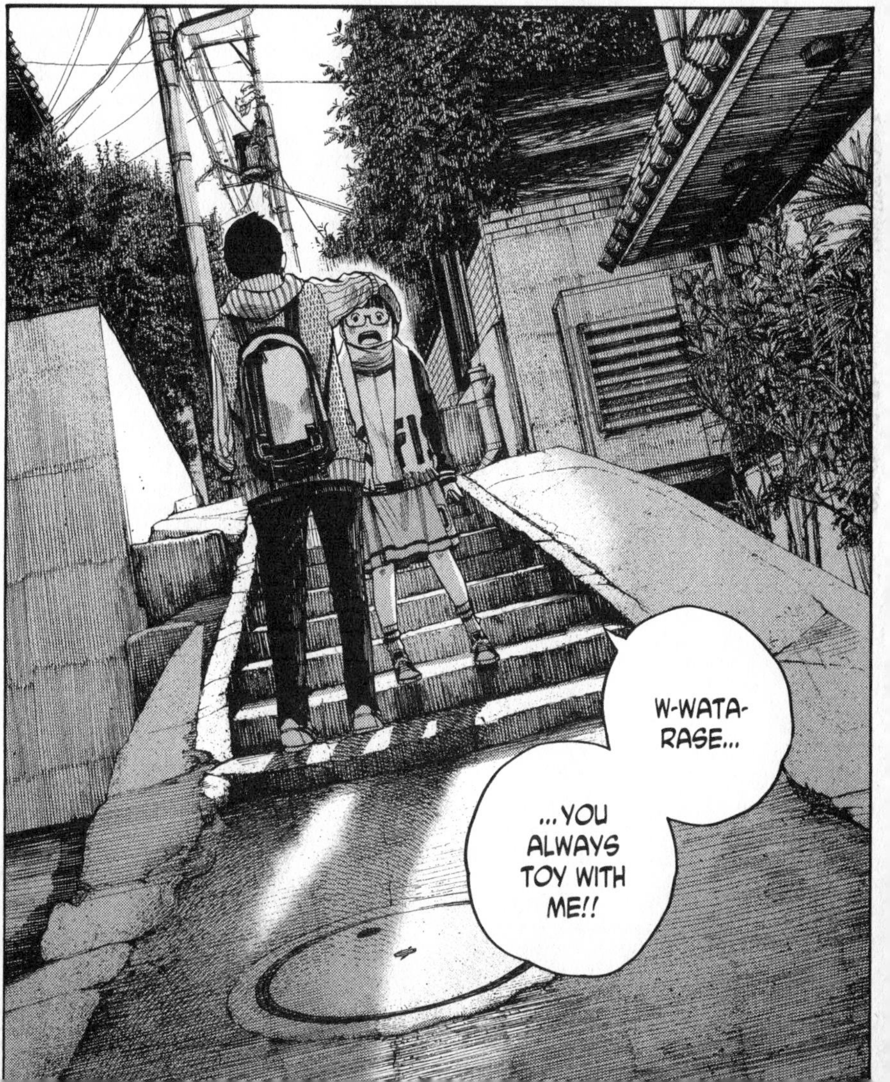
W-WATA-RASE...
...YOU ALWAYS TOY WITH ME!!

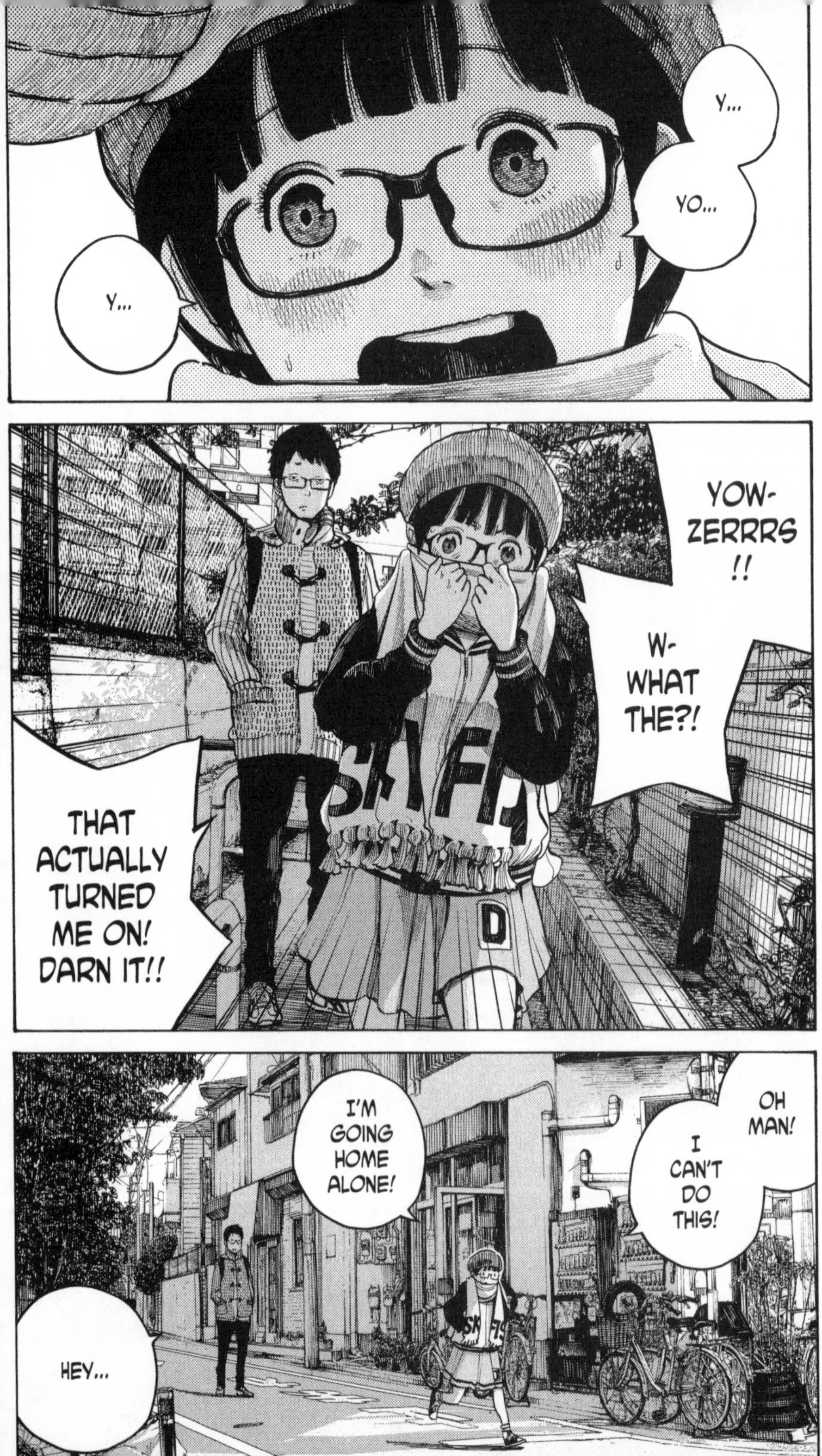
Y...
YO...
Y...
YOW-ZERRRS!!
W-WHAT THE?!
THAT ACTUALLY TURNED ME ON! DARN IT!!
OH MAN!
I CAN'T DO THIS!
I'M GOING HOME ALONE!
HEY...

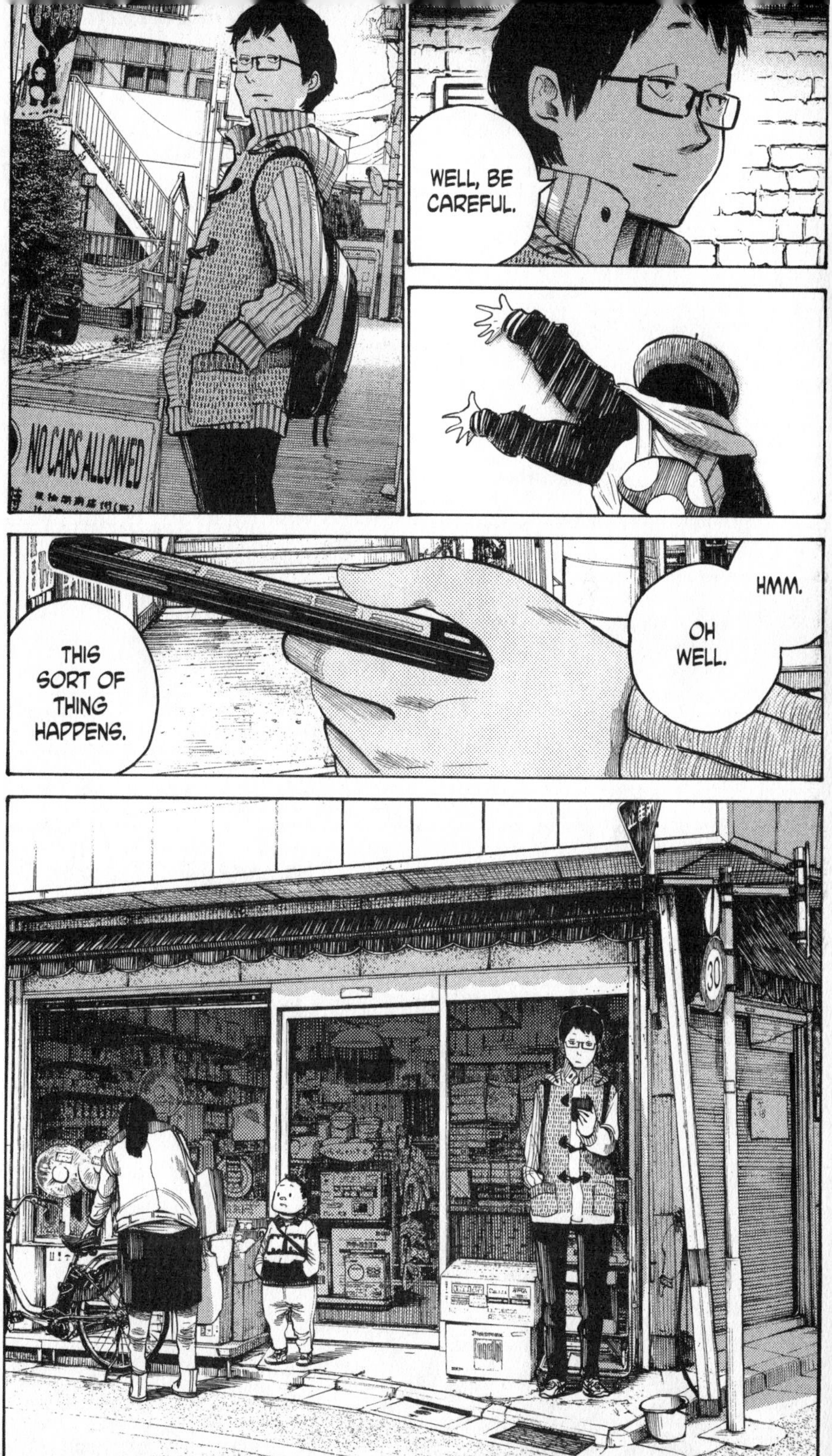
WELL, BE CAREFUL.
NO CARS ALLOWED
HMM.
OH WELL.
THIS SORT OF THING HAPPENS.

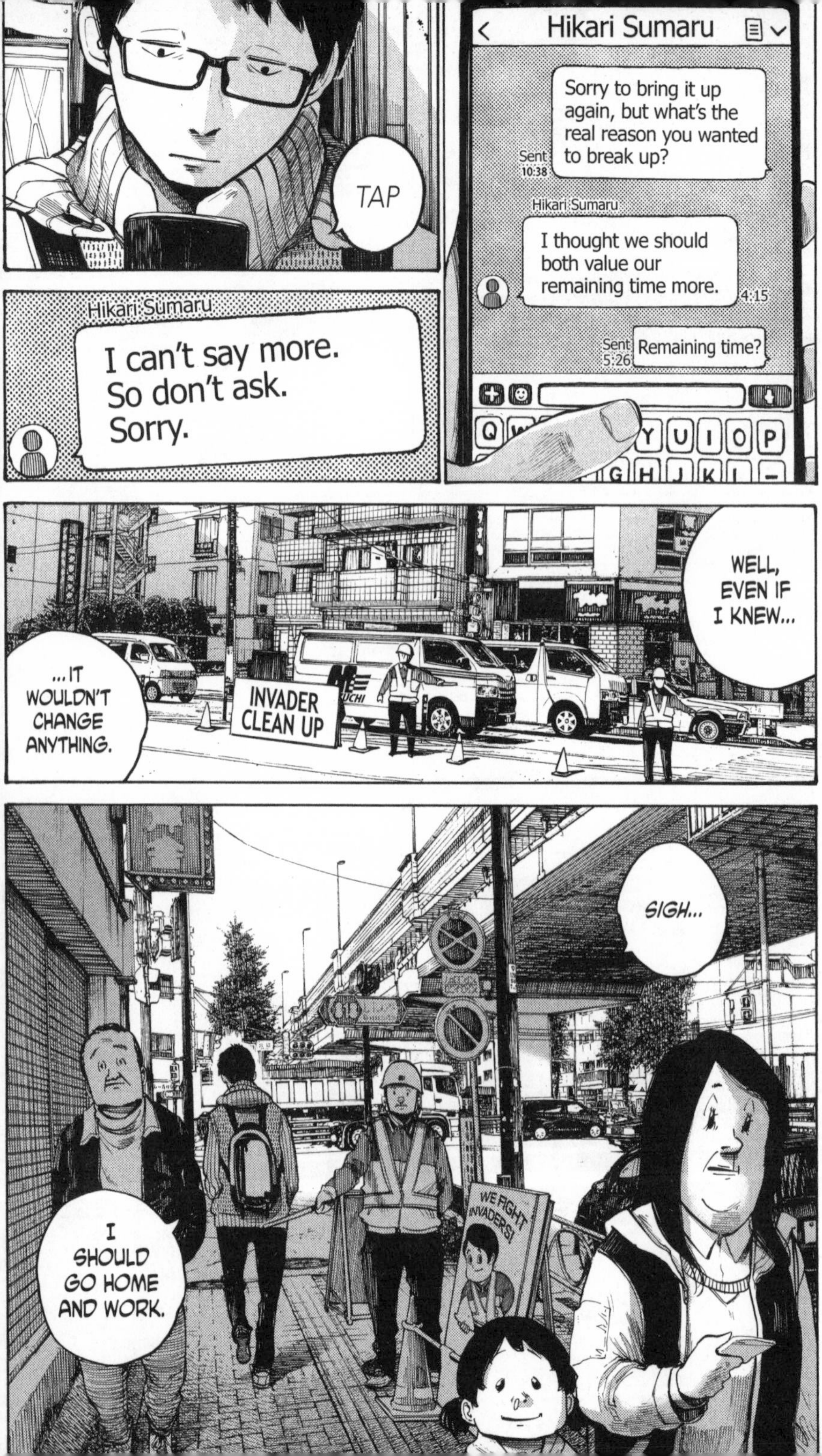
Hikari Sumaru
Sorry to bring it up again, but what's the real reason you wanted to break up?
Sent 10:38
Hikari Sumaru
I thought we should both value our remaining time more.
4:15
Sent 5:26
Remaining time?
TAP
Hikari Sumaru
I can't say more. So don't ask. Sorry.
WELL, EVEN IF I KNEW...
INVADER CLEAN UP
...IT WOULDN'T CHANGE ANYTHING.
SIGH...
WE FIGHT INVADERS!
I SHOULD GO HOME AND WORK.

CHAPTER 31

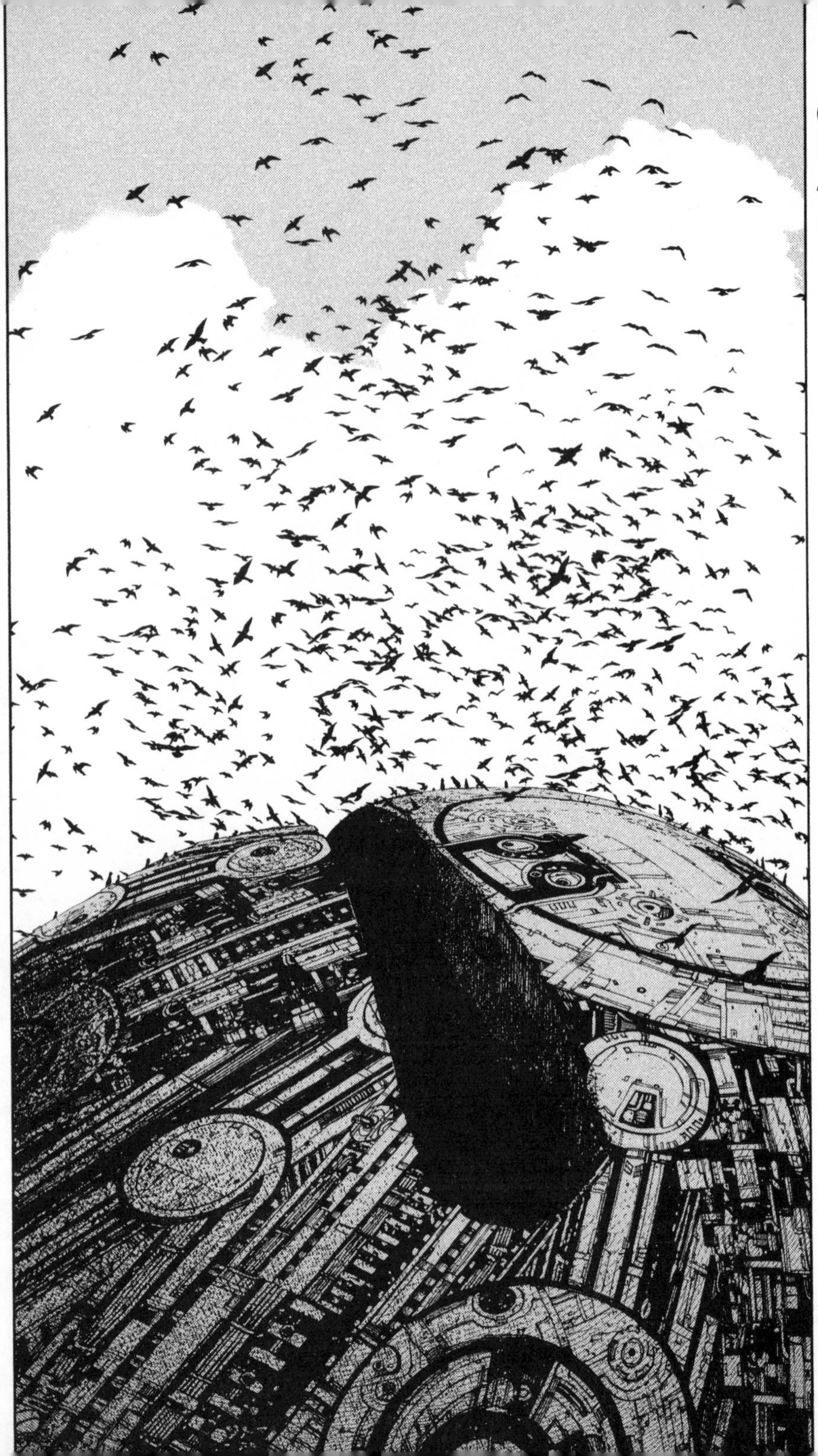

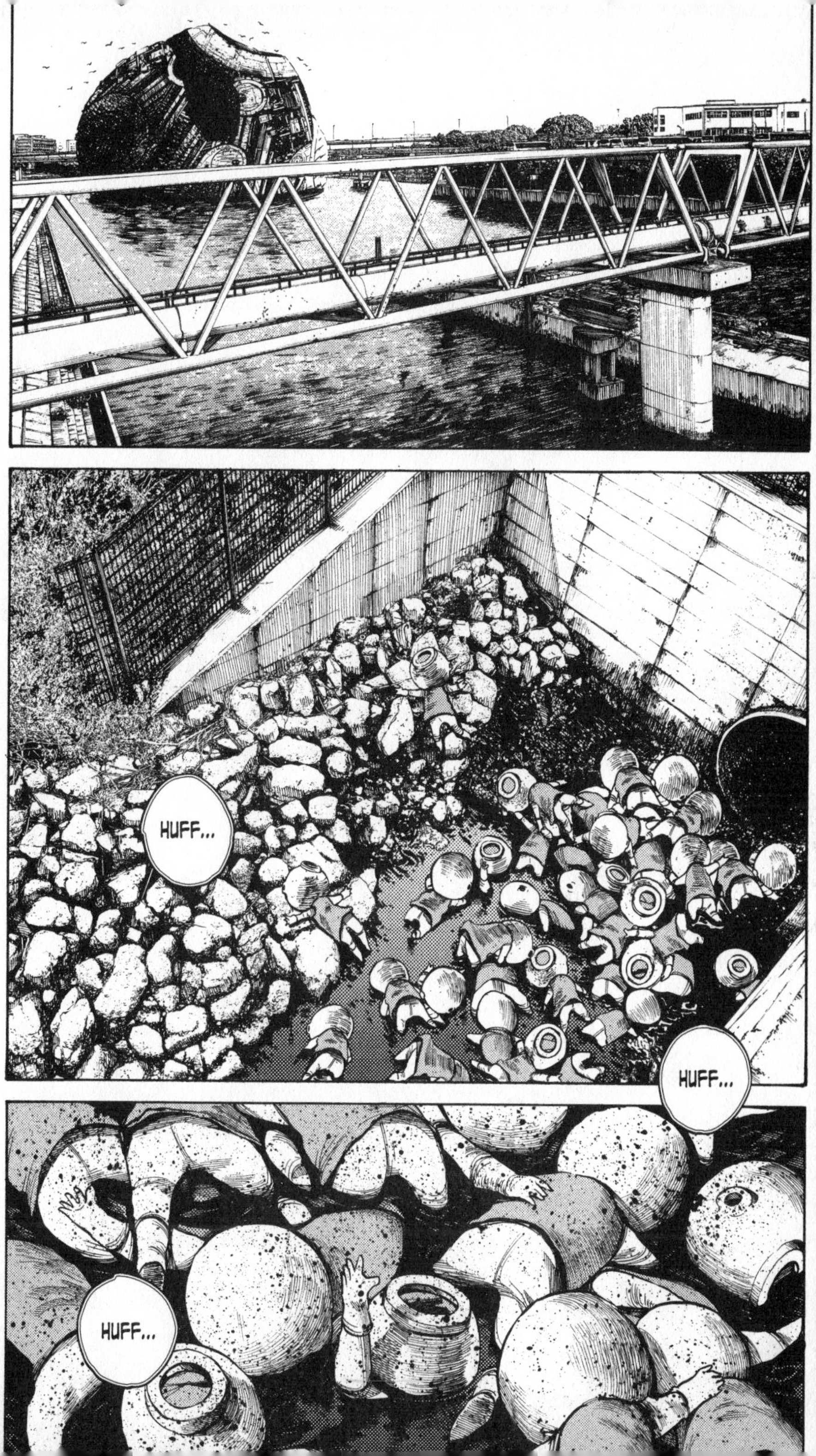
HUFF...
HUFF...
HUFF...

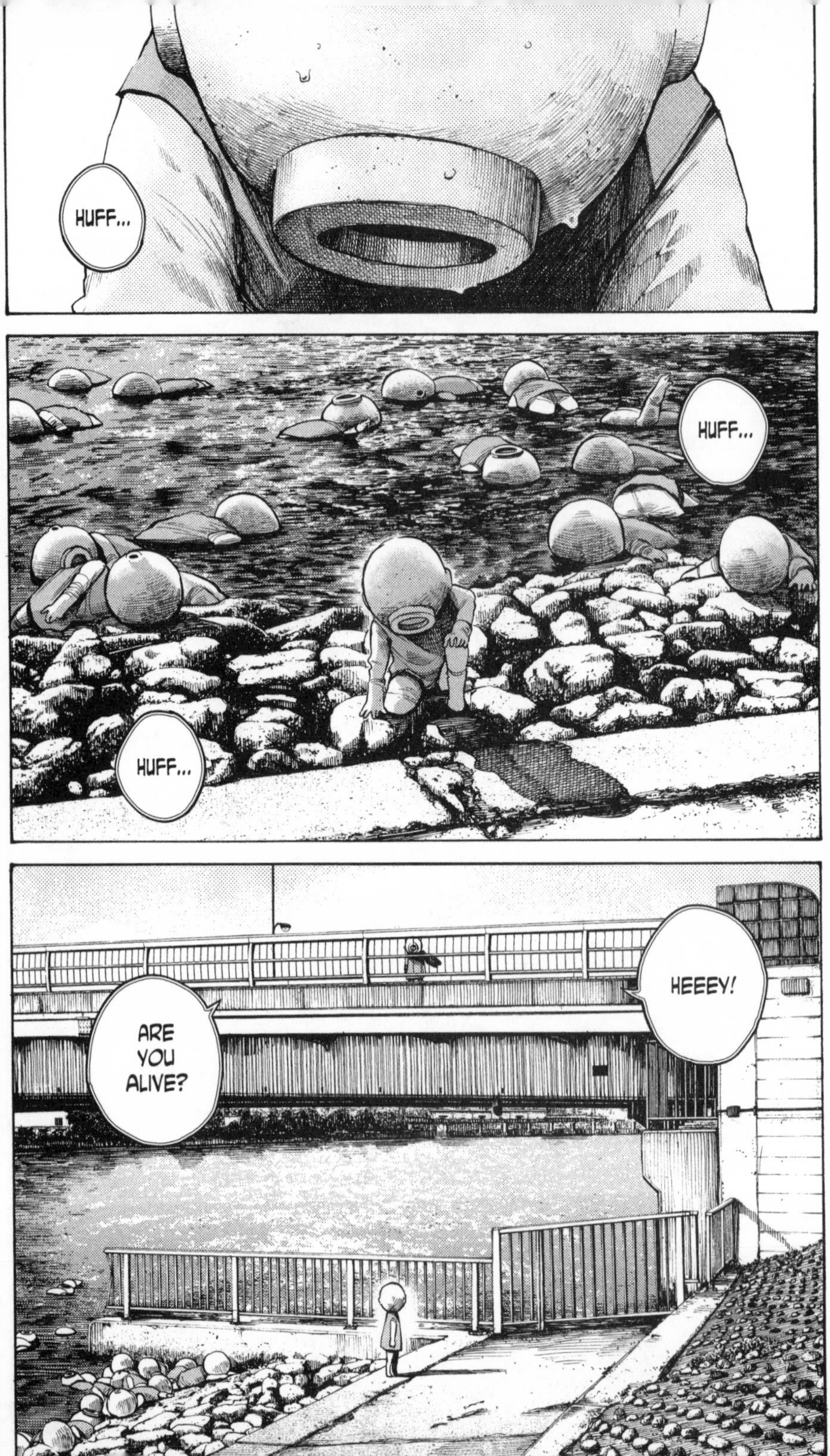
HUFF...
HUFF...
HUFF...
HEEEY!
ARE YOU ALIVE?

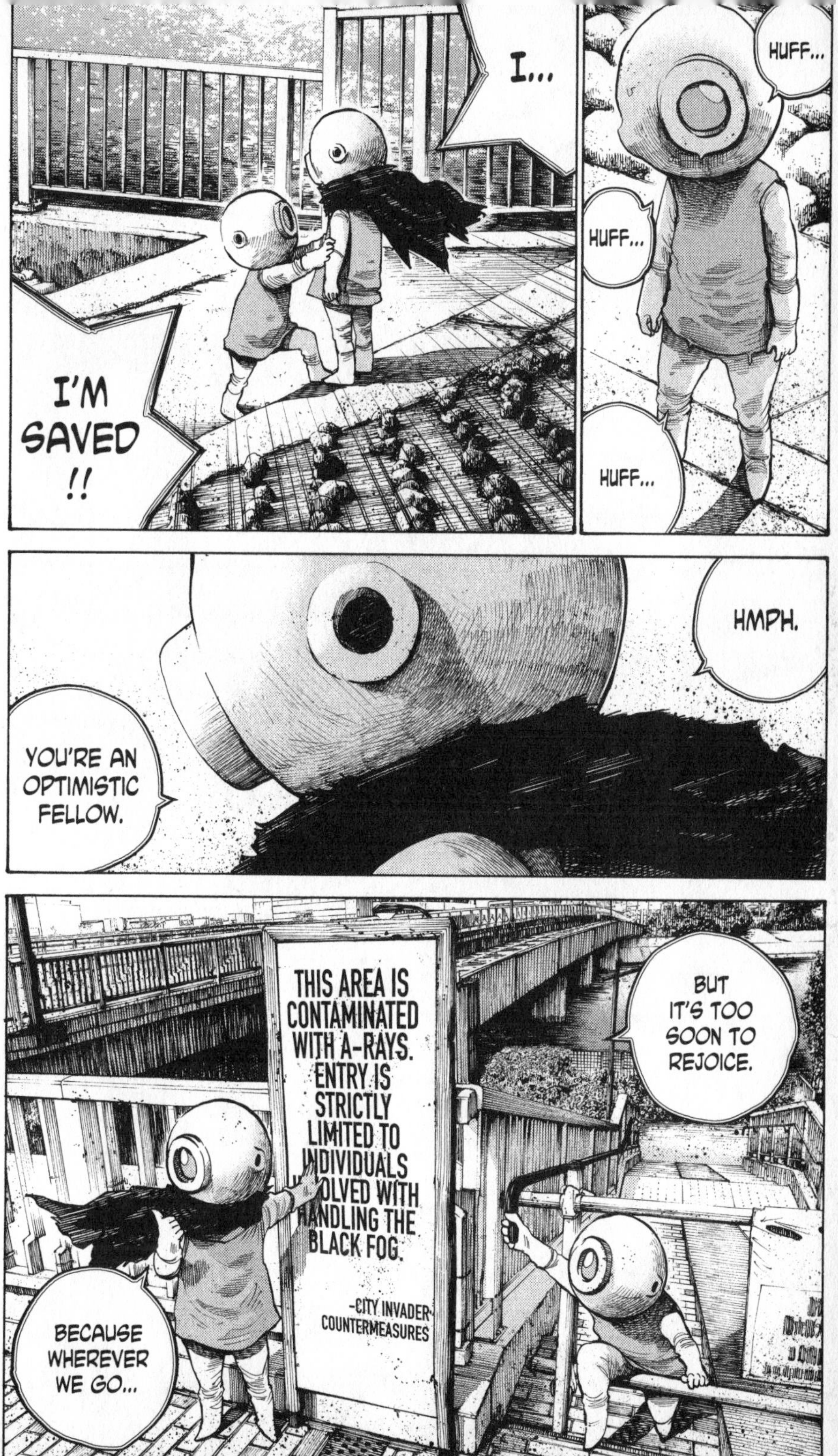
HUFF...
HUFF...
HUFF...
I...
I'M SAVED!!
HMPH.
YOU'RE AN OPTIMISTIC FELLOW.
BUT IT'S TOO SOON TO REJOICE.
THIS AREA IS CONTAMINATED WITH A-RAYS. ENTRY IS STRICTLY LIMITED TO INDIVIDUALS INVOLVED WITH HANDLING THE BLACK FOG.
-CITY INVADER COUNTERMEASURES
BECAUSE WHEREVER WE GO...

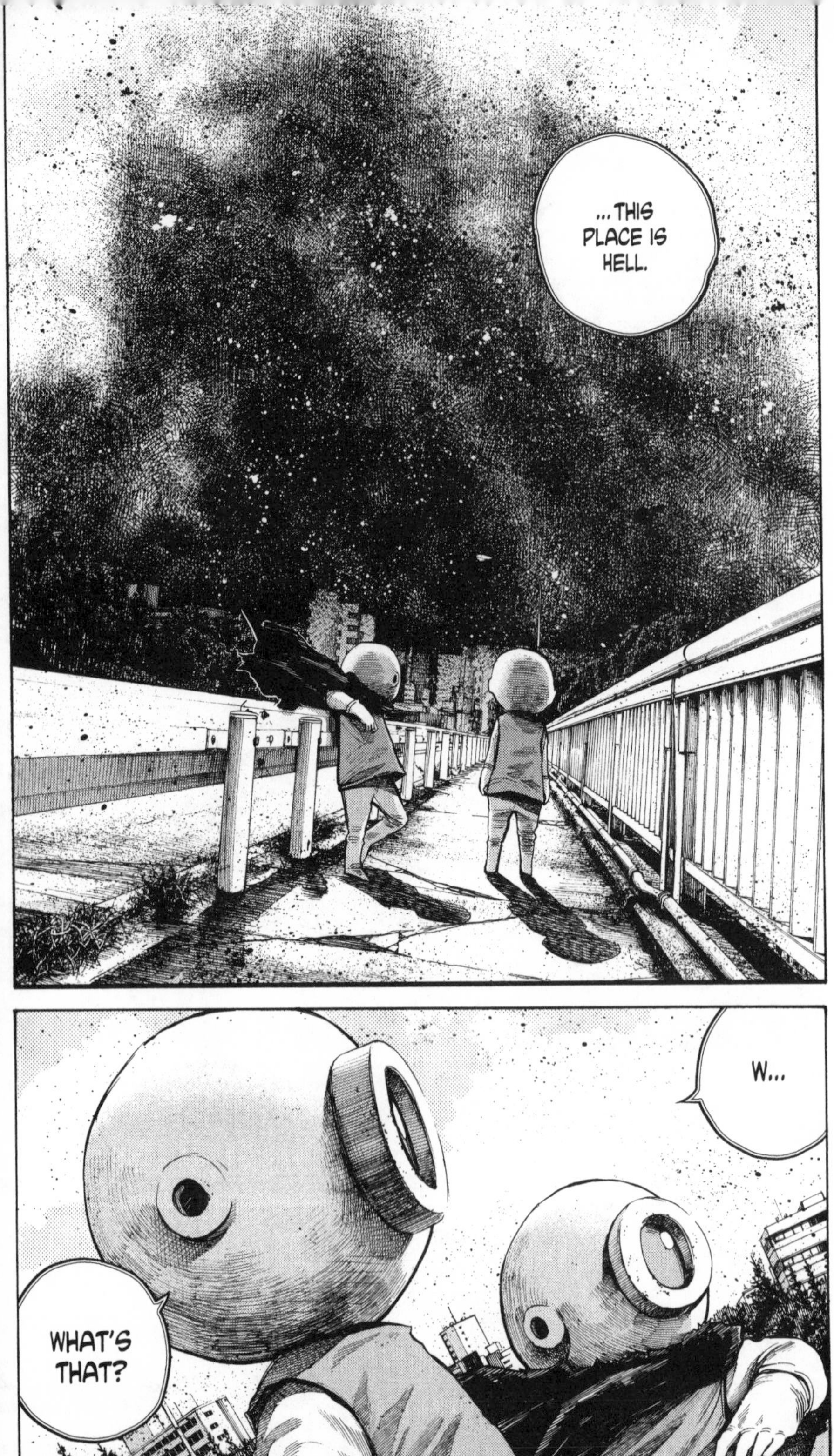
...THIS PLACE IS HELL.
W...
WHAT'S THAT?

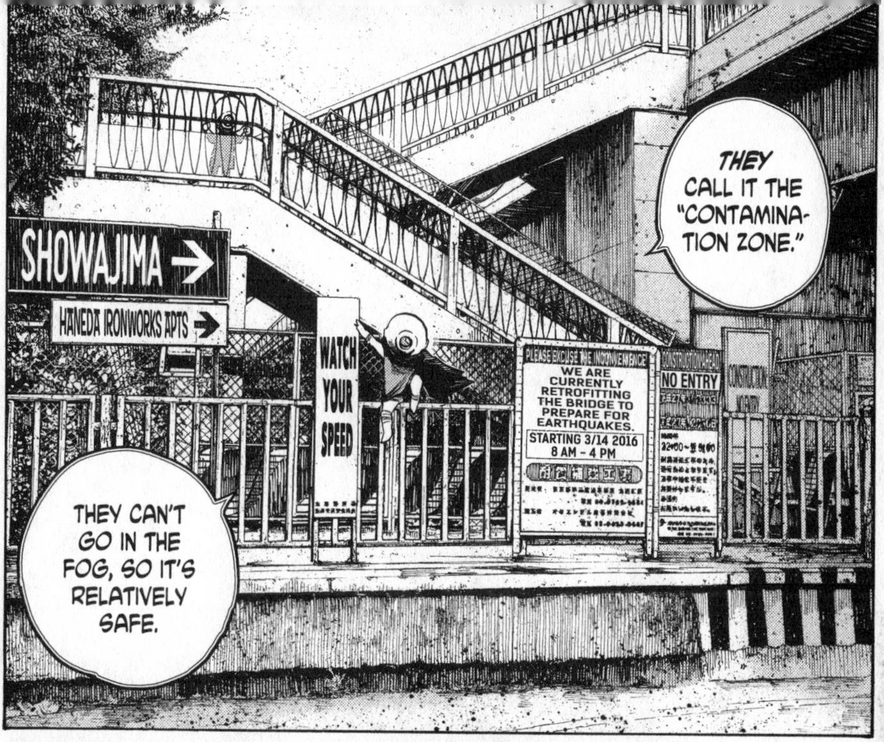
THEY CALL IT THE "CONTAMINATION ZONE."
SHOWAJIMA →
HANEDA IRONWORKS APTS →
WATCH YOUR SPEED
WE ARE CURRENTLY RETROFITTING THE BRIDGE TO PREPARE FOR EARTHQUAKES.
STARTING 3/14 2016
8 AM - 4 PM
NO ENTRY
THEY CAN'T GO IN THE FOG, SO IT'S RELATIVELY SAFE.

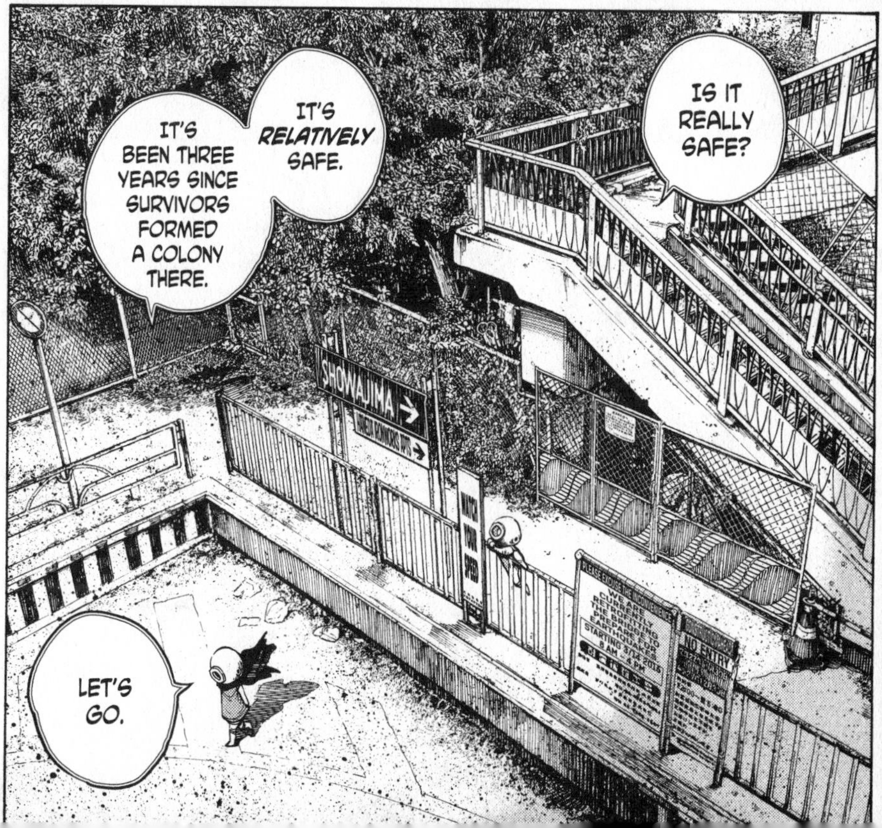
IS IT REALLY SAFE?
IT'S *RELATIVELY* SAFE.
IT'S BEEN THREE YEARS SINCE SURVIVORS FORMED A COLONY THERE.
SHOWAJIMA →
WATCH YOUR SPEED
NO ENTRY
LET'S GO.

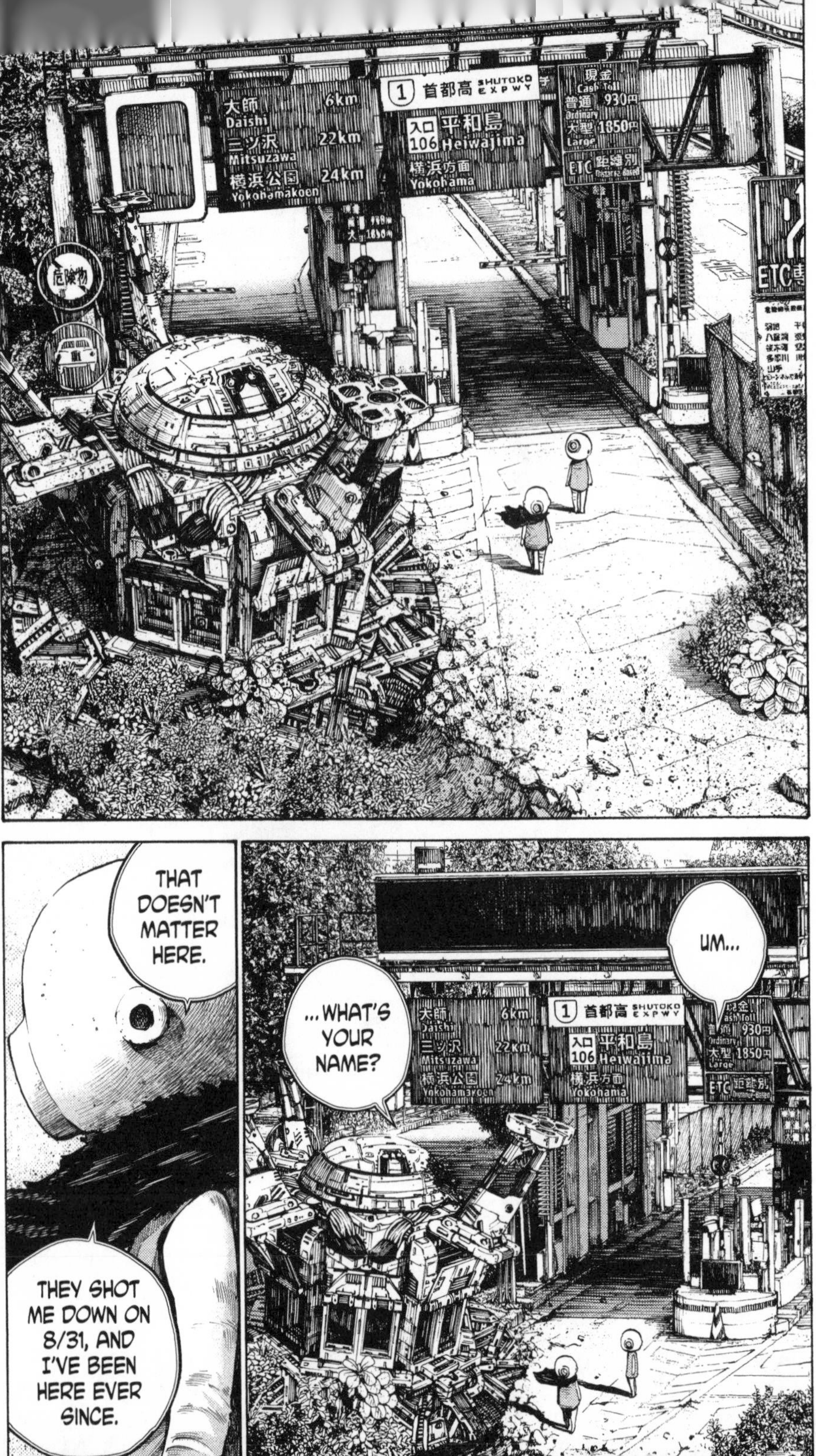

1 首都高 SHUTOKO EXPWY
大師 Daishi 6km
三ツ沢 Mitsuzawa 22km
横浜公園 Yokohamakoen 24km
入口 106 平和島 Heiwajima
横浜方面 Yokohama
現金 Cash Toll
普通 Ordinary 930円
大型 Large 1850円
ETC 距離別
UM...
...WHAT'S YOUR NAME?
THAT DOESN'T MATTER HERE.
THEY SHOT ME DOWN ON 8/31, AND I'VE BEEN HERE EVER SINCE.

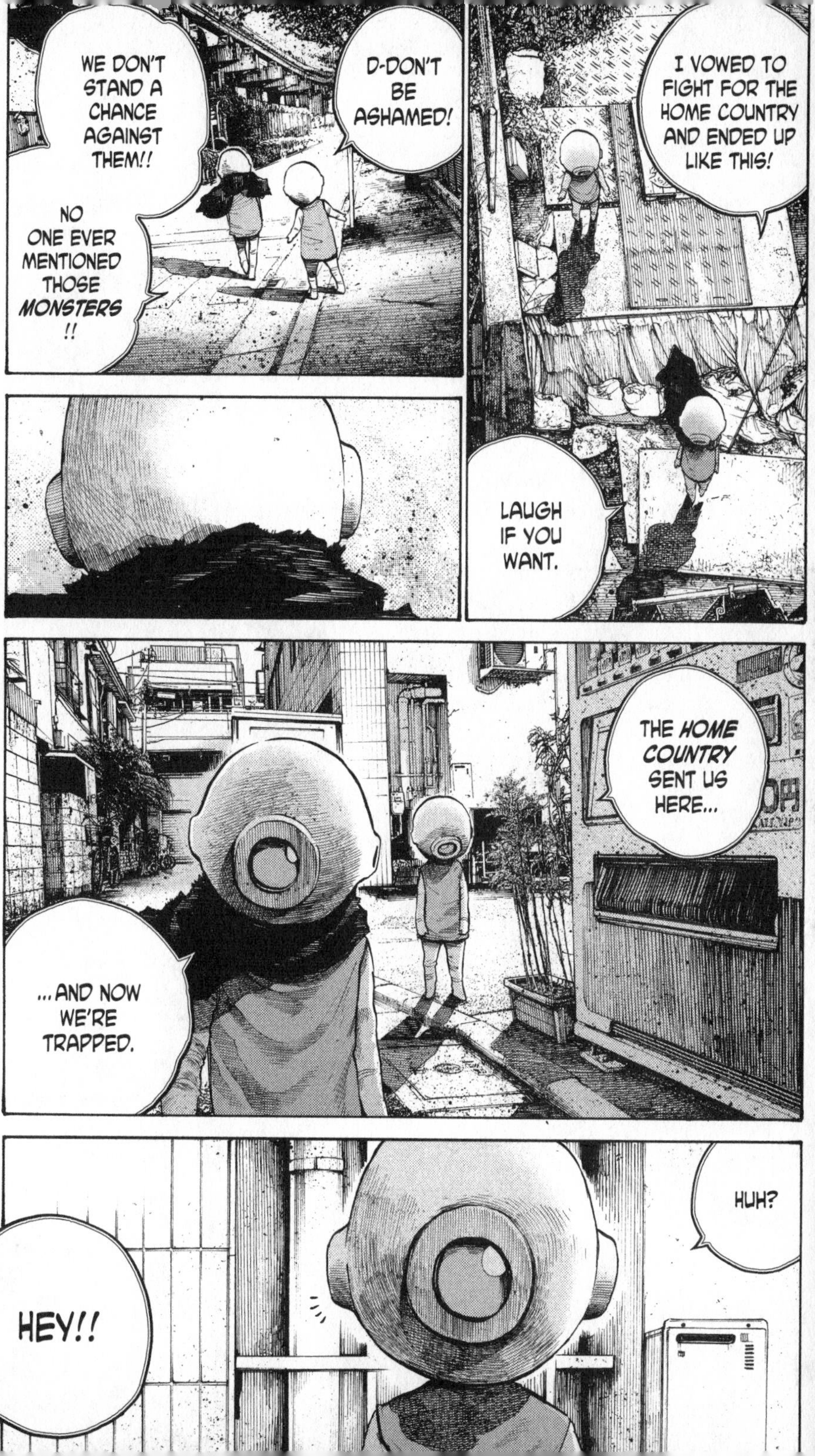
I VOWED TO FIGHT FOR THE HOME COUNTRY AND ENDED UP LIKE THIS!
LAUGH IF YOU WANT.
D-DON'T BE ASHAMED!
WE DON'T STAND A CHANCE AGAINST THEM!!
NO ONE EVER MENTIONED THOSE *MONSTERS* !!
THE *HOME COUNTRY* SENT US HERE...
...AND NOW WE'RE TRAPPED.
HUH?
HEY!!

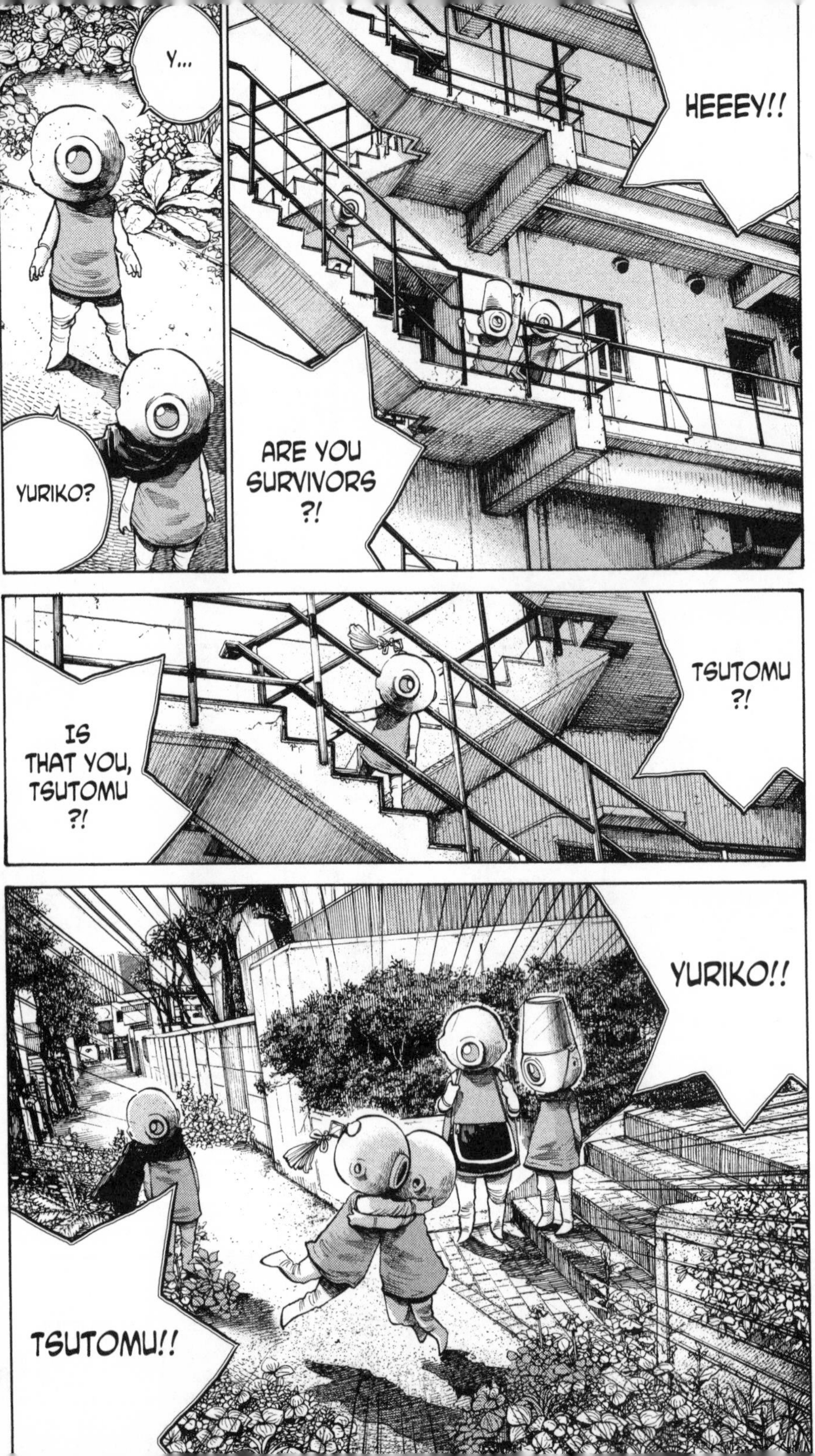
HEEEY!!
ARE YOU SURVIVORS ?!
Y...
YURIKO?
TSUTOMU ?!
IS THAT YOU, TSUTOMU ?!
YURIKO!!
TSUTOMU!!

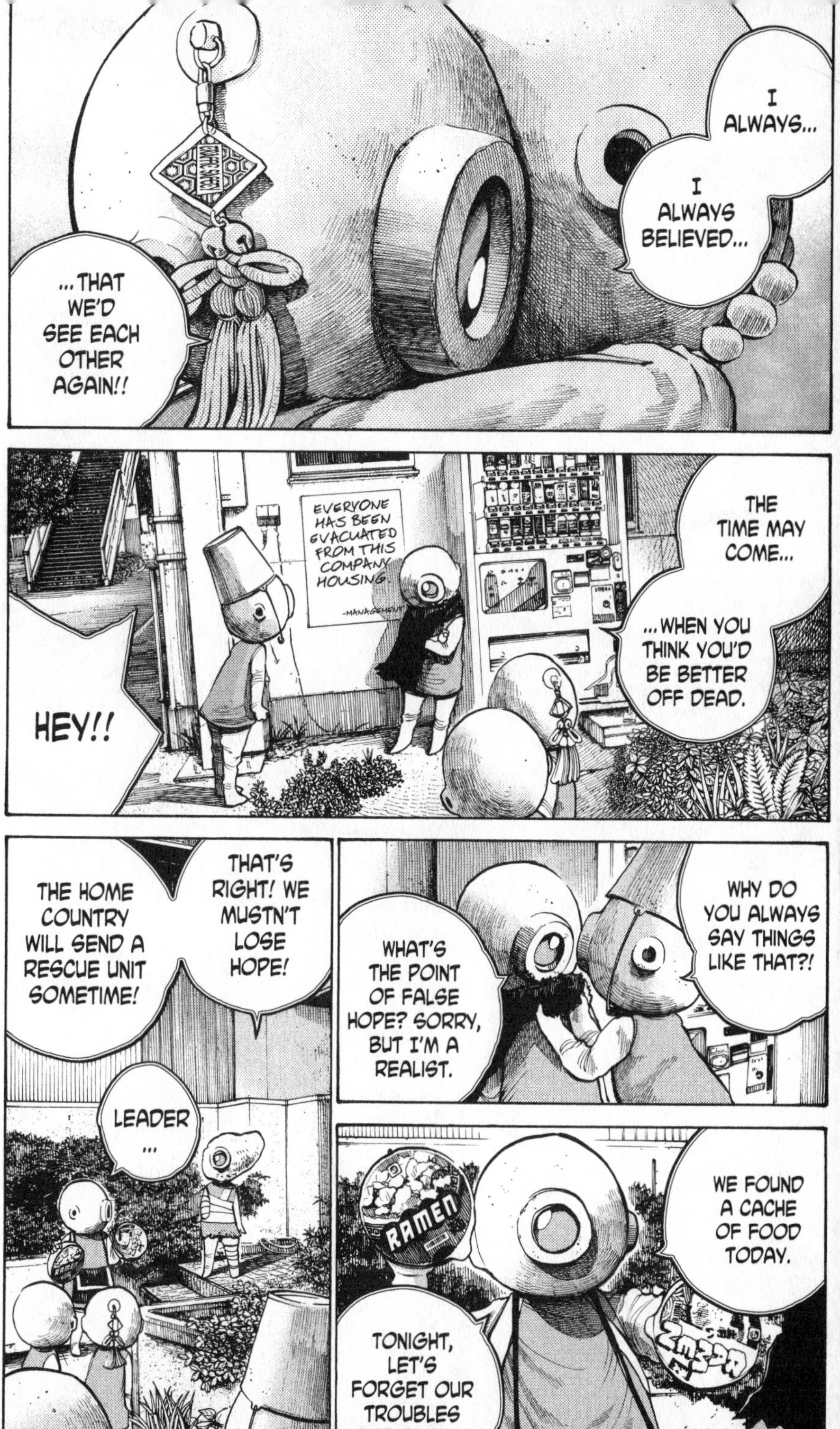
I ALWAYS...
I ALWAYS BELIEVED...
...THAT WE'D SEE EACH OTHER AGAIN!!
EVERYONE HAS BEEN EVACUATED FROM THIS COMPANY HOUSING.
-MANAGEMENT
THE TIME MAY COME...
...WHEN YOU THINK YOU'D BE BETTER OFF DEAD.
HEY!!
WHY DO YOU ALWAYS SAY THINGS LIKE THAT?!
WHAT'S THE POINT OF FALSE HOPE? SORRY, BUT I'M A REALIST.
THAT'S RIGHT! WE MUSTN'T LOSE HOPE!
THE HOME COUNTRY WILL SEND A RESCUE UNIT SOMETIME!
RAMEN
WE FOUND A CACHE OF FOOD TODAY.
TONIGHT, LET'S FORGET OUR TROUBLES AND PARTY!
LEADER ...

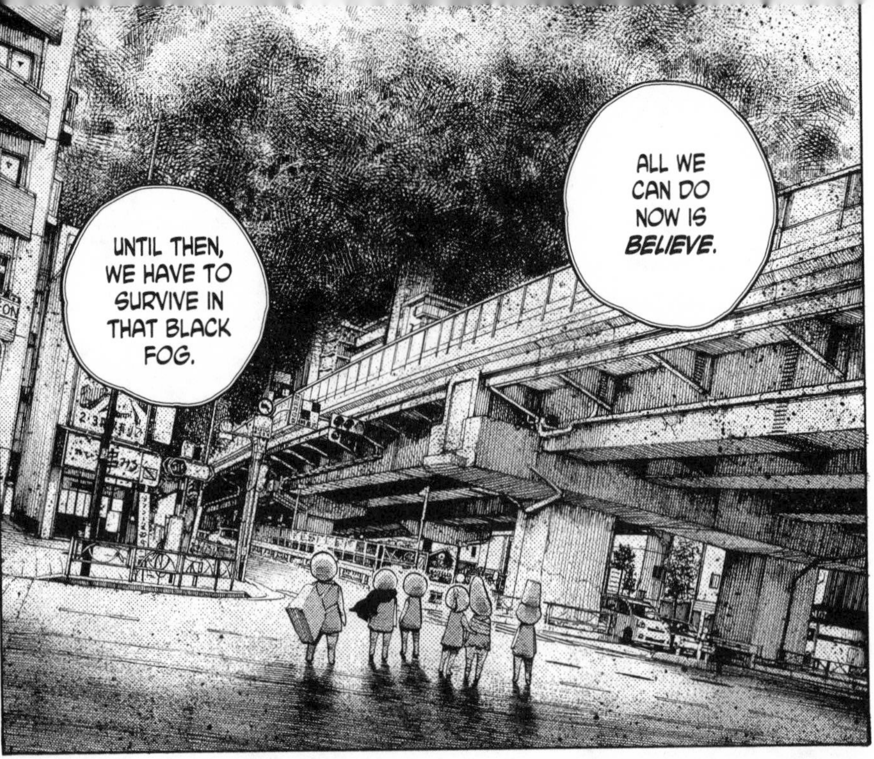
ALL WE CAN DO NOW IS ***BELIEVE***.
UNTIL THEN, WE HAVE TO SURVIVE IN THAT BLACK FOG.

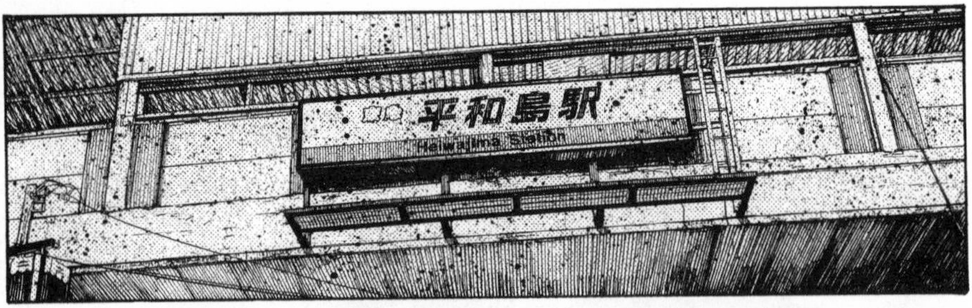
平和島駅
Heiwajima Station

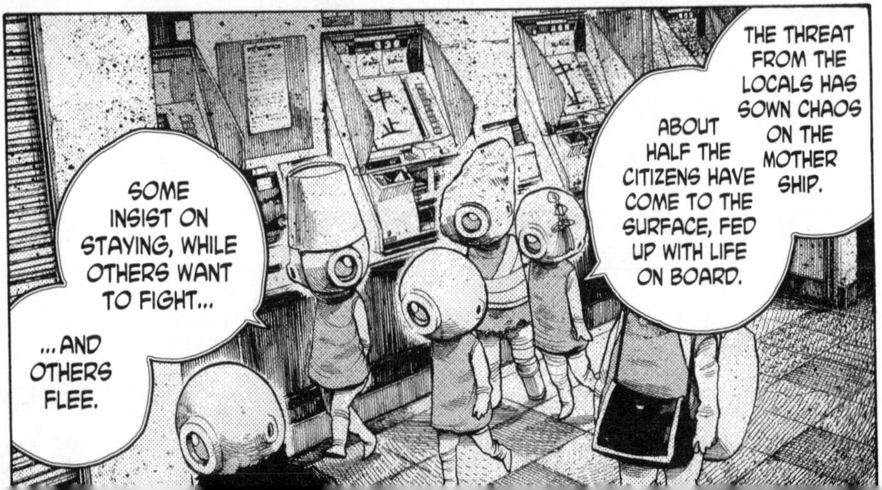
中止
中止
THE THREAT FROM THE LOCALS HAS SOWN CHAOS ON THE MOTHER SHIP.
ABOUT HALF THE CITIZENS HAVE COME TO THE SURFACE, FED UP WITH LIFE ON BOARD.
SOME INSIST ON STAYING, WHILE OTHERS WANT TO FIGHT...
...AND OTHERS FLEE.

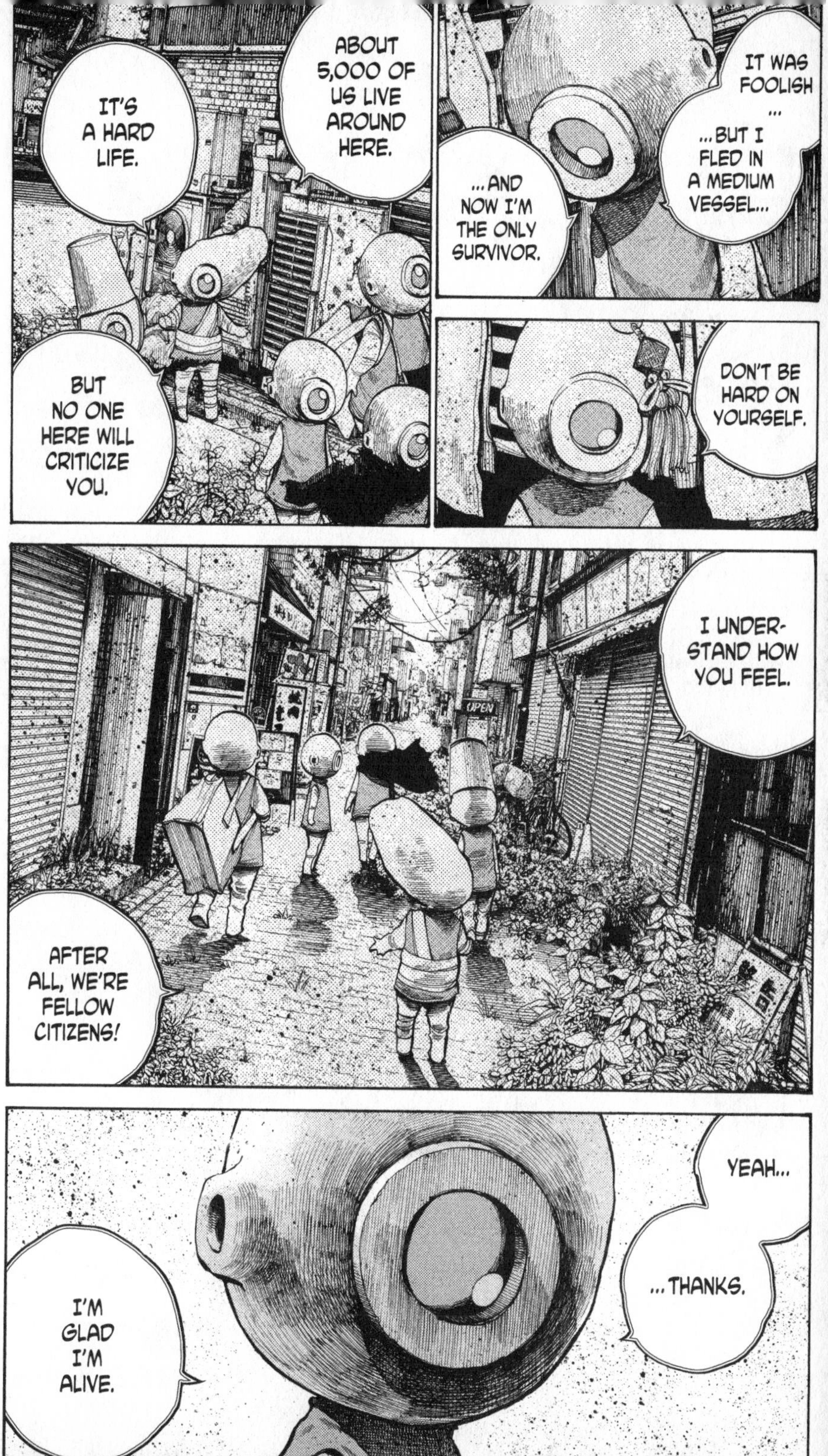
IT WAS FOOLISH ...
...BUT I FLED IN A MEDIUM VESSEL...
...AND NOW I'M THE ONLY SURVIVOR.
DON'T BE HARD ON YOURSELF.
ABOUT 5,000 OF US LIVE AROUND HERE.
IT'S A HARD LIFE.
BUT NO ONE HERE WILL CRITICIZE YOU.
I UNDER-STAND HOW YOU FEEL.
OPEN
AFTER ALL, WE'RE FELLOW CITIZENS!
YEAH...
...THANKS.
I'M GLAD I'M ALIVE.

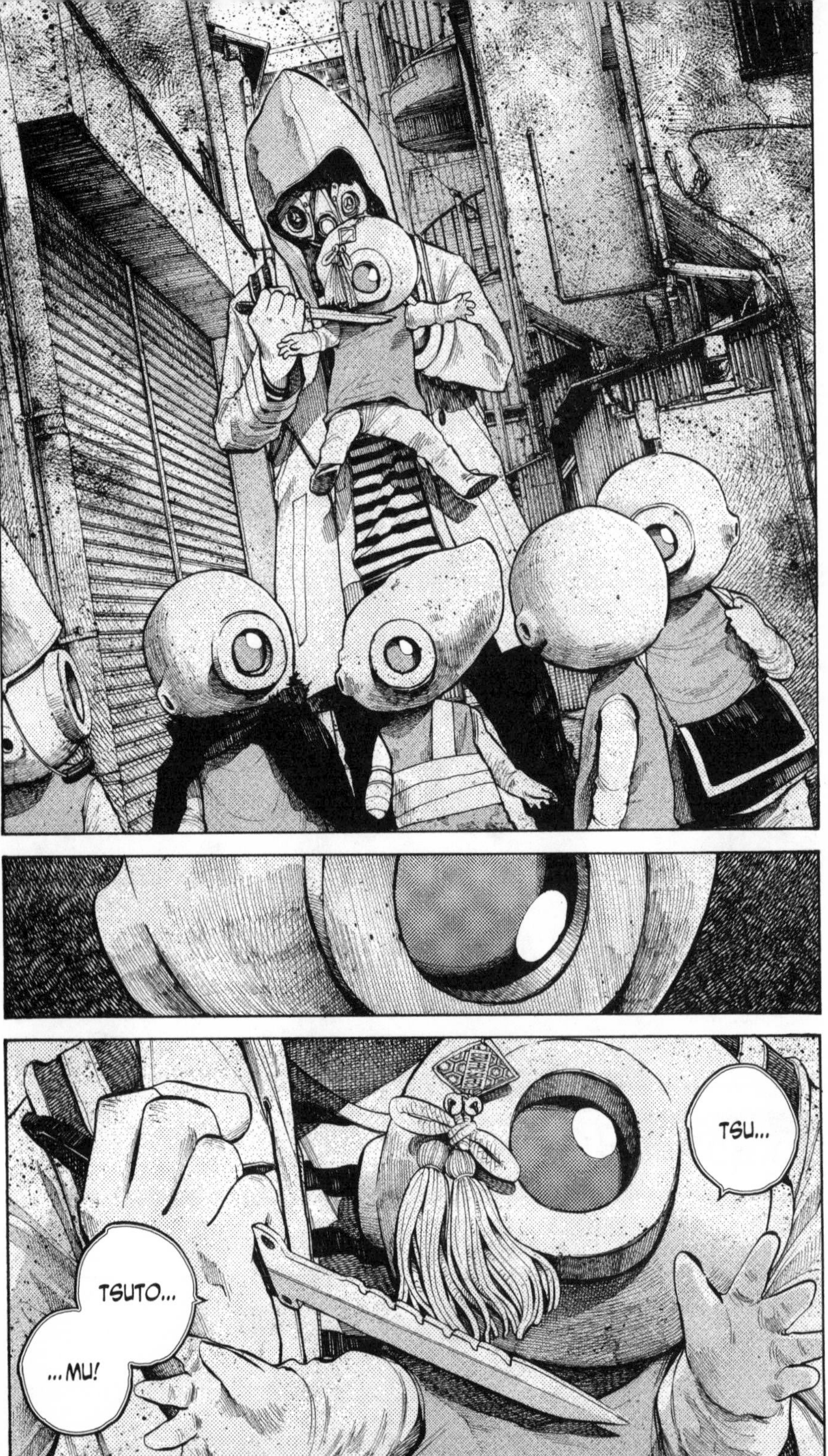
TSU...
TSUTO...
...MU!

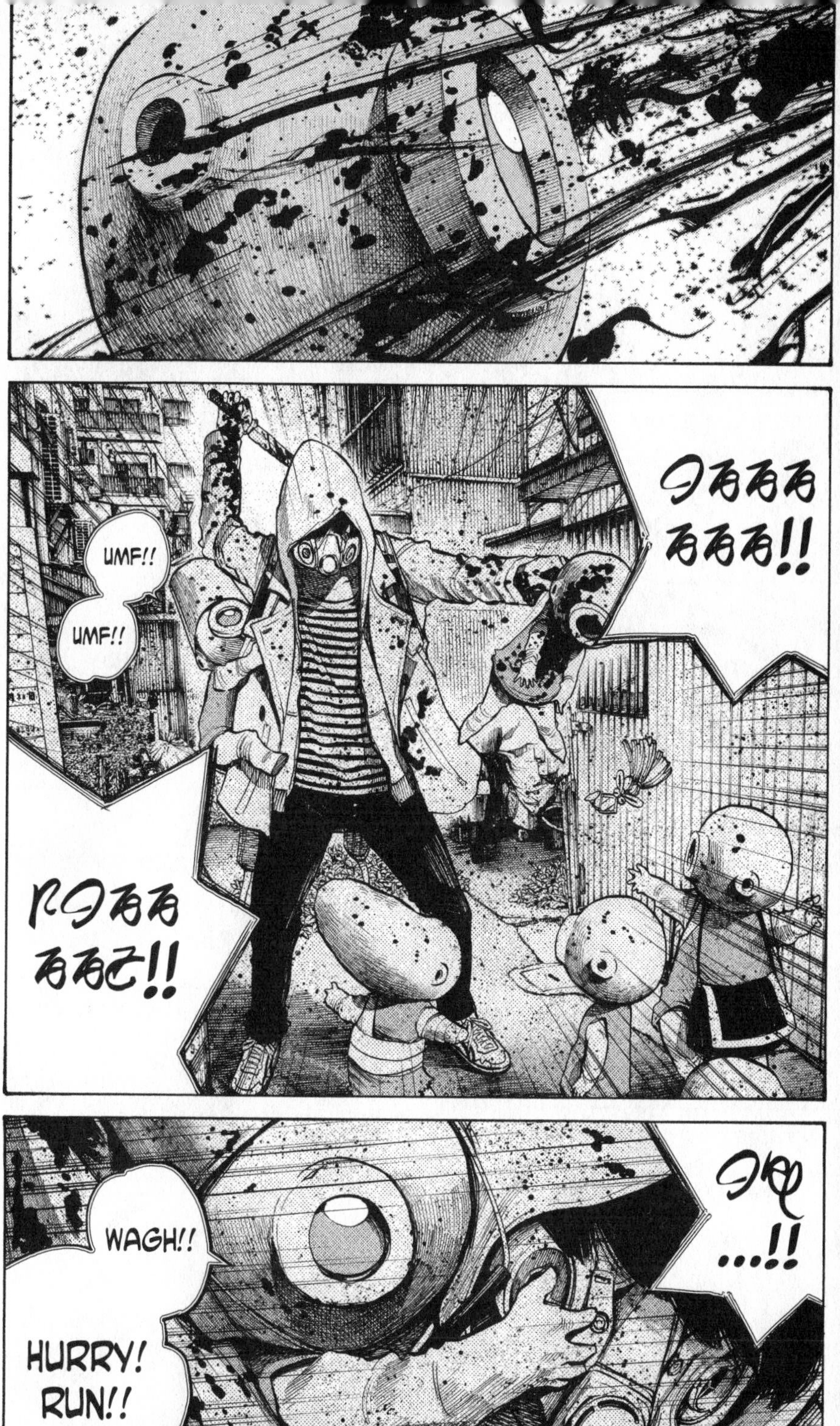
UMF!!
UMF!!
...!!
WAGH!!
HURRY! RUN!!

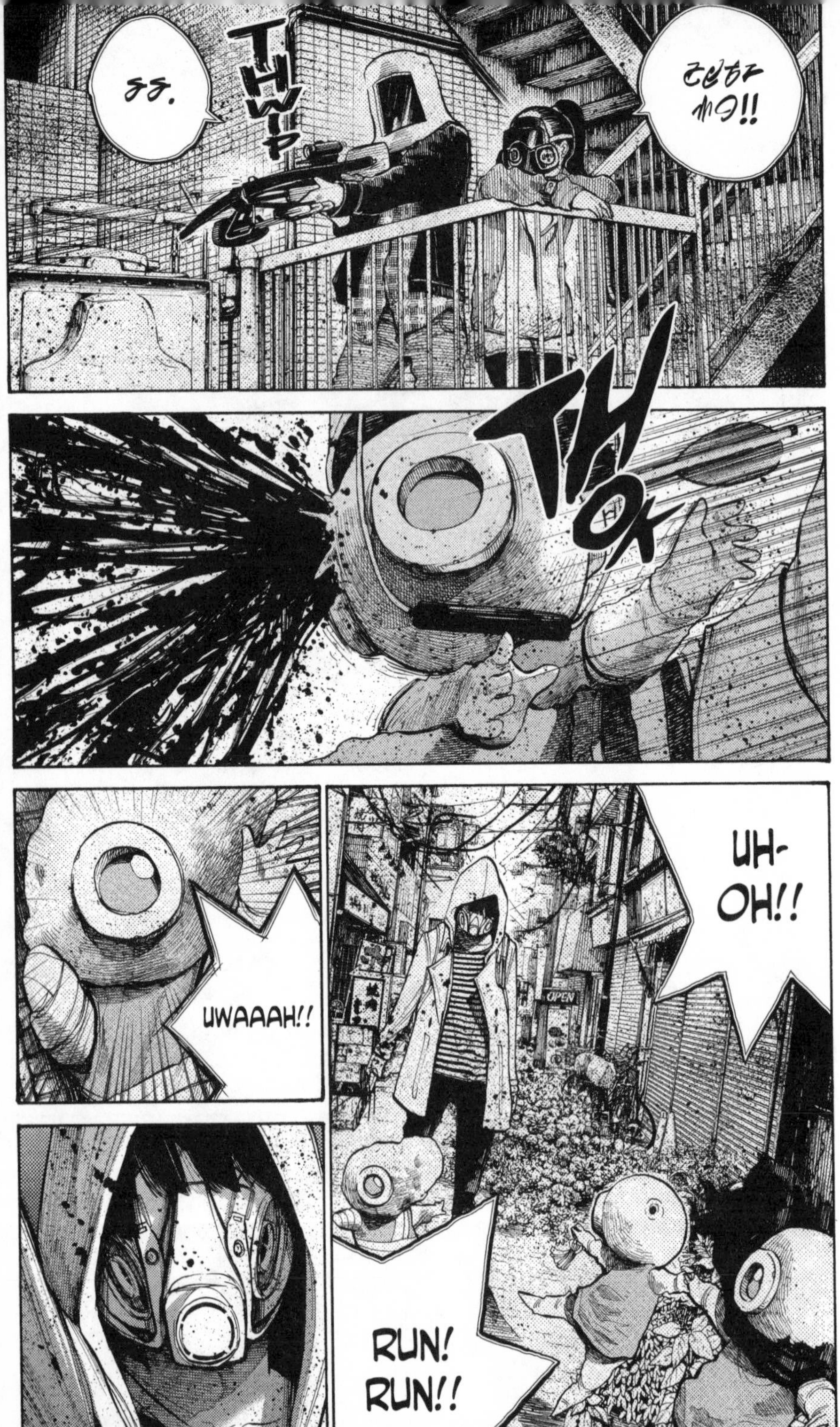
THWIP
THOK
UH-OH!!
RUN! RUN!!
UWAAAH!!

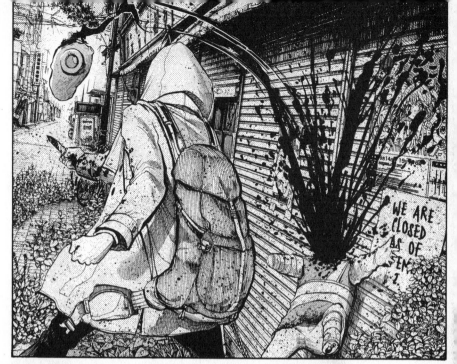

FORGET ABOUT ME! JUST GO!!

Y-YURIKO!!

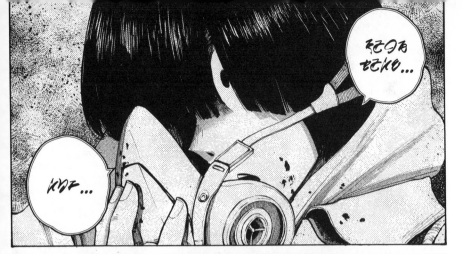

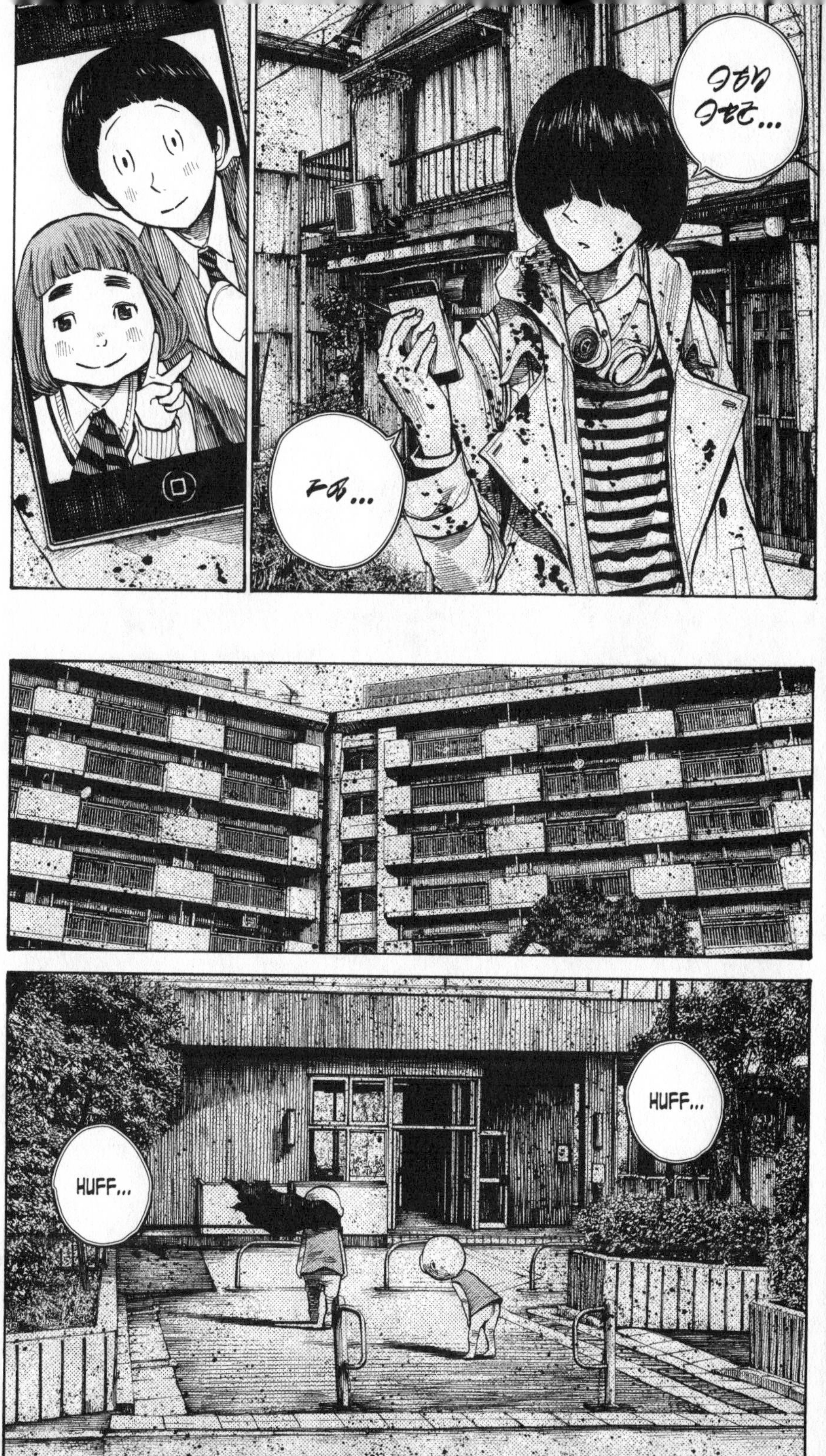
HUFF...
HUFF...

I TOLD YOU.

THE TIME MAY COME WHEN YOU WISH YOU WERE DEAD.

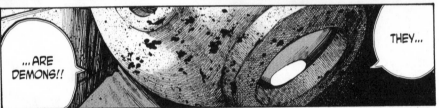

...ARE DEMONS!!

THEY...

YES...

...EARTH IS *DANGEROUS*.

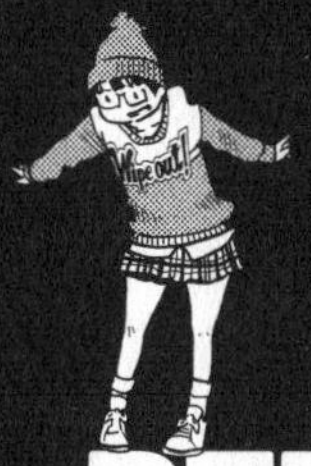

EDEDEDEDEDE DEDEDEDE

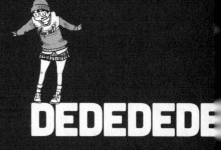

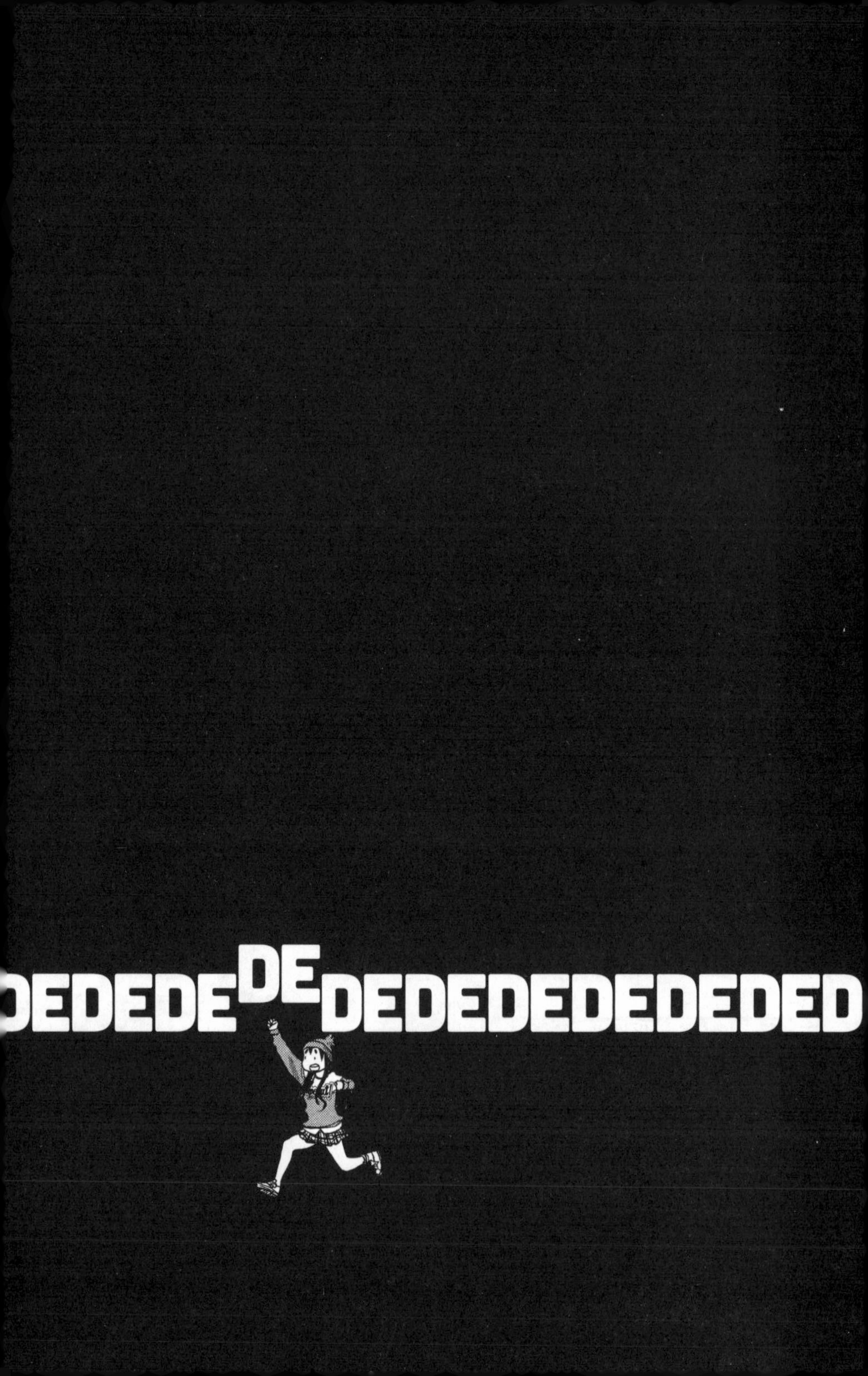

CHAPTER 32

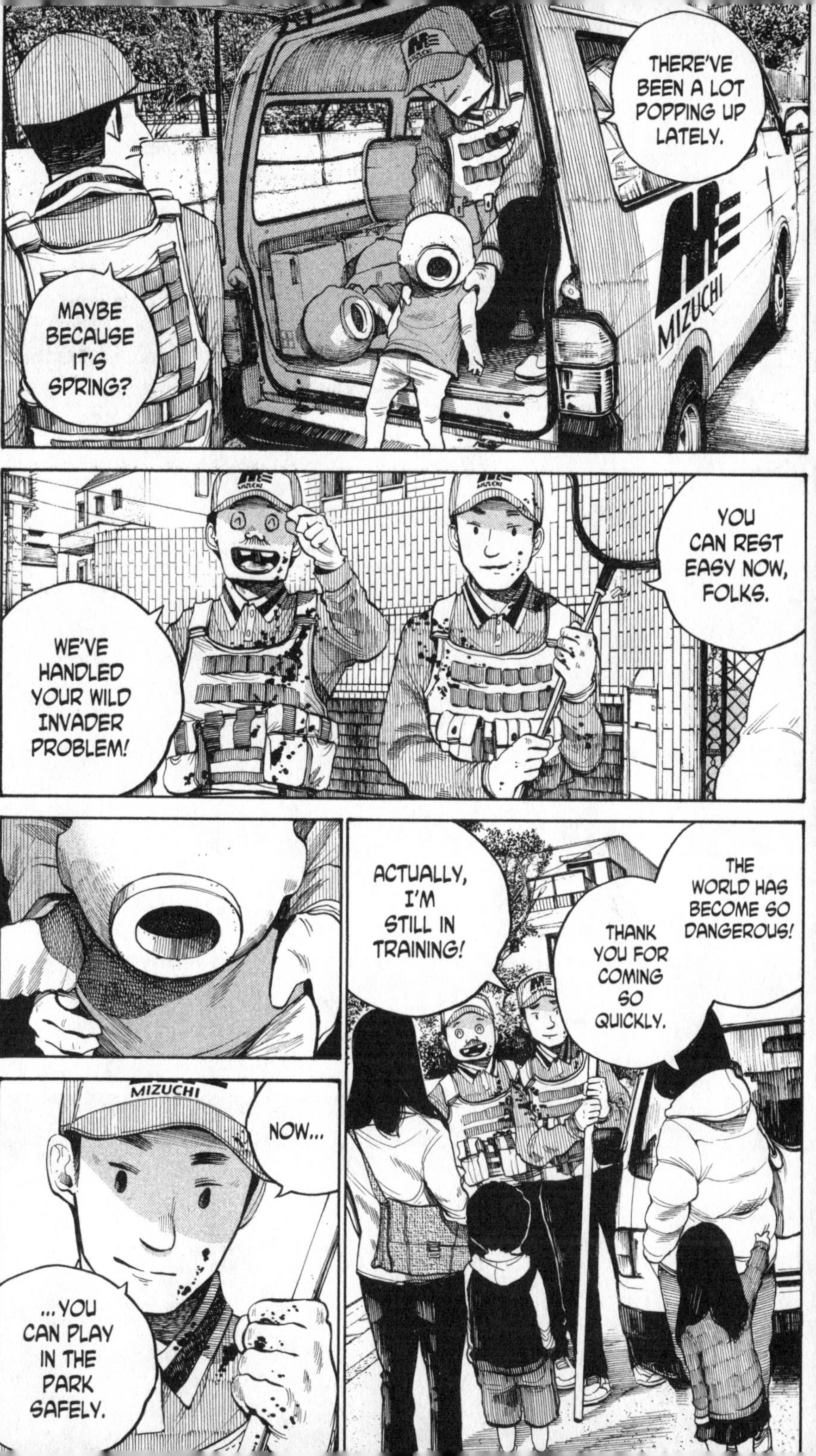
THERE'VE BEEN A LOT POPPING UP LATELY.
MIZUCHI
MAYBE BECAUSE IT'S SPRING?
YOU CAN REST EASY NOW, FOLKS.
WE'VE HANDLED YOUR WILD INVADER PROBLEM!
THE WORLD HAS BECOME SO DANGEROUS!
THANK YOU FOR COMING SO QUICKLY.
ACTUALLY, I'M STILL IN TRAINING!
MIZUCHI
NOW...
...YOU CAN PLAY IN THE PARK SAFELY.

WHEN I GROW UP...

...I WANNA BE LIKE YOU GUYS!

I'M GONNA FIGHT INVADERS AND SAVE PEOPLE!!

HA HA!

YOU'LL BE MORE DEPENDABLE THAN MOJIYA HERE!

MIZUCHI

AW, CUT ME SOME SLACK...

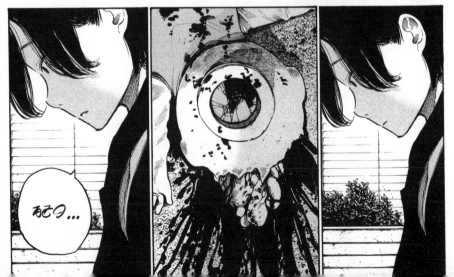

あむ つ...

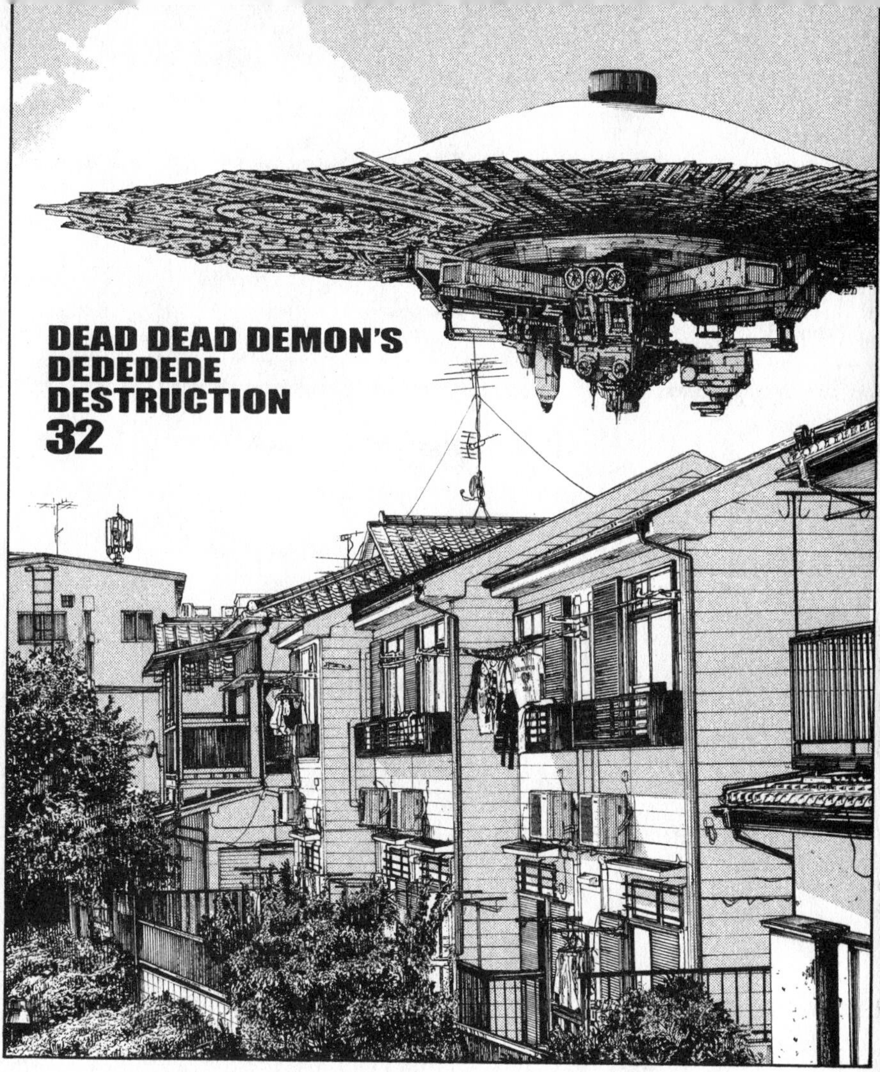
DEAD DEAD DEMON'S
DEDEDEDE
DESTRUCTION
32

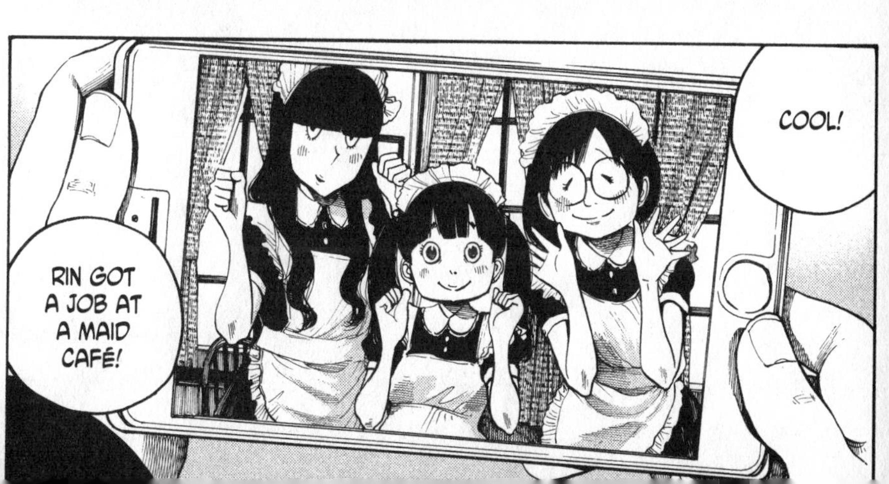
COOL!
RIN GOT A JOB AT A MAID CAFÉ!

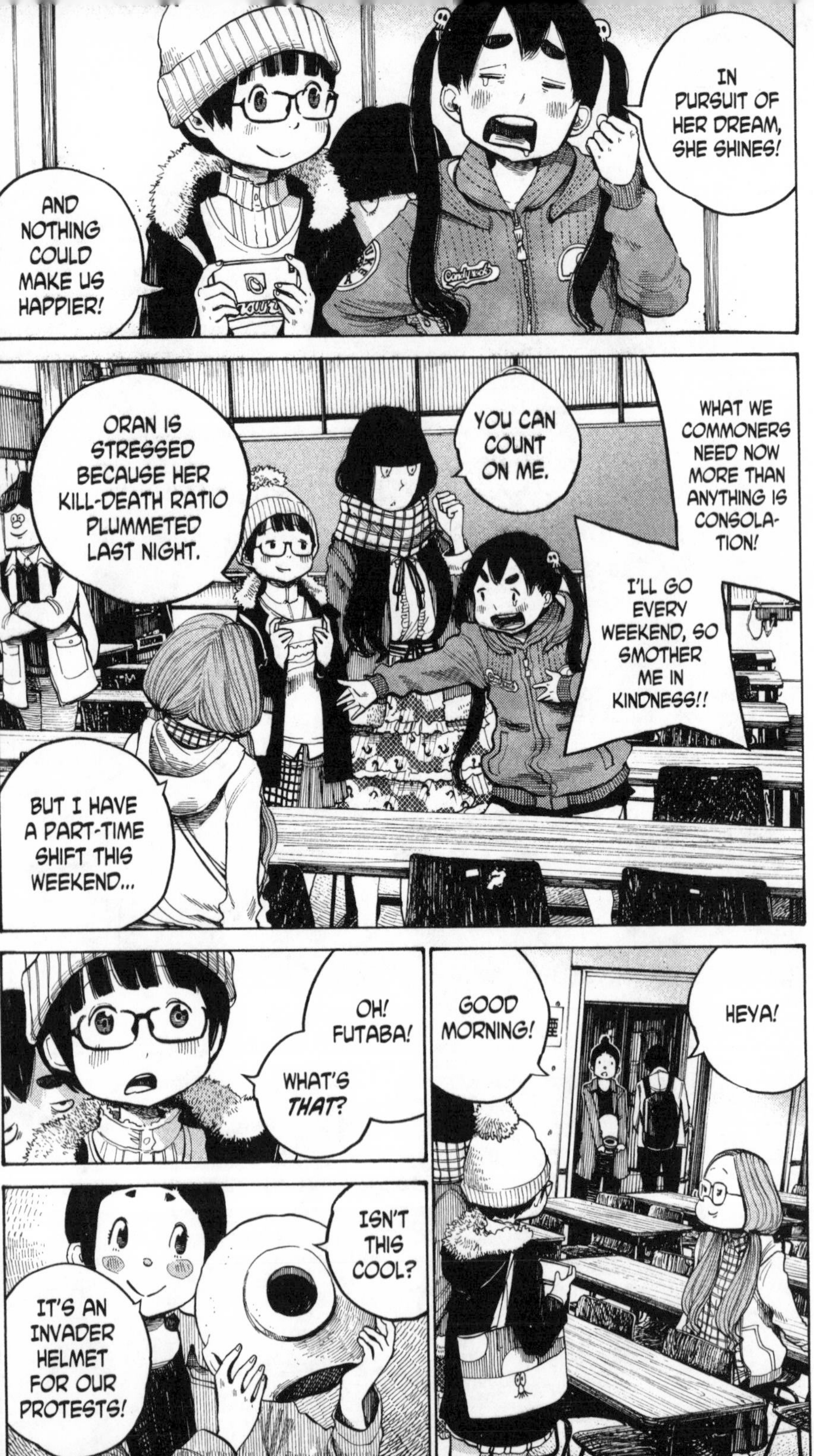
IN PURSUIT OF HER DREAM, SHE SHINES!
AND NOTHING COULD MAKE US HAPPIER!
WHAT WE COMMONERS NEED NOW MORE THAN ANYTHING IS CONSOLATION!
I'LL GO EVERY WEEKEND, SO SMOTHER ME IN KINDNESS!!
YOU CAN COUNT ON ME.
ORAN IS STRESSED BECAUSE HER KILL-DEATH RATIO PLUMMETED LAST NIGHT.
BUT I HAVE A PART-TIME SHIFT THIS WEEKEND...
HEYA!
GOOD MORNING!
OH! FUTABA!
WHAT'S *THAT*?
ISN'T THIS COOL?
IT'S AN INVADER HELMET FOR OUR PROTESTS!

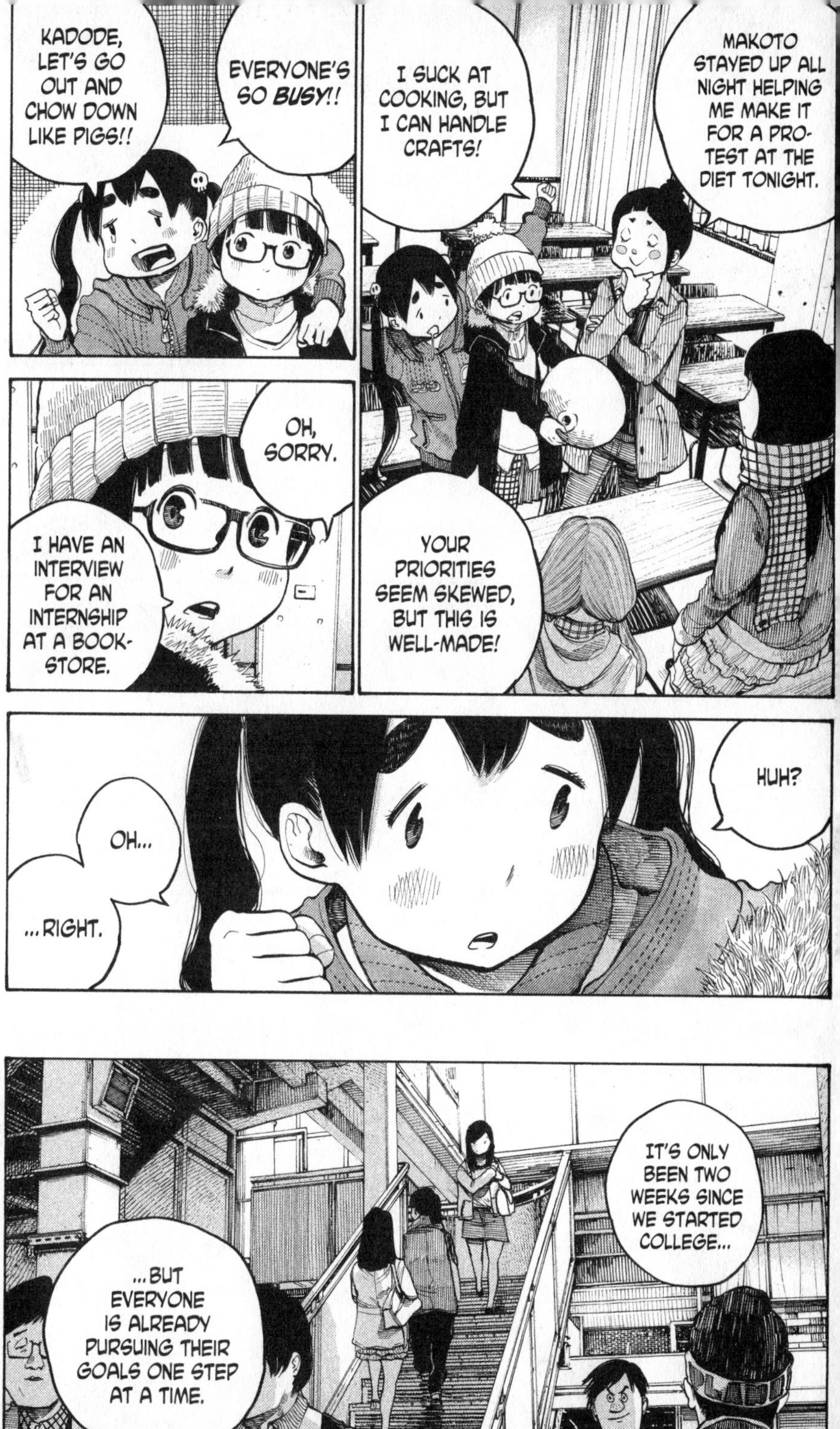
MAKOTO STAYED UP ALL NIGHT HELPING ME MAKE IT FOR A PRO-TEST AT THE DIET TONIGHT.
I SUCK AT COOKING, BUT I CAN HANDLE CRAFTS!
YOUR PRIORITIES SEEM SKEWED, BUT THIS IS WELL-MADE!
EVERYONE'S SO *BUSY*!!
KADODE, LET'S GO OUT AND CHOW DOWN LIKE PIGS!!
OH, SORRY.
I HAVE AN INTERVIEW FOR AN INTERNSHIP AT A BOOK-STORE.
HUH?
OH...
...RIGHT.
IT'S ONLY BEEN TWO WEEKS SINCE WE STARTED COLLEGE...
...BUT EVERYONE IS ALREADY PURSUING THEIR GOALS ONE STEP AT A TIME.

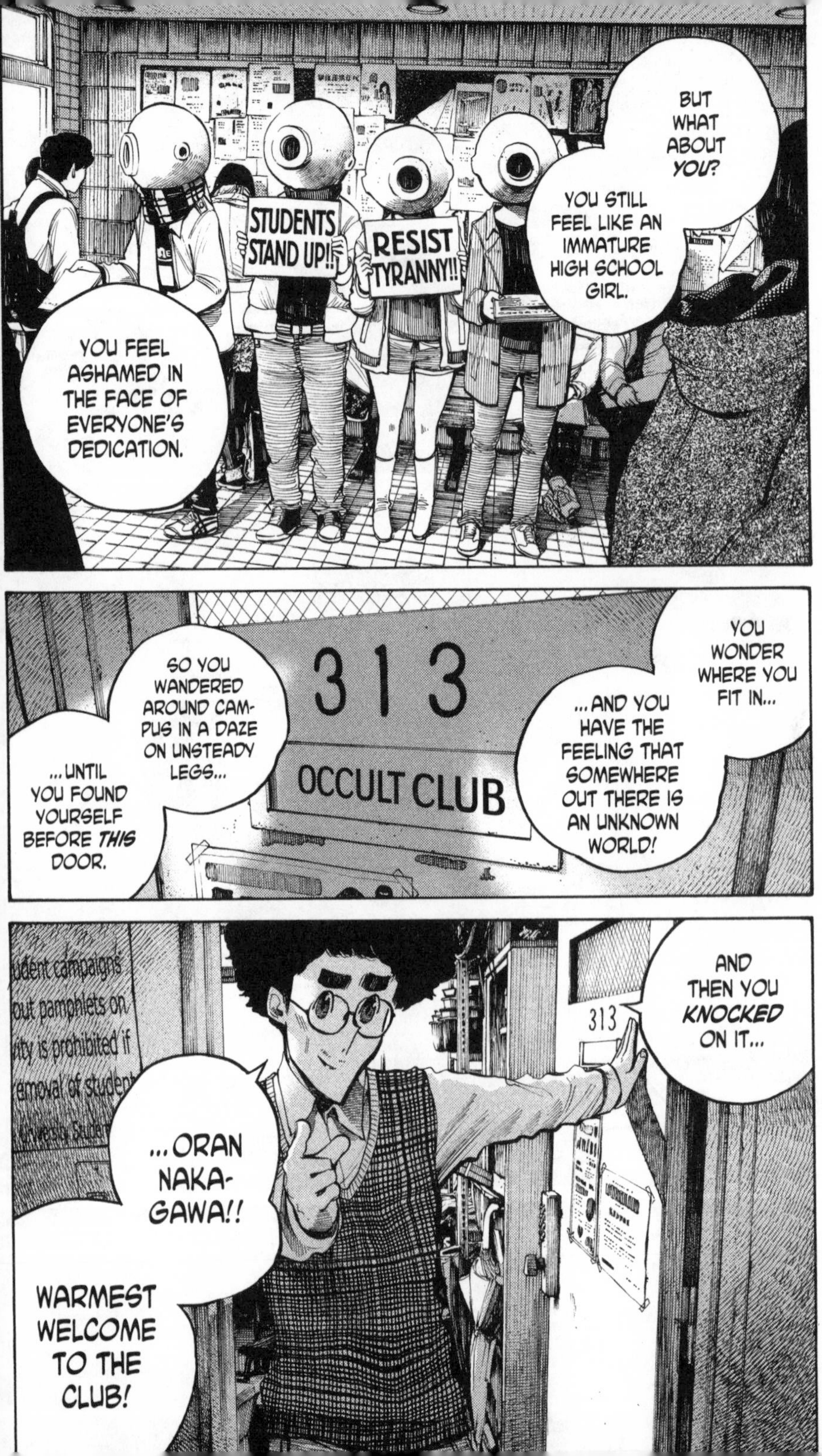
BUT WHAT ABOUT *YOU?*
YOU STILL FEEL LIKE AN IMMATURE HIGH SCHOOL GIRL.
RESIST TYRANNY!!
STUDENTS STAND UP!!
YOU FEEL ASHAMED IN THE FACE OF EVERYONE'S DEDICATION.
YOU WONDER WHERE YOU FIT IN...
...AND YOU HAVE THE FEELING THAT SOMEWHERE OUT THERE IS AN UNKNOWN WORLD!
313
OCCULT CLUB
SO YOU WANDERED AROUND CAMPUS IN A DAZE ON UNSTEADY LEGS...
...UNTIL YOU FOUND YOURSELF BEFORE *THIS* DOOR.
AND THEN YOU *KNOCKED* ON IT...
313
...ORAN NAKAGAWA!!
WARMEST WELCOME TO THE CLUB!

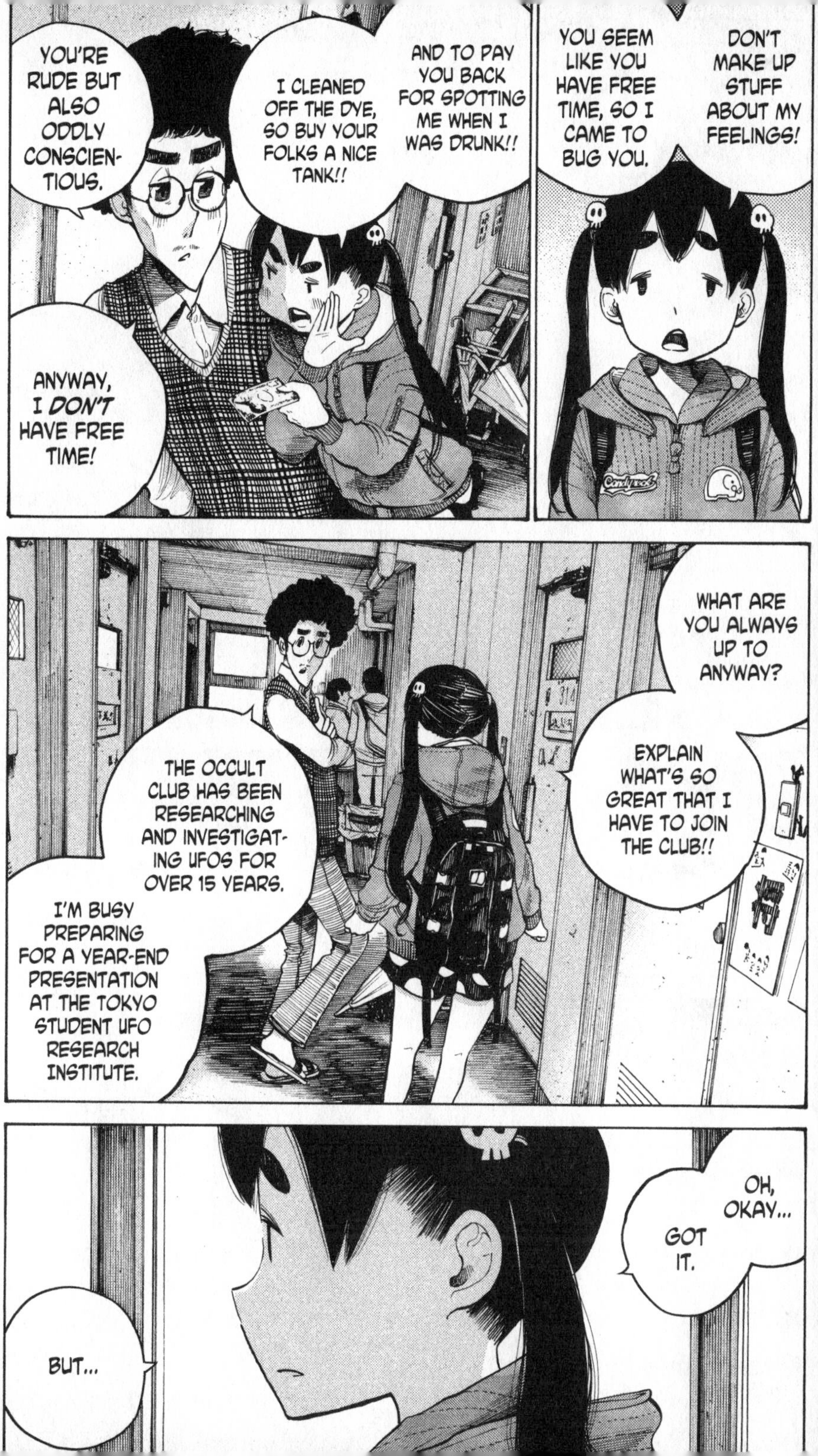
DON'T MAKE UP STUFF ABOUT MY FEELINGS!
YOU SEEM LIKE YOU HAVE FREE TIME, SO I CAME TO BUG YOU.
AND TO PAY YOU BACK FOR SPOTTING ME WHEN I WAS DRUNK!!
I CLEANED OFF THE DYE, SO BUY YOUR FOLKS A NICE TANK!!
YOU'RE RUDE BUT ALSO ODDLY CONSCIEN-TIOUS.
ANYWAY, I *DON'T* HAVE FREE TIME!
WHAT ARE YOU ALWAYS UP TO ANYWAY?
EXPLAIN WHAT'S SO GREAT THAT I HAVE TO JOIN THE CLUB!!
THE OCCULT CLUB HAS BEEN RESEARCHING AND INVESTIGAT-ING UFOS FOR OVER 15 YEARS.
I'M BUSY PREPARING FOR A YEAR-END PRESENTATION AT THE TOKYO STUDENT UFO RESEARCH INSTITUTE.
OH, OKAY...
GOT IT.
BUT...

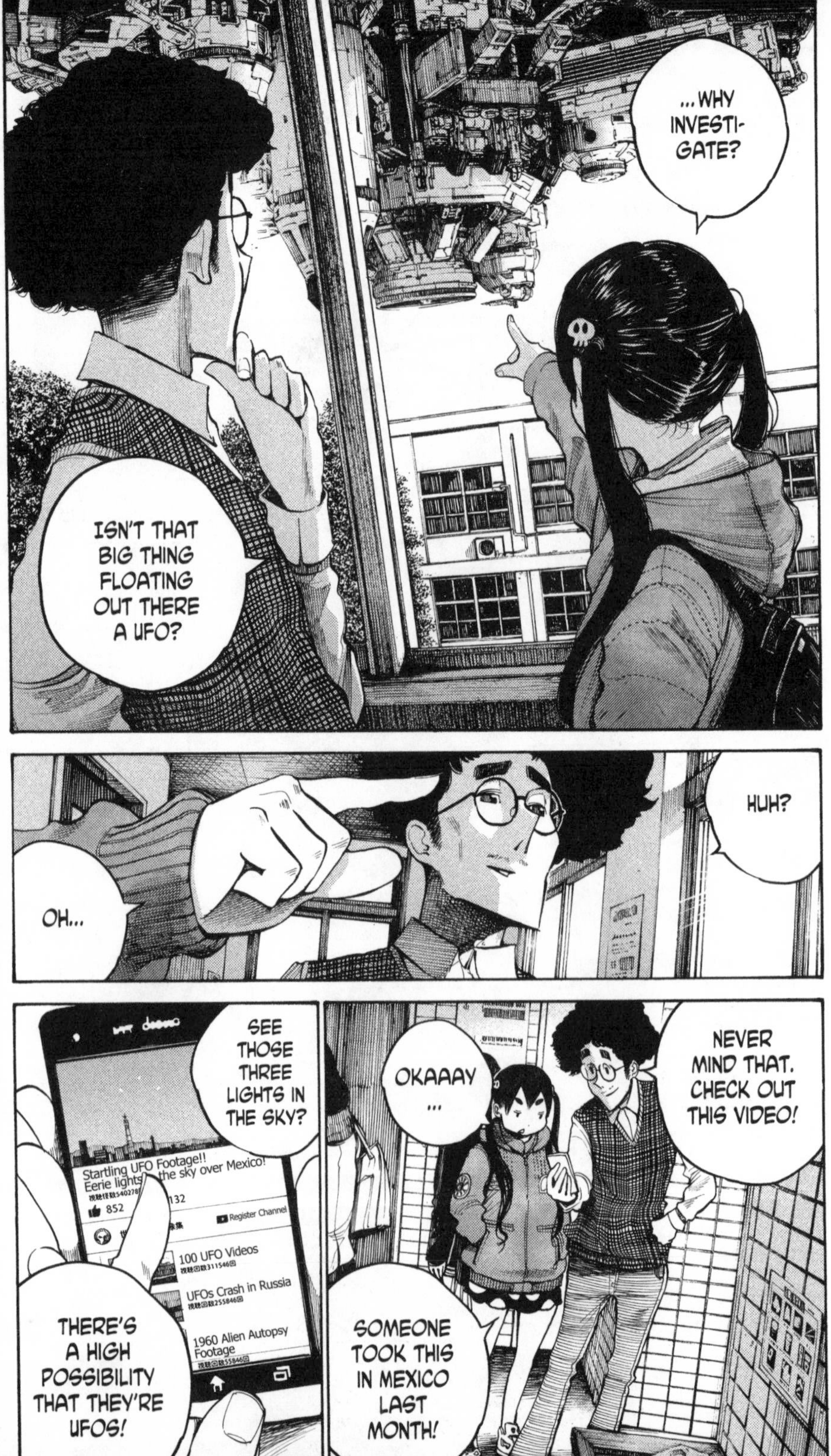
...WHY INVESTI-GATE?
ISN'T THAT BIG THING FLOATING OUT THERE A UFO?
HUH?
OH...
NEVER MIND THAT. CHECK OUT THIS VIDEO!
OKAAAY ...
SOMEONE TOOK THIS IN MEXICO LAST MONTH!
SEE THOSE THREE LIGHTS IN THE SKY?
Startling UFO Footage!!
852
Register Channel
100 UFO Videos
UFOs Crash in Russia
1960 Alien Autopsy Footage
THERE'S A HIGH POSSIBILITY THAT THEY'RE UFOS!

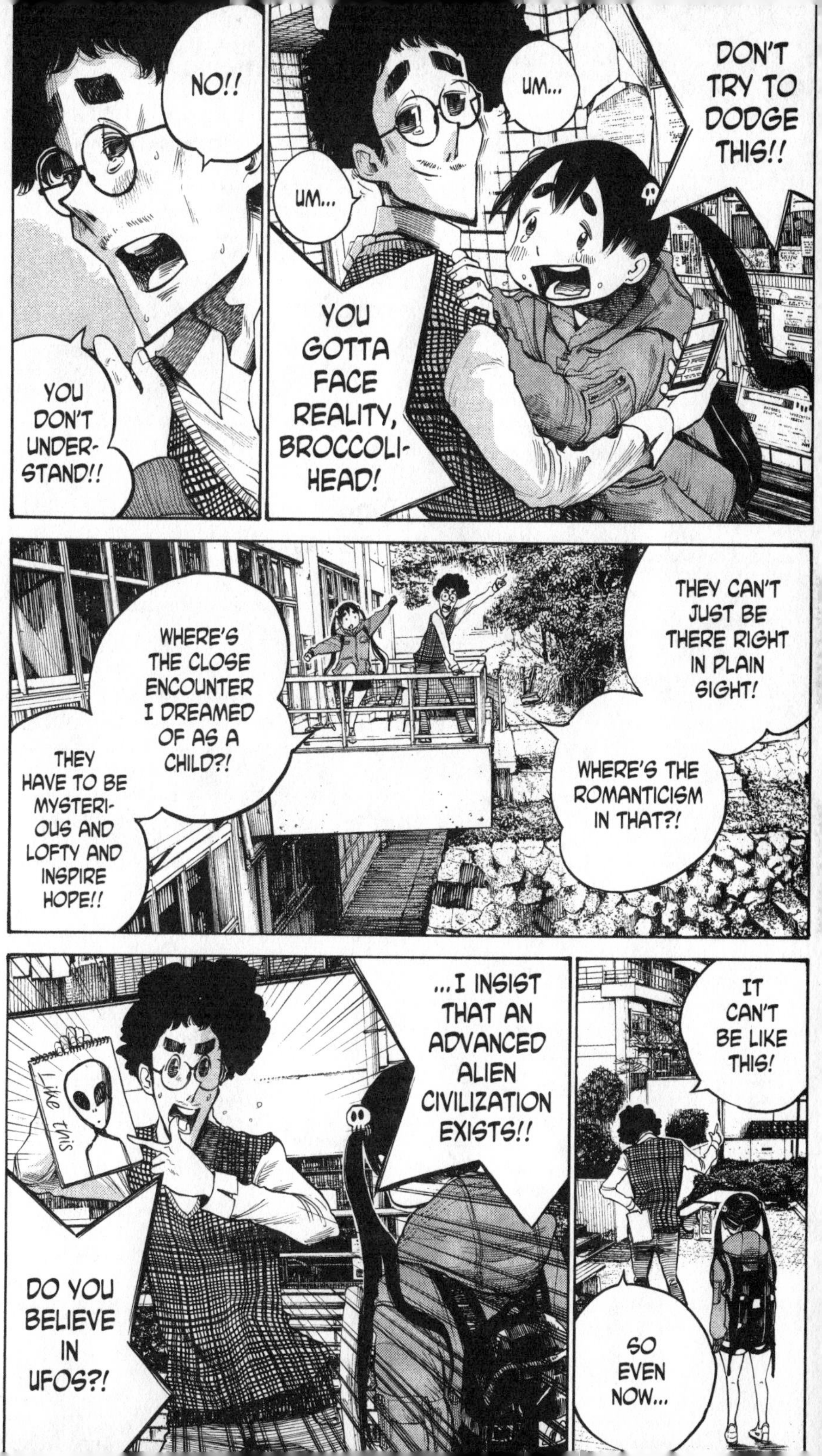
DON'T TRY TO DODGE THIS!!
UM...
UM...
YOU GOTTA FACE REALITY, BROCCOLI-HEAD!
NO!!
YOU DON'T UNDER-STAND!!
THEY CAN'T JUST BE THERE RIGHT IN PLAIN SIGHT!
WHERE'S THE ROMANTICISM IN THAT?!
WHERE'S THE CLOSE ENCOUNTER I DREAMED OF AS A CHILD?!
THEY HAVE TO BE MYSTERI-OUS AND LOFTY AND INSPIRE HOPE!!
IT CAN'T BE LIKE THIS!
SO EVEN NOW...
...I INSIST THAT AN ADVANCED ALIEN CIVILIZATION EXISTS!!
Like this
DO YOU BELIEVE IN UFOS?!

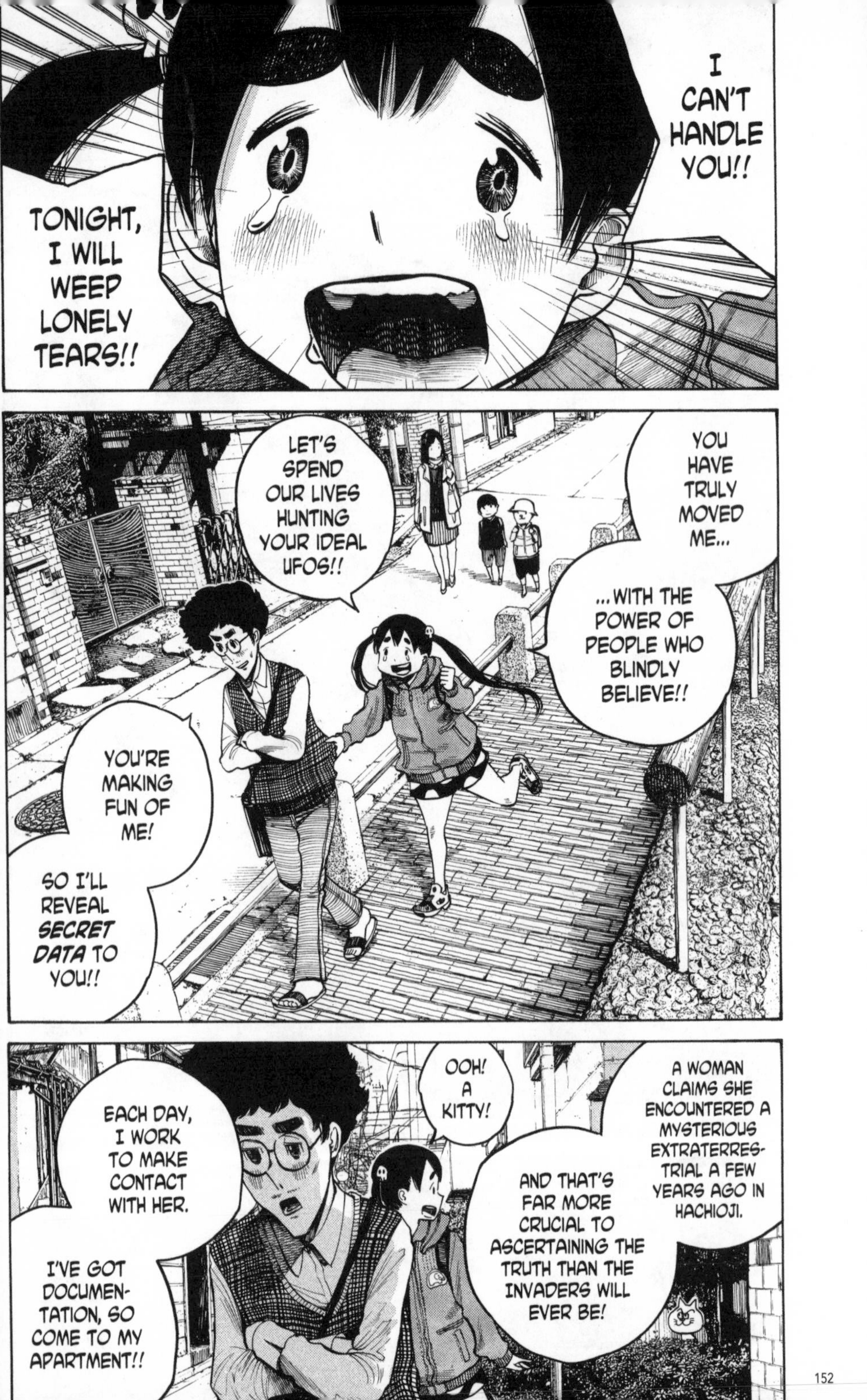
I CAN'T HANDLE YOU!!
TONIGHT, I WILL WEEP LONELY TEARS!!
YOU HAVE TRULY MOVED ME...
...WITH THE POWER OF PEOPLE WHO BLINDLY BELIEVE!!
LET'S SPEND OUR LIVES HUNTING YOUR IDEAL UFOS!!
YOU'RE MAKING FUN OF ME!
SO I'LL REVEAL *SECRET DATA* TO YOU!!
A WOMAN CLAIMS SHE ENCOUNTERED A MYSTERIOUS EXTRATERRES-TRIAL A FEW YEARS AGO IN HACHIOJI.
OOH! A KITTY!
AND THAT'S FAR MORE CRUCIAL TO ASCERTAINING THE TRUTH THAN THE INVADERS WILL EVER BE!
EACH DAY, I WORK TO MAKE CONTACT WITH HER.
I'VE GOT DOCUMEN-TATION, SO COME TO MY APARTMENT!!

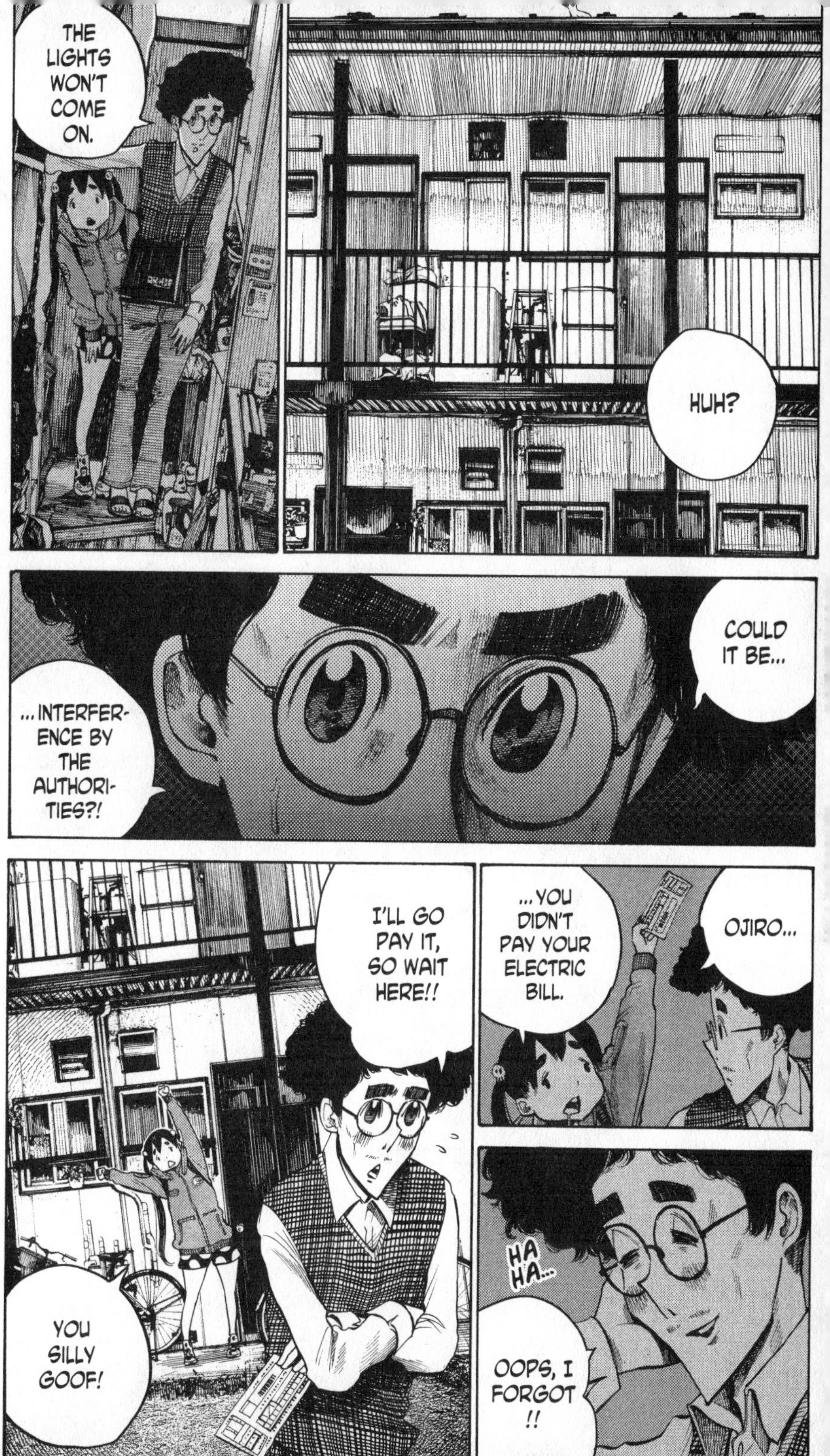
HUH?
THE LIGHTS WON'T COME ON.
COULD IT BE...
...INTERFERENCE BY THE AUTHORITIES?!
OJIRO...
...YOU DIDN'T PAY YOUR ELECTRIC BILL.
HA HA...
OOPS, I FORGOT!!
I'LL GO PAY IT, SO WAIT HERE!!
YOU SILLY GOOF!

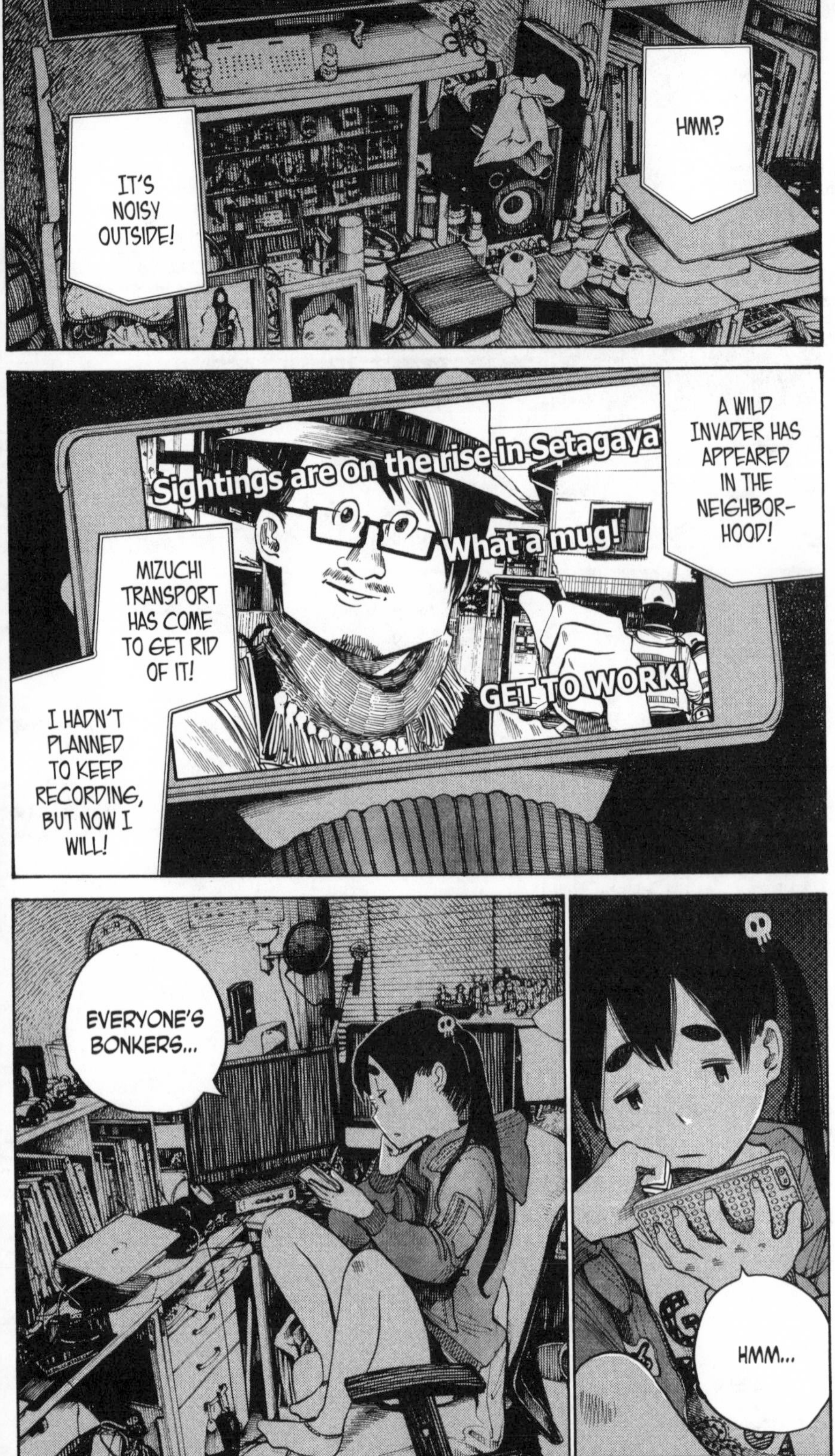
HMM?
IT'S NOISY OUTSIDE!
A WILD INVADER HAS APPEARED IN THE NEIGHBOR-HOOD!
Sightings are on the rise in Setagaya
What a mug!
GET TO WORK!
MIZUCHI TRANSPORT HAS COME TO GET RID OF IT!
I HADN'T PLANNED TO KEEP RECORDING, BUT NOW I WILL!
HMM...
EVERYONE'S BONKERS...

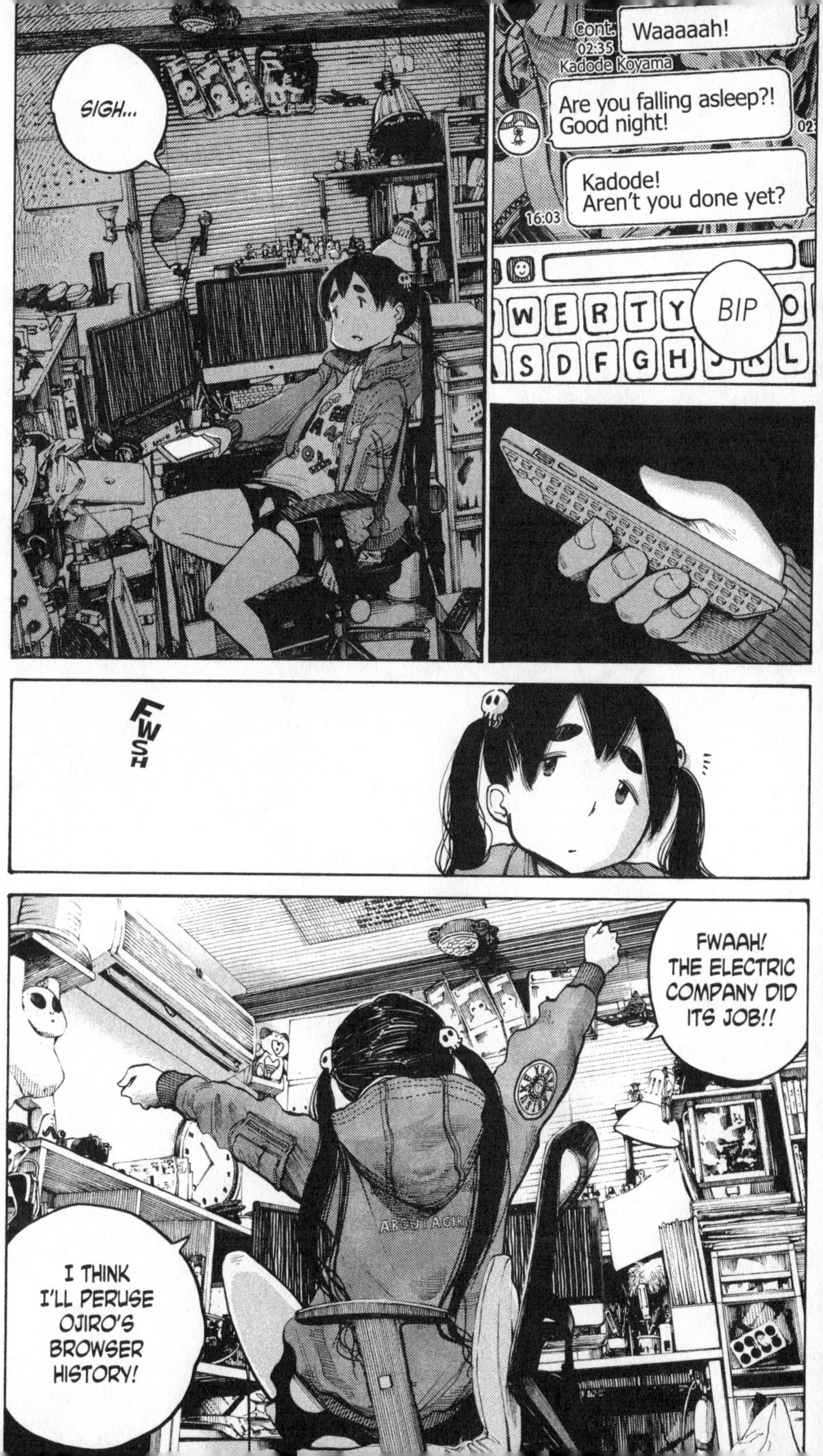
Cont. 02:35
Waaaaah!
Kadode Koyama
Are you falling asleep?! Good night!
Kadode! Aren't you done yet?
16:03
BIP
SIGH...
FWSH
FWAAH! THE ELECTRIC COMPANY DID ITS JOB!!
I THINK I'LL PERUSE OJIRO'S BROWSER HISTORY!

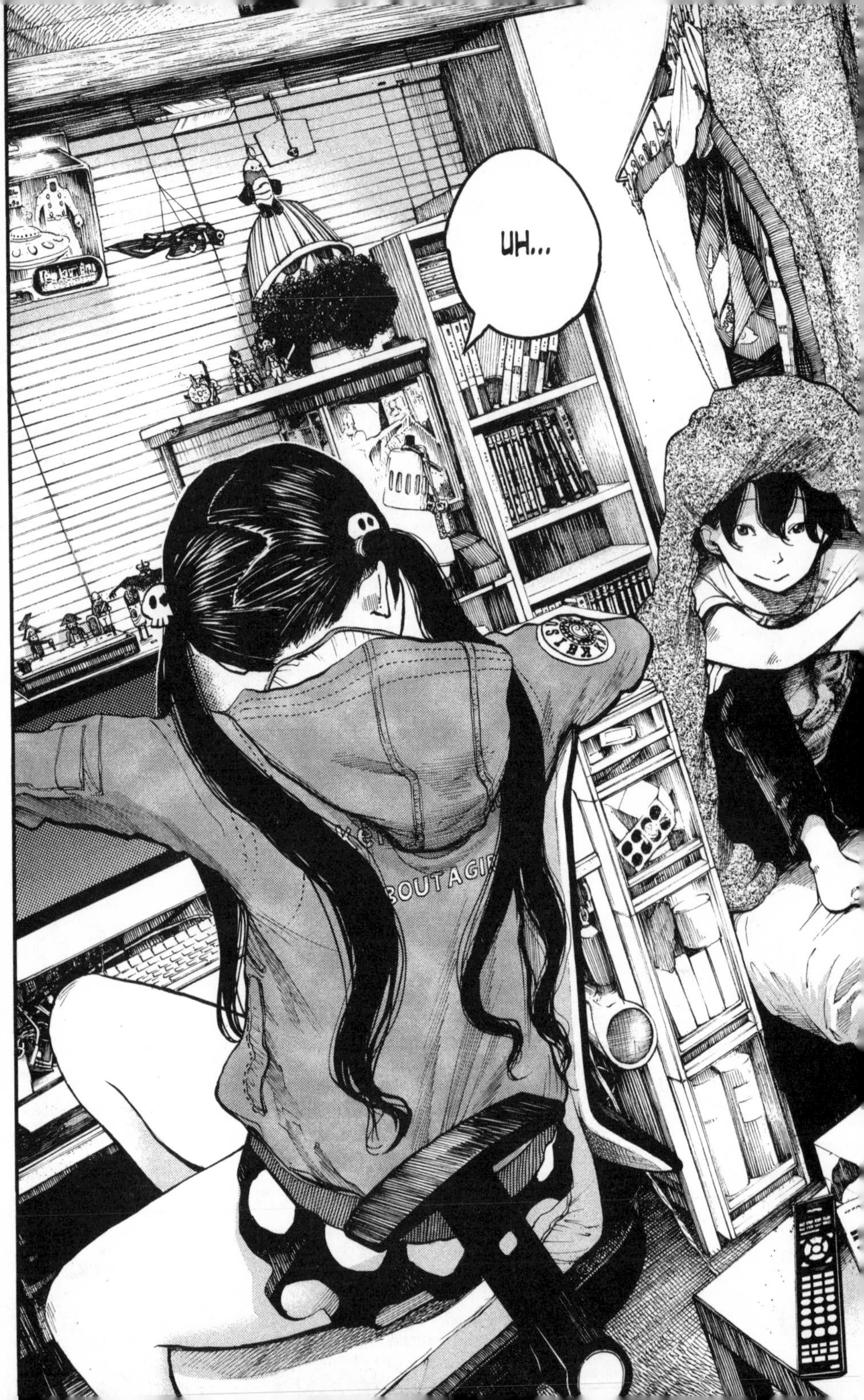
UH...

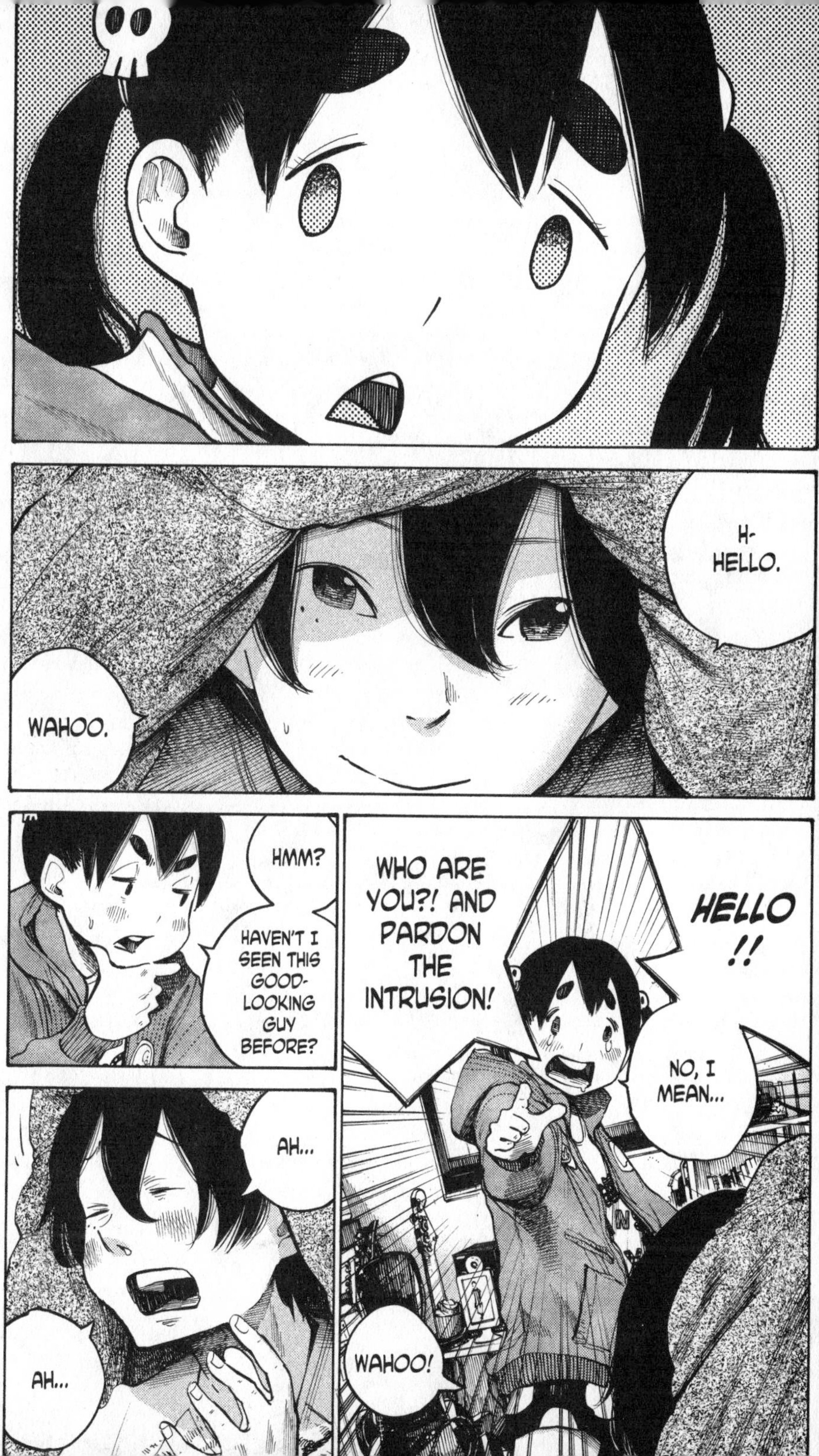
H- HELLO.
WAHOO.
HELLO!!
NO, I MEAN...
WHO ARE YOU?! AND PARDON THE INTRUSION!
WAHOO!
HMM?
HAVEN'T I SEEN THIS GOOD-LOOKING GUY BEFORE?
AH...
AH...

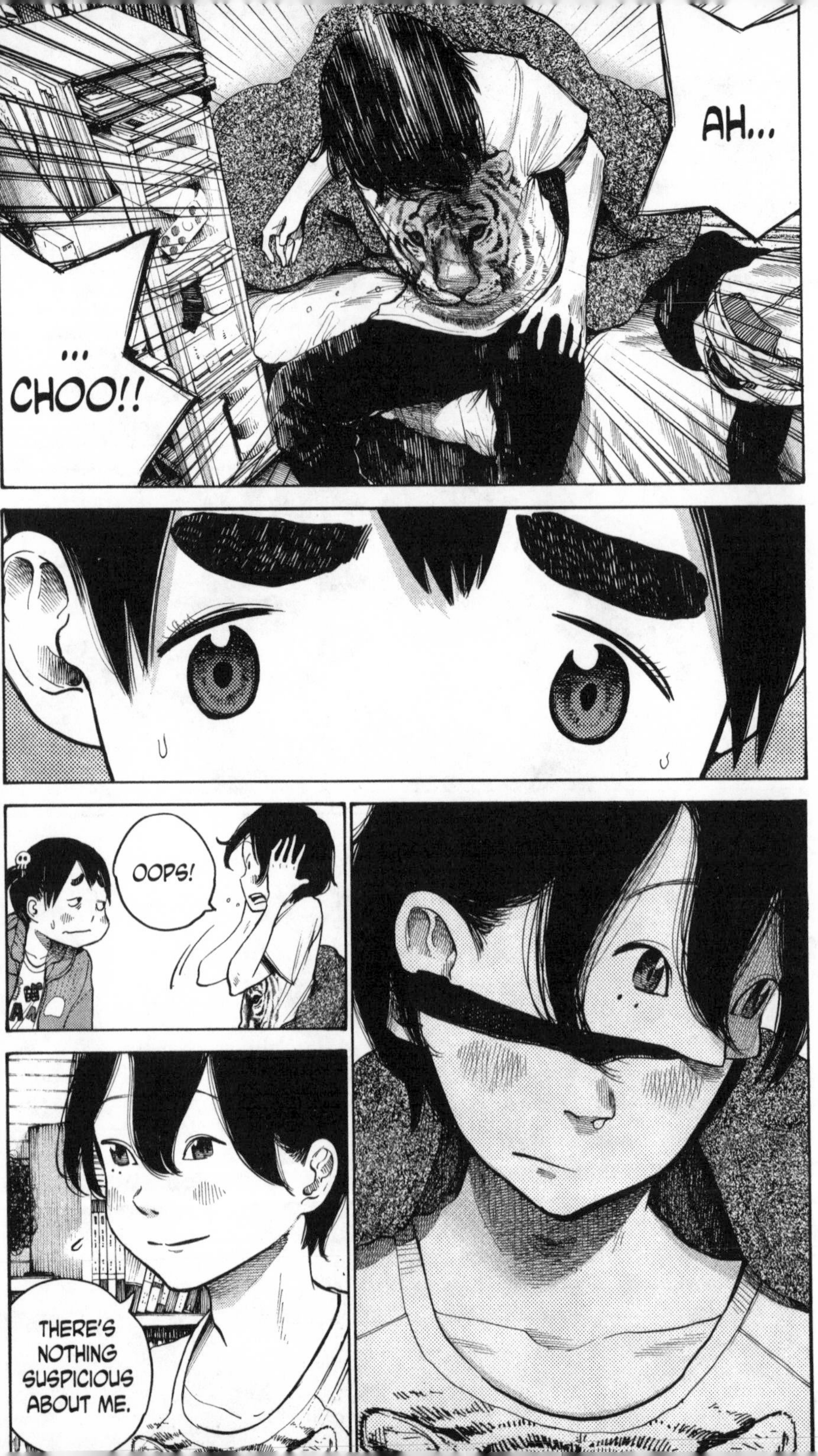
AH...
...CHOO!!
OOPS!
THERE'S NOTHING SUSPICIOUS ABOUT ME.

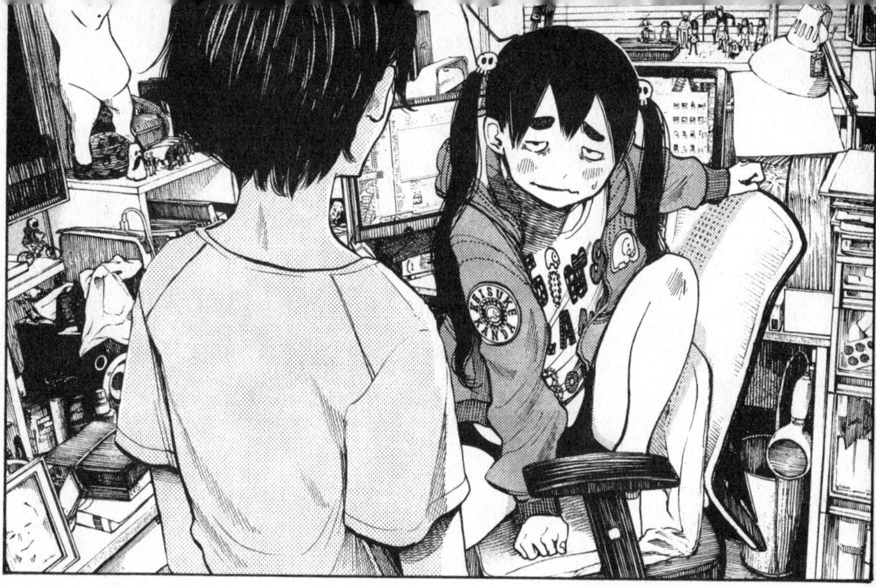
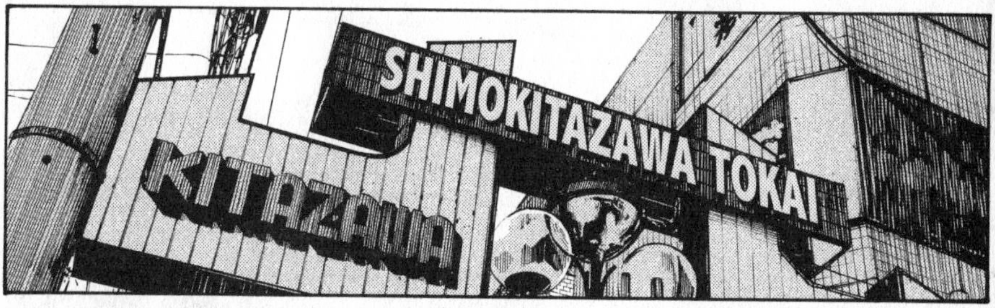
SHIMOKITAZAWA TOKAI
KITAZAWA
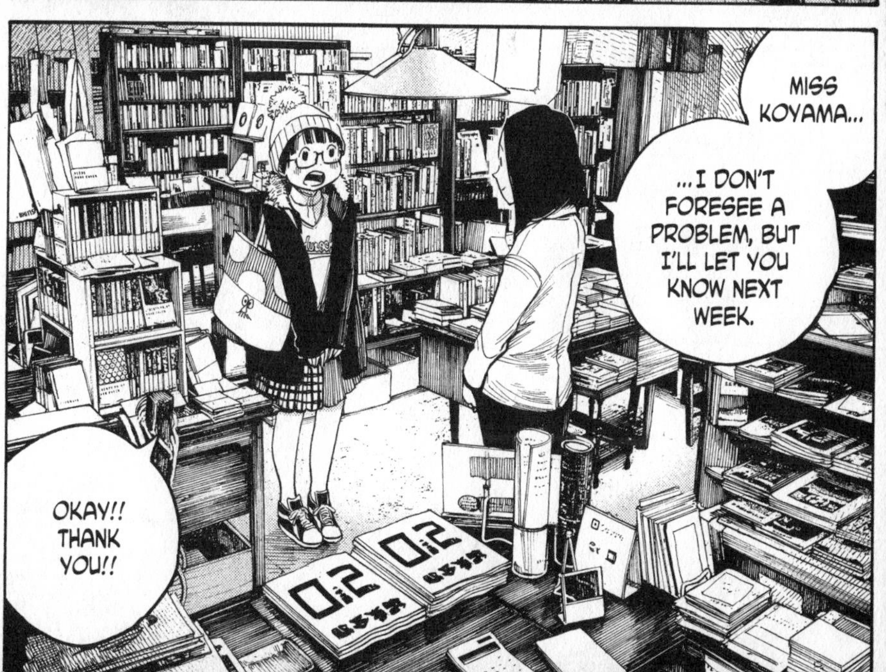
MISS KOYAMA...
...I DON'T FORESEE A PROBLEM, BUT I'LL LET YOU KNOW NEXT WEEK.
OKAY!! THANK YOU!!

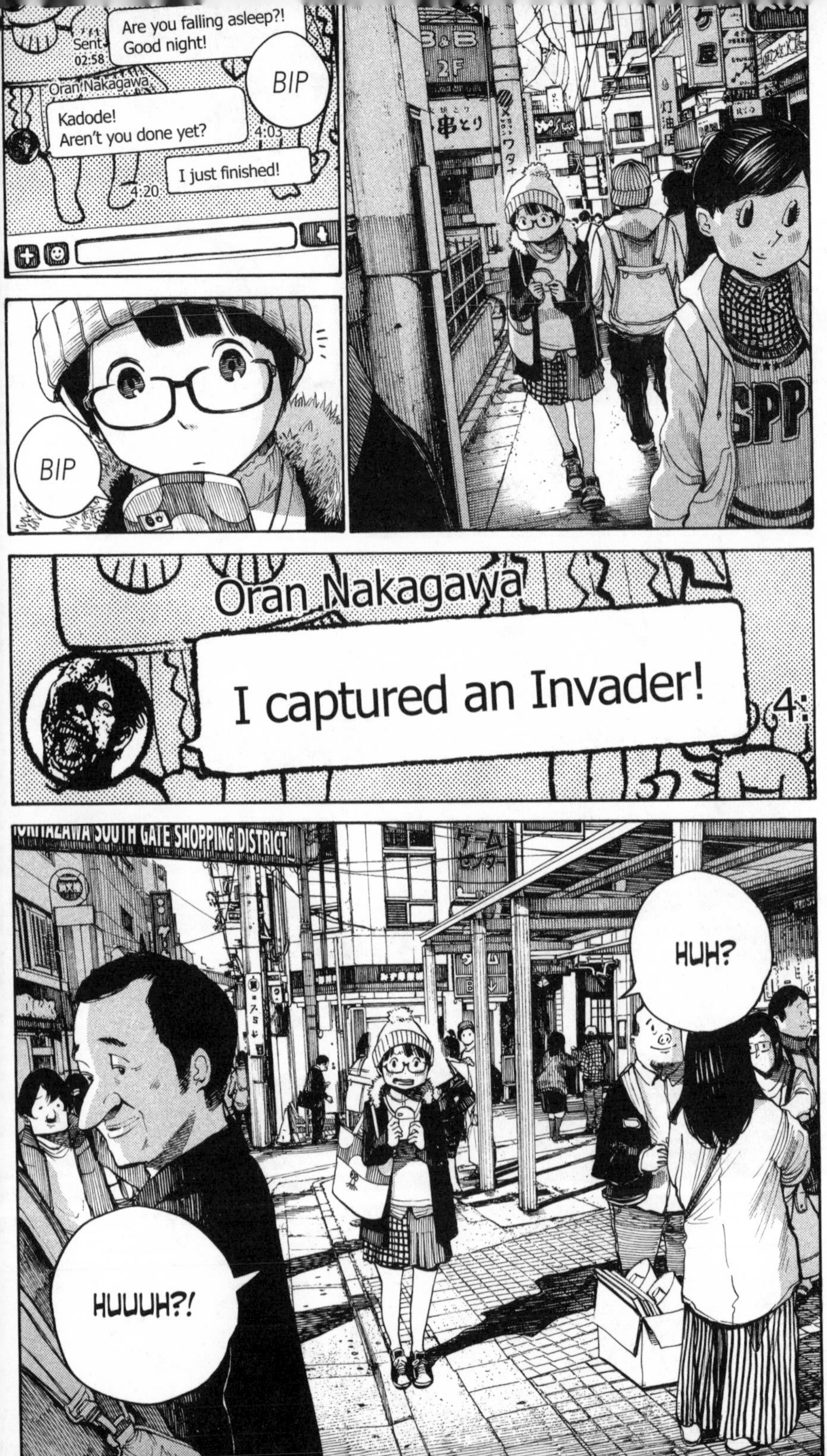
B&B
2F
Sent
02:58
Are you falling asleep?!
Good night!
BIP
Oran Nakagawa
Kadode!
Aren't you done yet?
4:03
I just finished!
4:20
BIP
Oran Nakagawa
I captured an Invader!
4:
SOUTH GATE SHOPPING DISTRICT
HUH?
HUUUH?!

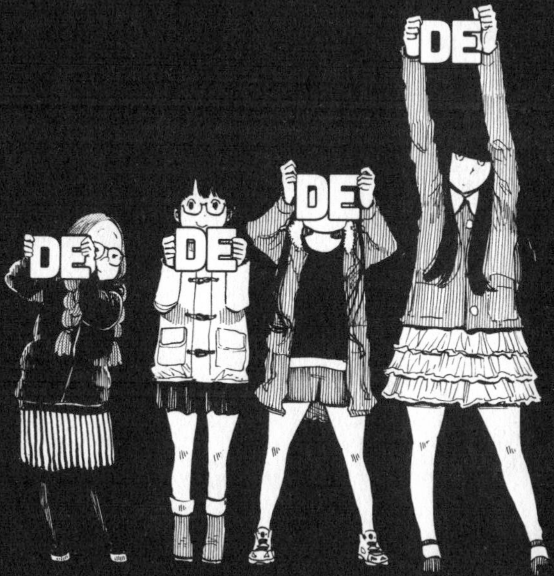
DE
DE
DE
DE

Dead Dead Demon's
Dededede Destruction Volume 4
Inio Asano

Background Assistants: Satsuki Sato
Ran Atsumori
Buuko

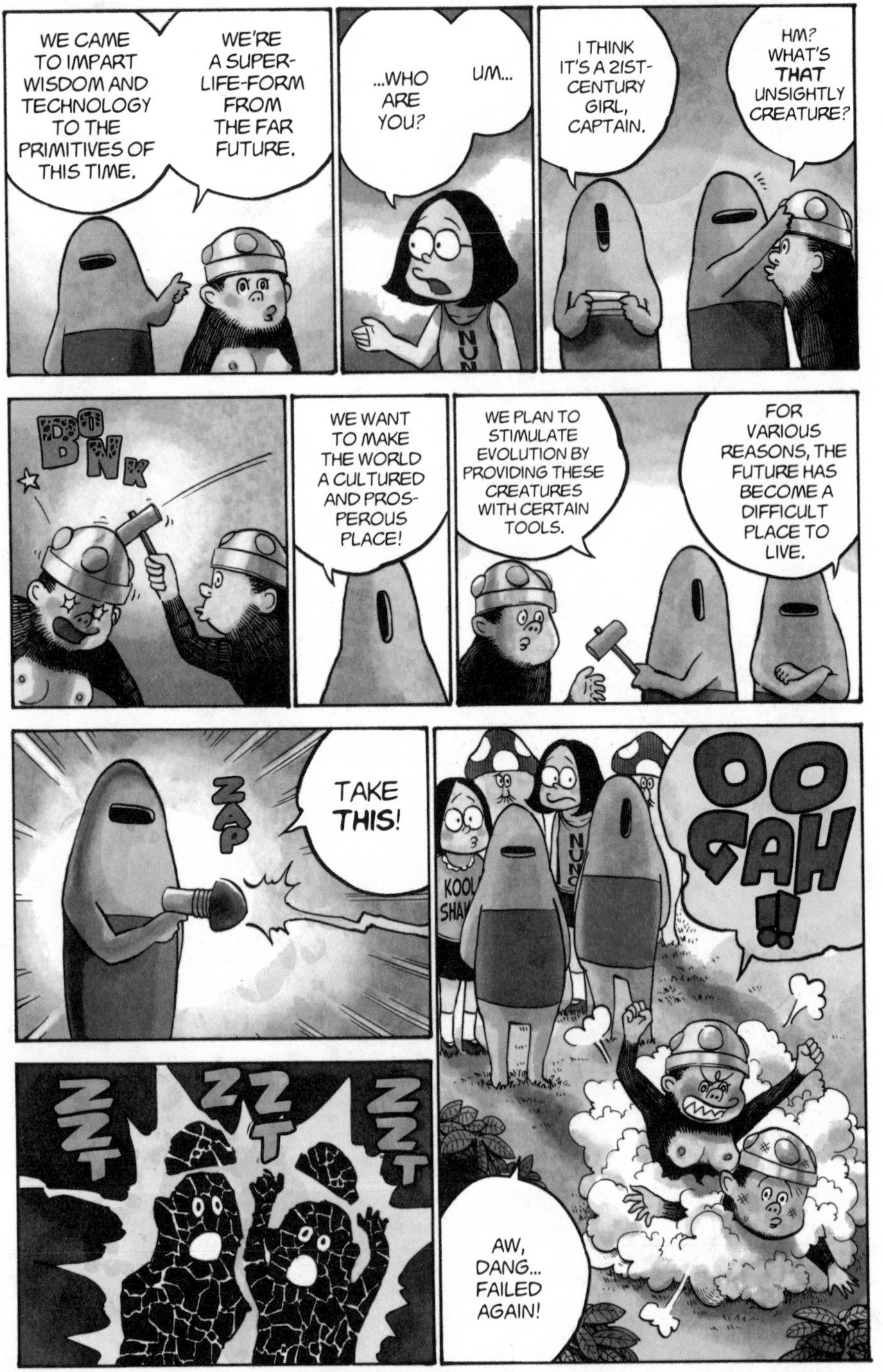
HM? WHAT'S **THAT** UNSIGHTLY CREATURE?
I THINK IT'S A 21ST-CENTURY GIRL, CAPTAIN.
UM...
...WHO ARE YOU?
WE'RE A SUPER-LIFE-FORM FROM THE FAR FUTURE.
WE CAME TO IMPART WISDOM AND TECHNOLOGY TO THE PRIMITIVES OF THIS TIME.
FOR VARIOUS REASONS, THE FUTURE HAS BECOME A DIFFICULT PLACE TO LIVE.
WE PLAN TO STIMULATE EVOLUTION BY PROVIDING THESE CREATURES WITH CERTAIN TOOLS.
WE WANT TO MAKE THE WORLD A CULTURED AND PROS-PEROUS PLACE!
BONK
OOGAH!!
AW, DANG... FAILED AGAIN!
TAKE **THIS**!
ZAP
ZZZT
ZZZT
ZZZT

☆ Volume 5 goes on sale April 2019! Keep your eyes peeled!

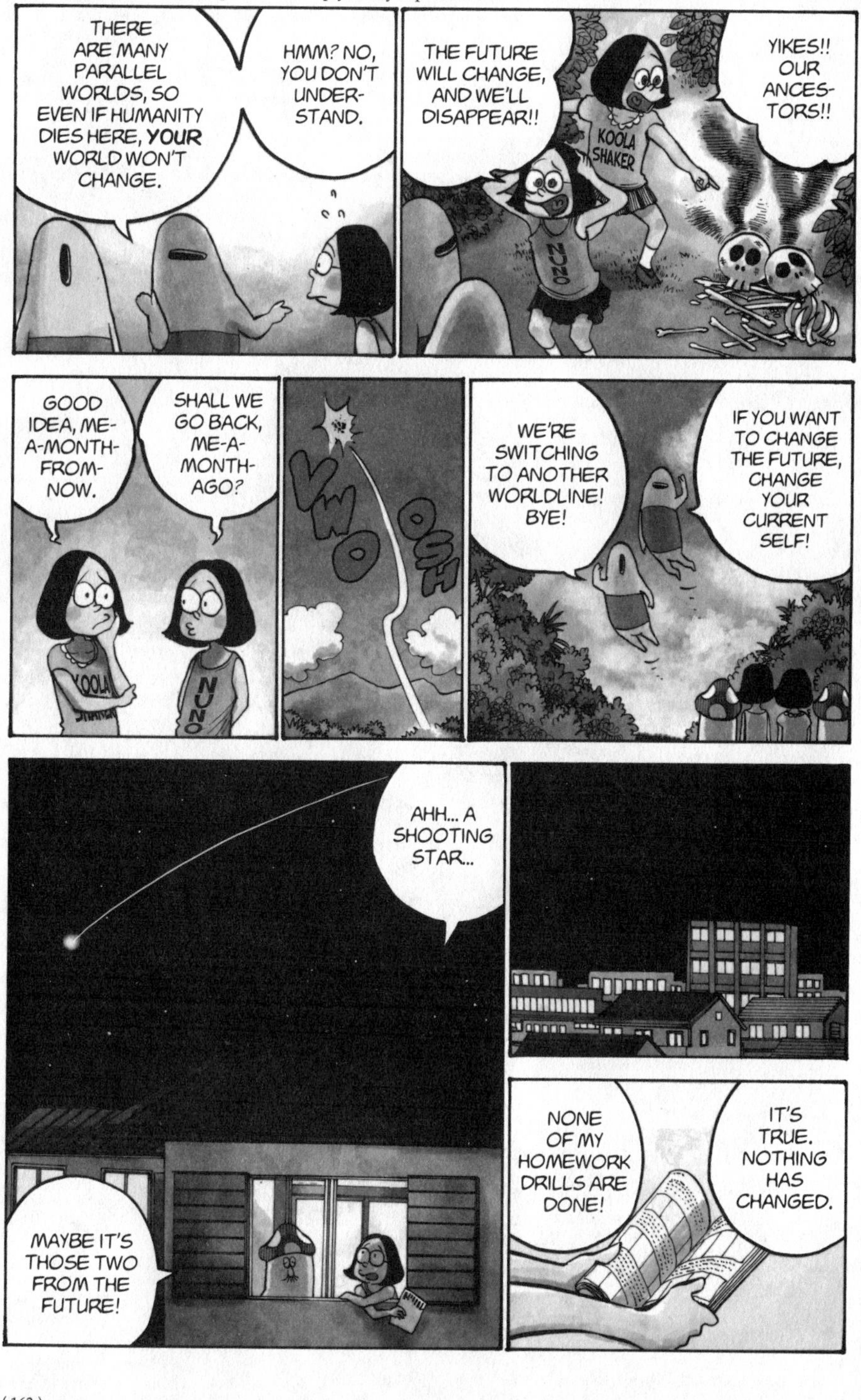
YIKES!! OUR ANCES-TORS!!
THE FUTURE WILL CHANGE, AND WE'LL DISAPPEAR!!
KOOLA SHAKER
NUNO
HMM? NO, YOU DON'T UNDER-STAND.
THERE ARE MANY PARALLEL WORLDS, SO EVEN IF HUMANITY DIES HERE, YOUR WORLD WON'T CHANGE.
IF YOU WANT TO CHANGE THE FUTURE, CHANGE YOUR CURRENT SELF!
WE'RE SWITCHING TO ANOTHER WORLDLINE! BYE!
VWOOSH
SHALL WE GO BACK, ME-A-MONTH-AGO?
GOOD IDEA, ME-A-MONTH-FROM-NOW.
IT'S TRUE. NOTHING HAS CHANGED.
NONE OF MY HOMEWORK DRILLS ARE DONE!
AHH... A SHOOTING STAR...
MAYBE IT'S THOSE TWO FROM THE FUTURE!

DEAD DEAD DEMON'S DEDEDEDE DESTRUCTION

Volume 4
VIZ Signature Edition

Story and Art by **Inio Asano**

Translation **John Werry**
Touch-Up Art & Lettering **Annaliese Christman**
Design **Shawn Carrico**
Editor **Pancha Diaz**

DEAD DEAD DEMON'S DEDEDEDE DESTRUCTION Vol. 4
by Inio ASANO
© 2014 Inio ASANO
All rights reserved.
Original Japanese edition published by SHOGAKUKAN.
English translation rights in the United States of America,
Canada, the United Kingdom, Ireland, Australia and
New Zealand arranged with SHOGAKUKAN.

Original Cover Design:
Kaoru KUROKI·Chie SATO+Bay Bridge Studio

Printed in Canada

Published by VIZ Media, LLC
P.O. Box 77010
San Francisco, CA 94107

10 9 8 7 6 5 4 3 2 1
First printing, January 2019

VIZ MEDIA
viz.com

VIZ SIGNATURE
vizsignature.com